"STILL NONE THE WISER"

(1952 – 1967)

Being the second and final part of the mid-century memoir
'NONE THE WISER'
A Twentieth Century Passage, 1932 - 1967

By
Paul Adamson

Bloomington, IN      Milton Keynes, UK
authorHOUSE®

AuthorHouse™ *AuthorHouse*™ *UK Ltd.*
1663 Liberty Drive, Suite 200 *500 Avebury Boulevard*
Bloomington, IN 47403 *Central Milton Keynes, MK9 2BE*
www.authorhouse.com *www.authorhouse.co.uk*
Phone: 1-800-839-8640 *Phone: 08001974150*

This book is a work of non-fiction. Unless otherwise noted, the author and the publisher make no explicit guarantees as to the accuracy of the information contained in this book and in some cases, names of people and places have been altered to protect their privacy.

© 2007 Paul Adamson. All rights reserved.

No part of this book may be reproduced, stored in a retrieval system, or transmitted by any means without the written permission of the author.

First published by AuthorHouse 3/21/2007

ISBN: 978-1-4259-7176-2 (sc)

Cover photo, Yendi, N. Ghana © Toby Adamson 1997

Printed in the United States of America
Bloomington, Indiana

This book is printed on acid-free paper.

Also by Paul Adamson:-

'None the Wiser' published 2004 by Hayloft Publishing Ltd.

Judge: "Having listened to your speech with
great interest Mr. Smith, I have to
confess that I find myself
none the wiser."

F. E. Smith: "Quite so My Lord, but I trust
Your Lordship is at least
better informed."

With drawings by Caroline Elkington

"STILL NONE THE WISER"

LIST OF CONTENTS

List Of Illustrations Xiii

Author's Introduction Xvii

Chapter 1   London, 1952 - 1954 1

In which the narrator returns to London, Civvy Street and a City Bank after 2 years in the RAF, emerging from the Far East under a cloud of (justifiable) suspicion, falls in love and decides to go to West Africa, aged 22.

Chapter 2   Accra, April May 1954 16

Culture shock on arrival in the Gold Coast replacing a young colleague who died only the week before I appear on scene. Life in a bachelors' mess. Will I survive?

Chapter 3   Work Is A Four Letter Word 28

Daily life in a colonial Bank. The hazards of the lunatics who roam the streets of Accra and sometimes the brassbound mahogany halls of Mammon. Am I mad as well to be here?

Chapter 4   'Diamond Run To Swedru.' 31

I am despatched up-country to collect a consignment of diamonds, by native transport with an armed guard. How the West African diamond trade worked in colonial times.

Chapter 5 Sekondi - 1954 37

I am posted to Sekondi at 24 hours notice to replace Humbert Plinge who has allegedly committed a social gaffe (retiring, naked, to bed on the snooker table in the Club while drunk, it was a formal dance night and the DC's wife was offended).

Chapter 6 'Sekondi - 1954-1956' 44

Life in small-town West Africa; a brief history of the Dutch, Portuguese and English who warred and traded along this stretch of coast since before Columbus 'found' America. A story of intrigue, violence and mayhem.

Chapter 7 'The Gold Coast - Sekondi - 1954/56' 50

More of the same, I establish my bachelor household, I am deeply depressed by the solitude of my existence, I resign. My resignation is refused. I come to terms with life once more and begin to enjoy a modest well-being.

Chapter 8 'Sekondi - 1955 - 'English Lessons' 56

The life of the young European bachelors working for the trading companies, Swiss, French, English etc., My new friend Jacques Spencer-Chapman and I attempt to improve their grasp of the English language and its idioms; confusion reigns.

Chapter 9 'Pidgin English.' 61

An account of the origins and importance of 'Coast Pidgin' in the everyday scheme of things. As explained by Burton, it is a separate language and a clear understanding of its complexities is vital. Plus the missionaries' version of the Book of Genesis.

Chapter 10 Leave - 1955-56...67

After 20 months I depart on leave via Tangier. O., the girl I left behind me in London declines to continue our interrupted romance. I patch up my broken heart by spending my accumulated savings on ski-ing in the Swiss Alps and later in Nice where I strike up a rewarding friendship with Fifi, a fan dancer in a cabaret. I 'dash' my way through a driving test in London and return penniless but more or less content to West Africa.

Chapter 11 Interlude For Light Relief 81

This is apocryphal 'Old Coaster' nonsense, including a parody of Kipling's 'I've taken my fun where I've found it' and an explanation of Secret Circulars A and B as issued by the Colonial Secretary in which he took exception to District Officers (pre-1914) indulging in concubinage. Not quite Sanders of the River material.

Chapter 12 'Tales Of The Silver Screen' 84

Hollywood and Bollywood and the open-air cinemas and the African reaction to films. My friend Gareth Plinge, drunk and exasperated by the noise, fires his shotgun through the cinema screen across the road, no-one notices.

Chapter Thirteen 'Tummy Palaver'............................102

The White Man's Grave may have become The White Man's Headache, but West Africa remains host to a multitude of deadly pathogens. I contract malaria, have a 'near death' experience and end up in hospital.

Chapter 14 'The Daily Grind' (Accra 1958) 116

After two tours in Sekondi and Takoradi I find myself back in Accra, now married to O. who finally made up her mind after four long years of saying "Yes and No!" I entertain Mr. and Mrs. David Rockefeller. A description of a West African surf port.

Chapter 15 'A Tale Of An Old Toaster' 129

'Money Doubling' and other scams originating in West Africa have a long history and continue to the present day. The world is full of gullible suckers.

Chapter 16 Sex And The Single Coaster' 135

A troublesome and age-old theme, young white men bedevilled in tropical climes – a cautionary tale or two. Thaddeus Plinge is saved by a lady policeman from the Vice Squad.

Chapter 17 'Ju-ju' 145

The importance and prevalence of Ju-Ju and 'fetish' in West Africa. Even white men become susceptible. Personal experiences involving witchcraft.

Chapter 18 'Of Cats, Dogs And Apes' 158

Tales of animal companions, of waifs and strays and their often tragic ends.

Chapter 19 "A Bit More Tether" 168

"The man who's spent his life building up trade and Empire in secluded spots is allowed a bit more tether than the man who stays home next to the Sunday School and selling insurance." Or so said Alfred Aloysius Horn aka 'Trader Horn.'

Chapter 20 'Office Palaver'..**173**
'Stuff' they never teach you in Business School. How to stop a mob from burning down the office. The use of violence in debt recovery. Gautier and the 'Bomb Marchers' in Tamale and Ouagoudougu.

Chapter 21 'Bat Palaver'...**188**
Bats: their unsatisfactory role as tennis ball substitutes, their fur, culinary properties and nuisance ratings.

Chapter 22 'The Crocodile'..**193**
Their natural history, personal experiences with and general all-round incompatibilty of the same.

Chapter 23 'Snake Palaver'...**211**
No African memoir is complete without its snake stories to send shivers down the reader's spine. Pythons, green mambas, a night encounter with a Gaboon viper, spitting cobras et al. Not for the squeamish.

Chapter 24 'Bee Palaver'..**244**
Barring man and the mosquito, wild bees are perhaps among the most dangerous creatures in Africa. A man is killed; O. and I are marooned in our house in northern Ghana.

Chapter 25 'Alas Poor Yaro – I Knew Him Well'.......**256**
An account of the African servants, cooks, stewards and nannies employed over the years, our mutual misunderstandings and a general discourse on their many virtues.

Chapter 26 Kano And The Bank Of The North.........**277**
In 1963 O. and I arrive in Northern Nigeria, where all is not as it seems. An account of the contemporary international diamond smuggling industry, its legal and illegal ramifications. Humbert Flange goes 'bush.'

Chapter 27 "In Nothing Else So Happy" 290
 Some of my African friends, hunters, politicians, lawyers, chiefs, traders, policemen, an appreciation.
Chapter 28 Lagos 1964 - 1967 312
 The day of the whiteman fades fast. In Lagos the opening stages of the Biafran War loom; assassinations, murder and military coups follow. Our own future now lies elsewhere. The End.
A Partial Bibliography 323

List Of Illustrations

1 Young City bankers, lunchtime late 1953. Author on left. 89
2 'Hell Corner' centre of young expat. culture in Sekondi, 1954 90
3 BBWA building opened 1916, except for the car still unchanged by 1954. 90
4 Fishermen on the beach. An unchanging scene. 91
5 Fort Orange, Sekondi, built by the Dutch c. 1670, finally bought by the British in 1872. 91
6 Richard Steimann 1954, timber-man, snake-fancier, photographer and obsessive fisherman. 92
7 Author fishing at Inchaban, 1956, catfish and tillapia were our more (or less) edible quarry. Note smart – almost 'natty' sporting attire.. 93
8 Catfish could be cooked in their own yellow fat from their diet of palm nuts. 94
9 View of Fort St. Anthony at Axim, Gold Coast, built by the Portuguese c.1490 besieged and taken by the Dutch in 1642. British in 1872. .. 94
10 Fanti drummer 1955. 95
11 My cook-steward for my bachelor years, Yaro Frafra on left and his 'brother' wearing I suspect, *my* suit and shoes *'borrowed'* for this studio portrait in 1956. 96
12 Jacques Spencer-Chapman on the Prah River in 1956. On this trip he and I got much further upriver than a Royal Navy steam pinnace in 1873 before it was peppered by Ashanti musket fire and forced to retreat. 97
13 akoradi airfield November 1956, I finally depart on leave. Jacques (right) has loaned me his splendid fur-collared coat with which to impress the natives back in Europe. 97
14 My 'old style' colonial house 1957 in Sekondi. Cool, dark and comfortable. 98
15 My 'modern' house later in Takoradi 1957, hot, unshaded, the rooms all airless right angled boxes and with no shutters or air-conditioning. .. 99
16 1958, back in Accra. With Jim Wright (right) at the Railway Station. Both of us hairpin thin. Were there no fat people around in the 1950s? 99

17 Picnic in the Shai Hills 1958. O centre with Paul and June Foot. Ludo the black labrador has dug a hole and is lying there to keep cool. 100
18 Tamale 1959. O. and I live in the bungalow on the 'Ridge,' Adamu the garden boy tends the coarse crab grass for the benefit of the camera. 101
19 Adongo Zurungu, aka 'Charles' our paragon cook-steward holds Sheba, the black cat we brought from Accra. 229
20 with Ferdie and Sid the baboon, both of whom we inherited in Tamale. 230
21 Sunday morning 1959, 7 a.m 'meet' of the Tamale Polo Club at our bungalow starts with brandy and ginger before hacking and return for 9 a.m.breakfast and more brandy. O. on left, Keith Hitchcock on Sindbad and Ralph Little on Tusker. 231
22 Probably 1960. O, Paul Gautier and I make unsuccessful hunting excursion up the Black Volta near Kintampo. We nearly capsize our tiny canoe, get lost for hours in the bush, all for one francolin which O. is holding. 232
23 Tom Gardner and I build the first powered boat to be launched on the White Volta above the dry season bridge at Yapei. We later receive note from Tom's UAC storekeeper in nearby village *'Dear Sir, I beg to assure you your boat is totally sunk. I have* 233
24 1961. O. with our daughter Isobel born in Tamale, on the stoep of our bungalow. 234
25 Author with rod and gun on the White Volta at Daboya, 1960.. Sporting dress standards have slipped since 1955. 235
26 1961, staff photo at Tamale. Wonderful N. Storph, then Chief Clerk, left centre. I was so ill I was carried out in my chair by Peter and Winfriend, the two messengers, front. 236
27 Visiting Yendi Branch 1961, Wonderful N. Storph, centre in tie, now manager. 236
28 Proper' (i.e. non-sport) Dagomba fisherman on White Volta displays catch. 237
29 1966 Lagos, Ikoyi, Oliver Eke our 'small boy' shortly before he left to return to the East as the Biafran War flared. 238
30 1965 Yoruba hunter with 'Dane gun' on banks of River Ogun. 239

31 1965 Benjamin Ladipo 'dressed to kill' with (dead) monkey near Ikorudu. He holds an antique English duelling pistol for reasons which now escape me. 240

32 'Fingal O'Plinge' and Ben Ladipo on Ogun River re-tracing Sir Richard Burton's 1860 tracks in same area. Note breakfast beer bottle to hand. 241

33 Jimoh Babatunde, Yoruba blacksmith holding flintlock musket he made for me in 1964. 242

34 1965, hunting dogs queuing to have their wooden bells hung around their necks. 243

35 1966, Paul Gautier and fellow 'Sunday hunters' in Ikorudu forest. Probably the last trip we made together before violence and unrest made such excursions too risky. 243

Introduction to 'None the Wiser' and 'Still None the Wiser.'

AUTHOR'S NOTE

"As we grow older the memories of early life brighten, those of maturity and senescence grow dim and confused. We prepare for our second childhood by re-living the first - and we are at last qualified to write about it."
(Anthony Burgess, "You've had Your Time")

In writing this book it is necessary at the outset to make simultaneously a confession and a statement of intent. I confess here and now that not everything you may read in the following pages is necessarily either one hundred percent factually true or historically correct.

Some of the events that I describe took place more than fifty years ago and also when I was a child, and I rely on childhood memory. Of the many extraordinary people that I encountered, particularly in Africa in later years, some known only briefly, many are dead. It is now impossible to recall in detail conversations or often to recall with whom or when they took place. Although I am sure that what I know to be correct is so, others who were present and who can still recall these situations will almost certainly differ in their recollections. Old friends' versions of what occurred at a particular time and place where we were present together often show up minor hiccups in my memory and gaping holes in theirs. I can also claim a legitimate excuse, common to many old West Africa hands. It is called 'Coast Memory,' a debilitating condition of the brain brought about by too long an exposure to the great heat of the sun on too many hot tin roofs, too many pink gins on Saturday mornings and too many daily doses of anti-malarial pills.

In memory time telescopes and expands; total recall is both impossible and at the same time what remains is highly selective. It becomes necessary to compound one's memory with imagination. Where memory conflicts with fact then I make no excuses and indeed prefer to rely on memory. In some instances I have forgotten names; in others it is perhaps diplomatic to change them, the same with places where perhaps feelings may still be sensitive even after the passage of years. If people who may think they recognise themselves or others in situations which they prefer not to remember, or feel offended or say. "That *was not* how it was," then I apologise and assure them that no malice is intended and furthermore that I am not referring to whoever it might be thought that it could have been. Several years ago my daughter gave me a little card on which I think was printed the following, "I know that you believe you understand what you think I said, but I am not sure you realise that what you think you heard is not what I meant." Or words to that effect.

For more than thirty years I kept a series of notebooks and disjointed and abbreviated diaries. Some of the contents are indecipherable and I have long since lost the key. As for the rest, some is of little consequence or no longer of interest, but some recall for me people, places and happenings that deserve to be remembered, if only as a piece of unimportant social history of Britain, the Far East and Africa. That about covers the confessional part of the preamble.

My intention in writing this account is not to create a connected narrative, although there is a thread, which is myself, but to describe what it was like to be a child from a particular background in the Thirties and during the Second World War subsequently growing up and participating in the final years of the British Empire at first hand, although in a very minor role. Insignificant role playing it may have been and one was invariably powerless to influence any but the most trivial events, but I was nevertheless interested and often felt myself to be a personally involved though impotent spectator.

Times and attitudes have changed so rapidly that I and many others of my generation have been caught unawares by the pace and rapidity with which old *mores* and ideals are not only discarded but forgotten. G.K. Chesterton wrote in 1904 "There is no more remarkable psychological element in history than the way in which a period can suddenly become unintelligible." He was in fact referring to the early and mid-Victorian periods, a lapse of a mere fifty years. The key, he said, had been lost. In his own words ".... the Crystal Palace is now the temple of a forgotten creed." In more recent times I believe the same quantum leap has taken place. The Thirties, the Forties and the Fifties with their beliefs and attitudes which in themselves evolved so rapidly with the catalyst of the war years, are now part of L.P. Hartley's 'Foreign Land' where things were done so differently, done in a manner that is often incomprehensible to many of those born and brought up since those times. I have heard it suggested that the 20th century did not really begin in Britain until 1940. Certainly most of the older generation responsible for my upbringing were themselves the products of an Edwardian or Victorian education although they were 'modern' in their own outlook and in their own time. In that respect I sit uneasily at the beginning of the 21st century amid its accumulated high-tech gadgetry and rapidly changing standards and beliefs. I find myself in the situation where the world in which I still have my being is becoming unrecognisable. I fear that one day I shall awake to find myself not just in a strange world but on an alien planet.

So much of value has now been discarded by the present generation without their being aware that it ever existed. Our modern 'heroes' acquire fame and celebrity unhampered by achievement. Those whom the younger generations aspire to emulate are as likely to die of drug-induced vomit or suicide as of natural causes. A real hero of this country's past, the great Duke of Wellington, that great reactionary die-hard soldier and statesman to whom this country owes so much, once said. "Progress is not always forward. Change is not necessarily always for the better," and as Field Marshal Montgomery added when reading the lesson in church, "..... And the Lord said unto Moses ... *and I for one, wholeheartedly agree with Him.*" Is it necessarily reactionary to regret the passing of differing values abandoned in the avalanche of progress? In my later life I have frequently been accused of being reactionary in times of ever increasing rapidity of change, because of the frequency with which I have urged the need to change only those things that it is necessary to change and to leave alone those things that do not need changing. The Americans put it more succinctly - "If it ain't broke, don't fix it!"* But then they ignore it just as we do. Continually re-inventing the wheel has always been one of mankind's failings and each generation in its turn is obsessed with the need to discard the old and to bring in the new. *(A more modern version of this is more likely to be "If it ain't broke – fiddle with it until it is!")

The attitudes, manners, habits and patterns of thought that I write about may surprise and shock present day sensibilities. With age I have myself discarded much that I once firmly held true. History, example and experience have changed me with the passing of the years. But it must also be understood that different times have different rules and that what is held wrong today was not necessarily so the day before yesterday. The immediate post-war years were a time of hope. A Brave New World was possible. Exploding populations, a damaged environment, famine, the destruction and desertification of vast areas of the globe, diminishing and threatened wildlife, the rise of despotic dictators in newly independent countries, these were all in the future. Had we in 1950 realised that in the first half of the 20th Century mankind had used (and largely squandered) more of the Earth's non-renewable resources than in the whole of previous history - it would have been interpreted then as 'Progress.' Such considerations did not really affect the mind of a young man launching himself upon the world at the age of eighteen in 1950. As an earlier example of such changing attitudes I have long treasured the memory of one John Newton, a pious and proselytising 18th Century Liverpool merchant who composed the words of that ever popular hymn

"How Sweet the Name of Jesus Sounds in a Believer's Ear," as he awaited the overdue arrival of his latest shipment of slaves from Africa. I am not trying to tell my reader that things were better in the past - just that they were often totally and incomprehensibly different.

Much of what I have to write in the later period (the second part of these memoirs covering 1952 - 1967) concerns West Africa during the last days of colonialism. It may be about Africa but it is not necessarily about Africans, it is about Africa from a very particular and perhaps peculiar, viewpoint, a West Africa that is now long gone together with those years when the British Empire faded into history. It is also about the early period of post-colonialism and independence that sadly and tragically in many instances briefly preceded a descent into profligacy, the corruption of fledging democracies by the pursuit of absolute power, the triumph of despotism and plundered economies. It is a period almost impenetrable to the generations born and educated since that time: indeed it is just as obscure to many of my contemporaries who led more conventional lives and whose careers followed more well-worn paths.

'Old Coasters' (as seasoned West Africa hands were known) after a while rarely reminisce - except with each other - about the more outlandish episodes that made up the warp and woof of their daily lives, that is to say they talk about them only to close friends and to those acquaintances who will neither question their veracity, nor in some cases their sanity. This attitude can be summed up by the experience of a friend who left West Africa in the 1960s to work in New York. When I saw him some two years later when he briefly re-visited the Coast, I couldn't stop him talking; it was as if some overstrained pressure valve had suddenly burst. After some months in America he came to realise that he was being regarded as a liar or as an unreliable and eccentric oddball, thereby placing his career in danger. The simple reason was that when he regaled his sober-minded Wall Street business colleagues with stories of everyday life in West Africa, he was seen by others as a victim of wild and fictional hallucinations. He therefore bottled-up his past life as if it were some previous criminal experience to be hidden away. When he met any old friends it all had to come bursting out from the floodgates of memory and common experience. Poor chap, perhaps he will be able to recall some of his exploits, triumphs and disasters which may (or may not) figure in these pages.*

---

* He might not, for example, care to remember the occasion when for an entire week one October down in the Niger Delta, he closed the Bank in order to celebrate Christmas with a group of American oil drillers.

"When dealing with Africa you can't write about the place or the people with a logical mind. You have to suspend judgement and education and see it afresh." So in 1987 said Ben Okri, then a new Nigerian writer making a name in London. That really sums up the problem. Truth is stranger than fiction. It is also weirder, more fantastic and tortuous in construction than we can generally credit. It is often pointless, self-defeating, circuitous and amazing. On the rare occasion it may help to achieve understanding. Africa is a harsh environment, the land itself, the people, the animals, all exist in a world away from the sheltered life we lead in the West. I look backwards sometimes in amazement, sometimes touched with guilt - and with regret - but things were different more than forty years ago.

If these following pages are memoirs, as I suppose they are, then both reader and I must tread warily to avoid the traps - or perhaps it is better to acknowledge them and trigger them off with due circumspection. Two quotations will serve to illustrate the pitfalls. As the late Robert Morley wrote in "The Pleasures of Age" - "In writing memoirs, it is not in the commercialism that the pleasure necessarily resides. That could be considered a bonus. The pleasure is in conjuring up the past - and amending it when the spirit takes one - that is so satisfying." The second comes from George Santayana - "A man's memory may almost become the art of his continually varying and misrepresenting his past according to his interests in the present." There is perhaps a third reason - "To put matters straight with God by revealing the Truth." "Ah yes" you may say - "but surely God knows the Truth already?" "Agreed, but not *this* version." There may be quite a number of people still alive, who knew me forty and more years ago in West Africa or elsewhere, who will say. "Why, the old bastard, saying that about X, or Y, he left out that time when *he* himself ..... etc. etc." Well, one would say that wouldn't one? It is the author's privilege to leave out the deeply embarrassing moments, or those split seconds that one would give almost anything to retrieve, to have that second chance. There are also matters of shame and regret, that long-dead albatross that we all carry with us hung around our necks. If I choose not to reveal certain matters, that is my concern, not the reader's. All I will say as a pertinent reminder is that life is not a dress rehearsal: there are no second chances. I have changed over the years. Many things that I did do, I would that I never had. In describing events of forty years and more past, it must not be assumed that I always approve - it is just the way things were.

Finally, as the years advance, I feel that I am becoming a member of an endangered species - not quite on the basis of a condom salesman in the Vatican - but simply in becoming old. My past is so much longer than my foreseeable future. The years stretch behind, full of incident and people and places, many now blurred - names and faces half-forgotten. But at least I know they existed and happened. The future has suddenly become finite, constantly shrinking. All of us, if we survive to become old, become different people, but by some strange enchantment we find that we have inherited a young person's memories. Life has one certain outcome of which little warnings, twinges, aches and pains bring to mind the fragility of our existence. Life has but one entrance and ten thousand exits; we all pass through many doors in a lifetime and before that final door opens I intend to try and bring some of those early memories to life in these pages. (This paragraph contains a series of clichés - it is a cliché in itself to say that such aphorisms are the distillation of mankind's wisdom and experience through the ages - so I will let them stand.)

Some readers may complain that the second and final part of this memoir – and the accompanying illustrations and photographs of West Africa have little to do with my then everyday calling as a banker. So be it. I was always ill-suited to that profession, I now realise it was but a temporary means to an end – and that end was often to get the Hell away from my office and see and do something else. In the Fifties and Sixties political correctness did not exist, we usually knew what was right and what was wrong without being obsessed with gender or race or equal opportunities – or thank God, 'Health and Safety' risk-assessment questionnaires. And finally, being young we did whatever we did with as little thought for the consequences as young people everywhere have done since Time began. I make no apologies.

I therefore ask the reader to accept the following history as in essence a basically truthful account of a personal Odyssey from the days of my pre-war childhood until I finally left Africa in 1967

I shall preface my narrative with the traditional disclaimer of the Ashanti story teller as he begins his tale.

*Ye 'nse se, nse se o."**

When he has finished the story, he concludes:

*M'anansesem a metaoye yi, se eye de o, se ennye de o, momfa bi nko na momfa bi mmera."***

* Trans. "We do not really mean, we do not really mean (that what we are going to say is true). ** This is my story which I have related, if it be sweet, or if it be not sweet, take some elsewhere and let some come back to me."

This is simply how your average academic ethnographer-cum-anthropologist would interpret it, instead of saying literally "This is how it is, take it or leave it!" as the storyteller intends. I think I shall direct my tale at a slightly less elevated pitch, perhaps somewhere half-way between that of the high-toned ethnographer and that of the BBC's 'Listen with Mother.' "Are you sitting comfortably, then I'll begin."

I shall leave you to be the judge.

This is my story.

Note: The name 'Walter Plinge' is, I believe, a fictitious name used to pad out theatre programmes to conceal the fact that one actor may be playing several roles. To avoid giving offence to any living person, some of my characters in these reminiscences might be taken as composite caricatures, see also 'Hamish MacPlinge,' 'Mimsie Borogrove,' 'Fingal O'Plinge,' et alia. Corporal 'Jonah' Plinge is based on several RAF NCOs of that ilk (see 'None the Wiser'). The incidents described are all true to the best of my recollection, compiled both from memory and my contemporary notes.

Dedication

I would like to dedicate this book to all those 'Old Coasters' (including more than a few doughty Madams deserving of that ilk), who went down to West Africa in the past, to those who survived without coming to some sort of grief and those who didn't. None of them - however brief their stay - will have escaped unmarked by their experiences. If I quote from Kipling (who knew a lot about Life, The Universe and Everything) then I think that those who have had direct contact with the Coast will understand something of what I have tried to say in the following pages. He says it much better than I could ever express it.

> *"I have written the tale of our life*
> *For a sheltered people's mirth,*
> *In jesting guise - but ye are wise*
> *And ye know what the jest is worth."*

(Prelude to Departmental Ditties)

Acknowledgements

I have to acknowledge again the forbearance and help of my wife without which this book would not have been completed. For critcism and encouragement my thanks go to Eric Robson for making the time to read the early manuscript. Percy Wood has been constructive and helpful in his detailed editing of the text, and hopefully he has steered me away from any libellous statements I may (unintentionally and without malice) have made in the course of my narrative. Especial thanks are due to my multi-talented god-daughter Caroline Elkington for once again 'coming good' with the line illustrations. Audrey Dunnett provided me with 'Genesis' and 'Application for Loan.' Tom Gardner continually prompts my failing memory. My son Toby gave me valuable help in sorting through far too many photographs and in editing them into a state acceptable to the final printing process. The late Richard Steimann of Thun, Switzerland took several of the better photographs of my early days in West Africa. In the end of course there are the many 'Old Coasters' and Africans I knew (of whom alas far too many are now dead) who provided me with a fund of stories and of experiences in that old West Africa that now only lives in the fading collective memories of a remarkable and sadly dwindling band of ageing eccentrics.

The author wishes to declare that this book may be considered unsuitable for vegetarians or for those of a nervous or sensitive disposition. To the best of his knowledge the author hopes and believes this book to be Ozone Friendly. Readers are also warned that at the time that many of the incidents herein described took place the concept of 'Political Correctness' was an as yet unformulated social theory.

Chapter 1
(London - 1952-1954)

*"A man can still be a London Banker
and yet have much spare mind."*
(Walter Bagehot, 1826 - 1877)

In October 1952 I completed my two years of National Service in the RAF, and was discharged honourably - but only perhaps by a whisker - if as I suspected, I was still under investigation by the RAF Special Branch following my involvement in a highly dubious incident in Malaya a few months earlier.* I was now to pick up the threads of civilian life once again although still a reservist. This posed little threat to either myself or to the RAF unless in the case of some extreme national emergency when my services, of such limited value as they were might once again have been needed.

I was now virtually penniless having used up my final RAF pay in settling my gambling debts incurred while playing cards on the month-long voyage home in a troopship from the Far East. The fact that both pay and debt were niggardly** sums was neither here nor there in those days when a five pound note was by far the better half of a week's wages back in Civvy Street. To recover any measure of solvency it was necessary for me to reclaim my old job almost immediately. My mother, recently divorced, to whose West Kensington flat I had now returned, was in no position to help.

I started back again at the City bank in Bishopsgate that I had left two years earlier, The Chartered Bank of India, Australia and China (as it was then), took me back, as they were obliged to, in my old position as a Foreign Staff probationer destined in theory (once I had reached the age of twenty-one) for an overseas posting. Unlike most of my contemporaries in the Bank who had also returned from their compulsory service in the Armed Forces, I did not get the two years' accumulated back-pay plus a £100 'loyalty' bonus that they were granted. Several weeks before I was called up, the period of compulsory National Service on the outbreak of the Korean War in June 1950 was still only eighteen months, very soon to be extended to two years. I was the first (being then, as now, 'alphabetically challenged') to be called in by the dour, elderly Scots Chief Accountant, to be asked if after my military service I intended to return to

---

* See None the Wiser, Part One, 1932 -1952.
**In our thin-skinned times this word is now politically incorrect. I stand by its correct meaning.

the Bank. Being totally unaware of the reason for this question, I had answered quite truthfully, that unable to see that far ahead, I probably would return - but equally I could not be certain. I was stunned when he said, with a certain grim pleasure (my unwitting folly having immediately saved the Bank some £500 – a small fortune at that time) "What a pity - had you said yes, the Directors have just decided to pay all the juniors away in the Services their full pay in arrears, plus a bonus when they come back." I was dumbstruck - the mean old Scottish bastard disallowed my furious back-pedaling - and dismissed me. Of course I told all the other juniors who were waiting to be interviewed and they all smugly took their unjust rewards two years later when they were demobbed, several of them returning for barely two months before resigning to go elsewhere, handsomely in pocket. It still rankles half a century later.

Working in a City bank fifty years ago was a vastly different field of endeavour to what it has now become. We were at the closing of that era of which in 1889 Jerome K. Jerome could write in 'Three Men in a Boat' *".... George goes to sleep at a bank from ten to four each day, except Saturdays, when they wake him up and put him outside at two."* Things had changed little. Apart from a few basic mechanical accounting and adding machines, plus a few tedious hand-wound calculators like miniature sewing machines - much slower than the wooden beads on a wire-stung abacus used in the bank's Far Eastern branches - we were entirely driven by pen and ink technology in monstrous leather and cloth-bound ledgers and account books propped up on sloping desks, our mental calculations being supplemented by ready reckoners and printed tables of discount and interest rates. It all worked remarkably smoothly and one consequence for the junior foreign staff who were moved from department to department every few months was that almost by a system of osmosis we soon came to learn how a bank functioned from top to bottom, even if we were sometimes short on detail. All very different to the end of the last decade of the twentieth century when many modern banks became casino operations trading twenty-four hours a day seven days a week, simultaneously risking both their own and their customers' capital, gambling on world-wide stock market fluctuations in commodities and currencies that gyrate according to the fickle electronic winds of politics and economics. 'As safe as a bank' they used to say. Alas no longer, but no doubt a banker's career half-a-century on is both more interesting and potentially profitable as well as infinitely more time-demanding to those who choose to graft for a decade or two (at the most - before retiring super-rich) in the halls of Mammon.

In 1952 when I resumed civilian life the City still presented the spectacle of massed bowler hats and rolled umbrellas. It was a time when those top-hatted kingpins of the Square Mile, the stockbrokers, rarely turned into their offices until time for lunch on Mondays (if pressed) or perhaps Tuesdays after their long and tiring weekends, departing in their Bentleys after lunch on Thursday or (if pressed) on Friday for their retreats in deepest rural Surrey. It was a time of steady and unfluctuating markets and strict Exchange Control, an age when as in Cobbett's time a hundred years before, *"The natural increase of money is five percent"* and prudent bank clerks could borrow at two-and-a half percent from their employers to mortgage their semi-detached houses in the suburbs, willingly donning the gilt-plated handcuffs that would shackle them to their desks and ledgers, assured of a job for life and a pension when they retired at sixty-five. Unless one was caught with one's fingers in the till, or was habitually absent from work it was a secure living. (At the Chartered Bank *pour encourager les autres* it was the accepted practice each year to sack those two juniors who most often missed the 9.30 am deadline for 'signing on' in the attendance register.) Britain's near bankrupt post-war economy still relied heavily on those great 'sunset' industries of coal, steel, shipbuilding and heroic engineering. The traditional markets of the Empire and Commonwealth still imported Manchester cloths and tin-plate hurricane lamps from Birmingham, Hercules and Raleigh bicycles, treadle sewing machines, brass band instruments from Boosey and Hawkes and cutlery from Sheffield. In other words business continued much as it had done since before the turn of the last century.

I had to borrow money from a colleague (who had his two years' back pay to conjure with) to buy a new suit, my old City blue-pinstripe suit from two years before was now skin tight, to be able to return to work, casual wear (sports jacket or blazer and always a tie) being allowed only on Saturday mornings. I now earned about £350 per annum, plus an annual bonus equal to an extra month's salary. Less than £30 was credited to my account each month-end and I was not yet allowed a cheque book still being under twenty-one, (neither could I vote – until I returned to live in the UK in 1968 I was effectively disenfranchised by living abroad. Since then I have religiously voted on every possible occasion – usually favouring whatever person or party whose policies I find the least offensive). This meagre sum together with the three-shilling (15 pence) lunch voucher each day was enough to live on, just, but it left no margins. At a City eating house the daily luncheon voucher would buy soup, meat and two veg. plus suet pudding with custard and a coffee, but many of the bachelor staff - and not a few of the younger married men - trod the well-beaten path to the nearest pub that would take the vouchers in exchange for a few pints of beer to set them up for the remainder of the afternoon.

The Bank also provided the mainspring of social life for the younger set. Near Hampton Court at East Molesey the Bank had a luxurious (for its day) sports club, it also offered residential catering for those bachelor staff from the further parts of the kingdom - and Ireland - who needed somewhere to live convenient to the City, and in addition, it provided a temporary base for single staff returning on leave from the Far East. There was a bar, tea-room, a ballroom and extensive grounds through which flowed the River Mole. There were tennis courts and playing fields for hockey, rugby, and cricket in season when the city interbank and finance house competitions were fiercely and sportingly contested.

I resumed playing rugger for the Bank's regular fifteen, foolishly offering my services as full-back in which position I had always enjoyed a modest success at school, realising that most players of that time, mere featherweight striplings (compared to the slab-muscled human bulldozers, shaven-headed and bulked up with God knows what who play the game fifty years later), could be effectively brought down by a low flying tackle. This tactic served me well enough, a puny ten-and-a-half stone weakling as I was then. As full-back one didn't have to run too far or too fast and the game would flow towards me without effort on my part. Until Nemesis struck. After several months of

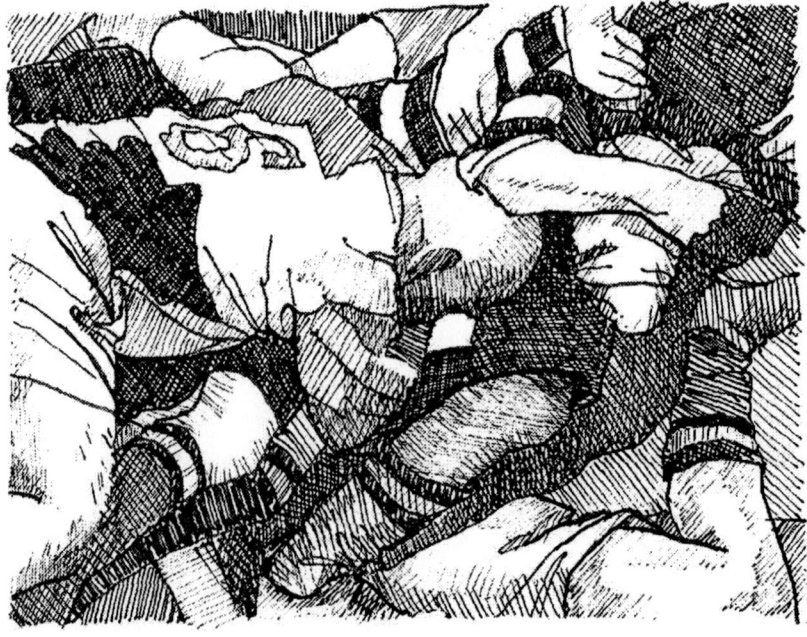

undistinguished and not totally unsuccessful playing - a 'friendly" match was arranged for one Saturday afternoon at Imber Court in Surrey. (We had cut-price sports railway tickets then, paid for by the Bank - a car was an almost unheard of luxury). Until the last minute I had failed to realise that Imber Court was the country home of the Metropolitan Police, and although it was only their 'B' team whom we played, as soon as the whistle blew it was immediately obvious that these great bruising hulks (for their time) were way beyond my strictly amateur abilities and they certainly had no concept of what might be meant by a 'friendly' game. (I would not be surprised to discover that the minimum qualifying height and weight at that time for the Met's recruits was six-foot-plus and fifteen stone). I shall draw a veil over the game. Suffice it to say that for what remained of that season I refused to play in any other position but wing-forward, and as soon as possible thereafter hung up my boots for ever with few regrets. I did not miss the hearty rugger social scene with its communal baths, scented with raw sweat and embrocation, deafened by endless choruses of songs along the lines of *"We'll be all right in the middle of the night, putting it in together!"* Nor did I miss the beer - in rugger circles, those ever-circulating chipped enamel jugs of draught bitter - funded by the 'pot' to which we all contributed equal shares. My capacity for English beer was limited, after two pints it has always made me nauseous and bloated while my companions at that time could cheerfully down six or seven pints without effect. Going equal shares as we did, it was never going to be an economic proposition.

Participating in amateur sport (or 'games' to put things in their proper perspective) in the early 1950s occupied a much greater part in a young man's activities than some fifty years later when self-styled 'sportsmen' are more likely to be couch-potato voyeurs wearing the latest soccer 'strip' rather than engaging in the real thing on the field. Television was virtually non-existent and professional players had a long way to go before becoming recognised throughout the land as highly paid stars and 'personalities.' Soccer and cricket had their own clearly defined seasons.[*] When the one finished, the other started. Football League matches were played on Saturday afternoons; most of the professionals had their weekday-jobs necessary to provide them

---

[*] Stanley Matthews (The Wizard of the Dribble) was a professional footballer from 1931 until 1965, playing for England 54 times, yet he was never paid more than £25 for any single match during his entire career. Denis Compton, England and Middlesex cricketer (and well-known advertisement for Brylcreem) also played for Arsenal as a winger, was capped for England and still found ample time to take well-earned holidays when neither cricket nor soccer were in season! If you think that this information makes me a sports fan, think again. I would rather attend a Sex Pistols concert than either a football or cricket match!

with a living. It would not have been thought unusual then for a major league player to finish his Saturday morning job as a garage mechanic or plasterer at 12.30, going to the pub for his dinner of steak and kidney pudding, settled with a couple of pints of the landlord's best bitter, turning up at the changing rooms half-an-hour before kick-off at 2.30. The kit was primitive, heavily studded leather boots to kick a soggy cow-hide ball weighing several pounds that put anyone heading such a monstrosity at serious risk of concussion or permanent disability in later life like a punch-drunk boxer. 'Goalies' as they were known wore flat gor'blimey caps, thick woollen sweaters, scarves and mittens to protect their chilblained ears and fingers. Successful players (if they were lucky) retired and took over the tenancy of a public house. Well-known cricketers pocketed the skimpy proceeds of their benefit matches and the more fortunate took up positions as cricket professionals or groundsmen at private and public schools – Fred Perry, pre-war Wimbledon and All England lawn tennis champion used to give extra-curricular tennis lessons to several of my prep school peers. Mid-century sport reflected the totally different set of values that drove the contemporary scene. Not better, not worse – but incomprehensibly dissimilar in present day terms.

My own social life however remained largely unaffected by my decision to give up team sports. The only loss perhaps was in missing the University matches, the internationals and seven-a-sides held in London, for which the Bank always gave time off on Saturdays and (sometimes) free tickets to the team members. I took up fishing again, an early love of mine, in the river Mole that ran through the grounds of 'The Wilderness' (the Bank sports club) which in those far-off days held abundant chub, sizeable pike and perch. On weekend evenings I joined the groups of young colleagues who used the club for tennis and cricket and on summer weekends whenever there were dances and with girl friends and young ladies from the bank one quick-stepped and waltzed to a local band or to the gramophone. It was I suppose all quite civilised - but somewhat tame after my recent time in the Far East.

Whenever one of our colleagues on the foreign staff was posted to India or points further east, we jointly celebrated his impending departure with a grand dinner at the Hong Kong restaurant in Shaftesbury Avenue. We were well known to the manager, an urbane Chinese, Mr. Yung, who invariably furnished us with a private room. He well knew that our party might be noisy (but never violent) and that at least one person would pass out at the table, face-down in the crispy noodles or the chicken chow mein. The foreign staff juniors took as their own personal anthem, that then current Guy Mitchell classic and polite enough for mixed company.

Still None The Wiser

> "I work at the Chartered Bank
> A respectable position,
> From ten 'til three they bring you tea
> And ruin your dispo-sit-ion."
> "Each night at Music Hall
> Travelogues I see,
> And there a pearl of a native girl
> Was gazing down at me."
> "Oh-h-h - she wears red feathers and a hooly-hooly skirt"
> Etc. etc.

In early 1953 the Bank opened its own residential staff training 'college' in a comfortable country house with its own grounds at East Grinstead. Some twenty or so of the foreign staff probationers were despatched there for six months to study full time for (and if possible pass) the Institute of Bankers Diploma. There was a Principal, the elderly, distinguished Sir Alexander Campbell, whose main claim to fame was having served on Lord Mountbatten's staff* after a long career in the Indian Army. There was a Bursar, a senior clerk from Head Office serving out his time to retirement and an almost full time lecturer in all the commercial subjects from one of the City Colleges. There was a Matron, a Mrs Napier, sensible and middle-aged, to supervise our laundry and our morals. It was really quite a doddle and we paid nothing for our keep. I suppose it was a way of sorting out some of the sheep from the goats, for although most of us passed in all subjects, some did so badly that they were obliged to leave, having seen the light, or simply reverted to the London staff or departed for pastures new - rubber planting in Malaya being at that time a favoured choice. Looking back I now realise that we were remarkably favoured employees and that several of us having taken all advantage of the Bank's good intentions, then subsequently left (myself included) was rather like a kick in the teeth for our benefactors, but as always, at the time there were good reasons, and we were young and in the latter part of 1953 I had fallen seriously in love with O. Our first major romantic encounter occurred at the Connaught Rooms, a formal occasion of dinner jackets (borrowed in my case) and long evening dresses at a Gala dinner dance thrown by the Bank to celebrate their first centenary - the entertainment being a performance by the young comedienne Beryl Reid in her persona

---

* Following the Dieppe fiasco in 1942 Lord Mountbatten was later sent to the Far East as Supreme Commander South-East Asia Command.

as the dreadful Birmingham tearaway, 'Marleen.' Later that evening along with a group of friends we decamped to the Panama Club in Windmill Street and in the early hours of the morning O. and I (by now totally bewitched) eventually wandered down to the Embankment to sit out what little remained of the night until the first Tube trains would take us back to our respective homes. It was a time when a dress code could still define the parameters in which one sought an evening's entertainment. To be abroad in the West End of London on a Saturday night in formal dress was only to be one of many.

I had become a banker by default rather by than by intention. Does any young person ever leave school fired by ambition to become a bank clerk? Perhaps there are such people, as there are said to be those whose dying words would be "I wish I'd spent more time in the office." Unlikely, but just possible. I became a banker - although at the time there were many other things I would have preferred to do - because there were no simple, easy or obvious alternatives. Becoming a bank clerk for the first time in 1949 a year before my National Service I had seen simply as a means to an end - to make a reasonable living in far-away places - starting at first with the Chartered Bank who at least offered the prospects of a career in the Far East, and secondly, in early 1954, with the old colonial Bank of British West Africa. By the time I went to West Africa I was already becoming aware that both emotionally and by temperament I was unsuited to most corporate environments, but I had little idea as to what I could gainfully do as a realistic alternative. By the time I finally left Africa in 1967 I think that the 'corporate environment' (then in its early flowering years) was making me ill.

Africa's later attraction for me, (apart from the immediate benefit of an eighteen-month tour as compared with the four years of an Eastern first tour - *some Far East firms did not permit marriage until two four year overseas tours had been completed* - enabling me in theory to resume my love affair with O. at an earlier date), was as it had been for many a young man since before the turn of the century, the prospect it offered of a life of modest adventure. Although most who took this route ended up on an office chair behind a desk, as banker or trader or government officer, there were still the opportunities either to be seized, or in some cases thrust unwillingly on those who in their heart of hearts might have preferred to commute from suburbia to a City office desk.

In the last few months (before I took up with O. I must admit) at the Chartered Bank, a friend - Donald Blacklaw - and I realised that with the recent influx of post-war graduates being given accelerated postings to the Far East over the heads of us semi-trained and qualified foreign staff probationers (who at least had studied for and passed our Bankers' Institute exams) our own expected postings were being further delayed. Donald and I pooled our researches and started thrashing about in the more obscure thickets of the plentiful job opportunities, looking around for other overseas employment.

Two (of many) alternative occupations that particularly took our fancy were firstly to join the old B.S.A. Police in Rhodesia - whose recruiting blurb that caught our eyes had a glossy cover featuring a booted and spurred mounted police trooper wearing a pith helmet surmounted by a spike and with pennoned lance at the ready - responsible, it was said, for single-handedly maintaining law and order over thousands of square miles of tribal Africa. The second option strangely enough also featured elements of equine locomotion with the West Indian sugar firm of Bookers to whom we both sent identical letters. Bookers replied by return offering us immediate employment as sugar plantation overseers in what was then British Guiana, on the South American mainland. The salary offered was only £400 per annum - but they added enticingly - "... the cost of living is low, both *white* and *dark* rum costs only one shilling *a quart*" - and what was more we would be provided with a riding mule for transport, plus an allowance for its maintenance! This was tempting stuff indeed.

But then Fate (or is it Nature?) plays tricks with young men, I met and fell in love with O. in late 1953 and my priorities changed. Donald was then told, as I was also, that we would soon have a posting to the Far East - for the Chartered Bank by now had found out the hard way that graduate recruitment had its pitfalls. They had earlier sent a classicist to Indo-China after only a few short months training in the Bishopsgate Head Office. After an equally brief residence in Hanoi or some such French colonial city, the trained and flexible mind of the Greek scholar had quickly weaselled out the weaknesses in the local banking system and he vanished from the scene, along with a small fortune in the local currency and one of the prettier Tonkinoise hostesses from the *bordelle* he frequented. It was several months before the gendarmes traced him to another remote town where with his partner - who presumably provided the technical expertise, he had invested his money in setting up another brothel. The Bank I believe, hushing up the matter, arranged for the French authorities to deport their former employee and sold off the brothel business as a going concern to re-coup their losses.

By the beginning of 1954 I was in something of a quandary. My continuing affair with O. had determined the course of events. Very sensibly O. said that she could not be certain that she would wait four years for my return from the Far East if I went off with the Chartered Bank - after all we had known each other a bare six months in London, however passionately we felt we had committed ourselves. We were certainly in no position to marry otherwise unless I improved our totally parlous finances.

The advertisement on the front page of The Times in the Appointments and Situations Vacant column read:-

> "**Bank of British West Africa** Limited have vacancies at their Branches in West Africa for single men between the ages of 20 and 25. Applicants must have a knowledge of Accountancy, and preference will be given to men with Banking experience. High standard of education is essential. Commencing salary £690 per annum, plus bonus (at present 10 per cent) and £120 Duty Allowance (total £879 per annum) rising to £860 per annum plus Bonus and Duty Allowance (total £1,066) at the beginning of fifth year. Annual increments thereafter according to ability. Low Income Tax. 18 month tours, free furnished accomodation and medical attention, three months' leave in England. £100 Kit Allowance. Please apply to the Secretary at 37 Gracechurch Street, London E.C.3 and give full details of experience &c."*

What red-blooded young British banker could possibly resist such an offer couched in these stirring terms? (Judging by the frequency of this advertisement in many relevant journals at the time – the majority regarded such a prospect with a degree of horror). However on the face of it this was a possible answer to my problem so I went down Bishopsgate and saw Mr. Kewley, the Secretary of the Bank of British West Africa in Gracechurch Street who welcomed me (figuratively speaking) with open arms. The advertisement was not intentionally misleading but it did leave much relevant information brushed to one side. I already knew that the Bank was perennially short of staff - West Africa was no health resort. It had a (deservedly) bad reputation all round and was pretty low down on the scale of desirability among the young and ambitious of the day. There were difficulties in persuading staff to stay on after their first tour of duty on the Coast - as recounted by a friend of mine, later a barrister, who

---

* My son-in-law recently remarked that that the ages given seemed remarkably young for the assumed responsibilities. My answer was that in 1953 a young man of 20 would have been considerably more mature and disciplined than his counterpart of fifty years later. Many had already served two years in the Forces and were making their way in the world of adulthood. Adolescence had been brief and barely tolerated by society at large. Also over the age of twenty five few young men would still find the 'idea' of West Africa enticing but more akin to enlisting in the Foreign Legion. The earlier one went to the Coast the better it was for all concerned.

on coming down from Cambridge with a degree in law and unable for the moment to find a place in suitable Chambers, arranged an interview with the BBWA with a view to becoming a banker. He was shown into the gloomy dark-panelled waiting room on the first floor of 37 Gracechurch Street with its musty display cases of West African *ethnographica*, copper bars and twisted iron rods and manillas (the early trading currencies of the region). While waiting to see the Secretary (the aforesaid Mr. Kewley) and the General Manager, Mr. Wright (an 'Old Coaster' nick-named 'Snakey'), my friend observed another young man also waiting to see 'Snakey.'

The young man was thin and ill-looking, with an unhealthy yellow complexion - and a definite tremor in his hands. He spoke to my friend, saying. "Are you by any chance thinking of going out to West Africa?" My barrister friend said, yes, he was here for interview to that end. The other chap, of such short acquaintance, leaned over and blurted out. "Don't go! It's *bloody* awful!!" It's a terrible place; I've just come back from there." He shuddered - or shook, "I'm here to tell them I won't go back under any circumstances." A messenger came by, whisked off the yellow and wasted young man before he could reveal more.

My friend, thinking over what he had just heard, quietly took his coat from the hat stand in the corner, crept down the stairs and slipped out furtively and unnoticed into the hustle and bustle of the City street.

When I handed in my notice to the Chartered Bank, the then Assistant General Manager, George Pullen - (who had originally been personally responsible for my recruitment), sent a messenger to summon me to his office. He was livid with rage.

The interview was short and not at all sweet. "Where are you going?" He demanded to know, I told him I was going to the Bank of British West Africa. He exploded with ill-concealed anger. "As far as I am concerned - they are welcome to you!" (Ironically, had I remained in West Africa for a few more years with the BBWA - as the wheel turned full circle with major bank take-over after take-over I would have ended up back again with Standard Chartered as my original employers had become at the end of the 1960s. George Pullen's attitude summed up what many people thought of the West African Coast and the people who went there at that time. With hindsight I find it flattering that he should have taken the time to carpet me and to give me a piece of his mind. The die was now cast.

I only spent only a few more weeks in London, getting kitted out, making my farewells, depressed at the thought of the coming parting with O.

It was in early 1954 at the age of twenty-two that I announced to my long-suffering family that I was going to West Africa. There were some quite strong reservations expressed. A visiting uncle said to me that when he was a young man the steamship companies invariably declined to sell return tickets to passengers shipping out to the West African Coast. It was, he said, considered unlikely that the return half would ever be needed for the homeward passage. My grandmother was quite thrilled and wrote to tell me that her favourite brother-in-law, my great-uncle Jackson Doughty, had been killed by the Boers while serving with the Imperial Yeomanry in 1900. He was buried somewhere on the South African veldt. My grandmother suggested that if I had a weekend to spare at some time I should hop on a convenient bus and go and visit his grave. Another uncle by marriage, who had gone out to the West Coast during the last war, I was told had been shipped home, wracked by drink, debauchery and fever. None of this advice and information did I find particularly helpful or encouraging. In later years I was reminded of this attitude by the comment of a retired soldier who claimed to have spent some years in West Africa during the war. *"Can't remember much about it, dear boy - all just a vague blur of black velvet tits and bottle tops."* I was in much the same state of confusion about my immediate destiny as had been Mary Kingsley before embarking on her first exploratory voyage to the Coast in 1893. She compiled what little information she had been able to glean from her (mostly ignorant) friends under the following headings:-

"The dangers of West Africa.

The disagreeables of West Africa.

The diseases of West Africa.

The things you must take to West Africa.

The things you find most handy in West Africa.

The worst possible things you can do in West Africa."

With the promise of my £100 Kit Allowance from the Bank I gave myself into the clutches of the London tropical outfitters. In those days the two principal emporia of this specialised trade were Bakers of Golden Square and Alkits of Cambridge Circus. (It was too much to hope that the Bank would *actually* make the allowance over to me personally. It was up to the suppliers to render the account to my employers and in any case, only £50 of this could be expended at home, the balance would be paid in West Africa, theoretically to be used there for setting up my household).

At Alkits the sales-floor had tempting displays of camp beds, portable canvas baths, water filters, brassbound oak and mahogany 'thunderboxes,' 'combination' knife-fork-and-spoon sets for the parsimoniously inclined, solar topees, knee-length mosquito boots and ant-proof tin trunks and 'chop' boxes to pack everything in. The condescending salesman was ingratiatingly attentive to my needs

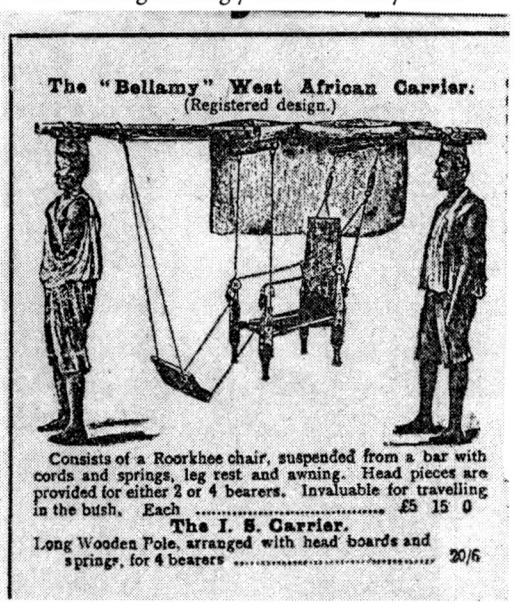

The "Bellamy" West African Carrier.
(Registered design.)

Consists of a Roorkhee chair, suspended from a bar with cords and springs, leg rest and awning. Head pieces are provided for either 2 or 4 bearers. Invaluable for travelling in the bush. Each £5 15 0
The I. S. Carrier.
Long Wooden Pole, arranged with head boards and springs, for 4 bearers 20/6

"And might *one* enquire where *Sir* has obtained a position?" I answered that I was going to the Gold Coast (which was to become Ghana in 1957 some four years later). I explained that I had really only come in for a 'Palm Beach' tropical suit, plus evening dress with a white dinner jacket, a dress shirt and one or two other items from the extensive list I thought I might need to supplement the khaki-drill shorts and woollen knee-length stockings the RAF had kindly allowed me to keep after my service in the Far East. (Before I left for Africa I was also obliged to write to the RAF requesting a release from my continuing obligations as a reservist, to which they reluctantly agreed on condition that I returned all my kit and the home uniforms in my possession and which still remained government property.)

"Ah!" Mused the salesman, a faraway look in his eyes, as he measured my inside leg. To bypass 'purchase tax:' then extortionately current, I could not take delivery in the U.K. and he explained that my goods (unseen) would have to be sent to my plane, only to be handed over to me at my destination - where it subsequently transpired an implacable and zealous colonial Customs Officer was to charge me full import duty - more than the tax I had so far avoided). "Ah! The Gold Coast - we *know* it well Sir, the *rich, red* earth of the Gold Coast makes it necessary to have one's trouser cuffs cut shorter than usual - it does not do to *trail* them in the dust and stain them."

In short order he then sold me a soft, long sleeved khaki flannel shirt ("... *Sir* must not allow himself to risk a chill after the heat of the day"). The washable white linen dinner jacket - which Yaro, the houseboy of my bachelor days ruined for ever when he first washed it without removing the shoulder pads and suffused a rich purple water-soluble dye (now fast) across much of the garment. "*Sir* must have a cummerbund for evening wear as well." He assured me that yellow silk was *de rigeur* in the Gold Coast. The only purchases I made there of use was the flannel shirt which lasted me for many years plus a few short-sleeved cotton shirts. The yellow cummerbund I discovered on arrival was only to be worn by government officials. As a 'civilian' protocol said I could only wear black. The first time I wore my Palm Beach trousers, the turn-ups and cuffs wrinkled around my ankles and dragged in that self-same rich, red dust I had been so particularly warned against. I wore the complete suit almost for the first time a few months later to fly to Takoradi when my fountain-pen discharged its ink reservoir across the inside breast pocket and into the armpit, ruining both shirt and jacket. (This was always one of the lesser-known perils of unpressurised flight). My dress trousers lasted a little longer, until Christmas 1954, when having driven from Takoradi to Accra with Gene Doyle and Jim Gilbert for the festive season, I inadvertently fell backwards off the verandah of the Accra Club into the shrubbery below, my trousers being irreparably shredded in the process.

There were however two notable purchases made at that time. O. and I entered an antique shop in Kensington Church Street run by two elderly and charming sisters. In a folder of ancient maps O. found a parting gift for me, a map dated 1715 of '*Zaara* (or the *Desart*), *Negroe-Land, Guinea etc.*' - whose topography and fundamental uncertainties were as vague and ill-defined as my own conceptions as to where I was bound. I pointed out to the two ladies where I would shortly find myself on their map. "Accra!" Said the one sister to the other, "How romantic! Is that not where King Richard The Lionheart was wounded by that *ever* so cruel Saladin during the Crusades?" "Ah yes! ..." agreed the other lady, "... Why! *So* he was - at the Siege of Accra."

The other lasting purchase was a pair of Lotus Veldtschoen boots that I bought in a City shoemaker. Lotus were so confident of the qualities of their 'Veldtschoen' brand of footwear that they habitually displayed them in a fishtank of water in their window. They cost me all of a week's pay, £8.10 shillings. They tramped their solid, comfortable and waterproof way over many scores of miles of assorted West African terrain until 1965 when O. and I went on leave to Connemara in the west of Ireland, that extensive area of bogland whose succession of 'grand, soft days' and relentless rains eventually sapped my boots' legendary impermeability to the point where my socks became noticeably soggy. When next in London, I returned my boots to Lotus for repair. "Your boots *leak!*" I said accusingly. "Even after eleven years Sir, *our* boots do *not* leak." and they repaired them for me free of charge. Thirty years later they were once again repaired for me by a proper, prison-trained cobbler in Glasgow who was so pleased to have "quality" on which to display his own craftsmanship that he begged the loan of them for several months to put them on show in his own window. Alas, with the passing years I now find them so heavy that I no longer wear them - but they still fit with all the comfort due from a well-worn glove.

All that was now left to me was to make my farewells and go.

CHAPTER 2
Accra - April/May 1954.

*"T'were like a posting to the Gold Coast - The White Man's Grave -
each year there counted for two anywhere else."
(Compo in BBC TV's 'Last of the Summer Wine')*

I took myself off to Heathrow via the airport bus from the West London Air Terminal in Earl's Court where one could then check in for the twenty hour flight to Accra. It was a Friday, the 24th of April 1954. O. did not come to see me off, very sensibly as it would have been too emotional. The pangs of separation for the next year-and-a-half were dismal and at the drop of a hat I felt prepared to abandon the whole enterprise and to stay in England. Parting had led to some awful moments of despair at taking off for so long into what seemed the wilds of Africa.

Heathrow Airport in 1954 was still a jumble of pre-fabricated Nissen huts (we have travelled so far in time since then that now I sometimes see the word 'Nissan' used in print as if they were a by-product of the Japanese car industry). Outside the Terminal buildings one walked past the statue of Alcock and Brown, the first men ever to fly the Atlantic non-stop - in 1919 in a lumbering Vickers Vimy bomber from Newfoundland to Ireland - where they crashed and nearly drowned in a Galway bog after sixteen hours and twelve minutes of semi-frozen flight sitting side by side in an open cockpit, scribbling messages to each other in the deafening din of their twin Rolls Royce Eagle engines. Very British heroes. Who knows or learns of them now? Where has their memorial gone? In 1954 long-haul flight was still an adventure. A mid-day departure for Rome would ensure that we overflew the turbulent high altitude winds of the Sahara by night en route for a dawn landing at Kano in Northern Nigeria the next day.

If there ever has been a true Age of Elegance in air travel it probably both came in and vanished with the luxorious flying boats that trundled along the old Empire routes. In 1954 BOAC still made a creditable effort with their Boeing Stratocruisers on the West Africa route. These 'air liners' were a civilian offshoot of the WWII four-engined Boeing Superfortress B29s that had delivered the first atomic bombs to Nagasaki and Hiroshima. They were a beautiful aircraft, fully pressurised for their usual altitude of 20 - 30,000 feet, two-deckers with a cocktail lounge slung below. The Bank then gave us no choice but to fly First Class. This was my first civilian flight on a luxury liner of the skies. Pampered and cossetted by stewards and hostesses (no common 'cabin staff' they, but chosen for their glamour and poise) we flew down across the Alps, the snow-covered peaks glowing in the late afternoon sun, to Rome. Sipping a half-bottle of champagne in the comfortable banquette seats of the bar I felt better already. Resurgent youth was resuming the helm.

While fuelling at Rome in the spring warmth for the overnight haul across the Sahara, I noticed that some of my fellow passengers, nearly all men, were already the worse for drink. From their conversation in the aircraft's cocktail lounge I had gathered they were returning to Government and commercial posts on the Coast and that many were obviously less than delighted at the prospect. My doubts were rekindled and not for the first, and certainly not for the last time in my life I was beset by that recurrent complaint of the hapless traveller. "*What the Hell* am *I* doing here?" This fleeting thought had never expressed itself all during my time in the RAF and in the Far East – with hindsight I suppose because as a serviceman I never had any real choice and was but a chattel at the disposal of the Crown. Now en route to Africa I was an adult supposedly capable of free will and could foresee many sleepless nights ahead pursuing such fruitless extensions of the above concept – plus such unanswerable questions such as, "Why am I *me*?" Or "Does God *really* believe in Himself?"

Flying at not much more than 20,000 feet one can still see the world below. The North African coast with its sprinkling of lights was soon left behind. With the stars bright in a black velvet sky above there was now no sign of any life apart from ourselves thundering south through the night. Wingtip lights flashing, the radiator cooling fins on the piston engines glowing red and from time to time the exhausts throwing out fiery sparks, the all enveloping space that surrounded our little world was broken only by the occasional brilliant streak of a shooting star. After wining and dining well and a nightcap in the bar (I always enjoyed airline food - in later years much to the irritation of my family) I slept fitfully, wrapped in a blanket, thinking of O. and whether we had a future together.

I can remember waking before dawn with a thick head caused by dehydration from too much free champagne taken at too high an altitude. No time changes or jet lag on that route, one flies almost down the Greenwich Meridian. The whole eastern sky was suffusing with a glowing pink from the still hidden sun. As the Stratocruiser began to lose altitude on its sixty mile run-in to Kano in Northern Nigeria, details of the land below slowly emerged. A grey, scrubby landscape appeared, sparsely wooded with occasional patches of cultivation, groups of grass-roofed huts, small villages and settlements, unpaved tracks and scattered herds of cattle or goats near the dwellings. The smoke from cooking fires and pinpoints of flickering yellow-red flames could be seen. As we lumbered down to the airfield at Kano the first rays of the sun pierced a thick haze of smoke and dust, lighting up the slopes of numerous curious pyramids outside the town. These were countless thousands of tons of groundnuts, stored in sacks and awaiting rail shipment south to the sea.

It was the morning of the 25th April 1954 and I was about to make my new landfall in Africa. (In Indo China at that very moment some 10,000 Frenchmen and their colonial troops - were facing odds-on death and destruction at Dien Bien Phu, that desperate battle once famously described as the 'last stand' of Rommel's Afrika Korps and the Waffen SS who filled the ranks of the Foreign Legion - but what cared I?)

Once the doors were opened, a thick, steamy atmosphere, thickly moist and redolent of God Knows What wrapped itself around me with a physical shock. Woodsmoke, dust, vaguely disturbing animal smells flavoured with some slightly putrid ingredients, soon drove off the crispy cool air we had brought down from the Saharan skies. It was the first scent of the real Africa I had come to find. It was rapidly displaced by a choking cloud of kerosene-based insecticide as a black official boarded and sprayed us heavily from a Flit-gun amid the groans and protests of the passengers and the cabin staff, (what pests could we have possibly transported from Rome to need such precautions?) Showing no visible signs of enthusiasm my fellow travellers who were disembarking in Northern Nigeria gathered their hand baggage and were led off on foot towards a huddle of distant buildings.

The rest of us went off to stretch our legs and to take the chance for a refreshing wash in the Airport facilities, leaving the aircraft to be re-fuelled for its final leg to Lagos and Accra. I can remember walking from the aircraft to the transit lounge bathed in a slather of perspiration. It seemed far worse than the heat I remembered from Malaya two years before. In the early morning light the heat, the dust and the scrub-surrounded confines of the airfield were not promising. The main airport concourse was deserted; the West African Airways, Sabena and BOAC desks stood abandoned and empty at this early hour. Two cleaners apathetically stirred the dust on the floor. A few scraggy vultures and kites lurched and scrabbled at bits of rubbish in the dust as we walked outside to the washroom. One of my companions, a middle-aged, grey haired man slightly the worse for wear from his night's carousing fumbled for the light switch in the still near-dark room - it was not to be found. I eventually traced it to the wall furthest from the door where it was mounted sideways rather than vertically. I managed to switch it on. Only one of the room's several naked and fly-speckled light bulbs worked.

The grey-haired man went to one of the wash basins where he turned on the single tap. Nothing happened except that an audible dry gasp of air whispered from the spout. '*AAAaaaaahhh*' it sighed - shortly to be followed by the remains of a small, dead, dessicated lizard. Looking at the fragmented dried-up corpse lying in the basin, he said resignedly. "We're back to the f*****g Coast again, laddie." He went to one of the lavatory cubicles, negotiating the tricky up-side down handle with practised ease, where he retched noisily for a while. I tried the other taps and basins for water without success.

Walking back to the transit lounge with my unused toilet bag I sat down eagerly to breakfast. A smiling, shiny-black steward impressively dressed in starched white drill with a scarlet sash and fez served our breakfast. It was a sort of glazed, lukewarm, hard-fried egg swimming in oil with a strip of tinned bacon. I quite enjoyed it, I was very hungry. My cup of tea was also only luke-warm and with a heavily chlorinated taste that was only slightly masked by the tinned milk, affording another reminder of my days in the Far East.

Opposite me one of my fellow passengers mashed the stub of his cigarette in the yolk of his unfinished egg. "Boy!" He shouted. "Take away this God-awful chop and pass cold beer, one time!" The steward appeared to understand this, to me, barely comprehensible request. He re-appeared with an obviously warm beer bottle, froth billowing from the top. "No cold beer Sah! Said the steward cheerfully. "Fridge 'e done die-oh." The man opposite looked moodily across at me. "I don't really care you know, it doesn't really matter. But if you're going to stay out here young man, make sure you get a kerosene refrigerator and sack the cook if he lets the wick go out. .... Trees, straight from the bloody trees ....." He tailed off and gloomily drank his warm beer.

I don't remember much more of the flight. Fatigue and a delayed hangover had now set in. The cabin staff had lost their crisp efficiency overnight. A few local passengers boarded at Kano for the final leg to Lagos and Accra. There was little to see, cloud cover lay below us all the way. The lingering fumes of insect spray hung over all and the bar had closed. The general air of depression deepened. Our landing at Ikeja, the airport for Lagos, was remarkable only for the fact that with the customary boiled sweets and cotton wool the stewardess gave each passenger a cellophane strip of anti-malarial tablets (this in itself was a foreboding - in my time in the Far East not one such tablet had passed my lips - perhaps West Africa really was still the White Man's Grave!). The heavy, damp heat was oppressive in the aftermath of a tropical downpour. I remember noting with surprise that in the arrival area where I had gone to stretch my legs, the immigration officials at their desks were white and British. (Nigerian

Independence was still seven years away in the future.) There was a joke then current, of the American businessman saying to the Immigration Officer on arrival. "They tell me that this dump is the arsehole of Africa." to which the official wearily replies. "Quite correct Sir, I assume that *you* are just passing through?"

The final leg to Accra took barely an hour. We had no time to gain height and flew onwards in the muggy atmosphere we had taken on board at Lagos. The cabin staff had given up by now and were themselves sleeping or dozing in the banks of empty seats. Below unrolled a flat grey-green landscape of muddy creeks winding through a wilderness of mangrove swamp mergeing into palms and forest. A few scattered tin-roofed villages could be seen along the waterways. We swiftly flew over Dahomey and Togo and then the countryside below opened out beyond the wide estuary of the Volta River. Low hills and grassy plains extended inland from the narrow sandy beaches and rocky headlands on which crashed the endless rollers of the Atlantic. A large slice of West African history is crammed into that short length of coast. English, French, Swedish, Portuguese, Dutch, Brandenburger and Danish forts and trading castles, many of them still standing and some inhabited; white stuccoed strongholds, but all of them long abandoned by the merchant adventurers who originally built them, lured to Africa by the magnet of slaves, spices, ivory and gold. Along the 200 mile shoreline of the old Gold Coast some sixty of these outposts of Europe (some handily within cannon shot of each other) had been established to trade and prosper – and equally to fail and squabble and fill their cemeteries with their despairing occupants. The French had even named their fort at Accra 'Crevecoeur' – or 'Heartbreak.'

It was about mid-day on Saturday when with a bump and a screech of tyres we were down and I was about to start my first weekend in Africa. I was twenty-two years old, rising twenty-three.

I was immediately struck by the noise and the heat. What particularly impressed me was the condition of the three colleagues from the Bank who were there to meet me. Don Fehilly, Dennis Christian and John Mason.. They were all three-parts (out of four) pissed. It was not yet mid-day.

Our first port of call was the bar of the Airport's famous - or notorious, 'Lisbon' Hotel. All three members of my welcoming party were still more or less the worse for drink and its after-effects and certainly fine-set from the continuation of the 'wake' following the sudden and recent demise of my immediate predecessor and his funeral a few days before my own arrival. It was not a particularly cheering reception. I remember quite clearly my own fatigue after the long flight from London and how particularly strong and refreshing were the long, fluted glasses of ice-cold Heineken beer so that our journey to my new quarters in the town leaves only a memory of heat and a bladder strained to bursting point.

My own state of mind, facing the prospect of eighteen months separation from O. was as gloomy as that of my companions. 'X' (my immediate predecessor) had barely lasted for three weeks in Accra (I am ashamed that I can no longer remember his name) when he became ill. His fever was initially diagnosed as malaria but by the time he was taken to the Ridge Hospital, it was polio - then endemic in West Africa and a great killer in the pre-Salk/Sabin vaccine days. (In one twelve month period during the late Fifties, Barclays DCO I believe lost three men to polio alone in the Gold Coast - out of a total expat. staff of about sixty.)

'X' died during the night following his admission to hospital. When placed in the iron-lung* as his breathing failed, there was either a power cut or the machine became faulty and the African nursing orderly detailed to operate the iron-lung manually, dozed off. 'X' died quietly while his nursing attendant slept. (Hans Mees was the MO at the Ridge Hospital a few years later in 1957 and 1958 and clearly recalled for me three similar cases of fatal polio when I spoke of it to him in Italy in 1986) and 'X' was, according to necessary custom, (no doubt triggering off a claim by the Bank on the Life Policy noted below) swiftly buried.

'X' was over six foot tall (or perhaps long?) and no local undertaker had a large enough coffin in stock. The Bank rapidly had one cobbled together by a carpenter in Makola market. The bottom was made of wooden slats from Carnation milk boxes, the late departed clothed in a large pair of pyjamas donated by Duggie Medcalf - the District Manager, nothing else being readily available. My 'greeters' had been pall-bearers, and although they hardly knew 'X' - he had been there such a short while and had spent much of his time out alone and 'on the town' - they had continued their funereal boozing for several days until my own arrival.

My friend Alan Craddock, when I told him this story, reminded me that in those days before we left London for the Coast, Bank staff were obliged to pay for a personal Life Insurance policy to provide the magnificent sum of £150 - the beneficiary being the Bank - the purpose of which being that if one died in West Africa, the Bank did not end up out-of-pocket in paying for their employee's funeral expenses. Crad,

---

* Probably donated by The Nuffield Foundation. Polio in the 1930s and until the late 1950s was such a worldwide scourge that Lord Nuffield's stated aim was to put an iron lung into every hospital throughout the Empire.

when he left the Bank of British West Africa after only a few years, with considerable foresight in one so young (at that time) persuaded the insurers to convert the policy to an endowment which some thirty years later yielded him a handsome sum on maturity. I had long forgotten that the Bank were such ungenerous employers in matters such as this.

The Bank had a 'chummery' for the more junior bachelor staff. This was in Adabraka, a more or less respectable commercial and residential area of Accra. Our Mess was a sprawling two-storied white stucco building within a compound surrounded by a high wall with an arched gateway. A single frangipani tree with its white, waxen, perfumed flowers grew from the hard red earth of the yard, nourished by a trickle of damp kitchen sewage which flowed down a green-slimed gutter out through the gate. At some time in the past I believe the building had been a stable. It was either rented by the Bank, or more likely seized in lieu of some bad debt or other from a Lebanese or Syrian trader.

The walls of the house were thick for coolness, the stained and peeling white stucco reflected the glare of sunlight and around the base of the walls was a rich terracotta stain where the torrential rain had splashed red mud up to a height of two feet or more. The living rooms, the dining area and large open verandah were upstairs. Down below at street level around the central courtyard were several small, airless rooms with slatted doors and wooden jalousies or shutters over the windows which had probably been the horse-boxes and were now the bedrooms. Each contained a bed, a chair, a mosquito net and a PWD** chest-of-drawers all standing on a bare red-cement floor (red 'Cardinal' brand polish once stained the floors of the entire Empire). Next to the room I was given was 'X's, still locked tight - presumed infectious and left until such time as his few belongings could be either sent back to London or disposed of.

The heat and the noise were trying. There was of course no air-conditioning and the racket filtered in from the traffic on the road outside and from the colourful African mammies at their pavement stalls. A group of 'talking' drummers from the Northern Territories, wearing jellybag caps or wide-brimmed leather decorated conical straw hats - like huge upturned funnels - with striped cotton smocks and baggy white trousers, leather amulets on their wrists, seemed to have taken up a permanent and

---

**: PWD. The universal acronym for the colonial Public Works Department - who made and repaired roads and bridges, operated the water and power supplies and made basic furniture in their workshops.

noisy residence with a couple of their 'dancing' horses down a side alley outside the gates. It was all difficult to come to terms with. Had I not already had some experience of the Tropics it would have been much harder.

Of the other three bachelors in the mess two were fairly hard cases in their late twenties. Don Fehilly was Irish - an ex-infantry officer. Dennis Christian, a former Captain in the Commandos, was already known to me by reputation. He had previously been with the Chartered Bank in London - with an enviable record of drinking and womanising. While still in London I had heard of his feat of 'balancing the books.' Late one New Year's Eve, the annual 'Balance Night,' near the hour of midnight, he staggered down the steps from the mezzanine floor into the main banking hall in Bishopsgate, with several heavy ledgers piled up on his head - so tight (from frequent visits to the nearby Kings Arms during the evening) as to be barely able to stand or to speak. Addressing the outraged Scots Chief Accountant thus - "I've balanced the books; can't we all go home now? *Hic!*"

It was shortly after that episode that Dennis had left the Chartered Bank in Bishopsgate, gone down the road to the Bank of British West Africa in Gracechurch Street and within a week or two he arrived in Accra, carrying on more or less from where he had left off in London.

John Mason was the third of the trio, aged twenty-three or four and just completing his first tour, most of which he had spent in Kumasi. I was shocked to find that he had already exceeded his eighteen-month contract by some two months - and still didn't know when he would be sent on leave. This was terrible!

At the Adabraka Mess, Don Fehilly was 'chopmaster;' responsible for the general messing, paying bills, keeping the accounts and hiring and firing the cook. He himself employed two young Ashanti lads as his personal houseboys, Kwesi and Kofi. They could not have been more than sixteen or seventeen years of age. Generally speaking Ashanti were not considered to make good house servants; they could be temperamental and were not always inclined to take instruction easily. Don used to tease these two young boys unmercifully to the point of tears whenever, as they often did, they would make errors of omission or commission. Don would gibber at them like a chimpanzee making grunting noises and scratching his armpits - which distressed them greatly. I found scenes like this offensive and embarrassing. West Africans and Ghanaians in particular often have a notable sense of humour but this doesn't extend to ridicule of their persons to which they are greatly sensitive - particularly from a *'Bruni'* a 'white man.' To call someone *'Kwasia!'* meaning 'fool,' is a dangerous insult and most extreme is to use the word 'clown' which has implications far exceeding the simple

English concept of the word. To use any of these terms can reduce the recipient to a foaming rage. Another expression which was a definite 'No-No' was to call someone a *"bushman!"* This always implied a very low opinion of someone's intelligence and suggested a recent descent from the trees*. (This latter fact alone explains the total, absolute non-marketability in West Africa of that well known at that time, British make of wireless - the Bush radio). Don was playing with fire with his two young Ashanti boys and his monkey imitations. *

By mutual agreement I paid half Kwesi's wages and shared his services with Don Fehilly - such as they were, washing and ironing, bedmaking and cleaning and waiting at table. Our meals were taken communally and were of very indifferent quality. If it rained while our food was being served, having been brought up the open staircase from the kitchen on the ground floor, the food arrived cold and damp. The menu was dominated by the general neglect on the part of the British bachelor in the tropics to pay much attention to what was served up by his cook. This problem was compounded by the lack of a native cuisine acceptable to European taste (with the exception of 'palm-oil chop' and curries), by the cook's ignorance of his employer's dietary customs and by his inevitable peccadilloes, such as milking the daily market money.

Our dining table was always dominated by a centrepiece - a large blue-and-white tin of 1,000 Paludrine anti-malarial tablets one of which we were each supposed to consume daily. The dining room was adequately equipped with basic PWD type furniture, sturdily made and practical but lacking in style. The windows were metal framed and shielded on the outside by green painted, slatted wooden shutters - jalousies, to keep out the glare and the noise from the streets outside. On a table in the corner was our sole piece of modern gadgetry, the 'Squawk Box,' the local Radio Re-diffusion set which was rented for 7s.6d a month. This broadcast via landline the local news in the seven principal languages of the Gold Coast: Ewe, Twi, Ga, Fanti, Dagbani, Hausa

---

* See Ward, "*A History of the Gold Coast*" and Rattray, "*Ashanti Law and Constitution.*" 'Abuse' is a serious matter to a Ghanaian/Gold Coast African where they can be extremely sensitive to ridicule and their childhood training inculcates this attitude. Historically speaking, many lives were lost, wars fought and bitter hatreds engendered over the centuries of European influence on the Coast - due to the failure of the white man to understand the depth of some of the African customs and cultural sanctions. The English proverb 'Hard words break no bones' is entirely contrary to native West African feeling. The word 'abuse' conveys many ideas besides the correct English meaning. The Akan languages (which include the Ashanti) contain many words signifying different kinds of 'abuse' many of which are simply untranslatable. An Englishman is hardened throughout his schooldays until he comes to regard 'silly ass' almost a term of endearment - call him a thief or a liar and he will be less tolerant. A West African's childhood training is all the other way, and what is to the one a mere childish trifle, becomes to the other a bitter insult.

and English - all of which took up quite a proportion of the daily available total of only seven or eight hours broadcasting in all. Endless record programmes of Gold Coast 'Highlife' (E.T. Mensah and his 'Tempos' Band) and West Indian calypso music (the catchy and ever popular *'Please Mistah Don' You Touch Me Tomato!'*) were played, but most importantly, Re-diffusion also relayed the BBC's news broadcasts which kept us in touch with the outside world. Only those who have lived abroad really know what those opening bars of the BBC World Service's signature tune *'Liliburlero'* fizzing, whistling and hissing through the short-wave static, meant to those far from home.

None of the bachelors in the mess seemed to have accumulated more than a wind-up gramophone and a few scratched 78 records at the best, or more than a few paperback books wherewith to lighten their cultural darkness. As to 'Culture,' the 'British Council Hour' - a programme on the Squawk Box that bemused the locals with such gems as readings of 'Beowulf' or once to my total amazement later in Sekondi, a free-verse English translation of a Chinese puppet play. The British Council tried hard on what was probably a very limited budget, in later years I heard the story of an International Festival of Culture organised in Kathmandu to which the USSR despatched a touring company of the Kirov Ballet. The British Council, responsible for such matters, managed to muster a team of two (the third being immobilised with acute diarrhoea) female clog dancers from Lancashire who performed on a table top in front of a large audience of Nepalese which included the King. The spectacle was received in bewildered silence.

The other main room in our Mess was a long sitting room on the first floor, almost a verandah, and again overlooking the street. The principal feature of this room was a large, humming refrigerator in the then current American style, a head-high and capacious machine of the sort depicted on Saturday Evening Post covers by Norman Rockwell. Its contents usually consisted of a half-dozen or so bottles of Heineken or Beck's beer, kept ice-cold, ice cubes (which themselves had to be made from boiled water) and sodawater perhaps, some fruit squash and a bottle or two of boiled and filtered tap water for general consumption. The cook may have had another small 'fridge in his kitchen, but on recollection I doubt it. All our food was either fresh or tinned and bought in daily from the market together with firewood for the simple wood-burning 'Dover' cooking stove. Any form of air-conditioning, apart from opening the window a bit wider or turning up the ceiling fan, was generally unknown at that time except in the houses of American missionaries and shipping agents.

Apart from the 'fridge, the rest of the furniture consisted of a row of wicker seats and 'steamer' chairs along the walls on both sides of the room. For some reason we all sat in the row of seats facing the fridge. There were a few small occasional tables for the ashtrays (everyone smoked cigarettes like chimneys in those distant days), drinks and 'small chop.' In the early evening before dinner we usually, if in, sat over a beer or two before showering and changing. Dennis Christian was often fairly well plastered by the time it was dark - about 6.30 pm - remaining topped-up until bedtime, unless he had other things on his mind.

Sometimes by 7 pm or so a girl or two, often a pair who claimed acquaintance with one or another residents of the Mess (usually Dennis again) would climb the stairs, and engage in idle chit-chat over a 'Fanta' or a cold beer. The girls always sat on the opposite side of the room flanking the 'fridge, trying to stimulate the bachelors' interest before they went on to one of the Accra night clubs. These Accra bar girls were very jolly and easy company and would have been upset to think of themselves as either prostitutes or call-girls in the European sense. Many of them had day jobs in places like the big trading company stores or Government offices. Out for fun and a bit of extra cash and a good time dancing and drinking in the night-clubs, (Kit-Kat, Lisbon, Seaview Hotel, Havana, the Lido - strange how all the names come back). Here the patrons of all races, European, African, Lebanese, drank and danced and made assignations - all for the entrance price of a bottle of beer (to keep out the penniless riff-raff) - later brought free to your table in exchange for your entrance ticket once inside.

My recollection of our mess food is that it was pretty awful. Very plain, badly cooked and sometimes unidentifiable. I remember one evening eating a nondescript piece of fish which I thought was probably a cutlet off a large snapper or some other firm-fleshed denizen of the local deep. I idly wondered aloud why the cook had prepared what I took to be gravy as an accompaniment for fish. This unusual combination also struck Don, who was our 'chopmaster,' as curious and he sent either Kofi or Kwesi to enquire the reason from 'Cuku.'

With some such message as "Mek you go ask Cuku now-now why he done pass gravy for fish?" The reply came back via the steward - "Massa, Cuku say 'e no be fish -'e be pork chop."

There is no satisfactory response to such an answer. It is the final move in an African dominated end-game over which one has little control. One simply continues eating to meet one's basic nutritional requirements.

Fruit, such as oranges, paw-paws, bananas, limes and pomelo, was plentiful but of fairly poor quality. Potatoes, being imported, were often unavailable and when these were scarce 'Cuku' would fry cakes of grated yam or cassava as an unwelcome substitute. Tough green beans and various species of local spinach seemed to be the only green vegetable and they were boiled to destruction. The bread was sweet and flabby with added sugar and powdered milk, baked for the local taste from American flour ('Robin Hood' brand - whose re-cycled flour sacks made excellent vests for local informal day wear). If not eaten within a few hours such bread would start to go green with mould. Milk for tea and coffee was provided by the 'Iron Cow' - watered down Carnation tinned milk. There was tough, fibrous, tasteless beef, skinny and strangely butchered pieces of goat and mutton, tinned peas and tinned diced mixed veg. - all copiously laced with Lea & Perrin's Worcestershire Sauce or ketchup. These were our mainstays.

British bachelors almost invariably ended up eating tinned soup and tinned vegetables as the cook's easiest way out, the daily ration of soup being helped down by a splash or two of 'Sherry Peppers' (red hot chillies marinated in sherry). Unless one was a French bachelor - with a French African cook from The Ivory Coast, or Togo, in which case you dined luxuriously, but off an oilcloth covered table. Few of the English would employ such a cook, it was reckoned they smothered everything in garlic and butter (these were the days when English housewives still pre-soaked macaroni and broken-up spaghetti in cold water before boiling it for half-an-hour or so). With a 'French' cook the 'chop' bills were said to be doubled, and besides they often spoke no English, not even Pidgin.

It was no better if one went out to eat at the Accra Club, or the Atlantic or Avenida Hotels. One could not escape the same dishes cooked in the same old boring way. Not a few bachelors - to avoid the inconvenience of hiring a cook and all the domestic hassle that this implied - ate all their meals 'on contract' at the Accra Club, but fared no better. For sweets or dessert - caramel custard was the staple resort of every African cook ever trained by an English 'Madam.' The general consensus seemed to be that the climate was too hot to be interested in food or to have an appetite. That was just for self-indulgent Frenchmen who didn't know any better.

CHAPTER 3

'Work is a Four-Letter Word'
(Anon)
" .... how earnestly are you set a-work, and how ill requited!
Why should our endeavour be so loved, and the performance so loathed?"
(Wm. Shakespeare - 'Twelfth Night)

We were usually up and about by 7am, six mornings of the week since the Bank opened for business at 8 am, on Saturday mornings only until noon rather than 1 pm. By the time we rose it was already hot and sticky, as it had been all night unless a rainstorm had cooled things down to the point where one reached for a blanket. Our breakfast (if one could face it) was invariably ripe paw-paw with fresh lime, followed by limp, translucent tinned bacon, eggs, all seethed rather than fried in warm oil, plus a slice or two of yesterday's mouldy bread dried into a cardboard replica of toast over the cook's wood-fired stove. A Paludrine tablet from the tin on the table washed down by a cup of weak tea tasting of damp, smoky wood and tinned milk and one was ready to go to work. A battered 'contract' taxi took the three of us who worked in the main Accra High Street Branch to arrive at the office by 7.30, and Don Fehilly departed in his pre-war Citroen Light 15 (black of course) for Tudu where he was Branch Manager.

At work in Accra, one was expected to dress respectably. A white, usually short-sleeved shirt and tie, slacks - probably locally tailored from white drill - was the order of the day. White drill was much favoured all round. With no air conditioning, suits or jackets were rarely worn except by some of the more senior African staff.

Fortunately the long-established Gold Coast Head Office of the BBWA had been built in the old colonial style, facing on to Accra High Street that ran parallel with the sea, one block back from the waterfront. The long three-storied building had overhanging eaves to shield the interior from the sun, with open verandahs to catch whatever sea-breezes there might be and tall green-shuttered jalousies over the windows. The top floor consisted of a few flats for expat staff. Inside, the high ceilings of the offices were fitted with a multitude of slowly circulating fans. On the ground floor the long mahogany counter with its gleaming brass grilles separated the public from the staff. All traditional and very practical. From his desk, flanked by khaki-uniformed messengers, the Accountant could command the whole of the Bank's public operation set out before him. African clerks perched on high stools toiled over huge hand-written ledgers and the European assistant accountants scribbled at their pigeonholed desks, banging on their bells to summon messengers to ferry fresh batches of account entries and documents to someone else. Personally I hadn't the faintest idea what I was supposed to be doing.

I was given a desk and told that from henceforth I should regard myself as an 'assistant accountant' but nobody really suggested what I might do. Bits and pieces of paper arrived from time to time. I would look at these carefully in a studied manner, sign or initial them, then spike them on a fearsome sharp piece of wire, or if it appeared appropriate, bang my bell in an authoritative manner and a messenger would appear as if by magic and ferry them elsewhere.

One of the more exciting things which occasionally varied the torpid monotony of sitting through a whole week of long, dull and stultifyingly hot mornings would be a sudden outbreak of shouting, banging of grilles and general upset from one or other of the African cashiers' cages along the counter. The clerks would stir uneasily, looking up from their ledgers. Dear old Stan Butcher, the imperturbable Accountant, invariably smoking his short stubby pipe, would issue an order and reluctantly the messengers would go out into the Banking Hall, grabbing a brush shank or a chair, en route towards the centre of the continuing uproar. There as often as not would be a gibbering, stark bollock-naked African, with his lunatic, long matted dreadlocks caked in mud and dung, body smeared with dirt and dust, would be shrieking and capering at the cashiers through their protecting bars. The cashiers, not unnaturally, were backing off, locking up their cages while returning equally vociferous abuse in the vernacular. The customers would scatter nervously, leaving the shit-covered madman well alone to his ravings. This was quite a frequent problem. It wasn't good for business.

Accra had minimal Social Services and if there was an Asylum for the mentally disturbed I never heard of it. Distressingly unhinged madmen roamed the streets, naked, filthy, living and sleeping in the deep storm gutters amid the garbage, and while few in number their appearance and behaviour gave them a conspicuous presence in the town. Often thrown out of their home villages and solely dependant on the chancy charity of their fellow countrymen, they found their way to the big towns. There was absolutely no mechanism for dealing with them. The hospitals refused to admit them, the police would not arrest them - they had nowhere they could lock them up except for their cells - and that caused more trouble than it was worth. Dirty, barking mad, aggressive and smelly, they were a frightening sight, but sometimes not so mad that they couldn't be bought off with a few small coins. At these times the police constable on guard with his rifle and bayonet outside on the portico steps of the bank would smartly vanish. The messengers would reluctantly approach the capering maniac, brandishing broom and chair and try to usher the dung-covered madman out of the bank. This ploy usually failed until Stan Butcher would reluctantly signal for the last resort - one of the messengers, keeping well away, would toss a small coin or two at the feet of the rancid lunatic - who would scoop them up triumphantly, to depart capering and gibbering on his way to his next port of call up the road. Stan would reluctantly sign a debit to sundry expenses to reimburse the messenger the few pennies expended. Peace would reign again. The police constable would re-appear at his post on the steps. Normal business (whatever that was, I had to find out soon!) was resumed.

CHAPTER 4

'Diamond Run to Swedru.'
"Goodness, what beautiful diamonds."
"Goodness has nothing to do with it, dearie."
(Mae West - 1893?-1980))

After I had been in Accra for a month or two, Stan Butcher, the Accountant, sent for me one hot morning. "Someone has to go to Swedru tomorrow to pick up a parcel of diamonds - it might as well be you." (Shades of up-country escort detachments in Malaya a year or two previously!) Before I left the office that afternoon I collected from the Chief Cashier a stout galavanised steel specie box (padlocked with an iron transverse bar running through the lid) I was not given a key, standard keys were kept at each Branch.

Instead of going off to work the next morning I took a rickety taxi up to the airport police station where I collected and signed a receipt for *'One escort policeman plus rifle, bayonet and 10 rounds,'* cost to be invoiced to the Bank. The 'escort' police, so called in the Gold Coast were the strong-arm branch of the law - armed paramilitaries, invariably either Hausas or Northern Territories tribesmen, often with little command of either English or the law, charged with riot and crowd control, guarding Government offices, treasuries, escorting gold and cash shipments for the mines and the banks and generally providing a bit more muscle wherever needed than the otherwise unarmed regular uniformed Police.

My young man was a Moshi from beyond the Northern Territories, his face boldly marked with elaborate tribal scars criss-crossing his forehead and cheeks like wheel spokes. He was dressed smartly in a red felt tarboosh with a tassel and bearing its polished brass Gold Coast badge with the palm tree emblem, he wore a blue woollen jersey with leather shoulder patches, (I always thought how itchy and uncomfortable these crew-necked, long-sleeved garments must have been in the heat). A brown polished leather belt with cartridge pouch and long Enfield sword bayonet, crisply starched khaki shorts with a scarlet stripe, blue knee length puttees and gleaming brown boots completed his turn out. He had a rolled-up blue cape strapped over his right shoulder and a small haversack. He spoke no English, or any other language that I could understand. He had obviously been instructed in his duties, and noticing him fiddling with the safety catch on his rifle - I gently took it from him (in accordance with the sound advice given to me in the Bank) and took the nine rounds from the magazine - plus the one already chambered 'up the spout' and put them in my pocket. I felt much safer as we took our rickety taxi back downtown to the lorry park in Makola Market.

At eight in the morning the market was already bustling with trade. '*Kaya-kaya*' NT 'boys' and labourers shifting sacks and bales of cotton cloth, vast shining blue-black market 'Mammies' slung about with sleeping babies tucked in their rainbow coloured cloth, stalls of produce and trade goods of every kind - mammies and piccans, swarming children shouting *"Akwaa'ba Bruni!"* ("Hello White man") - or "Dash me penny Massah, I be schoolboy," (this last, a patent untruth). The bus - I had been relieved to find it was actually a bus and not a 'mammy truck' I was to travel in - owned by the Syrian Adra Brothers Transport Co., was rapidly filling up with mammies with babies, baskets of chickens, a kid goat tethered to the seat behind, everything a riot of colour and noise in the morning heat. My guard and I seized a bench seat immediately behind the driver (First Class) - and we were off to Swedru, some fifty miles to the north-west of Accra, inland from Winneba, bouncing and bucketing along the dusty laterite road that swooped and twisted into the dark green forested hills.

It was a hair-raising journey. The rickety bus was wide open to the wind that rushed past; choking red dust covered us every time another vehicle came by. The driver who sat immediately in front of us was protected by steel bars (presumably to save him from assault by his passengers or the risk of a cascade of chickens or goats). He was elderly for a driver, a thin white curly stubble fringing his mostly bald pate - most unusual in Africans who frequently dyed their hair. Most alarming of all, when he turned around to peer at his cargo of freight and passengers, I saw he was wearing thick, myopically bottle-lensed spectacles of the type traditionally worn by Mr. Magoo or some archetypal sex-maniac offering a small child a bag of sweeties. He drove the ancient bus in the manner of Ben Hur hurtling his chariot with wild abandon around a Roman arena. On the roof of the bus his 'mate' who was perched on top of the deck cargo – stems of bananas, bales, boxes and baskets of livestock, I thought must have re-lived several lifetimes each journey as moments of terror were succeeded every few minutes by yet another intimation of impending catastrophe.

After the passage of fifty years I can still conjure up with startling clarity certain scenes from that journey. The driver hunched over the wheel - which I could clearly see had at least several inches of play which had to be taken up as slack before the direction of the bus was affected in any way. The total lack of any apparent braking power, this deficiency was made up for by the incessant use of the bulb-operated horn mounted on the side of the cab - this meant that for most of the time the driver only had one arm free for the gears and the wheel. The brilliant green of the foliage lining the road contrasted with the red laterite. We passed through swarming villages with mud 'swish' walls thatched with palm or rusty corrugated iron and roadside market stalls. We crossed dark, mysterious streams which emerged from the forest, over rattling single track bridges. Near villages the white sandy banks of the pools were busy with people bathing, washing clothes or collecting the dark clear water in tin drums and clay pots, the tops plugged with a tuft of leaves to stop the contents splashing over as the women hoisted them onto their heads. White sand contrasted with the black and shining skin of the villagers dressed in multi-hued cloth set off by white teeth and the pale yellow of the palms of their hands as they waved in greeting. My policeman soon lapsed into slumber. I quietly removed his rifle and put it under the seat with the specie box. To my intense surprise when we stopped in a village to unload and take on fresh cargo and livestock, the driver's mate on the roof, wedged in amongst the bananas, was also fast asleep!

We reached Swedru shortly after midday. The bus stopped in the middle of town in a dusty, pot-holed street with deep roadside storm ditches alongside a tumbledown mud-walled shack where someone had scrawled in uneven whitewashed letters - "NO URINATION HERE." The Bank was a five minute walk away in the commercial centre of the town by the cross-roads leading south to Winneba and north to Oda. There were a few tin-roofed Syrian stores, a concrete building or two, a few other houses verandahed and porticoed in the Brazilian style so common on the Coast and wooden-shuttered against the sun. The Bank was a four-square building, whitewashed and shaded by a low spreading roof over the upper floor.

I had a brief lunch with the Manager (Alex Barbour who later moved on to Sierra Leone) in his flat over the office. I can still see him, crisply dressed in starched shirt and white drill trousers as he took some small wax-sealed packages from his safe, locking them in my steel box. He showed me more loose stones in folded tissue wrappers which he had still to make up for another 'parcel.' These were nothing but dull and dirty looking chips of crystal to my untrained eye. One or two larger stones - although flawed - were of better gem quality but the bulk were simply industrial 'bort' of no great value, 'rough diamonds' in fact, like many of the traders who dealt in such commodities.

At that time before Independence (later in 1957 the government was to nationalise the trading part of the business), the Bank was still the main licensed buyer from the private diggers who panned and fossicked for diamonds and gold in the forests of the Gold Coast Colony and Ashanti. In the 1930s diamonds had been discovered in commercial quantities and via the Bank were shipped out to London for sale after cleaning and further grading. The managers of Branches like Tarkwa and Swedru were skilled buyers. After sorting and grading the stones, the manager estimated their worth, and then made advances to the miners of up to 70 percent of their value. Once the proceeds had been received back from London the Bank took a commission of seven-and-a-half percent and paid a further nine percent in Customs duty and a royalty to the 'Stool' (the Paramount Chief) and paid any remaining balance over to the miner. It was a very lucrative business for the Bank in the diamond boom of the early Fifties. Everyday banking transactions were the least of the manager's concerns in towns like Swedru when tiny diamonds almost by the bucketful, encased in dirt and grime, were dumped on the counter by grinning miners, greedy for their cash.

Back on the same bus again for the same hot, dusty ride back to Accra. My 'escort' fast asleep again for most of the journey - the risk of robbery or violence at that time was minimal. In the last fading days of Empire in Britain's showpiece colony in West Africa the writ of law and order was almost endemic as far as any organised criminal activity was concerned. I handed over my steel box to the chief cashier back at the Bank, gave my (by now) wide-awake policeman his ten rounds of ammunition, plus a packet of cigarettes in exchange for a smart salute, sent him off for a well earned rest and went back to the bachelor Mess for a shower to rinse off my first thick coating of African dust.

In Accra we used to go back to the Mess for a light lunch after the Bank had closed to the public at 1 p.m. In most up-country branches and places like Sekondi one stayed in the office until 1.30 or 2 pm or whenever the books were finally balanced and closed-off - then the office was locked up and one went back to the bank flat or bungalow, work now finished for the rest of the day. Then perhaps a snooze, or a late afternoon game of tennis at the Club - or whatever recreation took one's fancy. (This regime was known as 'keeping government hours').

In Accra and other main branches however, there was always extra work to be done and we often stayed on until 5 or 6pm. In early 1954 after closing off the books for the day in Accra all the junior European staff were expected to go and count the cash in the reserve strongroom - where serious shortages had come to light in £500 bundles of notes which had already supposedly been checked, double-checked and countersigned. This was a very boring way of passing an hour or two in the late afternoon and swiftly became intolerably boring.

All the book-keeping records were kept by hand in enormous ledgers, supposedly insect-proofed with their leather and cloth bindings impregnated with arsenic. Health and Safety regulations - what were they? Virtually nothing was mechanised or relied on anything other than simple pen-pushing. After the close of business each day a balance was struck to the nearest penny, the accounts were closed off - and the clerks then set-to again, writing up by hand the statements for each customer and filing the day's mountain of paper. It was all eminently straightforward and after a few months, even I with my slender knowledge and lack of numeracy began to grasp the principles and theory of how to run a bank. In a modern-day bank, computer-driven, with all-electronic transactions, mechanised, automated to the hilt as they are, I doubt if any single member of staff could encompass much beyond his own particular sphere, whereas it was a matter of simple fact that any one of us, almost without exception in those far-off days, knew and understood how the entire operation functioned.

When I say we went back to the Mess for lunch, that is most of us did. Colin Macleod who was acting as the relief manager at that time vanished to the Accra Club or some other watering hole for most of the afternoon with his 'Old Coaster' cronies. Stan Butcher, the much-badgered branch accountant would snatch a quick cup of tea across the road in the YMCA. 'D' would disappear most days for most of the afternoon to conduct one or more of his multifarious amours with various married European ladies - whose husbands were either out at work, or away on trek, or drilling the African soldiers of the Gold Coast Regiment - 'D' had a great penchant for the bored wives of the British NCOs and officers who were still there in some number.

Sometimes as we left the Mess after lunch to go back to the office, 'D' would race up in a taxi to tidy his room or to beg the loan of some clean bedlinen in anticipation of the imminent arrival of some lady friend or other whom he had persuaded in the lunch hour to visit him that afternoon and perhaps in all innocence expected nothing more than a cup of tea and light conversation at our Mess.

'D' was darkly handsome, with great charm and wit, but at the same time totally unreliable. Towards the end of his tour his afternoon 'rest periods' were seriously curtailed when he started to work in the District Manager's Office - by whom he was well thought of for some strange reason - perhaps 'D' amused Duggie Medcalf - as he did us all. By the time 'D' was due to go on leave, a few months after I arrived on the scene, he was broke as usual and in debt. I sold him (sensibly for cash) my smart blazer that I had brought with me from London and no longer needed so that he at least had a jacket to arrive with back in the UK. It was said that Duggie Medcalf, the District Manager, had lent him money personally to clear his debts at the Club and elsewhere. We had a great party when he finally left; toasting his expected return in three months time. No-one that I knew ever heard from him again.

CHAPTER 5

Sekondi - 1954

"The one Dutch success of the war (1783) was the capture of
the British fort (George) at Sekondi. By the Peace of Versailles of 1783
the status quo was restored, but the fort had been destroyed by
the Dutch and was not rebuilt."
(Dr. W. W. Claridge, History of the Gold Coast and Ashanti, 1915)

After only three months in Accra I was sent to Sekondi. I was to take over as branch accountant following some 'unexplained' (but seemingly traumatic) incident which had necessitated the urgent transfer of the incumbent, one Rollo Plinge, to Takoradi, a short seven miles further west along the coast. Whatever it was that had happened and nobody seemed to know, I was given barely twenty-four hours to pack up my few belongings, pay my messing bills, say my farewells to my new found friends and colleagues shake the dust of the city from my heels and go. Everyone said "You will like Sekondi - small town, great fun." Whatever I may have felt about this I cannot remember, but to be uprooted so swiftly was unsettling and made me even readier to pack in the whole African venture. O. was still writing to me almost daily - as I was to her - and I was missing her more than ever.

Being fairly brash and self-confident (with hindsight these qualities had little foundation in one so young and inexperienced), I decided I would introduce myself to 'Duggie' Medcalf the District Manager before I left. I was already a little taken aback that he hadn't sent for me for an introductory chat and pep talk since my arrival. Most remiss, I thought, and lacking in the social graces not to see a new junior executive and to make him feel at home. After all, there were only some fifty or so expatriates to run the whole chain of the Bank's branch offices in the Gold Coast for him. Never having met 'Duggie,' merely having seen him striding up the stairs to his office, I did not know how mistaken I was in my assessment of the situation. I was shortly to find out.

Douglas Medcalf was a gritty gentleman with an uncertain temper not improved by an ulcer. His cryptic DHM initial at the foot of a memo (I am sure it is still burned into the braincells of a generation of Gold Coast BBWA staff) could reduce an errant branch manager to a quaking jelly - often with good cause. His nose for smelling out 'iffy' loans and elliptical or evasive explanations on branch returns was deservedly notorious. In Accra since 1947, first as manager of the territory's main branch and in the district manager's hot seat since 1953, the year before my arrival, he had more than enough on his plate without my bursting in on him late one sweltering afternoon. His office was on the first floor at the back of the old colonial style building, facing away from any cooling sea breeze there might be. Green wooden shutters, half-closed, screened out the glare. A huge ceiling fan slowly circled above a large desk covered with damp papers held down by various heavy weights to stop them vanishing in any errant breeze. A black telephone handset with a crank handle, plus a bell to summon messenger or secretary was the sole concessions to modern technology. Brushing aside the urgent protests of both these latter gentlemen (female office staff were few and far between) in my determination to meet my Boss, I knocked on Duggie's door. "Come in!" This was I suppose on looking back, the high point of the brief interview that followed. From then on it was all definitely downhill.

"What are *you* doing in here?" He asked, in not at all an encouraging tone. I said who I was, that I was on my way to Sekondi and I thought it proper to introduce myself before I left.

The gist of the ensuing one-sided conversation indicated that he knew perfectly well who I was. That he hadn't sent for me. That he didn't wish to see me now. That he was sending me to Sekondi because I could most easily be spared in that my departure would make no difference to him or to the Branch, and that I had better do a damned sight better there than I had done so far in Accra. "Good afternoon!" I swiftly decamped.

It has long been a source of regret to me that in the days of my youth our seniors were generally regarded with a certain amount of awe as well as deference – and certainly more respect than some of them may have deserved. There were strict hierarchies in place and employees were expected to observe rank and status. I think that perhaps it followed on from the fact that nearly all of us had served in the armed forces at some time and our seniors saw it as no more than their due. By the time I myself reached more mature years and in my own opinion at least, had become entitled to the same respect and deference I had afforded to my predecessors – alas the whole system seemed to have collapsed in tatters even gone into reverse - informality and familiarity have ruled ever since. 'Luv,' 'Ducks,' or if lucky, 'Guv' perhaps or 'Squire' and the merest stripling youth or maid will now use one's Christian name on first aquaintance. We have never since come up with any satisfactory form of address to replace 'Sir' or 'Miss' or Madam' in the same way that our continental cousins have continued to shake hands with each other several times a day and to use their traditional and customary titles of respect in a manner that makes personal interaction so much easier to maintain even where familiarity rules.

Early next morning, hung-over more than a little from my farewells to the other members of our mess, I took a taxi out to the airport just after first light. Most of my sparse household kit was going through to Sekondi by road so I had little luggage apart from a change of clothes. The airport buildings were deserted. On the tarmac apron a Bristol Freighter and a Dakota, both twin-engined aircraft, were the only planes to be seen, lit up by the first rays of the sun. Outside across the road lay the verandah of the Lisbon Hotel, the tables empty, too early even for an early breakfast. In the dust the usual scavenging black kite and a vulture hopped and tussled without enthusiasm over the ownership of some desiccated scrap of rubbish. Overall, the immediate prospects were not exciting. My brief stay in Accra had been neither particularly enjoyable nor enlightening. My future seemed very uncertain.

I spotted a stirring of life. Comatose for the moment, under the sign of the 'Dumbo' look-alike winged green elephant of the West African Airways desk a clerk briefly stirred in his sleep. Waking him for a vital moment or two I checked in my luggage, established that he didn't know when my flight would depart and left him to his slumbers.

Finding a seat I settled down to await events while I pondered the information I had gleaned the previous evening concerning the reason for my precipitate departure from Accra. One of our small party had spoken that day to a colleague in Takoradi and had learned in the strictest confidence (soon undone with a little alcoholic lubrication) that Rollo Plinge, from whom I was about to take over as Branch Accountant had put up a serious 'black,' a social gaffe, after only a few brief weeks 'on seat.' The previous Saturday morning just past noon as the Bank was winding up for the weekend, Tony Carter, the manager, had said to Rollo as he was leaving the office. "Come up to the bungalow and have a beer before lunch." Rollo locked up, went up to his flat over the Bank, changed into shorts, discarded his tie and set off on foot for the Ridge where Tony Carter and his wife Edith lived. Not worth taking a battered local taxi. Having no car, it was only twenty minutes or so to walk down past the main Post Office in the tree shaded square with its memorial to some long dead Medical Officer who had once saved the town from an epidemic of yellow fever. Past the tennis courts, over the railway crossing and up the hill – there was the Sekondi Club in its grove of neem and flame trees off on the right - it was very hot in the midday sun - and Rollo decided to pop in and have a cooling beer before tackling the last stretch up the Ridge to the Carters' house.

Still None The Wiser

The afternoon came and went. Rollo stayed at the bar of the Club no doubt distracted by congenial company, pre-lunch drinks (and lunch) now long forgotten. By 8.30 that long ago Saturday evening he was still perched on his bar stool, still quaffing cold beer, well-pickled by now, blissfully unaware of passing time, comfortably sucking his thumb as was his habit, between draughts of Heineken. By now Rollo, if still aware of what was going on, strictly speaking should have decamped to the Cads' Bar in a side room at the back of the Club[*] where by established custom those still dressed in shorts or without a tie after 7 pm were expected to ensconce themselves, to avoid giving - or receiving offence. Rollo was either unaware - or beyond caring that this particular Saturday night was the Club's monthly Formal Dance Night. Gentlemen in white dinner jackets or in 'bum-freezers' and black tie, plus lady members, mostly wives, in evening frocks were assembling in groups at the bar before the evening's jollity properly commenced. Rollo was doubly conspicuous both by his obvious inebriation and his informal attire. The District Commissioner and his lady came in. The DC, President of the Club and a distinguished man as befitted his position, with a trim beard, swiftly summed up the situation and took command. He tapped Rollo on the shoulder. "My dear chap" he said, "don't you think it's time you went home to bed?" Rollo mumbled some reply, no doubt implying agreement, tottered off his stool, lurched across to the nearby (fortunately vacant) billiard table, discarding shoes, shorts, shirt and underwear en-route and before the assembled guests had time to more than gasp he had rolled stark naked on to the green baize of the table and was fast asleep, contentedly sucking his thumb once more before his head had touched the cushions.

---

[*] The whole ethos, etiquette, influence and lifestyle of the British colonial Club is deserving of a major work of research into the social history of the Empire. This is far beyond the scope of this memoir.

Still None The Wiser

By Sunday morning the palaver had reached Tony Carter's ears. Somewhat non-plussed by the outraged comment of the senior members of Government and commercial circles, (probably egged on by their ladies), who formed the Club's committee, he felt obliged to telephone Duggie Medcalf in Accra for guidance, no doubt exacerbating the latter's ulcer in the process. The solution was to move Rollo some *seven* miles down the Coast to Takoradi - where time and distance would supposedly alleviate the outrage. In the meantime I was to be despatched post-haste to take over from Rollo and presumably was expected to maintain more civilised standards. When I asked Rollo about this incident some time later he indicated that such was the effect of large quantities of pre and post-lunch beer on his personal space-time continuum that he was convinced that in the brief interim between the bar and the billiard table he had gone back to his flat over the Bank, undressed and laid himself down in his own bed. *What* sort of organisation had I joined? I asked myself.

But back in Accra it was now 7.30 a.m. and I was becoming anxious about my flight. There was still no sign of any activity. The airport remained empty and I was becoming restive. Of the two aircraft on the tarmac only the Bristol Freighter looked ready to fly. The Dakota still sported canvas engine covers while the Bristol at least had an open door with a stepladder up which had just climbed a cleaner with mop and bucket. Obviously my flight! Nursing my headache, intensified by the increasing glare and heat, I thought I might as well go and sit more comfortably while awaiting take-off. Wandering over, I climbed the steps, found a seat on the shady side and settled in, closing my eyes. The cleaner had vanished up above - the Bristol's flight deck was up top on another level over the front cargo doors. I sat for some ten minutes or so concentrating on my worsening hangover until the cleaner came down from the Flight Deck and eyed me with considerable curiosity as I sat in the empty, silent plane.

"Massa - dis ting no fit fly, 'e no go nowhere till dey fix-um." He said, kindly.

I walked back to the departure shack where a smartly uniformed African girl had now taken over the flight desk. She was considerably more efficient and told me that my plane was due in from Kumasi at any moment having been delayed and would then take off for Takoradi in short order. A tiny twin-engined De Havilland Dove swooped in out of the sky, taxied over, and a few minutes later along with a handful of other passengers, who had suddenly appeared, I was off to Takoradi.

The flight westwards along the coast at about 3,000 feet was interesting. I still remember it quite clearly. For about 200 miles, we flew over the long golden beaches on which the huge Atlantic rollers crashed endlessly, sweeping steeply up to the fringe of palms. Beyond the expanse of the Winneba plains, inland to the north were glimpsed low rolling hills, thickly forested. Then appeared the great trade castles of Annomabu, Koromantin, Cape Coast and Elmina, those gleaming white fortresses built by the Portuguese, the English and Dutch traders and explorers. The spectacular castle at Elmina was the first European building south of the Sahara that predated by some ten years Columbus's voyage to the Americas. Red laterite roads, muddy streams and rivers, villages and settlements – now we were over the wide Pra River leading up into Ashanti. Then the sweeping bay of Sekondi and a few miles further with a bump and a screech of tyres we were down at Takoradi.

Tony Carter, tall, fair, then aged about twenty eight, met me, driving me back to Sekondi along the coast road. By 11.30 I had unpacked my few belongings in the flat over the Bank, washed, changed and was sitting at the Accountant's desk with Rollo, taking over the code books, the safe keys, changing the combinations,, counting the Travellers Cheques and the gold bars, (the Bank sold gold by the ounce to licensed goldsmiths). It went on endlessly into the afternoon after a short break for lunch, checking the safe-custody registers, looking at the sealed glass jars full of ancient keys in gallons of Vaseline (deposited years ago by the departing owners of long since defunct and unprofitable up-country gold mines). All the duplicate keys for the Bank were withdrawn from Barclays Bank up the road, to be changed with the current set and thereby confirming in the process that both sets existed.

The safe held a large bottle of quinine tablets (was this for me - or for the staff - I wondered?) and two old-fashioned Webley revolvers with their curved 'bird's head' grips. Their ammunition was counted - I quibbled over this. The correct number of corroded .45 calibre hollow-nosed 'wog-stopper' cartridges (long since outlawed by the Geneva Convention) was only made up to quantity by an odd assortment of shotgun cartridges, a wartime 20 mm aircraft cannon shell and a few .22 miniature rifle cartridges and airgun pellets. Tony Carter re-assured me that this was of no matter, past managers had no doubt pooped off the missing rounds in unofficial target practice, and the Police had been quite happy the last time they checked this extremely odd assortment of ill-fitting projectiles intended for the Bank's defence and security. (These pistols were taken out whenever we shipped out the boxes of gold ingots we held in transit for the Ashanti-Obuasi mines, and they made a very uncomfortable pocketful in a pair of skimpy shorts.) The cash was all checked once the two cashiers had closed their books for the day when the Bank closed at 1 o'clock. Finally, the reserve cash in the strongroom was counted, bundle by bundle, bag by bag - dipping in to weigh and physically count sample bags, it was not entirely unknown in the Bank's chequered history for metal washers, gravel and stones to be substituted for coin!

At last it was done, Rollo was free; and I was officially the Branch Accountant. How the Hell was I going to do it? I didn't know the first thing about practical day-to-day banking, I was nominally in charge of a staff of some twelve or so very bright Gold Coast Africans - most of whom had been in their jobs at that Branch for several years. Mr. J. Harris Inkabi - approaching retirement, was the much respected Assistant Accountant - and looking back, was the man who actually ran the nuts and bolts of the Branch. Mr. John Wilson was the Chief Cashier - he was a sub-Chief of Axim in Appolonia province along the coast and had been with the Bank since 1911! Eshon I think was the second cashier; Mr. Turkson with his assistant clerk Essien - the latter a very smart young man, ran the Bills section; Dowuonah was the counter clerk, fat and jolly with a lisp; Mr. Arkaifie was the ledger clerk, there was Quansah - and then there were the two Kroo messengers, Peter and Tobi - and outside at the back of the yard was the Bank's carpenter, Dadzie - with a bright pink denture on which two large false teeth always seemed to be wobbling insecurely - who made all the wooden boxes for the Currency Board and the bullion shipments.

How did I cope? There was no such thing as a job description to give me any guidance. There was a thick book of 'non-user friendly' General Instructions into which I dipped from time to time, but otherwise I flannelled and fluffed my way through, learning as I went and most of the time managing to conceal my abysmal ignorance with a nonchalant air of supposed skill and expertise. It seemed to work, and several months later by dint of acute observation and subterfuge I had achieved a practical grounding in coarse West African banking methods. I had begun to understand how a Bank functioned in those long gone pre-computer days. I had also learned an invaluable lesson, that when one is out of one's depth one often finds that one is a far better swimmer than ever seemed possible. Experience is a great teacher.

CHAPTER 6

'Sekondi - 1954-1956'
*"The best view of the Coast is to be
seen through the bottom of a glass from the
stern of a ship heading for Liverpool."*
(Old Coaster - c.1954)

The Gold Coast properly faces almost due south. Looking eastwards from the lighthouse that caps Fort Orange, Sekondi bay appears very much like a bisected figure-of-eight. Almost immediately below the fort that stands on the headland lies the breakwater of the old harbour, jutting out to intercept the long Atlantic swells and which in years gone by allowed the surf boats ferrying in cargo from the freighters lying out in the bay, to beach in calmer waters. A ruined slipway, deserted warehouses and empty echoing godowns which had housed the old Ice Company before the trade was taken away to the vast new harbour built at Takoradi in the 1930's, lie baking in the sun. Above the sheltered beach and the empty warehouses in 1954 were the Police Lines, the barracks where the small whitewashed cement cubes housed the families of the guardians of the law. All was dwarfed by the ancient, brooding ramparts of Fort Orange, built by the stolid (but also hard drinking and frequently belligerent) Dutch burghers in 1670 and finally ceded to the British in 1872, after more than two hundred and fifty years of Anglo-Dutch bickering and frequent wars over the sovereignty of the Gold Coast trading forts and castles.

The first sweep of Sekondi bay encompasses the fishing village. A crescent of yellow sand with rows of dugout fishing canoes drawn up beyond the reach of the ceaselessly crashing breakers. The bulwarks of the boats - hardly canoes - many of them are more than 20 feet in length - are given extra freeboard with rough-sawn planks, carved and painted with Fanti names, biblical mottoes, gay patterns and whirls of Reckitt's blue, red oxide paint, glaring primary yellows and greens. Their masts are of mangrove poles, with patched and tattered sails of simple 'lug' design. Carved wooden paddles with scalloped blades lie propped against the grass matting screens in front of the fishermen's huts. Naked, blue-black, glistening children splash in the shallows. Pi-dogs, scabby and beset with flies doze twitching in the shade of the canoes. Vultures lurch and hop with flopping wings, squabbling over the remains of desiccated and decomposing fish. A small group of market mammies in brilliant cotton wrappers and head ties, squat in the sun, babies lolling contentedly behind them, secured in their mothers' waist cloths. Chipped enamel headpans lie on the sand beside them, waiting for the next fishing canoe to beach with its bilges swilling with croaker, cassava fish, herring, yellow-fin, horse mackerel, rays - the potentially dangerous stingrays with their tails already sliced off and small hammerhead sharks - swivel eyed and shovel mouthed. Shouting and jesting the mammies will fill their pans, arguing the price with the fishermen before hitching their babies firmly in their waist cloth, hoisting the laden pans on their heads and setting off up the hill to the waiting market.

Beyond the fishing village to the east rises a low ridge of sandstone cliff, where the seawall protects the bungalows above, set amidst neem and flame trees, dark glistening mango trees and drooping, wispy casuarinas. The old British trading post of Fort George built in 1680 also lies down here, barely above the tide line, a few rusted cannons quietly askew, its solid foundations now capped by a more modern dwelling. I wonder if the ghost of the long-forgotten English factor who feuded with his Dutch counterpart up the hill, over some 'mammy palaver' still haunts the site in 17th Century costume - fuming with rage over the Dutch Kapitan who had tempted away his dusky mistress. Mary Kingsley quotes from the log of the trading ship 'Hannibal' in 1693-94 commanded by Captain Thomas Phillips. *" ... calling at Secundel (sic) where we found (the factor) Mr. Johnson at the English Castle, in his bed, raving mad, in consequence of a severe domestic difficulty, in which the commander of the neighbouring Dutch castle, Mynheer*

Vanhukeline and a native lady played prominent parts." Mary Kingsley delicately (and somewhat surprisingly given her robust sense of humour) refrains from further detail, but I recall reading elsewhere, (the source now escapes me), that the Dutch Kapitan had turned the locals against Mr. Johnson and they set upon him one night, stripped and flogged him. When Johnson complained bitterly to the Dutchman, the response was that the English factor had brought the trouble down on his own head and that *"... he had no business to be out late at night!"* One cannot help wondering if he had been out looking for their mutual lady friend. Captain Phillips later reports in his journal that when his ship reached Shama at the mouth of the Pra River, they learned subsequently *"... that the Negroes having been set on by Vanhukeline, had surprised the English fort, cut poor Johnson to pieces, and plundered all his goods and merchandise."*

The traditional 'Asafo' warrior Companies of the Fanti and the Ahanta in the 1950s still paraded their huge, patchworked, fringed flags through the streets accompanied by thundering volleys from their Dane guns. Squads of dancers stamped and clashed their shell anklets in time to the booming drums and braying ivory horns surrounding the local chiefs in their palanquins. In the old town during the annual '*Homowo*' Yam Festival at the end of August, the rival warrior 'Companies' still pledged their various allegiances to 'Dutch' or 'British' Sekondi and no doubt still do so today. In earlier centuries they had forged defensive alliances with the Europeans in their forts and trading enclaves to counter the threat from their neighbours, and in particular the warlike Ashanti to the north who might at any time swoop down to the sea-coast to seize or exert control over the trade routes.

The town of Sekondi, Succundee, or even 'Secundel' has a long history of association with the European trading nations. First with a permanent presence were the Portuguese who arrived at El Mina in 1471 probably making their landfall at Shama at the mouth of the River Pra a few miles to the east of Sekondi which they named the Rio São João. It was probably down the Pra River that the gold they desired so much was traded by the Ashanti and other inland tribes. Later, and further to the west this time the Portuguese founded the great fort of St. Anthony at Axim - again near the mouth of the Ancobra, another river which also would have been a trading route for the native gold mines of Denkyera, Adansi and Wassaw. One hundred and fifty years later both the Dutch and the Portuguese built and occupied upriver forts on the Ancobra to trade for gold nearer to its source. These latter forts did not last more than a few years, interfering as they did with the African concept of trade - which was always based on 'middlemen' and control of the trade routes to the sea - which once achieved allowed a prosperous living involving little or no sweat of the brow.

Although the first cargo of slaves had been shipped from West Africa by the Portuguese as early as 1442 it was not the slave trade that had fired their cupidity but gold. The gold area of the coast was a bare 150 miles extending from Axim to Winneba, leading to a great concentration of forts, trading lodges and castles along the shoreline in the next two centuries. Between Keta and Axim, along the present day shoreline of Ghana there were at least forty-two of these European strongholds, some simply fortified 'lodges' with a factor and an assistant or two, but each with their own treaties and trading arrangements with the local chiefs and inland tribes. The Dutch historian Bosman declared in 1701 that it was the Portuguese who first "..... *served as setting-dogs to spring the game, which as soon as they had done, was seized by others."* By 1642 the Dutch - who were at war with Portugal (Brazilian affairs being the *causus belli*) took over the last of the latter's castles (Axim) and the Portuguese were ousted, after their flag had flown for 160 years without a break along the Gold Coast. They left their mark on the country, both in the profusion of Portuguese words in 'pidgin' - 'Dash' and 'Palaver' for example (from neither of which is there any escape in West Africa) are no more or less than the Portuguese for 'give' - and 'Palabre' speaks for itself! More important perhaps is the long list of plants they introduced from their other tropical posessions - oranges, lemons and limes, rice and sugar cane, maize, tobacco - and most importantly, cassava. They introduced cattle to the coastal plains, formerly inaccessible from the north because of the tsetse 'fly belt' that sealed off the forest.

In later years after O. and I had finally left the Coast, we lived for a while in Canada, in Montreal - where I found little or no sense of past centuries or history - or even of artefacts older than a century or two at the outside, much less in fact than there had been along that stretch of the old Gold Coast. Here the Portuguese had built their great fortified castle of El Mina ten years before Columbus 'discovered' the Americas in 1492. It has even been propounded (by the 17th Century chronicler Barbot) that the French merchant adventurers of Dieppe had first traded as far south as Elmina in 1346, carrying back to France great quantities of Guinea pepper and elephants' tusks - whence the old Dieppe trade of carving ivory for which the town was once famous. The Dons had later kept clear of West Africa, for by the time Spain was unified and powerful enough to interfere, they were pre-occupied with their New World conquests and in any case in 1494 the Treaty of Tordesillas had divided the world east and west of longitude 50 degrees into separate spheres of Portuguese and Spanish influence. Both Brazil and West Africa being granted to the Portuguese; of which fact the English, the French and the Dutch took no notice.

Still None The Wiser

When I first arrived in Sekondi I loathed the place. Loneliness was the main problem. I knew nobody, I had no car. After the office closed each day in the early afternoon there was nowhere to go and nothing to do. I engaged a cook-steward, Yaro, as my houseboy. I bought a modest supply of linen, crockery, beer, gin and cooking pots from the United Africa Company's Kingsway Stores in the centre of town, using what was left of my £100 'kit' allowance, half of which had already been spent before leaving London. The Bank supplied little in the way of any furnishings or comforts except for some basic PWD-style furniture (including tall lampstands for oil-lamps), a four-poster single bed and a mosquito net. I tried to settle down in the barn-like three roomed flat, - one of four above the Bank - the others all empty except for the one occupied by the Manager of the West African Drug Company, who rented part of the Bank building and the old Bank warehouse in the compound below. My kitchen, 'small room,' bathroom and kitchen were all out on a narrow covered verandah which looked out to a bustling market place where trade seemed to be mostly in sacks of charcoal, whose black dust mingled with salt spray streaked the glass panes in my windows. The Bank at least provided hard, shiny toilet paper, stamped with the motto "BBWA" which gave one a certain satisfaction.'

The high points of my daily existence were the almost daily letters I still received from O. Mine to her, equally as frequent, no doubt expressed my despondency. It was a bad time. I stuck it out for six weeks, wrote out my letter of resignation and gave it to Tony Carter, the Manager. Fortunately - or not, who knows? He declined to forward it to Accra, keeping it in his safe for a few days, by which time I had changed my mind - and we tore it up.

From then on things improved. Jacques Spencer-Chapman, (a nephew of Colonel 'Freddie' Spencer-Chapman the then famous author of 'The Jungle is Neutral') and the same age as myself, newly arrived with the old established Liverpool traders, John Holt's, came to live in the adjoining flat. I met the French and Swiss residents of 'Hell Corner' up the road. Jacques and I drank and played ping-pong with the reclusive Norman Welch - the West African Drug Company's manager, who lived in the other flat - reading the Latin texts of Tacitus and Caesar in the hot darkness, curtains drawn in daylight, the while listening to scratchy 78 rpm records of the Italian opera singer Gallicurci, his other grand passion. Norman, a bachelor, of slender build was a former Spitfire pilot. Because of his small size and weight he had flown high-altitude reconnaissance missions. He had a silver plate in his skull, the result of the crash which brought his flying career to an end. Jacques and I could sometimes persuade Norman to take us around in his then 'state of the art' Morris Minor, in which he later taught me the rudiments of driving.

After six months or so, the pangs of separation from O. had eased. I was still in love with her, but each of us had our lives apart to get on with. I began to enjoy myself again.

Jacques Spencer-Chapman sometimes had the use of his Agent's car at weekends, a hump-backed Standard Vanguard in which he drove us at high speed through the adjoining towns of Sekondi and Takoradi out along the bumpy laterite roads west to Axim and Dixcove, or eastwards to Elmina and Cape Coast - the ancient trading towns and castles of the old Gold Coast. In my memory these journeys were always verging on disaster, such was Jacque's style in those days. He had held a private pilot's license since the age of seventeen - which had once been suspended when he flew underneath the power lines on the sea coast near Worthing. I think in retrospect that he was one of those people, like Lord Byron, 'mad, bad, and dangerous to know' in that he was entirely lacking in any sense of natural caution or perceptions of risk or danger. His moral values again had much in common with Byron's. He was urbane and charming - but sometimes curiously detached from what I considered to be normality. You accompanied him at your peril. His mother was French and lived in England, his father English and lived in France. Jacques had been a 2nd Lieutenant in the Fifth Dragoon Guards for his National Service, although while serving in Germany he had once been arrested by the French Border Police as a deserter - having dual nationality they regarded him as 'one of theirs' and liable for conscription and it was only after lengthy argument that they accepted that serving in the British Army was sufficient reason for him not to be handcuffed and taken to the nearest French barracks. Jacques and I met up again some ten years later when we both lived in Lagos. He hadn't changed. Like myself he was now married, to a charming French girl he had met in Cameroon when working for a French oil company and by now they had three small daughters. His personal life style - flying, diving, and fishing far out to sea in dangerous waters, conducting extra-marital affairs - with his usual disregard for safety or convention - remained almost unchanged from his bachelor days. We lost touch in 1967 when O. and I with our own children left Africa for the last time. Considering his life-style, that Jacques is still alive I doubt, I would be delighted if he were.

CHAPTER 7

'The Gold Coast - Sekondi - 1954/56'

*"A man who does not mind his stomach
is unlikely to mind anything else."
(Samuel Johnson)*

As I read what I have written so far in these pages it occurs to me that some readers may find it frustrating that there is sometimes too much eating and drinking, '...all this buttoning and unbuttoning' and too little incident. Rather like life itself perhaps and therefore disappointing from much the same causes. I shall make no excuses, for the older I have become so have these matters become more interesting to me in recollection. The regrets I have are that I wish I had been less conservative when I had the opportunities to be radically adventurous in such matters. As age advances, the powers of my digestion decline in the face of so many delicious hazards that I can no longer surmount them without dire consequences.

There is a saying on the Coast that a good pepper soup should burn a man three times: once in the mouth as he eats it, once in the stomach when it's swallowed and the third time when ... well, it would wouldn't it? There was Maurice Lonergan's cook in Takoradi, Kofi, whose culinary repertoire included a pepper soup that met all these criteria. It was a clear, pale-red liquid, fiery and salty enough to make the sweat pop out of a corpse - and to make M's eyes behind his steamed-up spectacles bulge until he was almost cross-eyed. The soup lapped around a large dollop of pale blue cocoyam fufu set in the middle of one's plate. M. used to sit at the table wearing nothing but a large Turkish towel spooning up this stuff and drinking iced beer to replace the pints of perspiration that poured off him. I tried it once but had to give up after several mouthfuls while Kofi fussed around clucking with disapproval at my lack of appetite.

I recall one occasion going out with Jacques and his then lady friend, the delightful half-Greek, half-Fanti Diana who was married to a Government doctor, for a 'country chop' one Sunday to a palm-oil plantation out on the Axim Road west of Takoradi. Our hosts were Herbert Plinge the plantation manager - who later made off with Adjoah, the African nanny to his three lovely children - Herbert's wife, a plump and jolly lady whose name escapes me although I remember her quite well, and an Old Coaster who managed another plantation nearby. We sat down to a traditional Sunday 'palm oil chop' made with guinea fowl, messes of fiery hot peppers, onions, okra, spinach, all stewed together for hours and served in a huge tureen swimming with the dark red juice of fresh-pressed palm oil. The palm oil gave everything a distinctive, noticeably soapy flavour which some never liked. I always found it delicious, served with a multitude of side dishes and a mound of rice - and beer of course. The children sat with Adjoah at a separate table, they weren't given the 'palm oil chop.' I remember saying to the eldest child. "Don't you like it?" "No," he piped up, "it gives us a hot bottom." Well, you can't argue with that.

After our lunch Jacques and I fished for catfish in the small lake below the house where a stream had been dammed. We soon became fed up with catching small, spiky black-whiskered catfish with every cast, our hooks baited with bits of offal and we went up back to the house where we complained to Herbert that we were used to catching much bigger fish at Inchaban using earthworms for bait. (Worms were always difficult to find either in the garden or bush and one had to find a choice spot and mark it for future use). *A propos* of this Herbert said that he had once read a report in a Government agricultural paper saying that one reason for the poor fertility of Gold Coast soils was the fact that *"there were no earthworms at all throughout West Africa."* Herbert had been so enraged by this display of ignorance that he dug up a biscuit tin full of worms from a patch in his compound's garden and despatched them by parcel post to the 'expert' in Accra who had written the report - relying on the slowness of the mails to ensure that they were suitably putrefied by the time they reached their destination.

European expats in general were not very adventurous when it came to sampling the African cuisine. The English at home remained firmly stuck in the rut of a strictly 'meat and two veg.' diet. This is not surprising considering that by the mid-Fifties even garlic was still lumped together with other 'foreign muck' by the average British housewife and small vials of olive oil only came from the chemists as a remedy for earache. Elizabeth David had barely reached the fringe-consciousness of the middle classes. West Africa has a native cuisine, but the way in which it was often presented was almost guaranteed not to appeal to any English 'Madam.' Bachelor households were perhaps more likely to come across local foods, these were often acceptable to a palate jaded by the tropics. However in general 'Black Africa' south of the Sahara, lacks a cuisine that appeals to the European taste - unlike Morocco or Egypt - and what there is remains generally unpalatable to most European tastes without considerable modification and imagination.

'Kenke' was balls of cooked maize flour. 'Fufu' was yam, plantain or cassava, peeled, boiled and pounded and made into balls of gooey stodge. It was often better than imported and expensive potatoes - particularly the blue-tinged fufu made from coco-yam. Good fufu should be both plastic and pliable in texture rather like bread dough or chewing gum. One test made by European bachelors when eating it with palm-oil chop or 'palaver' sauce, or pepper soup was to take a small lump of it and throw it at the wall or ceiling - if it stuck, it was good. 'Gari' is the poor relation of these basic starches being nothing more than grated cassava, or manioc, dried to the texture and flavour of sawdust. Gari is poor stuff indeed and requires a lot of soup or sauce to make it palatable. Its sole virtue is bulk rather than nourishment and as such it is no doubt responsible for much of the *'kwashiorkor'* suffered by West African children, caused by protein deficiency.

Some excellent fish and meat stews were made with fresh palm-oil. 'Palaver' sauce was a mess of vegetables, egg-plant, okra, peppers, tomatoes and spinach all stewed together with palm-oil and fowl or fish; which was often prepared from imported, dried stockfish or salt cod.

The traditional Sunday lunch-time 'Palm-oil Chop' was by my time becoming less common with the expatriate community and being replaced by the West African curry. This resembled in style and presentation the Dutch East Indies or Indonesian 'Rijstaffel' - a fairly mild curry of meat or fowl accompanied by rice and a myriad of side dishes or 'gages'. These consisted of everything imaginable, ranging from pounded white chilli seeds of frightening heat to bland chopped bananas via 'stinkfish' (another name for the much-favoured imported dried stockfish) and dried river prawns and bowls of okra (for *"Power!"* - this expression being accompanied by an uncompromisingly upright thrust of the fore-arm). Onions and shallots, dry-fried or chopped, in half a dozen styles, coconut in various forms, peppers of many types, dried, sliced; pounded; minced and pulped fruits; groundnuts dried, boiled, fried and fresh. To have twenty or thirty 'gages' was commonplace and a matter of pride for the cook as well as the host. I once saw a small saucer of gunpowder placed on the table as a joke – or it may not have been. It was sometimes wise to ask how a dish was made.

It was usual to start by helping oneself and sprinkling a generous spoonful of pounded and dried red chillies on the bottom of one's plate as a good foundation, this then followed by a mound of rice, which was heaped high with curry and sauce topped with a generous selection of the side dishes which would be returned to again and again. Overall would go a topping of another spoonful of chillies or cayenne. Alas, my tolerance for those fiery gastro-intestinal delights has been burned away long since.

A Sunday curry or palm-oil chop, following a late morning's intake of several ice-cold bottles of Beck's or Star beer, or pink gins - the latter being drunk 'Coast style' by the tumblerful topped up with ice and soda water - was one of the week's highlights for the Old Coasters of yesterday. After lunch, a large brandy would be *de rigeur*. By late afternoon. the cane chairs of the host would support the groaning bodies of the participants, some sunk deep in swinish slumber, others smoking and mumbling incomprehensible rubbish to each other before retiring to their respective bungalows, to emerge at 7 am on Monday morning, usually fresh and ready for another week's toil. The weaker brethren, of whom there were a few, might complain on the Monday morning of "a touch of fever, old boy," requiring an early lunch time visit to the Club.

In general, Europeans avoided 'bush meat' - but not always, I have eaten 'cutting grass,' the giant cane rat, with Richard Steimann at Sekondi, as cooked by Essi, his wife (wedded by 'native custom' rather than with 'book and ring' as the saying went). It was delicious. Often known as 'bush rat' or euphemistically sometimes as 'rabbit' it is in fact a species of porcupine (*Thryonomys swinderianus*). The western press invariably highlights African famines with reports of the locals reduced to 'eating rats.' Well, so they also do in times of plenty, and very tasty they are.

Sir Richard Burton in the 19th century did not despise 'native chop,' writing that "neither monkey-fry nor boiled parrot are dishes to be despised - but it must be *wild* parrot, and it must first be skinned." I never ate monkey as far as I know, but I am guilty of having shot them in later years for my fellow African hunters. All the primates (including chimpanzees, mandrill baboons and gorillas) are hunted and eaten on a major scale throughout tropical Africa - probably creating thereby a pathway for some really serious viruses to enter into the human environment. Hence outbreaks of Lassa, Ebola, 'Congo' fever and Green Monkey diseases. AIDS and HIV it is now believed may first have 'crossed-over' in this fashion somewhere in Central Africa as much as thirty or forty years ago. Handling wild monkeys, dead or alive, is probably best not recommended. Long after I left Africa I recall reading in some guide-book or other supposedly giving 'safari' advice to the greenhorn, that it was "extremely unwise to handle by direct contact any wild creature, even birds and fish dead or alive - unless wearing rubber gloves, and that skinning, jointing and cleaning for the pot and trophy preparation should be left solely to one's African attendants." Well it wasn't like that in my day.

In 1958 shortly before my own arrival in the north of Ghana, my friend Paul Gautier, then a young man of twenty-eight, was the CFAO manager in Tamale - and a keen hunter and gastronome as befitted his French ancestry. Along with two fellow hunters and an African guide they succeeded in killing a large bush-pig, a Red River Hog (*Potamochoerus porcus*), somewhere deep in the bush north of Kintampo on the Black Volta.

"Nevair - *nevair* again! Jamais!!" Said Gautier when describing the incident to me in detail at his home in La Rochelle in 1997, the year before he died.

The pig weighed-in at not far short of a hundred pounds. They were several miles from the road and their pick-up truck. They bled and paunched the carcass on the spot, tied its feet together and slinging it on a freshly-cut pole started to carry it. Two of them at a time. Gautier said the pig was a tremendously heavy and awkward burden. The going underfoot was bad, with the long grass shoulder-high and broken ground and pig holes everywhere. It was very hot. They were surrounded by flies attracted by the blood and by tsetse flies pursuing Gautier and his two white companions who between them were forced to carry the pig two at a time, taking turns. "First on one shoulder, then on the other - until the skin was bare!" For when they had suggested to their African guide that he should perhaps carry his share of the burden - after all he was being *paid* - he had replied. "No! No! - That is quite impossible, you must understand that I am a Muslim. It is entirely against my religion to touch, or even to come close to a pig, it is unclean!" To this, Gautier and his companions had no answer, it was yet another example of African end-gamesmanship, succinctly summed-up by the expression then commonly used by exasperated expatriates as 'WA-WA,' i.e. 'West Africa Wins Again!' (I hear that the more up to date expression is 'TAB' – 'That's Africa Baby!')

They eventually reached Tamale long after dark, exhausted, hot, worn-out, blistered and thirsty. By now the pig had reached the state where it was essential to bring matters to a conclusion, to leave it overnight would have meant it spoiling, anathema to any true Gallic sportsman. Juliette, Paul's wife (also of course, French) was a competent butcher and knew how to dismember the beast and she stayed up until nearly midnight on the stoep of their bungalow until it was neatly parcelled-up and lodged in the freezer. However, Juliette was later found to have a tapeworm, almost certainly caught from eating underdone wild boar '*à la mode de Kintampo.*'

The average young English bachelor of my day however was usually stuck with nothing more exotic than 'roast knee of goat with bottled mint sauce.' Quite unlike the French who possess no scruples or boundaries in the pursuit of gastronomy. I once called on my friend Louis Pugnet in Takoradi to find him eating a tasty groundnut soup in the middle of which floated the remains of a tender guinea pig, bought in the market for a shilling. But for most of us it was that always evocative flavour of Lea &

Perrins Worcestershire Sauce with which we drenched our tough and fibrous steaks, tinned sausages and bacon, tinned diced veg. and stringy, tough green beans, followed by egg custard or tinned *'flute'* salad and undiluted Carnation milk from the old Iron Cow if we were lucky.

CHAPTER 8

'Sekondi - 1955 - 'English Lessons'
"Here will be an old abusing of God's patience,
And the King's English."
(Shakespeare - Merry Wives of Windsor)

'Hell Corner' was so named by Howard Christian*, the urbane Winchester and Balliol educated Gold Coast lawyer who lived in genteel poverty further down the road below the damp-stained stucco ramparts of Fort Orange, the 17th Century Dutch trading stronghold which dominated Sekondi from the headland. 'Hell Corner' because of the sporadically riotous habits of the small group of French, Swiss and other expatriate bachelors who 'lived over the shop' in that corner of the old town.

Jacques Spencer-Chapman and I lived down the hill from 'Hell Corner' over the Bank. Louis, Phillipe, Simon and a few more young Frenchmen, (one of whom, dark, surly and incommunicative, the son of a Marseilles butcher, was reputed to have knifed a rival in love and to have been exiled to West Africa as an alternative to prison or the Foreign Legion), occupied the shuttered and shaded upper floors of the French Company's lock-up stores below which sold fishing nets, lumps of 'cutch' (for dyeing the same), fish hooks, sealed tins of ship's biscuits and 'cabin' bread, treadle sewing machines, iron roofing sheets, tinned pilchards, nails, sacking bales of dried stockfish, cement and lengths of Manchester cotton cloth. Richard Steimann the Swiss timber buyer rented another flat from the French Company. Peter Lord, a young South African engineer was more upmarket - he lived in a bungalow up below the fort.

The French boys, all bachelors, lived simply above the SCOA stores on the corner - but then ate like gastronomes - none of their cooks (all from French territories) made any pretence at smartness - neither did their masters, they ate off grimy oilcloth with tin plates, not a cup with a matching saucer to be seen, but off such dishes that Jacques - himself half-French - and I could only marvel at with our 'English' trained cooks. They drank Algerian and Canary wines from wicker covered demi-johns - out

---

* Son of George (James) Christian (1869 - 1940) of Dominica, West Indies, who qualified as a lawyer in Britain c.1900, and later practiced in the Gold Coast. George Christian I believe was a forebear (great grandfather?) of the well-known British TV presenter, Moira Stewart. If you want to know how the author knows obscure facts like this, don't ask - he is a walking compendium of trivial and mostly useless but sometimes interesting information. See also Chapter 27.

of thick, greasy, chipped glasses, and ate delicious salads, fried fishes both large and small. Such things as *raie au beurre noire*, rare beef steaklets beaten tender and fried with garlic and butter - they had cheeses and sausages and coffee that was rich and dark, unlike ours which as often as not came out of a bottle of essence. Their cooks baked fresh bread each day. They made no concessions to being anything other than French. The bastards! But we did get our revenge on them by devious means.

We all drank together from time to time, whiling away the free hours and went to the cinema or to the local dances at the night clubs in the town. We conversed with each other in broken English, pidgin French, fractured German - or whatever combination suited the occasion. The French bachelors hardly bothered with the 'Club' life that the British usually followed. They indulged in a bit of Gallic roistering at weekends when matters occasionally got out of hand. Very rarely the odd bottle might fly out of the window and smash on the deserted street below and voices would be raised in argument. Their wind-up gramophone played endless 78s of calypso and French accordion music. Mrs. King's little bar across the road supplied fresh cold beers from her huge American refrigerator when their own supply ran dry. The ladies of the town would come to visit, to drink a cold Heineken or a Fanta before moving on elsewhere. It was all much more civilised than a similar bunch of British young men would have been, less rowdy and much less drink. The police didn't bother anyone in that part of town. The last days of colonial Africa were around the corner, the white man's supremacy was still in place for the moment but he was on the way out and no longer a threat.

One wet, steaming Saturday afternoon in the rains Jacques and I, Richard, Louis and Phillipe with nothing better to do, sat around idly drinking beer, smoking and talking of this and that. Richard's fractured Swiss-English was atrocious - learned in the timber camps in the bush and consisting mostly of four letter words. Phillipe spoke a form of English that was so garbalised - although he rattled away like a machine gun - that for much of the time it was incomprehensible. Jacques being of French and English parentage was of course fluent in both languages, although strangely enough like many young people raised to speak two mother tongues - his written grammar and spelling of both could verge on illiteracy at times. My own French was OK 'schoolboy' stuff about on a par with Louis' English.

Phillipe was concluding some outrageous story of his youthful sexual education of which we had understood about one word in three, when he said.

"An' zere was me - standing zere - completement *'narked.'*"

Jacques and I looked at each other, *'narked,'* what could he mean? Did he mean he was annoyed?

"Comprenez? Zere wizzout any cloth, rien du tout - nuzzing. *Narked!*" said Phillipe again.

"Ah-ha!" said Richard, as the penny failed to drop - "You mean you were standing there f.....g 'knackered.'" "Non, non, non!" interposed Louis, "I am *'knackered'* means 'Je suis fatigué.' N'est ce pas, mes amis?"

"Bollocks!" said Richard again - "Don't take any f.....g notice - 'narked' means you haven't any f.....g clothes on. 'Knackered' means tired - you stupid Frog bastard! Whoever heard of anyone being f.....g 'bollock *knackered?*"

These exchanges had reached a lower intellectual level than usual. Jacques and I looked at each other. Time for another English lesson, we had already been working on Phillipe for some time over the past weeks.

Richard lapsed into Low German - "Nackt! Means 'narked' - Dummkopf! Ohne Kleide - 'ow you say in French, Nu? Means bloody 'narked' nicht wahr? - No f......g clothes on! Like vot I f.....g said already."

Phillipe was getting a little annoyed. He shouted across at Richard "Hey, you! You sink I know fuck-nothing - I tell you I know fuck-everything!" Richard shouted back, "Fuck-all is vot you f.....g mean. Arschlock! Vos you borned stupid or has you been taking lessons?"

"Hold on, hold on," said Jacques - "Paul and I will put you right - Phillipe, listen, faîtes attention - you must learn some better English than that! Just imagine you are a guest in an English country house, polite society - toujours, mais *toujours* la politesse, comprenez? Not like we are here today. You must never speak like that."

"Bien" said Phillipe, calming down a little. "You teach, I listen."

"Now imagine it is late at night, your hostess is yawning - this is what you say. 'I go to bed now.'" Richard mumbled in the background "F..k off to bed your f.....g ...."

"Quiet!" Said Jacques. "Phillipe - listen! You say 'I want go to bed now, I am knackered. Ca veut dire je suis fatigué. And if you want to add a merry little joke, vous continuez 'as your English proverb has it - Early to bed and up with the cock!' Your command of good English will amaze everyone - also it is traditional in England as you say that, if you want to be considered a man of the world, un gai boulevardier, you must also wink, comme ca, right or left eye - n'importe quoi, and lay your right forefinger alongside your nose." We rehearsed Phillipe in the correct delivery of these useful phrases. The lesson continued, Richard and Louis listening attentively.

Colloquial terms were what we concentrated on. "Cobblers!" we explained was a universal polite English expression of mild surprise. The daily greeting "Bon jour" was usually translated and pronounced - easier to the French tongue, as "Good Morninge" with a soft 'g' as in the French word for orange. We pointed out that in polite society it was also acceptable for foreigners struggling with the English sibilant 'Th' to put their left hand in front of the mouth to avoid spraying unwary listeners with spittle.

To enlighten others of his profession as a French businessman and West African trader, it was in order for Phillipe to describe himself as. 'A man of affairs - with a finger in every tart' as the English phrase has it. "Oui, bien, précisement - exactement! You have put your finger on the fly in the ointment!" Said Phillipe triumphantly, recalling an earlier lesson. "Bravo!" We applauded.

We taught Phillipe a few English phrases commonly used in public houses - "Landlord! Pour me a pint of your best bitters on the house!" Or if he required a snack to ask for "Cheeses and peccadilloes." If he required accommodation he was to ask to inspect Mine Host's 'Private Parts - upstairs' before making a booking. Or if he fancied the barmaid - such tender phrases as "Please to lie down, I think I love you" as an opener would almost certainly guarantee her favours.

Poor Phillipe - even some four years later when we met again in Accra, both of us by this time respectably married - he still suffered from the effects of our earlier lessons. So much so that he had more or less given up altogether on spoken English.

Richard, the Swiss with his timber-camp pidgin was alas, too far gone for Jacques and me ever to improve on his own vocabulary or delivery. Some twenty years later he made a visit to my Lake District village. I had collected him from the railway station and was driving him over a narrow, winding fell road, we were held up by a car in front of us, meandering along on the crown of the road. "F.....g Hell!" Cried Richard. "Vy do you not horn him already? In my country I vould give him a blow with my f.....g trumpet!"

It is worth mentioning that Richard in his own turn had also acted as English tutor to the young Swiss bachelor trading assistants of the Union Trading Company, UTC, founded in 19th Century West Africa by the stern Lutheran missionaries of the Basel Mission. They lived in strict seclusion in their Mess near the Sekondi Club - their quarters being subject to random inspection by their senior (married) Agent, to ensure that they were not entertaining any undesirables, i.e. 'women.' I heard once that an unexpected visit late at night nearly led to the discovery of a naked lady of uncertain virtue concealed in a wardrobe, another having been already forcibly ejected through an upstairs window when the Agent was heard below. More than one infringement of this nature and they were liable to be shipped back to Switzerland in disgrace!

One formal dance night at the Club, the Swiss boys attended for a few beers before retiring to an early, (and almost certainly chaste), bedtime at their Mess. The senior Swiss decided it was time to usher out his compatriots. Drawing them up in a line, himself at their front, he came up to the District Commissioner and his wife. Thrusting out his hand, he clicked his heels in a formal bow, saying.

"Thank you Sir and Lady, I regret ve must a-fucking off to bed now."

CHAPTER 9

'Pidgin English.'

".... (the newcomer) hears people talking for some time without realising they are speaking English... it can be a very confusing language."
(Sir Richard Francis Burton 1820-1890)

One of the characteristics that marked newcomers to West Africa was the way in which they coped with Coast 'pidgin.' Those of a liberal bent would be annoyed both at their own inability to understand what a native speaker was getting at, and would adopt in return the age-old ploy of the British abroad of speaking plain English loudly and clearly, as if to a child, determined not to give in to what they mistakenly regarded as sloppy speech rather than a separate language with its own peculiar rules - but which confusingly gave a passing nod of recognition to English as spoken by the British. Out of sheer frustration the newcomer, would eventually give in to *force majeure* and, feeling slightly silly, would begin to wrap his brain around the complexities of learning a new *lingua franca*. More recent visitors to the Coast tell me that Coast 'pidgin' is becoming less incomprehensible to visitors from Europe and closer to English 'as she is spoke' because of the popularity and widespread availability of commercial videos which with the aid of a simple generator can now be shown almost anywhere.

One initial stumbling block was that the native speaker would invariably answer 'Yes' to a negative question. "Didn't you go then?" Answer. "Yes" meaning "Yes I didn't go." The principal affirmative is most nearly written as "Ennh." Surprise is a sharp, short, indrawn "Echh!" There was the word "Na" used pleonastically (ie as with the English constant "Like" or "Er,") on all occasions. e.g. "You na-go na dis place?" The vocative always ends in "Oh" as in "Mammy-Oh!" "Hear" as with "Savvy" is to obey or understand. "Catch" is the verb "to have." The word "done" is used as a past participle as in "I done finish for now," i.e. "I have finished for the time being." The word "dey" has numerous meanings, as in "Who dey?" answered "Me de-dey," "dey for up - or dey for down?" There is the definite "Aaah-hahh" on a rising inflexion as in "Aaah-*hahh* - now I go savvy dis-ting." i.e. "Now I understand." "Lib" or to live, to be found or to be in good health, or simply to be. "Done lib" means to die - or finish, as the cook would say, "sugar (or tea or matches or whatever) done lib."

Pidgin English (the word pidgin itself is a centuries old corruption of 'business') is very often a direct translation of various African dialects, *pure* English being too difficult for widespread use throughout such a large area. Pidgin became as much, if not more of a *Lingua Franca* than Hausa that is also widely spoken and understood throughout much of West Africa. Compared with the average Westerners, particularly the British, the Africans of the West Coast are impressive linguists, many of them will speak several native languages fluently apart from their mother tongue and many, if not most, will have at the least a limited command of English or French, the languages of education and of government inherited from their former Colonial masters.

One's ear gradually became attuned to Pidgin. Those who out of a false desire not to abase either themselves, their listener or the English language and who insisted on speaking conventional English soon found themselves at a disadvantage until they finally realised that Pidgin was not just bastardised English but a living language with its own rules and usage. Once on being asked if he had brought something his master had asked for, I heard a steward reply. "I look am, I find am, I no see am." Told to go and look again he came back with the desired object exclaiming "Massa - 'e dey like 'e no dey, I no fit see am!" Pidgin is - or can be very logical. There are a lot of shortcuts to a basic understanding of its uses within a relatively limited vocabulary. It is not a language within which one can necessarily express abstruse moral concepts; although I have no doubt that various missionaries have used it to great effect. It has some similarities to, but is considerably different from the other two main branches of Pidgin, the South Pacific version - as in Papua New Guinea and the old China Coast 'trade' pidgin.

Pidgin is always innovative and often very much to the point. In Freetown, in 1941, when Vichy French aircraft from Dakar bombed the harbour and the town, a local was heard to say "Steam chicken dey for topside drop plenty bad shit for we."

In Lagos I once achieved a certain cachet with a newly arrived Australian when in my hearing he asked a messenger to "Please turn off the main office air-conditioning unit." This was received with blank non-comprehension even after various further instructions and explanation. Having reached total impasse both turned to me for elucidation. Pointing to the air vent I said to the messenger "Mek you kill-am now-now." "Aaah-*ha* - I de-savvy now, I go quench-am one time." The messenger replied.

In 1964 when hunting in the bush near Ikorodu with my friend Benjamin Ladipo, Ben stopped, sniffing the air delicately like a well-trained pointer, turned to me and whispered. "You hear dat smell? Monkey dey. Ahhaa-*ha*! Now I see am, he dey for up. Dey for dat big stick, you fit see am?" Sure enough there it was and a few moments later Ben shot it out of the upper branches of a towering forest tree.

The expression "Wait small!" means "Wait a bit longer" as used on the occasion when the English 'Madam' went to the loo early one morning, was just about to sit down on the thunderbox seat when the hatch below and behind was whipped open, the bucket removed by "Dan the Sanitary Man" (coming round with the pre-dawn 'honey cart') and an authoritative black hand patted her firmly on the bottom, saying "Wait small, I de-beg you Madam! I go come back one-time." 'One-time' meaning immediately.

A friend told me that staying in the Rest House at Jos in Nigeria, the steward pulled the light cord switch - no light came on. "Echh!" exclaimed the steward in surprise. " ... String 'e no catch fire at all."

To extend an adjective such as "small" it becomes "small-small" which is even smaller. Distance becomes "far-far." To like something is "Sweet," as in "'e sweet me too much," i.e. "I like it." "'E sweet too much pass-all, pass Takoradi corn' beef," was at one time in the Gold Coast (following the introduction of wartime tinned meat) just about as far as one could go in expressing appreciation. "'E sweet me bad," is the reverse, i.e. "I don't like it." It is a very literal language, as in Odege Market in Nigeria, Lesley Weatherley said to a butcher, pointing at goat carcass. "Give me a leg." The butcher replied. "No lef leg Madam, leg 'e done finish." "What's that then?" said Lesley pointing at the goat parts. "Dat no be leg, dat be *arm*!" A similar story involves the bachelor giving a dinner party to a married couple in his bungalow. After dinner the host offers a liqueur to his guests and the lady's request is passed on. "Steward, pass Creme de Menthe for Madam." The Steward vanishes with a slightly puzzled air and returns a few moments later with a tray bearing a glass of water, toothbrush and tube of toothpaste. This is entirely logical.

In the old Accra Evening News, the daily organ of the then ruling CPP (Convention People's Party) and mouthpiece of President Kwame N'Krumah, there was often a column written entirely in Pidgin. When you read this at first sight it is beyond comprehension - until one realises that it is meant to be read aloud to other listeners, who by themselves cannot read it. Professor Yaro is the author of "Zongo Gossip." (The Zongo being the Strangers' Quarter of a town - the old *caravanserai* where the traders stop.)

"Goodibinin mah frensh! Tuday I com bak again cam tauk sumall tin for ma big broddah Dorta Ankurumah. Him dat man de mik him burfday tuday. Lek I de telli you mah reedas Dorta Ankurumah no go grow old, for him go sity for dis worl long tiem. I de telli you proper, we de pass dis we momentus day. For Dorta Ankurumah lak him laf dis tiem ko de one way from de tiem him modah bornam mik him grit for true. Etc. etc."

To make any sense of this hero-worship of Osagyefo "The Redeemer" as President Doctor Kwame N'Krumah of Ghana was known to his followers, it must be read out aloud.

The Coast is a serious place when it comes to the old-timers' tales of administering justice. One 'Langa-Langa,' the pen-name of the English author of that splendid book "Up Against It in Nigeria" (1922) writes of executions where comedy linked arms with tragedy. On one occasion the Police constable also fell through the trap embracing the victim. On another the rope broke and a week later the would-be-deceased was explaining to another newly sentenced prisoner that there was really nothing to it, just a bit of a jolt, but last time he was back in prison in time for 'chop.' 'Langa-Langa' once witnessed the execution for murder of an Asaba youth, who on the scaffold burst into dance and song, the chorus of which ran "Goodbye-oh! I go die-oh!" before suddenly disappearing from view.

One of the classic pieces of West Coast Pidgin as used by the missionaries is this version of the biblical tale of Adam and Eve that follows.

The Story of Genesis

"For the first time no ting deh. And de Lord he done go work and for make dis ting dey call um Hearth. For six day de Lord he work-work and he done make all ting. Every ting he go put for Hearth. Plenty beef*, plenty cassava, plenty groundnut, plenty banana, plenty yam, plenty guinea corn, plenty mango - everyting he de-make plenty of. And for de water he put plenty fish and for de air he put plenty-plenty bird. (*beef = bush animals)

After six days de Lord he done tire too much and he done go sleep. An when he sleep, plenty palaver start for dis place dey call um Heaven. Dis Heaven 'e be de place we lib when we done die, if we be only small-small bad for dis Hearth. De Angel dey lib for Heaven and play de banjo and catch plenty fine chop and plenty palm wine.

De Headman for de Angel dey call um Gabriel. When dis palaver start for Heaven dere be plenty humbug, plenty hullah-hullah, by bad angel dey call um Lucifer. De Angel Gabriel done catch Lucifer an go flog um. An' palaver stop one time. De Lord tell Gabriel 'e be good man too much an' He go dash Gabriel one fine trumpet. An Gabriel go get licence for play dis trumpet and hit drum for Heaven. An Lucifer he go for Hellfire one time where he be Headman now.

Still None The Wiser

Den de Lord come go lookum dis time dey call um Hearth and he savvy dat no man dey for seat. So de Lord take small piece earth and he go breathe an man deh-deh. An de Lord he go call dis man Hadam. De Lord 'e say to Hadam "Hadam!" an Hadam 'e say "Yessah!" de Lord say "Hadam, you see dis garden? You look um proper. Dey call um Paradise. Everyting for dis garden 'e be for you - but dem mango tree dat be for middle of garden - dat no be for you, dat tree be white-man chop, dat no be black-man chop. You no go chop um or you go get plenty-plenty sorry for you belly. You savvy?" an' Hadam he say "Yessah Lord I savvy."

De Lord he done go back for Heaven to hear Gabriel play de trumpet an' Hadam 'e go walka-walka for garden where everyting be fine too much. Byemby de Lord come back for garden an' go lookum see Hadam, an' he say "Hadam, everyting be alright, you like um, 'e sweet you?" An Hadam 'e say "Yessah Lord everyting no be bad, but ....." an' de Lord say "Hadam - wassamatta, you done get small trouble?" An' Hadam 'e say "No I get no trouble Lord, Sah..... But I no get woman." An' de Lord 'E say "Ah-*hahh*!"

An de Lord he make Hadam go sleep for one place. An he go take one small bone for Hadam's side - dey call um wishbone. He go breathe - an woman deh-deh. An de Lord 'e go call dis woman Heava. De Lord wake Hadam an He say "Hadam - you see dis woman?" An Hadam 'e say "Yessah Lord I seem um - she be fine too much." An de Lord go way-way for up to Heaven an Hadam an Heava go walka-walka where dey do play plenty.

One day Hadam go for catch barracuta, Heava done take small walk as she meet Shnake. An Shnake 'e say "Hello Heava, Eckabbo!" and Heava say "Mushayo." Shnake 'e say "Wassamatter Heava, why you no chop dem fine mango from tree for middle of garden?" An Heava say "dat be white-man chop, dat no be black-man chop. Hadam 'e say we go get too much trouble plenty pain for belly if we go chop um." An Shnake 'e say "Ah-ha! He be one black fool, s'dat chop be good chop for black man. You chop um, you like um!" An Heava she done chop um an done like um too-too much. She put dem mango for Hadam's ground-nut stew - den dere be plenty palaver for Paradise one time.

Hadam and Heava dey done savvy dey be naked, dey no get cloth at all, so dey putem hat for head. Byemby one man dey call um Noah come for garden. Noah be Headman for Elda Dempsta boat - an he done take Heava for sail on lagoon an dey go make plenty humbug for Hadam.

Still None The Wiser

Den de Lord done come back for Hearth an he go call Hadam, but Hadam 'e no be for seat, 'e go fear de Lord too much an 'e go for bush one time. Again de Lord call Hadam an Hadam he say with small-small voice "Yessah Lord" an de Lord He say, "Close me Hadam, close me" and Hadam close de Lord. De Lord say "Wassamatter Hadam, why you go for bush?" An Hadam say "I no get cloth Lord, so I no want dat you done see me naked." An de Lord 'e vex too much. "What ting dis, who tell you you be naked?" Den de Lord say "Ah-*ha*!, I de savvy now, you done chop dem mango for tree in de middle of de garden!"

An Hadam he say "I no chop um Lord - dem woman you go make for me, she puttum for groundnut stew!" Den de Lord make plenty-plenty palaver, 'e vex proper, an 'e say "Make for pack your bag and go."

An de Lord he done drive Hadam and Heava from Paradise."

CHAPTER 10

Leave - 1955-56

*"He capers, he dances, he has eyes of youth,
he writes verses, he speaks holiday, he smells April and May."
(The Merry Wives of Windsor - W. Shakespeare)*

My tour dragged on. It was the end of November 1955 before I was free to depart on leave - two months over my eighteen-month contract. My earlier fears had been realised, few expats with the Bank in those days were released on time. At least I had been enjoying myself in the past year, and I had come to terms with the fact that my previous, passionate affair with O. was unlikely to be rekindled when I reached London once more.

Before my leave commenced I was obliged to sign an iniquitous (in modern day terms) document pledging myself to sign another contract to return to West Africa at the end of my leave. Without this, I would not receive one further penny of salary - and if I later reneged on this agreement for any reason I would be legally obliged to refund any pay made to me on leave. At the same time our salaries reverted to the basic rate. All allowances ceased the moment we left the Coast. In those days the Bank was not a generous employer and our so-called 'contracts' were simply a one-sided agreement in their favour.

I arranged to fly home direct from Takoradi on a three day flight with Hunting Clan Airways who operated weekly departures from Accra, with overnight stays in the Gambia and Tangier. The aircraft was a Viking, a civilian version of the RAF's twin-engined Vickers Valetta transport - itself a refined development of the old Wellington bomber, the 'Wimpy.' It held about thirty passengers and being unpressurised, flew at no more than five or six thousand feet up the West Coast of Africa. We landed that first afternoon at Yun Dum, the airstrip for Bathurst (now Banjul) and we were bussed off to the Atlantic Hotel, on the beach some way out of town. It was then brand new and the first of its kind. There was time for a walk on the deserted beach and a drink by the new swimming pool. Dinner was no great shakes - still the same old Coast menu of tinned ox-tail soup, rubber chicken and tinned diced veg. I shared a thatched rondavel, mosquito-netted and without air-conditioning, with a PWD man, who drank himself to sleep and who rose late the next morning with no time for breakfast except for a swift

Alka Seltzer or two, complaining bitterly of the noise as it fizzed in the glass. Today I remain totally unimpressed by the thought of the Gambia as a holiday destination though it is now so popular with Swedes and Germans as a winter resort.

We flew out of Yun Dum by 0830, timing our departure to arrive ready for lunch at Villa Cisneros on the coast of the former colony of Spanish Sahara - now disputed by both Morocco and Mauretania. Flying low over great wastes of crescent dunes, with no sign of human existence to be seen for hour after hour, the vast emptiness of this corner of Africa was impressive. We touched down on a bare, sandy airstrip, as flat as a pancake and trudged across the flat waste-land to a group of low white buildings in the Spanish style edged by a sprinkling of wispy palms. On the airstrip itself were drawn up a few ancient aircraft of the Spanish Air Force - Junkers 52 tri-motored transports and Heinkel He.111 bombers - the sight of which induced a slight chill amongst those who still remembered the Luftwaffe's depredations of a few short years before.

It was a classic scene, blue-overalled Spanish soldiers sat slumped under the trees in the thin shade. Clutching their rifles, cigarettes drooping from their unshaven lips and chins, they evinced no interest in our party as we walked by. One of our lady passengers remarked to our pilot who accompanied us on our way to what turned out to be the Spanish Officers' Mess. "What on earth possesses these poor men to stay in a place like this - how can they possibly stand it?"

"It's very simple Madam," replied our captain - "this is a punishment station for dissident Spanish soldiers. You will observe over there, about a mile away, the sea and that rickety jetty. There are no boats and the water is full of sharks. In the other direction," he pointed beyond a small square fort in the distance, "is the desert. There is no water for hundreds of miles. There are no roads. The local inhabitants do not much like the Spaniards, if they escape that way they either die of thirst in the sand or are captured by the tribesmen - who may, or may not, depending on how they feel bring them back, either 'intact' or perhaps minus a few body parts, in exchange for a small reward. There is no Spanish equivalent of the old 'Goolie Chit' system we British so sensibly operated on the North-West Frontier[*]. Apart from these factors, there is nothing to keep them here at all!"

---

[*] In the 1920s and 1930s RAF airmen who crashed their unreliable biplanes over tribal territory on India's North West frontier carried 'goolie chits' which promised payment of a substantial reward if the bearer of such a document was returned to the British authorities 'intact' i.e. in good working order.

Our lady passenger looked quite shocked at these revelations. We had a modest lunch of cold meats and salads with beer and wine and returned to our aircraft and feeling more sympathy with the lounging, idle soldiers. Several years ago in a small travel ad. I saw again the name Villa Cisneros (long since changed to Dakhla, I believe). The potential holiday visitor was offered *'sun and sandy beaches in romantic, unique surroundings.'* After two or three days I imagine the average package tourist would be pleading for complimentary 'Goolie Chits,' ready to risk the desert to escape!

By late afternoon we had touched down again outside Tangier, then in its sunset days as the international hideaway of the rich, of the big-time smugglers of the day and the last resort of half the exiled homosexual writers and washed-up piss-artists and sleazy con-men of the western world - in other words a totally fascinating and slightly dangerous destination, both picaresque and fashionable. Unfortunately our brief overnight stay at the small Hotel Mirador on the esplanade gave us little chance to sample these tempting delights. After dinner a small group of us ventured into the narrow alleys of the Casbah; keeping one another closely in sight. We went into a bar or two and were tempted into the souks to be shown rugs and brassware. The deeper we penetrated the better were the rates of exchange everywhere displayed for all the world's currencies. For us poor Britons this was small comfort, restricted as we were then to an allowance of no more than an annual £75 for travel outside the Sterling Area. My room-mate, the PWD man again - disappeared the moment we checked into the hotel, leaving his overnight baggage unopened in our room and only turned up again the next morning, in the last few minutes before take-off. As our 'Hostess' tut-tutted over the absent passenger on her checklist a battered taxi screeched to a halt at the still open cabin door. Our missing PWD man, dishevelled, clearly over-tired and emotional, fell out onto the tarmac in an untidy heap. He was hauled on board, strapped firmly into his seat where he groaned and snored all the way to our final re-fuelling stop at Bilbao.

Arriving at Heathrow was an anticlimax. It was bitterly cold and raining on a wintry afternoon in late November. I was wearing my now somewhat ravaged 'Palm Beach' linen suit, but for extra warmth at Bilbao - being forewarned, I had taken my pyjama trousers from my bag and wore them under my tropical suit. I was also profoundly grateful to Jacques Spencer-Chapman who had loaned me a splendidly fashionable fleece-lined three-quarter length coat with a fur collar.

O. met me on arrival, if only to confirm that our 'affair' was over and she and I went home to my mother's flat in what was then still 'British' West Kensington, for dinner. It was a fairly bleak homecoming and I remember wishing I were back again in Africa. The prospect of the next three months was not promising.

In the event parts of my leave were great fun. One common problem of the young, footloose chaps on leave from the 'Colonies' for three months and more, with saved-up money to burn was with whom to burn it. One had lost touch with one's contemporaries at home and anyway they had to work all week for their living unlike myself. During the past twenty months I had scrimped and saved from my salary of £750 per year, the huge sum of more than £300 which I had intended to put to our now abandoned marriage plans. I was - in those days, for a twenty-four year old - almost conspicuously wealthy. The average Briton then was still trapped in the UK poverty and currency restrictions as if it were still wartime. Young people in particular often suffer from the usually erroneous and almost universal belief of supposing that everyone else is having a more enjoyable time than themselves. I now intended to disprove this.

I needed a UK driving licence as I intended to buy a car on my next tour and this was a less complicated and expensive way to obtain a licence for the Gold Coast, than inevitably having to 'dash' and grease various palms to facilitate 'passing' the local West African driving test. This was always a tedious process, the 'pass' dash (whatever one's ability) was usually £20 - a lot of money in those days. So I booked myself a 'crash' driving course in West London with a reputable driving school. How this turned out I will recount later.

Another friend from my earlier Chartered Bank days in London was also as I discovered on leave from Nigeria, having made much the same career change and decisions that I had as to the Far Eastern alternative. We shared the cost of a hired car and he drove us up to Edinburgh and back again over the course of the next few days. It wasn't much fun. We discovered over that New Year that the festival of Hogmanay mainly consisted of Scotsmen being sick in the street and that the Scottish pubs and small hotels that we stayed in offered little in the way of entertainment or congenial surroundings; and this was even before the days of tartan carpets and TV fixed to the wall. The roads may have been empty in those days, but the winter driving conditions were frightful and our hire-car had no heater, this in 1955 being still an optional extra on most models.

As soon as I came back to London I left again by train for a two week winter holiday to Wengen in Switzerland. The Swiss Franc then stood at twelve to the pound sterling - I was rich! Our group had some pretty girls, 'l'aprés ski' and the partying was a revelation. The snow was fresh and crisp, the skies blue, one swished and schussed across the sunny pistes with delight in our new found - and well taught skills. For most British visitors after the gloomy post-war years it must have been heaven. I swiftly met Gertie, a German girl from Zurich also on her first winter holiday - who helped banish the last of the blues from my bruised and tender heart.

At the end of the two weeks' ski holiday there seemed little reason to return to London. Gertie had invited me to stay at her home in Zurich - so why not? I needed more foreign currency - my meagre UK travel allowance now exhausted, so I bought up all the unused travellers cheques from my own small tour party - giving them cheques on my London account in exchange - thereby obtaining an adequate fund of Swiss Francs with which I subsequently bought more travellers cheques in US Dollars. I had not become a banker for nothing! I amazed myself at my own perspicacity.

Zurich was not a great success. Gertie worked as a physiotherapist at the Childrens' Hospital and was out all day. Her parents, both retired German Protestant missionaries from Surinam in South America, although friendly and pleasant - and satisfyingly curious about my life in Africa, were a trifle wearing, perforce all our conversation in Gertie's absence was in German. Gertie's father, somewhat mystifyingly, pronounced me to be "*Ein ganz Tropen-Mensch.*"* The small, cramped flat, with the four of us, meant that a considerable damping-down now occurred in the blossoming relationship between Gertie and me, so carefully nurtured in the previous freedom of the Alps.

After several days, (Zurich was too Swiss and sober-sided to be an exciting daytime city for a young man intent on pleasure), Gertie and I parted, promising to write to each other. I flew on to Nice, thinking that rather than return to the mountains for another spell of ski-ing perhaps the fashionable Côte d'Azure would prove to be the ticket.

I booked myself in, demi-pension, at the Hotel Bristol which was cheap and quite respectable although small and obviously favoured by British visitors. I was gratified on the second day, when speaking by chance to another English guest at a nearby table, to discover that until then because of my facility in speaking French to

---

* Lit.Trans. "*a complete tropical type.*"

the hotel staff - and not least because of my splendidly Gallic fur-collared fleece-lined coat so kindly lent to me by Jacques - that the British in the hotel had up until then taken me to be French!

I stayed no more than three or four days as I needed to return to London for my driving lessons. The mornings in Nice were spent exploring the town, lunching pleasantly at small cafés and restaurants and walking on the Promenade des Anglais in the sun. Sitting at an outside table at the plushier hotels like the Negresco, watching the elegant passers-by as I sipped my sophisticated glass of vermouth and Campari known as an 'Americano,' my own elegant coat of course draped across my Daks and Simpson-clad shoulders . To complete the image I also sported dark, shaded sunglasses that I had worn while ski-ing. I had become an unashamed *poseur*.

My second evening I went to the ballet then playing in the theatre of the Municipal Casino. It was the dance company of the Marquis de Cuevas - whose premiere danseuse was the statuesque Marjorie Tallchief (reputedly of Red Indian extraction - one was allowed to say this at that time, rather than the presently mandatory 'native American' - her sister was another well-known dancer, Maria Hightower). I had been introduced to the delights of the ballet a year or two earlier in London by O. Being somewhat poverty stricken we had perched ourselves in the gallery slips - high above the stage and the rest of the audience, (I think the tickets were then no more than a shilling or two). With O I had seen most of the classical performances of the day. In Nice, I decided I would 'push the boat out' and I bought myself a seat in the first row of the stalls. I do not remember what was danced, it was modern.

Anyone who knows anything about the ballet will immediately realise the error of my ways. Nobody, but nobody, sits in the first few rows of the stalls to watch ballet dancers perform! I found myself sitting below the stage, separated from the dancers only by the narrow orchestra pit. I was ensconced in solitary splendour in the centre of the first row. The nearest members of the rest of the audience were several rows back. The orchestra sawed and fiddled away, so close that I could hear the rustle of the pages of music being turned and the conductor's exhortations. Across the musicians' darkened pit the dancers on stage huffed and puffed, grunting audibly with strain as their feet squeaked and thumped on the boards. I could see the perspiration beading their brows as they twirled and pirouetted, wafts of body odour drifted liberally across the pit together with occasional droplets of sweat. To add to my discomfiture during the first act, two 'ladies of the town' came down the aisle and sat beside me for several minutes, attempting to proposition me. I assured the first to arrive that for the moment my sole interest lay in the performance on stage in front of us. She left, only to be followed by a second young lady who perhaps thought that I was just playing hard to get. After the first interval I found myself a seat a little further back and managed to enjoy the rest of the performance. Covent Garden (in my time at least) had never been like this!

After the performance I soon left, casinos have always bored me and gambling; both cards and horses I had already discovered were tedious and could be expensive. I wandered around, was it the Place Garibaldi? The names escape me now, but I found a night-club - more properly perhaps a cabaret, near the centre of the town which was more to my taste. I went in, depositing my splendid fur-collared coat at the cloakroom.

Night clubs, cabarets, of this type have long since vanished into history. So-called 'clubbing' today, or 'substance'-fuelled disco-dancing, swilling cans of pop-and-vodka mixes to deafening music is solely a pastime of the young - no-one else could stand the noise. It is as different from the night clubs of the Forties and Fifties as is a Bingo Hall from a Palm Court Orchestra. In a 'club' of the type I now entered there would be a cocktail bar, a small dance floor and a competent band, comfortable plush seating at discreetly lit tables and booths and black-jacketed white-aproned waiters. Every hour or two there would be a cabaret show - a singer perhaps, jugglers or acrobats, 'exotic' dancers or a small chorus line - judging from the photos on the street outside, this would be a typical French version of those I knew from London, a little expensive perhaps, but after all I was a young man, well off for those days and I had nearly two years of West Africa to get out of my system.

The cabaret was only thinly patronised at that hour and it was mid-week. I ordered a drink (probably an 'Americano' again). I lit a cigarette and listened to the band, a small Gypsy orchestra in tight, flared trousers and flounced, frilly shirts playing *Zigeuner* airs on fiddle and accordion. All very French and sophisticated. A few chic, well-dressed and very attractive girls sat chatting at the bar. It was impossible for me not to be aware of them.

It was not long before a dark, exceedingly pretty girl came over and asked permission to join me; I was not made of stone. She was in no way forward or obvious as had been the ladies in the casino. We chatted pleasantly, having introduced ourselves. For the purpose of this narrative I shall call her Mam'selle Fifi LaPlinge. After an hour or so of pleasant conversation, a dance or two on the cramped floor (for someone as clumsily ham-footed as I, it is remarkably easy to sway romantically to French accordion music), we sat at our table once more until the waiter whispered briefly in her ear. Fifi excused herself, saying she would return in a few minutes.

The lights dimmed, the band struck up and a spot-lit *chanteuse* - another of the girls from the bar - gave a passable imitation of Edith Piaf to polite applause. Next, a pair of athletic, acrobatic dancers juggled and contorted themselves into impossible positions to cries of "*Hoop*-la!" and "*Allez-oop!*" Then as they exited, the drummer crashed out a triumphant roll and the lights dimmed even more - and then to a roar of applause - the audience had increased since my arrival, the spotlights focused on two huge scarlet ostrich feather fans in the centre of the floor. As the fans slowly parted, they revealed to my intense delight and pleasure, a small but perfectly formed dancer's body, as naked (but for a tiny jewelled G-String) as the day she was born. For a moment or two I quite failed to recognise the features of Mam'selle Fifi - the highlight of the cabaret!

What else was a respectable Englishman in such circumstances to do but to sit back and enjoy the show? In London in earlier years I had seen Miss Phyllis Dixie tastefully displaying parts of her 'all' - behind her enormous feathered fans - in her famous stage shows, a stately British institution to whose performances one could have safely escorted one's elderly maiden aunts. In 1953 at the Prince of Wales variety theatre in the West End a chum, 'Jimmie' James and I had actually gone to see the fabulous black American dancer known as 'Baby' Scruggs - built like a pocket Venus, dressed only sufficiently to allow various fringes and tassels to be attached (presumably glued) to her anatomy. 'Baby' Scruggs strutted and shook parts of herself that until that moment a properly brought up young man had only been able to imagine - if he dared. Her performance concluded with contra-rotating tassels on her bosom, rhythmically swinging fringes wobbling and shaking with wild syncopation while the audience went mad!*

Mam'selle Fifi's act fell somewhere between those two extremes. I shall not dwell on it. She returned to my table once the cabaret was finished. After the last show she explained she was free - but desired a late supper if I would care to accompany her. She explained that her act was exhausting and left her famished and she preferred to eat elsewhere than in the club.

By now I was anxiously assessing the state of my wallet. Cash was the immediate problem. During Fifi's absence I had changed a couple of my Swiss-purchased US dollar cheques with the club's obliging cashier - receiving in return what I thought was a remarkably generous bundle of French Francs. This was just as well as a few minutes later the Gypsy band began to thread their way around the tables, pausing to serenade the prettier girls and their companions. I watched with a certain amount of dread, for it was quite obvious that while the customers appreciated the music - they

---

* I think that the then Lord Chamberlain's office, the censor of theatrical morals since Shakespeare's day, later demanded that Ms. Scruggs tone down her performance or the theatre would be closed.

were having to tip the musicians to make them go away or to play their own choice of tune, and the longer the fiddlers and accordionist scraped and squeezed their respective instruments - the more it seemed to cost the object of their efforts.

The quartet of moustachio'd and frilly-shirted gypsies reached our table. Fifi was clearly the apple of their collective eyes for without prompting they played a medley of what were obviously her favourite, and I feared expensive, pieces. Turning to me, the violinist simpered unctuously, did *M'sieu* have a favourite tune?

My mind went blank. Unlike those appearing on the popular BBC radio request programme of that time. 'Down Your Way' I could not even come up with that all-time favourite choice of the musically illiterate public-at-large, Handel's 'Largo.' I retreated deeper into shock, as the violinist, interpreting my silence for indecision rather than ignorance, said. "Ah - but of course, *you* are English!" Turning to his companions he waved "Un - deux - trois!" They broke into a spirited *'zigeuner'* version of what I finally realised was 'It's a Long Way to Tipperary.' I fumbled in my wallet, deeply embarrassed as I paid them handsomely, carefully judging the amount necessary to make them go away without encouraging them to continue with anything else from their English repertoire - perhaps 'Boiled Beef and Carrots' or 'My Old Man Said Follow the Van.'

Fifi was pretty and charming. We found a late night café-bar, where for the first time in my life I ate oysters - at her insistence. No wonder that so many young Englishmen came to France to complete their education if so many young French women were as delightful and graceful as Fifi was with me. We walked back arm-in-arm to my hotel, with new found assurance I tipped the night porter who ushered us into the lift for my floor.

To say any more would be to break my early pledge to tread with circumspection in matters such as these. Fifi left again in the early hours of that morning after we had arranged to meet for a late lunch the next afternoon.

I remember Fifi with affection. Sophisticated, totally French, completely feminine. We continued our brief and passionate affair the following evening, following much the same pattern. This time at the club I managed to circumvent the musicians. I cashed more US dollar cheques with the obliging cashier and without checking the rate of exchange I once again received a satisfyingly fat helping of francs. I suggested to Fifi that I cancel my return flight to London the following day to stay with her a few days longer. "Alas" she sighed, "c'est pas possible." At the weekend her wealthy protector - an 'industrialist from Lyons' would be in town.

"He is old, but rich - tu comprends? A girl has to live, Cherie." As I said, she was a sophisticated and practical girl. French to her delicate fingertips.

The next day I flew back to London, surprisingly with what seemed like plenty of money in my pocket. I still had my 'crash' course of driving lessons to follow up. Time was running out and soon I would have to return to West Africa.

Several weeks later after I was back in the Gold Coast, in Sekondi, the mystery of my unexplained wealth in Nice was explained. I received a tearful letter, in French, from the cashier at the cabaret. She explained she had obtained my address from Mam'selle Fifi herself (who must have obtained it from my hotel) - who sent fond kisses (a fat lot of good they were at that distance!) The Travellers Cheques she had exchanged for me, she had mistakenly assumed were in Sterling rather than US dollars for which the rate was then something like $2.40 to the English pound. I had received almost two-and-a-half times as much money in francs. No wonder I had thought I was rich! The cashier explained that she was being obliged by her employer, the cabaret owner, to make good the quite substantial difference from her own pocket. Alas, she was but a poor war widow with fatherless children to support - she was sure that as an English gentleman, I would oblige and honour the debt she had incurred on my behalf.

Still None The Wiser

How could I refuse such a tender plea? I had enjoyed my stay, spending money both liberally and literally on wine, women and song. Jacques was about to depart on leave and would be visiting the south of France to see his father, in his turn wearing the splendid fleece-lined fur-collared coat that I had returned to him. So I gave him the money that was due, charging him to deliver it in person in Nice together with my personal introduction to Fifi.

When Jacques came back to Sekondi some three months later, he confirmed all had gone well, the cashier had been deeply grateful. Fifi, he said, was not really his type - and besides she had her 'industrialist' protector watching her like a hawk since her indiscreet behaviour had been reported to him. But, as he said, the cabaret's resident *chanteuse* had quite stolen his heart, however briefly, away.

After my jaunts ski-ing in the Alps and in Zurich and the South of France I had left myself little time to take my UK Driving Test. I had already booked myself a few 'refresher' sessions with a driving school in West London to bring myself up to scratch sufficiently to meet - as I thought - the examiner's demands. All I needed to do now was to take the test. I was supremely over-confident. The instructor's dual-control car was a Morris Minor 'Moggie' the same as Norman Welch's car back in Sekondi of which he had bravely allowed me to take (sole) control and drive along the wash-board laterite roads to Cape Coast and back once or twice. En route one passed a few mammy wagons, skirted the major pot-holes, avoided running over goats and piccaninnies in the villages - or falling off the Pra River bridge at Beposo - and that was that.

Driving in London I found was much more difficult. Even by 1956 one was already beginning to need eyes in the back of one's head to navigate the crowded streets. I tried in vain to book my driving test before my rapidly approaching departure back to the Coast. My driving instructor, a mild and mostly calm little man, suggested that I take an Automobile Association test - in urgent cases such as mine they were at that time authorised to conduct driving tests whose results were accepted by the Ministry of Transport (similarly, passing a military driving test entitled one to a full civilian license). I arranged a test immediately with the AA.

The day of the ordeal arrived. It was to take place at the AA's Headquarters in Leicester Square which meant driving to the West End with my instructor in the dual-control Morris Minor. I drove as far as the Albert Hall when my instructor, by now visibly nervous and sweating (we had not ventured outside of quiet back streets until now) made me draw into the kerb. He spoke briefly and to the point.

"Mr. Adamson - I have to say that without several more lessons you haven't a snowball's chance in Hell of passing the test!" He paused. "I do have a possible solution (here he coughed nervously) - I will drive now from here to Trafalgar Square, to ensure we actually arrive there in one piece. Er, er - umm, I er - actually know your examiner. These chaps are very badly paid for such a responsible job - or so I am given to understand. If you could see your way to letting me have a fiver, I'll have a few words with him beforehand and explain why you need a license so urgently. All that stuff about graft you told me about in West Africa etcetera."[*] I took two fivers out of my wallet and passed one over. "The second one is for you when I pass." I said, my time in the Gold Coast had taught me much.

My instructor parked carefully in Leicester Square and disappeared inside the building. After an age, during which time the 'Moggie' became firmly boxed-in front and rear as other cars squeezed in, my instructor came out with a dark-suited, grim looking little man. I was not encouraged by his demeanour - until from behind him I noticed my instructor giving me a broad wink and a discreet thumbs-up. If what follows, in terms of the traffic flow seems impossible today, one must remember that everything has changed radically in the past forty-odd years. My examiner took his seat. I pulled away from the kerb with some difficulty, banging the cars behind and in front quite vigorously before I was out into the stream of traffic. The examiner said little except, "Turn here, down there, LEFT! LEFT!! LEFFTT!!!" I obligingly turned left at the top of the Square making for Piccadilly - in the process bumping over the pavement and forcing a policeman to move smartly backwards before I ran over his boots. Thinking to conceal my car's number plate as the bobby fumbled for his notebook I put my foot hard down and swung into the outside lane towards Piccadilly Circus. "LEFT! HERE!!" I obeyed the examiner's instruction and swooped across the inside two lanes of buses and taxis and drove relatively smoothly and without further incident gathering pace down the Haymarket. "LEFT!!!" He shouted again and we shot at speed into Pall Mall, past W.W. Greener's gunsmith's shop. He guided me without further incident back through Trafalgar Square and I pulled up at last, stalling the engine in the process, outside the AA Headquarters building. We sat in a frosty silence for some minutes.

---

[*] Not perhaps as much as I found out in later years viz. that almost every man has his price, that the 'honest' man is therefore by definition, the most expensive. Most people can be bought, not always necessarily with hard cash – with the alleged exception perhaps of the citizens of Afghanistan of whom it was said "You can only rent an Afghan - and they won't always tell you when the meter runs out."

There was no sign of my instructor, he was obviously hiding inside. At last the examiner spoke; he had remained virtually speechless apart from his sparse directions during our brief ten minute test drive.

"I am obliged by the Regulations to ask you some questions on the Highway Code." He did so, posing three simple problems clearly, from the samples then set out in the few brief pages that then comprised the Code. I was quite unable to answer any correctly; my mind had gone a total blank.

We sat in what seemed to me a doom-laden vacuum for a further few minutes while he jotted down notes in his pocketbook. "Your instructor, Mr. Plinge, tells me you are leaving the country in a few days to return to Africa?" "Yes, quite correct, I'm flying out again next week!" I replied. "Well, Mr. Adamson - I tell you what, you're obviously a gentleman, (thus confirming the French war-widow's opinion of me in Nice). If you will give me your word of honour and promise faithfully not to drive anywhere in the UK before you leave - you can have your license."

My instructor took his own fiver, driving cheerfully back to Kensington. He said "You're very lucky you know. The last time I tried on that dodge with old Fred, it cost twenty quid - but then the candidate was an Indian Maharajah - and neither of us could be certain he would keep his promise not to drive!"

CHAPTER 11

Interlude for Light Relief

*"Captain Stokes told us that notwithstanding the country of Gambo
is so unhealthy, yet the people of that place live very long, so as the
present King there is 150 years old, which they count by rains because
every year it rains continuously four months together. He also told
us that the Kings there have above an hundred and fifty wifes a-piece
and offered him the choice of any of his wifes to lie with,
and so he did Captain Holmes.
(Samuel Pepys - Diary, 16th January 1662)*

The District Officer's Lament
(with apologies to Rudyard Kipling)

(According to my 1954 note this is sung to the tune of 'The Eton Boating Song'

"I started as A.D.O. Bende
As shy as a girl to begin
Till I bought me a fine Ibo virgin
For the price of a bottle of gin.
Ugly, and oily and smelly,
Savage and sullen she were.
She give me a fright on the very first night
-But I learned about women from 'er."

"An' then I was posted to Lagos,
Where I was told that they didn't do such.
But to see all those bush lamps returnin'
From Ikoyi, every night, was too much.
So I went to the Chief Secretary
To find out the way to begin -
'E said "First you must see Secret Circular B" (**See Note**)
- An' I learned about women from 'im."

"An' then I was sent up to Yola,
Where I swore I would try to be good.
Till I met me a snappy Fulani
An' I did just as other men would.
Proud like, and 'aughty, and 'andsome,
Sort of ambitious she were
- Never saw 'er again when the Resident came.
But I learned about women from 'er.

"I've taken my fun where I've found it
An' His Honour 'as 'ad the last word.
For now I am D.O. Forcados
An' my increment's being deferred.
But oft of a Saturday morning
As I'm drinking my seventeenth gin,
I cry 'Ain't it a shame!' But still - all the same,
I KNOW MORE ABOUT WOMEN THAN 'IM!"

Note: The notorious affair of the Secret Circulars 'A' and 'B' was but one result of the 'fraternisation' of Colonial Officers with African women - much more common apparently on the West Coast than in East Africa where a stricter code was thought to be observed. Secret Circulars 'A' and 'B' were promulgated by the Secretary of State for the Colonies in 1909: 'A' declared that *"It had come to His Honour's attention that a certain number of government officials were living in a state of concubinage with native women and a very serious view would be taken of people living under these circumstances."* Whereupon all sorts of unpleasantness beset the whole of the government service and a hurried follow-up Circular 'B' was sent round saying that *"With regard to my last Secret Circular 'A', it now appears that **not** such a serious view will be taken of government officers living in a state of concubinage with native women."* **Further Note:-** In August 1966 I saw a letter in The Times from Margery Perham asking for unpublished personal letters or Mss relating to government service in the Colonial era. These she wanted for the archive being compiled at Oxford for the University Colonial Records Project. I sent her a copy of the above, but perhaps unsurprisingly received no acknowledgement. I have since lost the complete copy I wrote down in 1954 at Sekondi when Malcolm Midgeley stayed with me at the end of his final tour (after eight years in West Africa he confided that he had "had enough") en route from Hohoe to the UK and in his cups regaled me with a fund of 'Old Coaster' stories - most of which I have long forgotten. There may have been one or two more verses but these are all I can recall.

CHAPTER 12

'Tales of the Silver Screen'

*"That's what they used to call it, 'The Arsehole of the Empire' - yes, and B****e was about seven miles straight up."*
(Gareth Plinge - 'Reminiscences in his Cups' c. 1965)

In the late Fifties or very early Sixties my friend Gareth Plinge was with BBWA in Sierra Leone, posted to a dreadful town called B****e - in a muddy, fever-ridden swamp on Sherbro Island lying off the coast to the south, where he was the manager. The main business of the Bank there lay in letters-of-credit for piassava exports, piassava being a coarse, stiff fibre cut from the leaf stalk of a palm that flourished in the swamp - much used for bristles in brush manufacture, (including the particular brush head on the long, sturdy rod supplied by the Swedish firm of Bofors for scrubbing out the barrels of their ever-popular 40mm AA guns). Gareth was one of the few resident Europeans - the other non-Africans were mostly Syrian or Lebanese and Indian traders who plied him with drink and offers of women in expectation (mostly unrealised) of easier credit with the Bank. To term B****e a dismal dump is to flatter the place. Gareth said he was frequently drunk and depressed, not surprisingly. His sole recreation (apart from drink and women - and the latter he said were so unprepossessing that after a lot of trial and error he subsequently came out of the closet and decided to be 'gay') was to ride his bicycle off into the swamps to shoot wild duck. There were few cars as the roads were simply muddy tracks leading off into the spiny piassava thickets.

Gareth lived in a dreary flat over the rented Bank premises in the middle of town. The night-time noise was appalling. Adding to the cacophony was an open-air Indian-owned cinema across the road - he could clearly see the screen from his balcony. There was no air-conditioning to block out either the noise or the heat. Gareth when sitting drunk in the evenings, as he often was, if the noise from the cinema became more unbearable than usual, would unload the lead shot from his duck-shooting cartridges, reduce the powder charge, replace the shot with solid hard-dried lumps of the stodgy local bread that he made for this purpose - and then at moments of catharsis in the film when the audience would go wild, Gareth would take careful aim and discharge his gun across the street at the cinema screen. He said that nobody ever took any notice. In daylight, so he told me, his bread-shot holes in the screen were quite clearly visible through his binoculars, which gave him a certain amount of satisfaction. He spent, I believe, six months in all at B****e, barely managing to retain what little sanity he still possessed at that time. On leave in UK, being told he was to go back to B****e he resigned and came out to the Coast again with UBA (a French bank in Nigeria).

Several years later in 1966 during the period of unrest preceding the early massacres that finally led up to the Biafran War, Gareth was at Port Harcourt which was where he finally flipped and went totally round the twist. Late one Saturday night, drunk, dancing and capering on the flat roof of the Bank in the centre of town overlooking the street below, he was throwing firecrackers into a jeering crowd who had gathered, shouting at them "YOU'RE ALL DOOMED!" (According to Malcolm Muggeridge, D. H. Lawrence shouted this at Bertrand Russell across the dinner table). Shortly after this incident Gareth cracked up completely and was flown home in a pretty dire and highly nervous state. He was relieved by another friend, Finnbar O'Plinge, who with three small children and his wife heavily pregnant with their fourth - subsequently had to drive her to the hospital in labour, through riots and dead bodies littering the streets when the local Ibos retaliated in kind against the Hausas and Northerners, exacting retribution for the similar slaughter of Ibos in Kano.

On the subject of cinemas in West Africa, most were in the open air relying on the natural darkness of the tropical night - but reluctant to refund their customers in the event of either torrential downpour or brilliant moonlight. Some of the films were incredibly ancient, but none the less popular for that, familiarity being greatly valued by the African audiences as they could chant along with the dialogue and anticipate the high-spots. That fine 'imperialist' film 'Sanders of the River' was hugely favoured until it was banned by Dr. Kwame N'Krumah in Ghana in 1959 or 1960 - probably at the direct request of the star, the singer Paul Robeson and also of the Kenya Prime Minister, Jomo Kenyatta, who had been an 'extra' in the film (except for a few back-projections of African locations 'Sanders' was mostly filmed on a Thames backwater upstream of Teddington Studios). Both Robeson and Kenyatta for years had been seeking to buy up every surviving copy of this classic film to destroy them. Oddly enough the local African audience always sided with Mr. Commissioner Sanders, singing along with Paul Robeson and jeering at the villainous tribesmen. Finally, when Leslie Banks who plays Sanders mans the Maxim gun on the bridge of his gunboat, "Zaire" and mows down rows of Africans - the Gold Coast audiences would go mad, jumping on the seats, shouting, cheering 'OSAH!! OSAH!!' and 'KILL 'AM SANDI, KILL 'AM!!! I still think it was a great film.

Still None The Wiser

In Tamale in 1959 John Wood (sadly, long since dead) and Ralph Little (happily as I write still much alive) both of Tamale Motors conducted a controlled experiment. One Saturday afternoon having as usual consumed several lunchtime beers (quite frequently as much as a case of a dozen large Beck's between them) at the Club, they equipped themselves with a big brass handbell and a wooden rattle normally used in combination as their motor workshop's fire alarm and took themselves off to Captan Brothers' Cinema (indoors) to view some immensely popular Indian film which was showing - advertised as "All Blows!" Gaining entry to the balcony they watched the film show, hooting and hollering along with the audience at the appropriate moments, furiously ringing the bell and twirling the rattle. Not one person took a blind bit of notice. Having suitably satisfied their curiosity, they returned to the Club and resumed their interrupted beer consumption until the late afternoon when it was time for John to open the bar at the Polo Club and for Ralph to go home and change into boots and breeches to play a chukka or two on the old Police parade ground.

At Takoradi in 1956, the cinema most frequented by European audiences was open-air, on a knoll that overlooked the vast harbour below, and run by the Seamen's Mission. Bright moonlight, rain, wind, thunder and lightning, mosquitoes and swarms of flying ants, all occasionally limited one's concentration from time to time, but not necessarily one's enjoyment. At the Mission cinema in 1954 I watched Randolph Scott and Binnie Barnes in 'The Last of the Mohicans,' the very first film I remember seeing - as a serial at a Saturday afternoon matinée in the Colosseum Cinema in Wallasey in 1937 or '38.

Another film, now regarded as a Sci-Fi classic, called 'The Thing' was popular at that time and brought prolonged cheers and hoots of laughter from the mainly European audience when the US Air Force hero, shivering on the screen amid frozen (cardboard) Arctic wastes, delivers the deathless line "Gee - I sure wish I was back in Accra City, Gold Coast, like I was in the War!" At the Gyandu Palace Cinema in Sekondi, open-air for the masses below, there was a tin-roofed balcony above for the cream (those prepared to pay two shillings or so) of local society, black and white. There I recall watching 'Under Two Flags' (1939) - in which the heroine, 'Cigarette,' darling of the Foreign Legion and of Ronald Coleman, played by Claudette Colbert, mysteriously expired in a hail of bullets at the beginning of the film when the reels were shown in reverse order. The same happened with 'The Charge of the Light Brigade' where Errol Flynn charged the Russian guns and sabred the villain in the opening reel. No one ever complained. No excuses or explanations were ever offered by the management.

It was also at the Indian-owned Gyandu Palace Cinema in Sekondi that I saw at first hand a mass panic, or stampede. As I watched the film from the balcony above the common *hoi-polloi* below - suddenly without the slightest warning instant chaos erupted. Seats and benches were overturned, the entire audience below us scrambled for the exits, screaming, shouting in fear, pushing and scrabbling at the walls in heaving mass-packed rugger-scrum formations at the (of course) locked and bolted emergency exits. It was a classic display of mass hysteria. To me the most impressive aspect of the incident was the instantaneous manner in which the audience reacted. One moment they were watching the film from their seats, the next instant they were standing four deep on one another's unwilling shoulders attempting vainly to scale the walls. It was a miracle no-one was injured. Within several minutes a measure of calm was restored and the film resumed after an ill-written notice was projected on the screen saying **"Sorry pleese. Recent disturbances due to small fire of sugar box in projector room."**

Cinema handbills advertising the attractions of the latest Hollywood and Bollywood programmes were an art form in themselves. The African audiences adored Indian films, often un-dubbed or untitled into any local language - but lavish with colour, music, dancing, with complicated plot and sub-plots in profusion, full of simulated outlandish violence and of suggested (but never-to-be-consummated) sex. The Cinema hoardings on the street outside would proclaim their offerings as **'ALL BLOWS!'**

The Venice Cinema in Sekondi was Syrian owned and as well as being inside a hall and therefore weatherproof showed fewer Indian films, more Hollywood productions and doubled as a dance hall when required. I have only to hear the opening bars of 'The John B Calypso' played anywhere in the world and I am instantly conveyed back to 1954, listening to a scratchy 78 recording of E.T. Mensah's Tempos Band played over and over again before the performance could start. The Venice was slightly up-market compared to The Gyandu Palace. For a start it was weatherproof, but otherwise any comparisons were only measured in degrees of audience discomfort and fewer smells than at the Gyandu Palace which emanated from the nearby dark, viscous and often seething Sekondi lagoon. A visiting American was overheard one evening at the Gyandu Palace's box office, exclaiming to his companion through the folds of a handkerchief clutched to his nose. "This *stink* - how can you stand it? You some sort of *pervert* ... or what? I mean this is seriously like where God farted!"

The handbills that circulated advertising each week's coming programme were masterpieces of misleading shorthand:

RETURN OF THE CORSICAN BROTHERS
Richard Greene   Paula Raymond

Explodes in a fury of swashbuckled action! Island of Voilence! (Sic) Where vengeance explodes with every hoofbeat and the mediterranean ran red with terror! No man could match his

daring When a Woman like This was the prize!

See the daring duel of the daggers!

The brutal strappado torture!

RATES 2/6., 1/6 & 1s.

Sometimes they were more puzzling, less direct, as if the local copywriter had grappled with the action and the dialogue and had failed to come to grips with the essential plot:

NO ESCAPE
Starring......Lew Ayres.....Marjorie Steele

"Get your hands up! Your fingerprints are of the murder weapon

You have no way out you shayne." Mascular stars vealistic

thrills and tingling lige or death climax in U.S.'s No Escape

I am eternally grateful that I have never managed to sit through or have endured in its dreadful entirety that old Hollywood 'weepie' starring John Payne and Maureen O'Hara:

SENTIMENTAL JOURNEY

What a dathetic drama! ... Can love cross the barrier of death? A picture of such sweep and passion one cannot afford to miss. Fancy yourself to be the poor, mourning widower and seeing the vision of your wife whilst her familiar song "Sentimental Journey" is being played. What would you do with the trained,

Grief Stricken and Adopted

girl left behind by your wife to take her place?

Such theatre as this latter piece promises I have always held was more than normally sensitive flesh and blood could stand at one single sitting. In retrospect I find it strange that these older Hollywood romances - the epitome of one man/one woman, almost asexual, and certainly doom-laden relationships amounting to obsession - no double beds, at least one foot on the floor in bedroom scenes, were apparently so popular with their African audiences. The entire concept was so foreign to West African cultural and social and sexual structures, where extended family relationships, matrilineal succession - polygamy, collective parenting and to western eyes a much looser moral code where multiple sexual partners were accepted as the norm. How could such films and plots be so popular? I have no answer. Violence, revenge, action, right versus wrong - all these themes have a universal appeal - but romantic, almost 'courtly' love often with a strong undercurrent of tragedy - make strange bedfellows with the basic and practical relationships of most non-western societies where these old 'Weepies' were shown.

1 Young City bankers, lunchtime late 1953. Author on left.

Still None The Wiser

2 'Hell Corner' centre of young expat. culture in Sekondi, 1954

3 BBWA building opened 1916, except for the car still unchanged by 1954.

Still None The Wiser

4 Fishermen on the beach. An unchanging scene.

5 Fort Orange, Sekondi, built by the Dutch c. 1670, finally bought by the British in 1872.

6 Richard Steimann 1954, timber-man, snake-fancier, photographer and obsessive fisherman.

Still None The Wiser

7 Author fishing at Inchaban, 1956, catfish and tillapia were our more (or less) edible quarry. Note smart – almost 'natty' sporting attire..

Still None The Wiser

8 Catfish could be cooked in their own yellow fat from their diet of palm nuts.

9 View of Fort St. Anthony at Axim, Gold Coast, built by the Portuguese c.1490 besieged and taken by the Dutch in 1642. British in 1872.

Still None The Wiser

10 Fanti drummer 1955.

Still None The Wiser

11 My cook-steward for my bachelor years, Yaro Frafra on left and his 'brother' wearing I suspect, *my* suit and shoes '*borrowed*' for this studio portrait in 1956.

Still None The Wiser

12 Jacques Spencer-Chapman on the Prah River in 1956. On this trip he and I got much further upriver than a Royal Navy steam pinnace in 1873 before it was peppered by Ashanti musket fire and forced to retreat.

13 Takoradi airfield November 1956, I finally depart on leave. Jacques (right) has loaned me his splendid fur-collared coat with which to impress the natives back in Europe.

14 My 'old style' colonial house 1957 in Sekondi. Cool, dark and comfortable.

Still None The Wiser

15 My 'modern' house later in Takoradi 1957, hot, unshaded, the rooms all airless right angled boxes and with no shutters or air-conditioning.

16 1958, back in Accra. With Jim Wright (right) at the Railway Station. Both of us hairpin thin. Were there no fat people around in the 1950s?

Still None The Wiser

17 Picnic in the Shai Hills 1958. O centre with Paul and June Foot. Ludo the black labrador has dug a hole and is lying there to keep cool.

Still None The Wiser

18 Tamale 1959. O. and I live in the bungalow on the 'Ridge,' Adamu the garden boy tends the coarse crab grass for the benefit of the camera.

CHAPTER THIRTEEN

'Tummy Palaver'

"Beware and take care of the Bight of Benin.
There's few come out, though many go in!"
(Ancient Proverb)

"The Coast is pestilential, the natives numerous and unmanageable."
(Lord Kimberley, Colonial Secretary, to Consul Hewett in Lagos, 1883)

When I look back over the years I am amazed at the self-assurance and equanimity of youth apparent in the manner in which most of us accepted, or perhaps ignored the inherent risks to our short-term and long-term health which we incurred willy-nilly on the Coast. In spite of all the advances of medical science, the West Coast has never been noted as a health resort. By the 19th century it was a virtual charnel house for Europeans. To quote that eminent and eccentric Victorian explorer and traveller Sir Richard Burton. *"The annals of the Wesleyans in West Africa read more like a necrology."* Burton had a poor opinion of most missionaries - blaming their committed abstinence for their poor survival rate, writing of one. *"He died two years later of a confirmed teetotalism. In these lands the habitual water-drinker is even more short-lived than the habitual drunkard."*

Mary Kingsley held much the same views at the end of the 19th century although she allowed more sympathy for the missionaries' enterprises, in particular for the famed Mary Slessor of Calabar who was instrumental in bringing an end to the practice of killing new-born twins (based on the premise that as one twin was an evil spirit - but it being impossible to determine which, both were exposed in the bush and allowed to die to settle any future doubts). Before embarking on her first exploratory voyage to West Africa in 1892 Mary Kingsley had been counselled on sunstroke and quinine and advised to seek an introduction to the Wesleyans as *"...they are the only people on the Coast who have got a hearse with feathers."*

In 1860 Burton wrote of the assembled missionaries of Abeokuta as resembling nothing more than *"galvanised corpses."* At the same time he described the British Consulate at Lagos as *"..... a corrugated iron coffin or plank-lined morgue, containing a dead consul once a year."* In the 17th and 18th centuries when quinine was virtually unknown the death rates were even worse, 'unseasoned' new arrivals from Europe were often struck down within a few days of landing through the surf, fever, death and funeral all being over within a few days. West African malaria whose causes were then unknown was of the non-recurrent type taking the form of a single, severe attack that was often fatal. If an officer of the Royal African Company manning the trading castles along the Coast survived a full year, he was then regarded as 'seasoned' but fewer still beat the odds and survived for more than five years at the most and rare indeed was the Briton who lived to retire with his wealth to his native heath – unlike their fellow adventurers who followed the more well-worn road to India and the East.

In early 1954 at the age of twenty-two I had announced to my long-suffering family (as I have written elsewhere), that I was going to West Africa. There were some quite adverse reservations expressed. An uncle said to me that when he was a young man the steamship companies invariably declined to sell return tickets to passengers shipping out to the West African Coast. It was, he said, considered unlikely they would survive long enough to claim their return passages. Until the introduction of more effective anti-malarial drugs after the end of the war in 1945 (the accelerated research was prompted by the need to keep large armies in the field in malarial zones) fever and sickness were part and parcel of the white man's baggage involved in living in West Africa. The names of the successors to the simple quinine sulphate tablets trip easily off the tongue; Atabrin and Mepacrin (which both turned one's complexion bright yellow), Darraprim, Nivaquin, Paludrine, Chloroquin. Quinine itself, although effective enough when administered in precisely calculated doses as a curative, was much less successful as a prophylactic. It had two great drawbacks - if too much was taken over an extended period, it could induce a permanent degree of deafness; if too little was taken at the onset of a 'touch' of fever there was always a risk of encouraging the much-feared 'blackwater' variety when the malarial parasite retreated to the kidneys and the patient subsequently pissed away these invaluable organs in a stream of bloody urine, usually leading to the condition that I believe is now described in politically correct medical terms as: *"The patient failed to achieve his maximum wellness potential."* i.e. He died.

I read a recent obituary of a distinguished former West African colonial officer of whom it was said. *"He much regretted the post-war introduction of the daily Paludrine tablet, in the days of quinine people were noticeably nicer and kinder to one another, as you never knew when your neighbour's help and assistance to see you through a bout of fever might prove vital to one's survival."*

That old but interesting humbug, 'Trader' Horn, wrote in his inimitable fashion in 'The Ivory Coast in the Earlies.' "*Old Coasters are a dying breed. There isn't that sort of person any more. There's plenty of 'em down alongside the tombstones, but they aren't making them any more and there ain't no call for 'em, more's the pity.*"

At Sekondi there were 'plenty of 'em down alongside the tombstones' in the old European graveyard on the low cliff-top above the aptly named Cemetery Beach. The tilted and sunken headstones were gangrened and stained with damp and mildew, many garlanded with the bright green, fleshy leafed convolvulus with its conical pink flowers. Bearing their names and ages 'Aged 22,' 'Aged 23,' 'Aged 26.' 'Much Beloved,' 'Not Forgotten.' 'Mourned by his friends,' 'Forever Cherished Memories.' *Forever?* Finis.

Africans talk to their dead, they bring them token gifts of food, of yam and cassava, they dribble gin and palm wine on their graves - as much to keep them quiet as for any other reason. They pass on family news to stop the possibly troublesome dead from wandering about to find out what is going on away from the spirit world they now inhabit. Eventually the dead will lose interest in the affairs of the living and rest quietly. But few people visit the graves of the legions of European dead, and West Africa is full of them, lying uneasily so far from home. No relatives come to tidy their graves - or to talk to them. Their friends soon forgot and were posted away to other stations or Home, or perhaps died in their turn. The tombstone - if there is one, tilts and settles. The heavy rains wash away the red topsoil - and as at Cemetery Beach, the gullies open up, a few termite-riddled planks may surface and the odd bone or two lies in the weedy patches with the snakes and the scorpions.

One Saturday night in 1955 I sat for an hour or two on such a grave in the hot moonlight, comfortably drinking whisky and water with Jacques and old Colin MacLeod (I called him 'old' then - he was no more than forty-four or five). We had all been invited to celebrate the opening of a new enterprise, the Handad Hotel, just across the road from the old European cemetery. This was the latest enterprise of a local big 'mammy' trader, Hannah Dadzie - who, Jacques and I suspected was perhaps a former intimate acquaintance of Colin from his wilder and earlier days. Colin MacLeod, dead these many years alas, was the quintessential 'Old Coaster' bachelor. A senior manager with the Bank, he had been almost everywhere in West Africa since before the war. He acted as relief manager at all the major branches. Virtually deaf (when it suited him* see **Note**) from taking too much quinine as a young man, a great golfer and when he retired, a pillar of the Invergordon Golf Club until he died in the summer of 1979, he was a ladies' man, drinker and raconteur extraordinary. The stories about him are legend wherever Old Coasters still gather. I greatly admired him and was lucky to work under him at Sekondi in 1955, later at Takoradi in 1957 and also at Accra in 1958 when O. and I were first married.

Back in Sekondi the three of us had arrived in Mac's car to find the party in full swing, a Highlife band in full blast, drinkers and dancers in kente cloth and colourful head ties and wrappers cramming all the available space to bursting point. The noise, the commotion, the sweat was altogether unbearable. Madam Dadzie saw Colin from afar, and forging through the crowd like an irresistible galleon under full sail, embraced him tenderly. She apologised for the crush, calling a passing steward to bring us a bottle of whisky, some water and glasses. She vanished into the throng once more, wobbling and shaking her magnificent haunches in time to the throbbing calypso drums of the Highlife band.

We sat companionably on a tombstone across the road, drinking our whisky and water in the bright moonlight. It was quite an elaborate grave from the 1930s - obviously the occupant had been well thought of in his day, but now it was like all the others, ill-kempt and untended, the lettering mouldy and illegible.

* **Note:** - The crime of Bank robbery was unheard of in the pre-Independence days of the Fifties - except for once at Kumasi where Colin was relief manager while the incumbent was away on leave. A Nigerian 'been-to' had returned from the UK and taking his example from watching television violence, he obtained a pistol and determined to rob the bank. Approaching a cashier's cubicle he drew his gun and without saying a word pointed it at the cashier's head and pulled the trigger. The pistol misfired; the would-be robber calmly broke the gun and replaced the defective cartridge. By this time the cashier, severely alarmed, had crouched down behind the counter. The other horrified staff now alerted to what was going on crept beneath their desks. The robber leaned over the counter ignoring the cash lying there (obviously having made up his mind to shoot someone) and shot the cashier in the back of the head (he survived - the bullet travelled down the rib cage beneath the skin and emerged from his lower back). The robber scooped up what cash he could reach and strolled out of the bank to hail a passing taxi. The policeman on guard duty outside flung down his rifle and fled the scene. It was said that in the moment of stunned silence in the Banking hall following the loud report of the gun - the only sound to be heard was Colin MacLeod's voice from his office shouting, "Come in! Don't knock so hard - I'm not *bloody* deaf you know!" The robber was later apprehended by an unarmed (except for a swagger stick) English policeman who was passing in the street, realising what had occurred

had hailed another passing taxi and caught up with the robber at a crossroads on the edge of town where both he and the getaway driver had stopped for a spot of 'shut-eye.' (End of Note).

Mac told us of a pre-war funeral he had once attended at Bathurst in the Gambia. As in most European burial grounds on the Coast, fresh graves (usually two) were always kept available - when wanted, they were needed quickly in that climate. They were covered with smart wooden hoods to prevent passers-by from falling in and to keep the weather out and the sides from crumbling. The deceased had died in the hospital the previous night of fever and his colleagues and friends had celebrated his passing with a superfluity of refreshment at the Club before assembling with the Padre at the cemetery in the early afternoon. The Padre was as inebriated as the mourners and pall-bearers who had stumbled and sloshed across the soggy graveyard from the hearse to the graveside. It was the middle of the rainy season and when they lifted off the wooden cover from the grave they found it full to the brim with water. Mac said that when they tried to lower the coffin into the grave it simply bobbed about on the surface, showing no signs of submerging. The Padre was of the old school and more than equal to the occasion, said Mac. He rooted out some long handled shovels from a nearby shed and found some stout mangrove poles, and while the assembled mourners held the coffin down below the surface with these implements, the Padre intoned the committal for burial at sea. They sang 'For Those in Peril on the Sea' and then 'Abide with Me', before- replacing the wooden hood over the now floating coffin and adjourned once more to the Club as the afternoon's tropical downpour resumed on time.

The music from the Handad Hotel - highlife, samba, pounding calypso rhythms bellowed out into the night, blotting out the shrill cicadas and whining mosquitoes. The dancers and drinkers spilled out onto the verandahs and into the garden. Shrieks, laughter, shouts of conversation filled the night air even across the road where we sat smoking and drinking in the graveyard. At last Mac held up the whisky bottle, now nearly empty, and ceremoniously dribbled the last inch onto the crazily leaning headstone. "There you are Matey - have a drink on us!"

Sir Richard Burton himself suffered many bouts of fever during his searches for the sources of the Nile and his later extended travels in West Africa (described somewhat scathingly by 'The Times' as mere *'reconnaissances'*) while acting (ostensibly at least) as British Consul at Fernando Po. But I cannot agree with him when he gives his detailed description of fever, the onset and initial attacks of which he found exhilarating. *"Profuse sweating after rigors and fever, the imagination raised to Parnassus, the intoxication similar to drinking strong green tea."* He cured himself with quinine and salts - as well as swigging back large quantities of his favourite nostrum 'Warburg's Drops,' of which the main constituent was opium (which could well have contributed to the *'Parnassus'* of his heightened imagination).

In 1957 while at Takoradi I suffered the only really serious attack of malaria I remember enduring in my thirteen years on the Coast. One frequently felt unwell from a myriad of possible causes and the usual unvarying sameness of the coastal climate. As a precaution at such times one simply upped one's intake of anti-malarial pills. On this occasion however I was struck down almost without warning one evening. The classic rigors, fever, headache - the latter only one of a multitude of bone-cracking aches and pains. I retired to bed with aspirin and Paludrine and as I sweated and alternatively froze with icy chills I piled on every blanket I could find and waited for the morning.

I either slept or passed out eventually, enjoying (if that is the correct word) what would now be termed a 'Near Death Experience.' I said nothing about this for many years until in more modern times the reports of such occurrences have become almost commonplace. In my delirium I hallucinated an out-of-body vision during which the entire secret meaning and driving force of the Universe (it was, for the record, mathematical,[*]) was revealed to me in a great blaze of dazzling light towards the source of which I was travelling effortlessly and happily. Everything became blindingly and brilliantly simple, I knew and understood *everything* and felt a tremendous sense of elation. When I awoke at dawn, my sheets and blankets were drenched with sweat, wringing wet. For the moment my fever had broken. Sadly however much I racked my brains I could not recall the single and most crucial detail of the mystery that had been revealed to me - but I was still consumed with the most stupendous sense of all-embracing euphoria I have ever experienced. This euphoria sadly faded over the next months together with the feeling which although in diminishing degree has remained with me over the years. It is that both in life, as well as in death there is no need for fear, that in some strange way everything is 'taken care of.' I think that perhaps Burton must have experienced something similar - and if so I can understand his wish for repeat performances. But one pays a high price for the admission fee.

My steward Yaro, padded in with my early morning tea. "Massa" he said, "I tink you be plenty sick." I despatched him to fetch my neighbour, a colleague, who taking one look packed a bag for me and took me off to the hospital where I remained for the next several days. The worst parts of the cure were the generous tumblerfuls of

---

[*] Douglas Adams in the 'Hitchhiker's Guide to the Galaxy' years later also confirmed (wrongly) the mathematical answer as 'Forty Two.' The vortex of dazzling light climbs up steeply towards the right.

gaggingly bitter quinine and salts I was expected to down several times each day until my personal population of malarial parasites were once more reduced to acceptable levels.

A strange part of life on the Coast for the average expat in more modern times was that in fact, death in its many forms was now relatively rare, but all the more shocking when it struck. It is true to say that the West Coast by the mid-1950's was no longer 'The White Man's Grave' but was more 'The White Man's Headache.' Unlike life (and death) in the English village I have lived in for the past thirty-five years, where there is a constant cycle of birth and death, of children being born, of the elderly and infirm dying each winter (and sometimes the seemingly hale and hearty), of the churchyard slowly filling with ever more familiar names - in West Africa the Europeans were almost without exception people in the prime of life. There were only a few young children up to the age of five or six when they were invariably sent home to school. The adults ranged from the healthy twenties to the mid-fifties (when compulsory retirement rather than infirmity usually removed them from the scene). It was sudden disease and accident that took away one's contemporaries on the spur of the moment.

Road accidents took their toll, chipping away at the unwary. In my earlier years polio still ravaged the un-vaccinated (there was no vaccine until the 1960s), my immediate predecessor in Accra having died from it after a mere three weeks in West Africa. Two more acquaintances died of the drink, one of pancreatitis, the other of cirrhosis when his liver finally gave up the ghost. The latter expired in his bath, fully clothed, of a massive haemorrhage, with a bottle of whisky for sole company. He was a tidy chap and had filled the bath with warm water to the overflow, leaving the tap running. There were suicides, both failed and successful - which could have been prevented but for the remoteness and distance of those reduced to such extremes. Typhoid and cerebral malaria were not uncommon - two friends from Tamale both fell victim to the latter - fortunately while on leave in England. Dick Chadwick the Game Warden from Damongo regained consciousness in a Liverpool hospital bed to find a jolly Ghanaian nurse leaning over him washing him down. Believing himself back on the Coast, he grappled with her in an attempt to drag her (protesting loudly) into his bed before once more lapsing into delirium and unconsciousness. Ralph Little, the wiry polo player from Tamale fell sick in Harrow after a few weeks on Home leave. Coming to for a brief lucid moment in hospital, he found the staff, unable to make any diagnosis and concerned by the violence of his delirium, preparing to strap him into a strait-jacket - he was *compos mentis* just long enough to tell them to get their skates on and get him to the Hospital for Tropical Diseases - which to their credit they did.

Mike Cundy nearly died of typhoid at Hohoe, losing, I seem to remember him telling me, nearly all his hair in the process. (Many of us deliberately failed to keep up our six-monthly boosters for typhoid inoculation - the unpleasant side effects of which closely mirrored the disease itself.) My successor at Tamale, Douglas Edwards, had a year or two earlier, nearly died at Tarkwa from cerebral malaria, being saved against the odds by the skill of Hans Mees, the Dutch MO then stationed there and later to become PMO at Tamale.

In Sekondi in 1954 or 1955, Jacques Spencer-Chapman went down with fever. Shaking, sweating, alternately either burning up or freezing, he declined to be taken to the hospital. Norman Welch, our immediate neighbour and pharmacist, and myself piled every blanket on him we could find when he froze, sat up with him through the night until the fever broke, mopped him down with damp towels when he burned, while Norman plied him with anti-malarial pills and potions - Jacques admitted later he had been carelessly 'hit-and-miss' with his daily Paludrine, but that episode concentrated his mind and thereafter he paid more attention to the blue-and-white tin that always used to sit next to the salt and pepper on every expat's dining table.

There were too many obscure and easily mis-diagnosed diseases, such as dengue and sandfly fevers; West and Central Africa's climate incubated a complete encyclopaedia of morbid pathology, a paradise for the serious student of tropical disease and parasitology. Hepatitis and jaundice were common. The Africans sickened and died in and out of their season of measles, of TB, of influenza, or of cerebro-spinal meningitis - which each year followed the bone-dry Harmattan wind off the Sahara in late November - and then flourished in the crowded confines of the traditional huts of the Northern Territories until relieved by the onset of the rains. I remember one such epidemic when Government loudspeaker vans toured the northern towns warning the populace of the symptoms of CSM, principally a blinding headache, stiff neck and fever. The small hospital in Tamale was swamped by queues of patients pleading these all too common symptoms. In isolated areas there were still pockets of smallpox that occasionally spread to the towns, perhaps at times in Nigeria where there was a smallpox '*fetish*' being deliberately spread by the priests of the cult. The entire town of Elmina in Ghana was quarantined in 1954 or 1955, the coastal roads barred and blockaded by health officials who ruthlessly vaccinated everyone passing through - spreading God knows what else in the process. There were less life-threatening afflictions like bilharzia, kraw-kraw (scabies), parasitical guinea-worm and hook-worm, filaria and tropical ulcers. There was the *tumbu*-fly whose maggots hatched out in human flesh (one doing so in the small of my back where I still have the scar). There was '*Glossina*

Mortitans' - the tsetse fly that feeds harmlessly on wild game, keeps to the shade and is host to the deadly trypanosome that infects people and cattle, insidious and eventually fatal if untreated - I was painfully bitten many times in the bush but seemingly never by a carrier insect.

During the colonial era the government medical departments often performed near miracles in both treatment and large scale preventive programmes for the indigenous populations. Post independence the former colonial powers ceased to pump money into health schemes that they saw as no longer their problem. For the same reason the global pharmaceutical giants have seen no future in continuing to develop 'Cinderella' drugs for a third world market with its own specific diseases, whose rapidly expanding populations have a chronic inability to pay for the medicines they need. That was fast becoming the reality of the situation many years before AIDS appeared on the scene and delivered its hammer blow to the teeming millions of sub-Saharan Africa. Intractable diseases such as River blindness, Sleeping sickness, Leishmaniasis, flesh-eating tropical ulcers, guinea worm infestations and bilharzia are never going to be researched for new drug treatments by the pharmaceutical industry – for as they say in Yorkshire, "It'll bring nowt in – there's no brass to be made."

When O. and I first arrived in Tamale in late 1958 we learned of one of those interminable domestic arguments which pre-occupy small expatriate communities in remote places. Government, commercial and the Army all knew each other's business. The garrison quartermaster, a British Warrant Officer, was conducting an ongoing feud with the Battalion MO, one Captain Hector MacPlinge MD, well known for his occasional eccentricities, who was alleged amongst other matters to have permanent and unauthorised possession of one of the Quartermaster's store's two re-useable coffins kept 'on charge.' It was rumoured that in his small military hospital the MO was in the habit of assessing his African patients' condition and then galvanising the most seriously ill either into recovery or into a swift and terminal decline by storing the disputed coffin beneath their sickbed. The QM maintained that this was highly irregular and that the coffin should be kept in his store and only issued on production of a death certificate, and to be promptly returned following the burial. (If you really want to know, the African deceased was removed from the coffin at the graveside and buried simply in a shroud according to Moslem practice). The matter was never resolved.

Hector MacPlinge was also famous for his own particular translation of the standard British Army lecture on VD into pidgin English, complete with unmistakable (and probably obscene) gestures, which he customarily delivered to the appreciative African soldiery. Another MO, Dave Morrison of the 5th Battalion, reckoned that he quite possibly owed his life and those of his fellow officers to his own delivery of Hector's lecture while serving with the United Nations forces. This was performed at dawn to a company of mutinous Ghanaian soldiers on a Congo river steamer. The officers, African and British, plus the loyal African Sergeant Major, having passed the night below, consumed a case of warm brandy (to prevent it falling into the hands of the mutineers) while the soldiery on deck uttered their dire and murderous threats. The Colonel called a pre-dawn Officers' Conference. It was then decided that the MO, Captain Morrison MD - being the only person present not responsible for discipline, was therefore the only officer the soldiers might be persuaded to listen to. Dave, roused from a drunken slumber, suffering from a horrendous hangover, (having his throat slit in such a condition he later said would have been a merciful release) in the hot Congo River dawn, having drunk more than his share of the warm Belgian brandy, was rudely thrust out on deck. His mind a blank, he managed to attract the soldiers' attention. Unable to think of anything better to say or do, standing on a hatch cover he then commenced his delivery of Hector's much polished VD lecture (with gestures). This saved the situation from disaster, the soldiers started to fall about with laughter, ceased carving chunks from the woodwork with their bayonets - and when the Sergeant Major crept out as the performance ended - responded once more to his orders, discipline temporarily restored.

There must have been a well-stocked European cemetery in Tamale, for in 1939 there had been an epidemic of (supposed) yellow fever which had carried off the majority of the Government officers, but I never looked for it. One result of that incident was that all the old-style government bungalows in Tamale were gloomy and airless, the windows, doors and verandahs being heavily wire-screened against mosquitoes.

Child mortality among the local population was high. John Fox, when I first met him was a twenty-year old second lieutenant, growing up fast in Africa while doing his National Service with the RWAFF in Tamale. Years later he is the founder of Welfare State International and co-publisher of 'The Dead Good Funerals Book.' He wrote movingly in the Guardian in 1996 of how as little more than a schoolboy, suddenly transferred to the harsh realities of Africa ".... *Naively I collected empty ammunition boxes for burying the bodies of the dead babies or the still births that were frequent in the families of my 30-strong platoon of soldiers.*"

Among my own staff in the Bank I was aware that deaths among their families were frequent, but commonplace and if of young children were accepted almost without comment. Measles and diarrhoea kept infant mortality high.

Shortly before the birth of our daughter in November 1960 in Tamale I developed appendicitis (not unnaturally I was widely accused of having a 'sympathetic pregnancy') which necessitated an operation. With hindsight neither event is recommended in such circumstances. O. should really have returned to England a few months earlier, but as they say, ignorance is bliss, and in the event all went well. It was only much later that we learned that Hans Mees the MO had arranged for suitable blood donors for O. to stand by if needed. Had our second child, a son born in England in 1963 with major complications, been born in West Africa it is almost certain that both O. and the baby would have died.

I was prepared for my own operation in the small West Hospital for government officials near the Army Lines, packed in a stretcher in the back of an open Landrover, driven in a haze of morphine through the dusty streets to the General Hospital, decanted from the vehicle and stretchered up into the wire-screened operating theatre in the centre of the hospital compound. All was open to public view, goats and chickens scavenged and children played in the dust outside. There was no air-conditioning, but I noted no flies inside. There were not enough staff to lift me onto the table and in my semi-conscious stupor I climbed up and lay down under my own steam. The surgeon was Italian, wearing no more than a gown, gloves, mask, his Y-Fronts and short green gumboots. It was stupefyingly hot. I was relieved to see that Hans Mees, the PMO, had put in an appearance to, as he said, "keep an eye on things." I was more disconcerted to find that the anaesthetist was an African male nurse, a customer of the Bank to whom I had recently refused an overdraft. This worried me until oblivion intervened. Dave Morrison, the army doctor of all those forty years ago recently wrote to me following a visit in 1999 to Ghana. *"The old civilian hospital in Tamale is now abandoned having been replaced ...... The netted windows brought back memories of having to lean over patients while operating to protect them from the fog of dust which came through every time a lorry went past!"* Perhaps it is not surprising that my own wound became infected.

O. had some minor trouble with her eyes and consulted the Indian ophthalmologist at the Hospital (where she also visited and distributed small comforts to the African patients, many of them with dire and distressing conditions). This particular doctor later sent me his personal bill at the Bank for five guineas. I disputed this pointing out that in the Northern Territories all medical treatment by government doctors was free. The doctor acknowledged this was correct, but pointed out that as an expatriate, my employer would pay. Not so, I replied, the Bank was fairly stingy in this respect and would only cough up for tropical illnesses. "No problem" said the doctor

- "I'll write you another bill." The next post delivered a revised bill for twenty guineas and a letter certifying that O. had contracted and had been treated for *'onchocerciasis'* - or 'River Blindness' - caused by an insect-borne parasite common in the north. "Don't worry" he said, "once cured, nobody can tell she's had it!" Perhaps unreasonably, perhaps because I was approaching the end of my tour and becoming more than usually irritable, I still declined to pay.

In the old days, Mary Kingsley alleged that men had died of 'sheer funk' on the Coast, having arrived after a long sea voyage during which they were frightened half to death by the Old Coasters' tales of the dangers of fever - " *... particularly if you happen on a place having one of its periodic epidemics, soon demonstrates that the underlying horror of the thing is there, a rotting corpse which the Old Coaster has dusted over with jokes to cover it so that it hardly shows at a distance. .... Many men when they have got ashore and settled, realise this, and let the horror get a grip on them; a state briefly and locally described as funk, and a state that usually ends fatally.*" She goes on to quote a classic case where a young man, never out of England before, took up a position as a book-keeper down in the Bights. The factory was isolated and he was put ashore in a ship's boat with his belongings and a case or two of goods, the ship's officer was in a hurry and pushed off again through the surf."

"*There were only the firm's beach boys to meet him - he was left alone with a set of naked savages as he thought, but really of good kindly Kru boys. He could not understand a word of what they said, so he walked up to the house and on to the verandah to try and find the Agent he had come out to serve under. He waited in vain for someone to turn up. Sundry natives turned up and said a good deal, but nothing he could understand. In desperation he made a bolder tour and noticed a most peculiar noise in one of the rooms and infinity of flies going into the shuttered window. Entering he found what was left of the white Agent, a considerable quantity of rats, and most of the flies in West Africa. He then presumably had fever, and he was taken off, a fortnight after, by a French boat, to whom the natives had signalled, and he is not coming down the Coast again. Some men would have died right out from a shock like this.*"

Miss Kingsley continues, writing. "*The cemeteries of the West Coast are full of those people who have said that Coast fever is 'Cork' fever and a man's own fault, which it is not.*" In more modern times the arrival of the almost daily air services to and from the major towns of West Africa has meant that the unsettled newcomer, the tyro, not liking what he finds, simply hops on the next plane home to Europe.

One final cautionary tale. I was feeling unwell one morning, but definitely not 'Cork' fever. I called in at the Army MO's surgery. He was quite happy to treat 'casual' civilians (this was the young Dave Morrison who was, and is still a good friend and later became a NHS consultant). He said. "Probably a touch of malaria" and he wrote out a prescription (being a civilian I was not entitled to the Army's drugs) which I later collected from the pharmacy in town, taking the first doses at my desk. By early afternoon I was distinctly unwell. My vision was blurred, I had lost my balance and my extremities were fast becoming numb. I phoned my friend T., the UAC District Manager who swiftly came round to my office, locked up the strongroom and the safes for me, and drove me home. O. had already called the young army doctor who was on the spot as I was helped into the bungalow. After prodding me with pins, tapping me with his rubber hammer, shining lights in my eyes (by now I was also virtually blind), Dave took O. on one side and to her great alarm and fortunately not in my hearing, said. "I cannot rule out either polio or a brain tumour."

I slowly regained my vision, feeling in my legs and arms returned over the next several hours until I was able to stand up without falling over in a fit of vertigo. I still had my 'touch of fever' and considered taking more of the pills which I had neglected during the crisis. Idly I read the leaflet which the pharmacy had left in the packet. "Possible side effects" it read, *"Do not exceed stated dose. Dizziness, vertigo, loss of feeling in extremities, severe visual disturbances."* The dose I had taken it transpired was exactly double that intended. The Army's own pills were half-sized compared with the version I had taken!

> *"If you have no time to attend to your illness,*
> *you get time to die."* (Gold Coast Proverb)

CHAPTER 14

'The Daily Grind' (Accra 1958)

".... which being my proper business I never neglected. If it ended soon, I would sometimes take a trip to the neighbouring Towns, and returned home to supper, after which I amused myself with writing, reading, or visiting with friends till bed-time, where I was commonly treated with Palm Wine, Honey Wine, or else a fruit called Cola, which relishes water. I used frequently to go a-shooting, which was principally Doves and Partridges. Guests I used sometimes to have in plenty, some being Traders, and others being messengers from the Great Men of the neighbouring Kingdoms. At the four corners of my bedstead I set up four poles to support a kind of pavilion made of thin cloth for keeping out the musquetoes.

(*Francis Moore: 'Travels into the Inland Parts of Africa.'- London 1738
   *Agent for the Royal African Company's Fort George, Gambia River)

When I first went to West Africa, the newcomer was invariably thrown straight in at the deep end, to sink or swim by his own efforts - or perhaps merely to flounder. By the simple virtue of having a white skin in the Gold Coast in those distant pre-Independence days one was immediately cloaked with both a measure of power as well as with sudden responsibility. Being a white man in black Africa at that time was a position carrying a lot of baggage with it that was not always apparent to the novice Coaster. It was the final twilight-twitching hours of the old Empire. Since just before the turn of the century the British had acquired a quarter of the world's land surface and could behave with a privileged immunity in much of the rest. It was a heady inheritance - to know with a quite unreasonable assurance that wherever one found oneself a true Briton was never 'just another foreigner.' Senior grey-headed African clerks as well as houseboys and servants deferred to the young whiteman (whatever they might say behind his back among themselves) in a manner that could swiftly inflate the tyro's own fat-headed and overweening self-importance. It was usually up to one's elders and betters to prick the bubble. It was a difficult transition to come to terms with for many a twenty-one year old who just a few short weeks before had been merely a trainee in some company Head Office at home.

In later years as travel to and from the West Coast became easier with the advances in air transport, I always had a sneaking regard for those recruits who, often without previous experience of either the tropics or of West Africa in particular, would arrive at the 'Big City' airports of Lagos or Accra - only to recoil in horror at the heat, the chaos, the smells, the noise - to the point where, digging in their heels they would demand to be put on the next flight back to Europe, even in some cases refusing point-blank to leave the airport. Some might even stay a day or two before demanding release from their contract having found their initial misgivings confirmed. I remember one such in 1965, a deeply distressed young man who having arrived in Lagos had been ferried from the airport at Ikeja in a series of battered taxis, from the last of which he was dumped unceremoniously outside our block of flats in the residential suburb of Ikoyi Island. He had been given no help coming through Customs and Immigration, the Bank's official 'Mister Fixit' having missed him on arrival. That was shattering enough and he had then been milked of large sums in bogus fees and charges by the various Nigerian officials who simply regarded him as a heaven-sent innocent cash-cow ripe for plunder as he struggled through the hopeless maze of petty corruption that can ambush the unwary traveller in such Third World backwaters. He had been allocated a small part-furnished ground-floor flat in our block until better accommodation was made ready.

O. and I felt sorry for him and asked him up to our own apartment for drinks and dinner on the night of his arrival in an unsuccessful attempt to cheer him up and to try and re-assure him that it was really quite possible to live and survive in Lagos. Somewhat the worse for drink he staggered down the staircase later that evening only to find that the door lock had been forced on his temporary lodgings and most of his belongings stolen. We managed to calm him down again with more drink and he retired to bed, air-conditioning full on as he found the heat and humidity oppressive. During the night the air-conditioner burned out, awakening him with a resounding 'CLONK!' as the electric motor seized. With the room full of fumes from the scorched wiring he opened the windows and resumed his disturbed and drunken slumbers.

In the morning he awoke, hot, sweaty and covered in mosquito bites, to find that during the hours of darkness an active termite nest - nearly a foot high and bustling with large ants, had appeared in the middle of his bedroom floor. After a breakfast of sorts in our flat he took a taxi into town (with what remained of his baggage) went in to the General Manager's office and refused to budge from there until instructions had been given for an immediate return flight to London.

Even expatriates who might have two or three tours tucked away behind them as bachelors in 'bush' towns up-country sometimes fell foul of the same syndrome when they married and brought out their pink-cheeked brides, fresh from some leafy garden suburb. The culture shock that could be experienced by an ill-prepared bride could only be imagined by the more stout-hearted 'madams' who first came to West Africa in any number during the 1930s and 1940s. This was why in the late 1950s the old Bank of British West Africa restricted newly married expatriate staff to the larger towns and cities (O. and I finally married in February 1958 at the end of my second leave) on the tenuous ground that the wives would (in theory at least) be happier in such centres of civilisation.

In 1956 or '57 one such, Mimsie (neé Borogrove) married young Peveril Plinge after a whirlwind romance while the latter was enjoying a well-earned three months Home Leave. Do you remember the mid-Fifties? Those flounced multi-layered petticoats, the first bee-hive hair-dos? Panty-hose and rubberised foundation garments worn by the young ladies at the Tennis Club Dance night? Much of the fashionable underpinning worn by the female of the species at that period was a young man's nightmare come true. Inexpert fumbling was incapable of penetrating anything but the outermost ring of defences. A friend of mine from that time recounted the sad tale of how one late spring day he had inveigled one such young lady into a recumbent position on the grassy bank of a bluebell wood. After a while the girl said, suspiciously. "And exactly what may I ask; do you think you are doing?" To which the ardent young man, thinking that candour was probably the best approach, replied. "I'm fondling you in a suggestive manner!" "No you're not!" she retorted. "I think you're just warming your hands!" Storming to her feet she left, flouncing off in a whirl of armour-plated petticoats.

The expectations inspired in the young and newly-married by those early black-and-white TV advertisements were of a high degree - Ford Prefect saloon cars and Twin-Tub washing machines. I don't know what Peveril had told his bride about 'Life' in West Africa either before their wedding or during the brief honeymoon, but before she knew where she was, on her first trip abroad in her entire life - Mimsie was with Peveril in his small, battered second-hand car, plus their suitcases and whatever was left of her husband's bachelor household kit, driving northwards some four hundred miles from Accra via Kumasi and the Yeji ferry across the Volta River towards Yendi in the far north-east of Ghana where her husband was to be the Bank's manager.

'*Amor*' does not '*Vincit Omnia*' with any certainty in such circumstances. By the time they reached Kumasi, staying overnight in a small, hot, African hotel room with no air-conditioning, Mimsie was badgering Peveril that this was not what she had been led to expect - nor indeed did it match up in any way with the life-style she had led back in the leafy suburbs of Home. She had already removed several ants from her bee-hive hair-do. Peveril pleaded with her not to be too hasty - after all, they were getting on for near a third of the way to Yendi. He was sure that Mimsie would feel differently in the morning.

By the time they reached the ferry across the Volta at Yeji at mid-morning the next day, Mimsie was in tears. By the time they reached the small town of Salaga, halfway to Tamale - Mimsie was hysterical. Her lacquered hair had collapsed, the red laterite dust from the road was liberally transferred to her crumpled dress, her cheeks were streaked with tears and sweat and the temperature stood close to 110 degrees F. She was developing a fine prickly heat rash. That night in the Tamale Rest House, with the rats scurrying in the thatch of the rondavel, the geckos 'chic-chacking' on the ceiling, Mimsie spelt it out to Peveril - he could stay if he wanted, in which case the marriage was over - or he could resign from the Bank tomorrow, and they could both take the first flight home. There was no way she could possibly stay in this dirty, smelly, dusty, hot, uncomfortable, tropical dump full of strange people, unpalatable food, lumpy beds, bumpy roads and ...."BATS!!!! - PEVERIL! EEEEKK! .... THERE'S A BAT IN THE ROOM!! I HATE BATS!!!! PEVERIL - DO SOMETHING!!!"

Peveril and Mimsie never completed the final sixty or seventy miles to Yendi the next day. They turned back and drove back south to Accra where Peveril resigned. The two of them flew back to London and a happier life in Acacia Avenue (for Mimsie at least) within the week. Who is to say that they were wrong? Not I! I would not dare to presume.

After spending my second tour in Takoradi I went on leave in December 1957. It was then proposed that I would return to Ghana (The Gold Coast having gained independence in March 1957) as Manager of the Keta branch, a town on the coast near to the eastern border with Togo. Keta (prior to 1914 for a few brief years it was a part of German Togoland) lies in open country on the seaward sandbar of a large, brackish lagoon near the estuary of the Volta - noted for the record rod-caught barracuda once landed there by a former Colonial Chief Secretary of the Gold Coast.

Keta has a long history and there had been an active Danish trading fort established at Keta in 1784 - and from there they no doubt supplied the inland tribes with the long-barrelled red-painted flintlock 'Dane' guns and muskets, in exchange for slaves and for gold. The Danes could not have traded many slaves from here for in 1792 Denmark became the first European nation to prohibit slavery, thereby placing themselves in a difficult situation, as all the neighbouring tribes persisted in carrying on the trade and the Danes lacked sufficient force at their disposal to discourage it. In 1847 the Danish sergeant-in-command of their trading post at Keta was provoked by a renegade Portuguese who openly marched a 'coffle' of slaves past the fort along the strand. The series of scuffles, skirmishes and 'palavers' that ensued then resulted in the eventual killing of the sergeant-governor in a sortie against the Keta people who deeply resented this interference with their business affairs.

Reinforcements for the beleaguered Danes soon arrived by land from Christiansborg Castle in Accra. From their fort the Danish cannon now bombarded the town of Keta, setting it on fire and virtually destroying it. The angry townsfolk in turn then besieged the fort, starving the Danes near to submission. Fortuitously a French warship, the *'Abeille,'* arrived and seeing obvious signs of trouble lay offshore while the new governor attempted to swim out to the French man o' war. He was wounded by musket fire from the Keta men further up the beach and was forced to return to the shore. Another man however, safely made it to the the ship, explained the hazardous situation whereupon the French sent in a landing party through the surf and plucked the remaining Danes to safety. Of course it didn't end there. The Danes later recovered the fort with a sea and land expedition from Accra, but the town lay derelict as long as the Danish local control lasted. It was eventually rebuilt in 1850 when the

British finally took over from the Danes. The Portuguese slaver who sparked off the incident was almost certainly an associate of the notorious Brazilian, Francisco Félix de Souza* - known to the Africans as 'Cha-Cha.'

I never made it to Keta. It could have been interesting - if for no other reason than the fishing. While on leave at the beginning of 1958 I asked the Bank as my employer for the necessary permission to marry O. (a satisfying conclusion to our four year blow hot, blow cold relationship). Imagine such a scenario some forty years later! 'O' was 'interviewed' by the General Manager to determine her suitability (as were all the foreign staff would-be-brides at that time). This procedure may well have arisen because of a series of recent fiascos such as that noted above involving Mimsie (neé Borogrove) and Peveril Plinge - but who knows? O. was quite disconcerted to be ushered into the Bank's imposing boardroom on the first floor in Gracechurch Street, to find the newly-appointed General Manager, J. C. Read, sitting at the end of the long mahogany table with a clear plastic tube emerging from his left nostril, which was then taped vertically to his forehead in the manner of a snorkel. Obviously the poor man was being treated for some sort of sinus condition. As O. later said, it was impossible not to find one's eyes becoming fixed on this odd protuberance. I was also present and such was the effect of this strange sight that neither of us could subsequently remember any substance of whatever conversation passed between the three of us. The subject of - or reason for the 'snorkel' was studiously ignored by Mr. Read and in the circumstances it would have been presumptuous for either O. or myself to have mentioned it first.

The outcome, O. presumably having 'passed' the General Manager's quizzing, was that in short order I received a letter confirming our flight to Accra (via Rome where we stopped off for a week's honeymoon) and that I was now posted to Accra where I would take over the Bank's Clearing and Forwarding operations. I had already done a stint at this esoteric occupation in Takoradi on my previous tour so I knew that it was a 'cushy number' - one was virtually one's own boss, no-one else had the vaguest idea what was involved and to absent oneself from the office at any time was a simple matter of saying "I'm off to the Queen's Warehouse/the Customs Longroom/the 'Beach' - (or whatever) - back in an hour or so!" - the while one took oneself off for a cup of coffee in the YMCA over the road (where one was just as likely to find Colin MacLeod - then acting as Accra Manager - ensconced at a table taking coffee and biscuits with one or other of his 'Old Coaster' chums) or off to browse through the books and records in

---

* Fictionalised by the writer Bruce Chatwyn in his novel 'The Viceroy of Ouidah' - and as played by the wildly eccentric German actor Klaus Kinski in Werner Herzog's weird 1988 film 'Cobra Verde.'

the UTC or Kingsway Stores. What was more important still - being attached to the Bills Department there was no need to hang around until all hours of the afternoon or evening until the accounts clerks had struck their balances and closed off the day's books - an obligatory procedure in those days of hand-written ledgers when everything had to balance to the penny - unlike modern computerised book-keeping where both major and minor 'black holes' are both tolerated and simply set-off against an accumulating surplus or deficit to be written off in the annual accounts.

I was fortunate that I took over a well-run section, part of the Bills Department, from Jim Wright, seconded from London Head Office for a couple of tours or so. Jim was (or so he seemed to me, then a mere stripling of twenty-five) a middle-aged bachelor, hairpin thin (as I was myself in those far-off days). Jim had spent much of the war as a POW, captured in Greece in 1941 when as a medical orderly he had volunteered to stay behind with the wounded while the British army withdrew in disorder to Crete, those surviving the subsequent debacle there, escaping to Egypt.

The main work of my section, staffed by several clerks and a gang of labourers, was to clear cargo from the Accra beach on behalf of the Bank's clients, once it had been landed through the heavy Atlantic surf from the ships lying a mile or two offshore, then either to forward it by rail and road up-country or to deliver it to customers in Accra. As frequently as not it would also taken into the Bank's own stores and warehouses to protect the UK shippers from defaulting consignees failing to pay up on presentation of the shippers' demand drafts. The Customs equally, given half a chance, would sell off at auction any cargo left uncleared for more than a few weeks – this was a system wide open to sharp practice. For example a shifty consignee could tip the wink to a friendly Customs officer, getting the latter to bring forward a swift sale of uncleared cargo, buying it up for a song and leaving the unwary UK shipper whistling for his money. We had to watch the weekly Government Gazette like beady-eyed hawks to pick out any cargo offered for sale in which we might have an interest. The section's Chief Clerk, Mr. J. Harris-Acquaye, a middle-aged gentleman of much experience handled all this with great aplomb and skill, leaving me little to do but sign huge piles of Customs Bills of Entry and to deal with the correspondence. I had ample time to ponder the many Mysteries of Life and the Universe and to visit the beach warehouses or to take coffee with Colin MacLeod across the road from the Bank in the YMCA - where he would also take refuge from the cares of the Manager's office.

There was a measure of humour, whether unconscious or not, on the part of those officials who composed the weekly Government Gazette of Orders-in-Council and sundry notices and I have long treasured the recollection of the Customs auction list which included the item:

"Qty. 1 case of Castor Oil, consignee: - . Officer Commanding Movements, Ghana Army."

As I have said, Mr. Harris-Acquaye was a man of parts, greatly respected by both the African clerks and the expat staff, and we were taken aback when one morning he returned to our office from the beach warehouses, heavily bandaged around the head, his shirt bloodstained. He had been passing through the old quarter of James Town not far from the Bank when a rally of demonstrating workers had been charged by the Mounted Riot Police - and having been caught up in the meleé willy-nilly - this most respectable and respected senior African clerk was walloped around the head by a mounted policeman's baton which nearly ripped his ear off. For once his equanimity was disturbed and he fulminated not only against Doctor N'Krumah's CPP government but the fact that he had been struck by a 'savage' N.T. (Northern Territories) horseman. There was still a perceived rift at that time between the more educated Coast Africans and those they regarded as the 'wild men' from the far north.

I left almost all the staff problems to Harris-Acquaye, but even he was exasperated one morning when I asked why Ashie, one of the young clerks was absent. He produced a letter he had just received, for me to read, the while grinding his teeth. The letter read:-

Accra, 26th Sept. 1958.
Dear Mr Acquaye,
It is a pitty but I really cannot attend business today.
The reason being that I had a strong fever yesternight.
I look a bundle of nerves this morning and I think I shall
be a thorn in the flesh, sitting drowsly in the office.
Please pardon me for being absent and by God's Grace
I hope to report for work tomorrow.
Yours faithfully,
D.K. Ashie.

Harris-Acquaye alleged this touching missive had been lifted verbatim from some 'business' correspondence course that the absentee clerk was studying. I told Harris I found it an admirable piece of blank verse worthy of inclusion in any modern anthology.

It was while I was still working as Beach Master for the Bank that Duggie Medcalf, the District Manager, sent for me one morning. It was a more relaxed meeting than the memorable occasion when I had first brought myself to his notice almost five years earlier when leaving Accra for Sekondi. Duggie was quite affable for once. In his office were a smartly dressed couple in their early forties[*] I guessed. Americans almost certainly at first glance.

"Adamson," said Duggie, "meet Mr. and Mrs. Rockefeller. Take my car and driver. Show them around the town, they particularly want to see the surfboats."

David Rockefeller (grandson of the great John D."*God gave me my money*", the 19th century American 'robber baron'[*] who founded Standard Oil was the youngest of the five sons of John D. Junior) was then in fact only thirty-three, his wife was probably younger. He was already chairman of the Chase Manhattan Bank, the Rockefeller's own Bank, later to be known as 'David's Bank' - the fact that he was a 'Big Wheel' and both then and later seen as the mastermind behind several 'world conspiracy theories' quite passed me by at the time. His stratospheric status was beginning to reach its heights, quintessential American aristocrat and on first name terms with most of the great statesmen of the later twentieth century. The David Rockefellers were both charming, as only those born to unimaginable wealth can afford to be (and not always are so), to the minions and flunkies who attend them.

Medcalf and the Rockefellers were 'David-ing' and 'Duggie-ing' each other - it was a business trip, no doubt exploring closer links in the upper echelons of the banking world. The Rockefeller connection with West Africa went back many years and indirectly had probably saved the lives of many of the Bank's staff, both black and white. As early as 1920 the Rockefeller Foundation had funded an extensive research programme to develop effective yellow fever vaccines and in 1928 four unfortunate researchers had killed themselves in the fine tradition of testing their own experimental

---

* When one is young, one always thinks older people are much older than they are.
* The Rockefellers, the Guggenheims, the Vanderbilt, Astor, Carnegie and Mellon families epitomised 19th century American capitalism, all of them founding members of the 'fuck it/them' school of laissez-faire economics. "Liquidate labour, stocks, the farmers, real estate etc., people will work harder, lead a more moral life. Values will be adjusted and enterprising people will pick up the wreck from the less able."

serum. This eventually led to the production of the first safe vaccine at Yaba in Lagos, in 1931. (I remember later discovering that in Tamale nearly all the resident white government officials had died in the 1939 epidemic of yellow fever). By the post-war years, yellow fever had ceased to be a major threat to Europeans in West Africa, although the disease has also modified itself sometimes manifesting a milder and less lethal form resembling jaundice.

Ali, Duggie Medcalf's driver, tall and equable (unless offered a glass of beer which would then render him swiftly unconscious), with myself sitting alongside him in the big Morris Isis estate car (in American terms probably regarded as a small 'compact'), gave the Rockefellers a swift tour of the city's (Accra in 1948 had a mere 135,926*[*] population) teeming streets and markets. After an all too short visit to the Accra Museum which delighted them both, passionate art collectors that they were - we then drove down to the Beach. I flashed my Harbour permit to get us through the gates and as we left the car our nostrils were assaulted with the customary and unforgettable hammer-blow blend of free-flowing African sweat (euphemistically called 'Fleur d'Afrique' by the French), plus the rich, ripe stench of fermenting cocoa beans and the unmistakable near-toxic effluvium emitted by the ubiquitous bales of Icelandic and Norwegian dried stockfish that lay around. "Oh MY GAAHD!!" Exclaimed Mrs. Rockefeller, clapping a delicately - and certainly insufficiently - scented lace handkerchief to her nose as this obnoxious mixture held together by sticky sea-spray flowed around us.

I must have spent the best part of a year working in and around the Accra harbour complex along the James Town waterfront. It was simply a part of my everyday life. I never took a single photograph of what is now a long vanished way of life, the traditional West African surf port - the hubbub of the godowns and warehouses just above the tideline and the short breakwaters and jetties that sheltered the steep sandy beaches from the last of the roaring Atlantic combers that rolled in endlessly, breaking in a welter of foam as they neared the shoreline.

The cargo boats lay at anchor a mile or so out to sea beyond the line where the breakers gathered their powerful forces. It took the Rockefellers' exclamations of amazement and delighted wonder at the spectacle to bring home to me the extraordinariness of what I had come to see as a commonplace and workaday scene.

---

[*]Whittaker's Almanac of 1959 is remarkably precise as to the Accra population count taken in the last colonial census some ten years earlier. By 1959 it was probably nearer 250,000, by 1999 it had reached more than two million. No modern urban infrastructure can cope with that scale of increase.

Through binoculars they watched the clinker-built surfboats being loaded far out to sea from the derricks of the ships 'working cargo', the big sea-going double-ended craft rising and falling against the ship's sides in the long, regular swell, the semi-naked boat crews agilely manhandling the bales and crates that were hoisted and swung out from the holds. As the surfboats rose and fell, paddlers with their trefoil shaped blades kept them in position, until at last, loading completed they set out for shore, half-a-dozen men on each side, paddles rising and falling in unison, flashing in the sunlight, rippling muscles on heavily built torsos and straining arms. All grunting and chanting in rhythm as the blades bit into the water, responding to the helmsman's urging as he stood on the stern controlling the steering oar. It was a sight that had little of the modern world in it. Except for the silhouettes of the merchant vessels out to sea it was an unchanged scene from past centuries. At times the surfboats vanished from sight in the trough of some towering Atlantic comber, only to re-appear again on the summit of the next as the helmsman at his steering oar judged his moment to urge his paddlers into furious action to catch the all-important breaking crest to surge triumphantly the last few hundred yards into the safety of the shelving beach.

Once safely beached the boats were swiftly unloaded of their bales of Manchester cottons, bags of cement, iron sheets, dried fish and flour (all the staple imports of West Africa) by teams of shouting labourers, the cargo of bales and crates borne off as head loads and on man–hauled wagons to the Customs sheds. We watched a sailor or perhaps a passenger being carried ashore through the shallows, borne on the shoulders of a porter - not only having been precariously disembarked over the ship's side in a mammy-chair slung from the derricks - but probably sea-sick and soaking wet from the roller-coaster voyage from ship to shore. The major trading companies and the shipping lines all employed their own boat crews and labourers to man these graceful and seemingly fragile shells. It was said that in good conditions as much as 4,000 tons of cargo could be landed on the Accra beach in a single day. Even cars were unloaded from the ships' holds in a wholly frightening operation, being lowered by derrick onto pairs of surfboats rafted together and then taken ashore through the relentless Atlantic breakers.

As the Rockefellers rolled their ciné camera until the film ran out and then clicked away with their Leica I explained that many of the surf-boat crews were traditionally from the Kroo tribes of Cape Palmas and the Windward Coast, that many of them could swim no better than a dog-paddle, barely sufficient to stay afloat, that drownings were frequent when boats overturned - and that apart from the risk of a watery death - their working lives on the surf boats were limited to a few short years because of the tremendous physical stress imposed on their bodies. In previous centuries the Kroo 'boys' had been so valued for their seafaring skills by the coasting European traders that they were always exempted from the risk of purchase as slaves – their distictive tribal scars a guarantee of their liberty in the Whiteman's eyes. That was not to say that they would have been exempted from debt slavery or other forms of bondage within their own society arising from criminal or cultural transgressions but simply that no American, Brazilian or European slave trader would ever lay a shackle on them but paid them handsomely to help work their ships up and down the West African coast.

Even more dangerous than landing cargo, I told the Rockefellers, was taking a loaded boat out through the surf, laden perhaps with several tons of cocoa beans in huge sacks sheeted over in the bilges. Not only did sea-soaked cocoa spoil fast, but it also posed a very real threat to the ship that loaded it, from the risk of fire from self-combustion. A moment's inattention or an error on the part of the helmsman could equally spell total disaster. As we watched, an unladen canoe made its way out to sea again, climbing each breaking wave in succession bows-on, pointing almost vertically in the air, in a welter of breaking foam, until at last it was free and surging powerfully out to sea, the glistening paddles rising and plunging in perfect time. The grunting chant of the crew coming fitfully back to shore.

Mrs. Rockefeller turned to speak as we left to go back to Ali in the car. Like me Ali had seen it all before and was chaffering and joshing with a comely young mammy selling fruit at the roadside.

"Tell me, how long have you been here Mr. Adamson?"

"Just about five years now since I first came out to the Gold Coast."

"Gee! You really must *love* Africa Mr. Adamson!"

There is really no answer to such a statement; I let it ride without further comment. With hindsight, it contained more than an element of truth.

Note: *Thirty-four years later, another half-a-lifetime in the future, the widely diverging paths of the Rockefellers and me (nearly) crossed again. O. and I found ourselves in a remote and slightly spooky jungle camp for eco-tourists on the cusp of the Orinoco-Amazon watershed where Brazil borders on Venezuela near the mining town of Icábarú. Where the only others apart from our small party who had dropped in for a cold drink and some stodgy cheese empanadas, was the unexplained presence of a South African woman of seemingly frail health and her young German minder, plus a red-haired Scots lady from Ecclefechan. The* *somewhat spaced-out manager (squatting bare-foot on the floor and plaiting a straw mat) suddenly said apropos of nothing "David Rockefeller and his wife were here last month" and he showed us the visitors' book marking their stay.*

I would have liked the opportunity to remind the now aged couple of that long ago morning in West Africa, watching the surf boats riding the breaking crests of the Atlantic rollers with the pale smoky-grey terns hovering overhead, forked tails streaming in the wind as they sought out their prey, plunging down to scoop up tiny fishes from the maelstrom below.

CHAPTER 15

'A TALE OF AN OLD TOASTER'
(or 'How to Double Your Money')

"There is some ill a-brewing towards my rest
For I did dream of moneybags to-night."
(Skakespeare - 'Merchant of Venice')

In the days of my youth nearly fifty years ago the practice of money-doubling was thought to be a peculiarly West African phenomenon - simply a localised manifestation of universal human greed and gullibility. Many Africans half-believed in it, many more believed in it implicitly. Some Europeans and Lebanese used to think they knew how it was done - and foolishly dabbled in it, sure that they could beat the game and come out on top. I see from my readings of recent newspapers that modified versions of these basic scams, many of them originating in West Africa, have resurfaced in Britain, a fair illustration perhaps of national decline both in the field of intellect as well as of Empire.

On the West African coast where I lived for so many of my formative years the gaols held a generous seasoning of African clerks and petty officials. They were more victims than practitioners (usually having borrowed other people's cash in preference to using their own). These unfortunates firmly believed they were on to a sure thing until the final pay-off - or rather the lack of it - landed them in big palaver. I did hear of one European who together with a Syrian made it pay when they actually succeeded in beating the system. But only the once. They had the canniness never to try it again as it is too dangerous a game. Like playing poker with any card wild at the dealer's choice. Money doubling used to be big business in West Africa. Politicians were caught up in it, lawyers, traders, businessmen, bank clerks, farmers, peasants - you name them, it was all part of the rich warp and weft of West African culture.

The essential for the would-be practitioner in those days, the one vital qualification, was to be known to be on good terms with all the various spirits and to have the *ju-ju* necessary to the process, plus a little bit of 'seed corn' in the form of ready cash. The truly skilled professional, by juggling with his different clients and clever timing could start off with relatively little 'bait.' It is also helpful if the Money Doubler is preceded by a reputation as a magician or as someone with an extra strong fetish. This can be done by clever advance PR work, by sending in a 'John the Baptist' co-miracle worker type to hype the powers of the famous Money Doubler who will shortly be coming to town. The only attributes the punter needs is access to some ready money - combined with a temporary suspension of disbelief - plus of course the desire to be truly, *truly* rich. Was it not the great, late Bernie Cornfeld who first asked of potential investors in his Fund of Funds? "Do you *sincerely* want to be rich?" He then waited for them to form an orderly queue, anxious to hand over their cash.

Sometimes the client punter will even approach the practitioner direct and say "I've heard of your special powers, here is five hundred CFA Francs (or Pounds or Cedis or Dollars or Naira or whatever) please double this for me." To which the Magician replies, "Certainly Sir, only too pleased, come back tomorrow morning." Or the practitioner himself or a go-between will approach a Bank Cashier and say. "Lend me £xxxx from your cash drawer - and I'll bring you back double the amount by closing time and before your Manager checks the till." Or the cocoa farmer who has just been paid in cash is taken off into the bush by the money-doubler where they bury a small amount of cash with magic spells and ceremony at the foot of some suitable tree.

All the initial transactions are done with small amounts of money simply to prove the *bona fides* of the practitioner to the investor - and also to enable the former to assess the residual wealth, the degree of greed and the other psychological factors that are driving the party of the second part - i.e. the punter. To begin with all goes well; double the investment is dug up the next morning, or brought back to the Bank before closing time or to the store on the edge of the market the next day. I think you probably get the drift of how the scenario progresses. Larger sums will of course take longer to double because of the stronger *Ju-Ju* needed, until at last the Bank Cashier goes to jail, the cocoa farmer has lost all the cash he got for last year's crop, the trader ruefully checks his stocks and calculates how poor he now is and the Money-Doubler is nowhere to be found. Surprise, surprise all round!

Money doubling succeeds where the mass psyche is preferably consumed with greed and untrammelled by logic. Thus large segments of the populations of so-called civilised countries as well as the African native and the Asian peasant can simultaneously believe in both of two entirely conflicting facts. The writer Paul Theroux has partly explained this phenomenon by suggesting that people who are bilingual (as are the Welsh and also many African peoples) which is in itself a form of schizophrenia, thus allowing a person to hold two contradictory opinions at the same time - because they remain untranslated.

In 1965 the Lagos press reported how three dead men, all naked, had been discovered in mysterious circumstances in a locked room together with a dead sheep and other (unspecified) items.

"The Police," said the report, "*have decided that the deceased had almost certainly been involved in a money-doubling ritual which had gone badly wrong. The fact that a copy of the Seventh Book of Job (sic) was found to be missing from the scene was held to be near conclusive evidence.*"

It was widely held by those amongst my Nigerian friends whom I questioned that a copy of the Seventh Book of Job was a vital accessory to the ritual of a successful money-doubling operation which, almost without exception, they believed to be possible. All agreed that there were serious risks involved but considered that these were outweighed by the likely gains. When I later observed (after suitable research) that the Old Testament only ran to two Books of Job, this information was dismissed as being totally irrelevant. "The *Seventh* Book of Job" asserted one my clerks, "is one of the better known '*lost*' Books of the Apocrypha," thus showing up my ignorance of the Bible. (I wonder perhaps if the 'missing' Book is the one in which the Lord inflicts the ultimate punishment upon the unfortunate Job by giving him a computer?)

There is of course one particular question that must never in any circumstances be asked of the Money Doubler. This is "*How* come, if you're so clever you are willing to double *MY* money - why not do it with *YOUR* own money?" This question risks giving great offence and must be avoided or any deal will risk being called off in a fit of pique.

While I was in Sekondi in the Gold Coast - now Ghana - in 1954 there occurred a variation on the theme of money-doubling. Two gentlemen, no doubt also skilled at working the more normal double-your-money scams on their less educated fellows, approached a prosperous pharmacist in the town, adopting a high-tech approach. In the privacy of his office at the back of the store they demonstrated their marvellous apparatus. Plugging in the small box-like machine to the electricity supply they showed the chemist a wad of blank paper cut to the exact size of a Currency Board £1 note. With a flourish they inserted a blank sheet in each of the two slots in the top of the machine, switched on, and - Hey Presto! Up popped two pristine, consecutively numbered, absolutely genuine new one pound notes! The druggist was hooked. After another quick demonstration to convince him, he came round to the Bank, withdrew £200 in cash from his savings and whizzed happily back to his store to conclude the purchase of the magic money-making machine plus a starter pack of ready cut blank paper. Re-assuring the now happy client that in no time at all he would re-coup his outlay - the sales team left, insisting that the 'magic' would not work unless the machine was allowed a full half-hour to recharge itself.

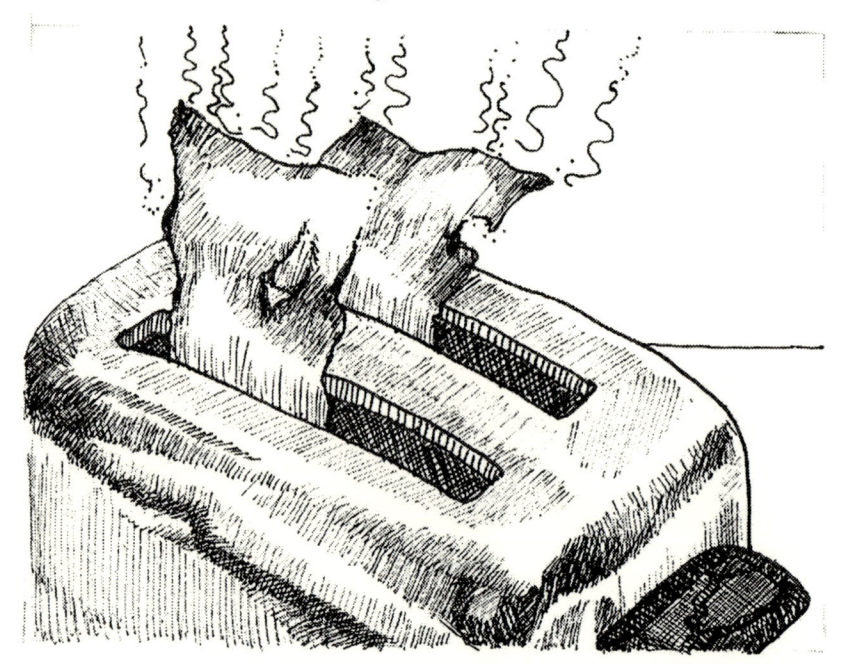

Eagerly our friend watched the clock, barely able to restrain himself. On the dot of the half hour, he switched on the machine, inserted the paper and - Hey Presto! Up popped two badly scorched pieces of totally blank paper. Desperately trying again and again with no success whatsoever he nearly set his office on fire. He had in fact become the owner of a two-slice electric toaster - an unfamiliar piece of kitchen equipment in those far-off days in West Africa. Swiftly realising that he had been sold goods of less than merchantable quality our friend took immediate action. Racing around to the Police Station on his bicycle he alerted the entire local force to a peak of concerted activity. The two magicians were arrested as they were leaving the town in a taxi, minus of course the pharmacist's £200 which was never seen again.

When this case came to Court, the Magistrate, finding the two con-men guilty, highly commended the Chemist as a pillar of society in being instrumental in bringing the two villains to justice, for as he said, "Criminals such as these place the entire national currency at risk!"

The spirit of those two master salesmen still lives on among us today. Not only on the wilder shores of West Africa but wherever the likes of Roger Levitt, Barlow Clowes et al. invite their clients to cast logic aside, to shelve disbelief, to hitch their investment wagons to the stars and follow them up the Yellow Brick Road singing as they go.

Things don't really change, there are always those who say that pigs *can* fly (despite fairly convincing evidence to the contrary) and there are always those ready to believe, particularly if there is the 'certainty' of a large profit in the offing. Is there a moral to this story? I suppose there is, it lies in the old maxim "When a man with money meets a man with experience - the man with the experience ends up with the money and the man who used to have the money is left with the experience."

It is worth remembering that Roger Levitt was sentenced to 180 hours of Community Service for the £34 million fraud he committed. Peter Clowes who defrauded 18,000 mostly elderly people of £16 million was freed after only four years of a ten-year prison term - rated at one day in gaol for every £11,000 stolen. If an investment sounds too good to be true, it probably is![*]

---

[*] Combined with my comments about playing cards for money while I was in the RAF i.e.'Who's the Patsy (See 'None the Wiser' p. 218, Hayloft Publishing 2004), this last paragraph's advice is worth at least double the cover price of this book.

NEWS IN BRIEF

Court frees man in £950,000 fraud case

A man accused of swindling an American millionairess out of nearly £950,000 by convincing her that pieces of black paper could be turned back into $100 bills with a special chemical was freed yesterday.

Mohammed Abubakar, 33, of Ealing, West London, allegedly spun Christine Griffith a tale of a disguised $150 million fortune and a mysterious money-cleaning brew, but he was released when the Crown decided to offer no evidence after hours of legal argument. Southwark Crown Court in London heard that Mrs Griffith, who is in her thirties, was left with blistered skin and a sink full of fast-dissolving "notes". To add insult to injury a separate bottle of the dearly bought chemical exploded in her fridge, she said. Mrs Griffith had told the jury she met Mr Abubakar while staying in an upmarket hotel, and claimed that they later became lovers.

The Times 10/3/2000

Banknote trickster jailed

A trickster who convinced his victims that he could turn paper into banknotes and duped two men into handing over £18,000 each, was sentenced yesterday at Southwark Crown Court to 18 months' jail for conspiracy to defraud. Claude Ismael, 41, from Paris, told businessmen that he had already made millions of pounds for President Mandela of South Africa. Jean Garta Dakou, 30, of Albany Street, Camden, north London, was also jailed for 12 months after admitting conspiracy to defraud.

Times – 24/12/96

Businessmen fell for magic banknotes

BY DANIEL McGRORY

BUSINESSMEN had been defrauded of thousands of pounds by confidence tricksters after believing that they could turn pieces of black paper into banknotes, it was claimed yesterday. At the businessmen were pressed between a strip of paper and £50 notes and dipped in genuine £50 and £50 notes was a secret solution. Ten minutes later, when the paper was removed from the liquid, it appeared to be a new banknote.

Dean Armstrong, for the prosecution, told Southwark Crown Court that the businessmen were allowed to take the sampler and spend them to make sure they were genuine. They would return with as much cash as they could muster on the promise of doubling their money. "What they did not realise was that the so-called fivers were in fact paper that had been dyed black by a chemical such as iodine and then washed clean in another liquid," Mr Armstrong said. "One of the victims was told that if he could give them £1 million, they could make it into £2 million."

The owner of a London recording studio and the head of a West End clothing business each handed over £18,000 after meeting the ringleader of the Nigerian gang. The two businessmen were told to return to an hotel in London later in the day to pick up the cash but found the room empty and their money gone.

Claude Ismael, 41, of no fixed address, Lazare Dinzambe and Guy Yomi-Nkemtchou, both 23, of Canning Town, east London, deny conspiracy to defraud between December 1995 and July this year.

The trial continues.

The Times 10/12/96

Friday. A former director of Islamic Bank had embezzled $245m with four colleagues while under the spell of black magic, they were jailed for three years. They stole the money to give to an African gang of convincing swindlers who promised to double it with magical powers.

Former wrestler 'tortured in bath'

BY ELIZABETH JUDGE

A 20-STONE former Olympic wrestler was held captive in a bath and tortured for four days by a man he duped into handing over £300,000, a court heard yesterday.

Rigobert Youmbi was allegedly attacked with a meat cleaver and threatened with having his hand hacked off during his imprisonment by Garth Robinson. His ordeal ended last May when police tapped threatening phonecalls made to Mr Youmbi's friends in France and stormed the house in Wembley.

Middlesex Guildhall Crown Court in London heard that Mr Youmbi, an illegal immigrant turned asylum-seeker, arrived in Britain in 1997.

He and his friend Pierre tricked Mr Robinson, 37, into believing that a cocktail of American chemicals, rubber gloves, buckets and banknote sized paper could be used to duplicate £10 notes.

Mr Robinson was successfully duped, and handed over £300,000, believing he would make a £600,000 profit, the court was told. Not long afterwards the two conmen fled Britain but two years later, Mr Robinson who was furious at being tricked, tracked down Mr Youmbi in Paris and decided to get revenge.

Alan Kent, for the prosecution, told the court that one of Mr Robinson's friends plied Mr Youmbi with tales of a wealthy individual who wanted £1 million chemically copied. He returned to Britain but when he arrived he was driven to a carpark and surrounded by a gang of motorcyclists.

Mr Kent said that Mr Youmbi, who once wrestled in the Olympics for his home country Cameroon, later told police that he was blindfolded and taken to the house in Wembley. He was hit over the side of a head with a meat cleaver, then stripped, gagged, bound hand and foot and bundled into the bath.

"He was also deprived of food and forced to urinate in the bath," Mr Kent said. During the imprisonment Mr Robinson telephoned some of Mr Youmbi's friends in France, threatening to cut off Mr Youmbi's hand if he didn't send him the money he was owed.

After police intervened, Mr Robinson was arrested as well as Terry Dixon, a 33-year-old former Olympic boxer. Both men admitted false imprisonment.

Stephen Solley, for Mr Robinson, said his client had invested the money in the scam out of desperation for his daughter to go to university. The case continues.

The Times 9/2/00

CHAPTER 16

Sex and the Single Coaster'
('Mammy Palaver')

*"... Singing, feasting and dancing, rum and gin - only lacking mutton and caper sauce.
Our hosts were perfectly civil and obliging, and so were our hostesses
- rather too much so I could prove, if privileged to whisper in the reader's ear.
But what would Mrs. Grundy say?"*

*('A Swarry up the Ogun River' as described by Sir Richard Francis Burton
From 'Wanderings in West Africa' London 1863)*

In Sir Richard Burton's day long before the turn of the century the main route to the gold mines at Tarkwa and Abosso (the French mines at Tarkwa then being managed by a Monsieur Bonnat) was via the Ancobra river, west of Axim. Some timber was shipped from here - but eventually abandoned because of the difficulty of rafting the logs brought down river across the bar. At nearby Dixcove and at Cape Three Points Burton noted that crocodiles were worshipped. In 1955 the crocodiles were still there and the fetish priests, for a small fee, would feed them scrawny chickens for the very occasional visitor to photograph. The mouth of the Ancobra River was probably the worst bar on a coast already notorious for difficult landings. The bar breaks up to four miles out and as Burton wrote".... *fine sharks fatten inside the river mouth."*

In 1955 I hooked a big fish here one day, baiting with a dead mullet in one of the tidal channels. I became fast to a sullen monster - possibly one of Burton's *'fine sharks'* - which surged relentlessly up and down the deep runnels. I lost the fish after some twenty minutes of a one-sided fight without ever catching sight of the leviathan. I had a very stiff sea rod and 40 lb.or 50 lb. breaking strain line - it was the steel-wire trace that gave up the ghost in the end. As always one remembers the big fish lost better than those one managed to land. Recalling some of the unpleasant, shovel-mouthed, razor-toothed and poison-spined, slimy horrors that Jacques, Richard and I pulled out of both fresh and salt waters of that region from time to time, I was probably the better off for not landing it.

That same day in a shallow part of the brackish creek when trying to catch more bait fish, Richard snagged a small six-inch silvery little catfish which slithered off the hook, fell head (and spines) first onto his bare foot - which then bled copiously and painfully for several hours leaving an obviously poisoned wound, very slow to heal. In later years I caught several of these in the Lagos lagoons and always treated them with great caution). But what, may you well ask at this point, have fishes to do with sex, the subject of this chapter?

That day Jacques was also with us. Richard and Jacques, who argued frequently, were talking together in French as they often did, perhaps finding each other more compatible in a neutral language. Nearby a gang of labourers were repairing a culvert beside the dusty laterite road and a semi-naked 'mammy' in a waist-cloth, middle-aged and with flat 'razor-strop' breasts, who was carrying head pans of dirt for the gang, overheard Richard and Jacques speaking and came up and conversed with us for some time in passable French.

She was a lively and amusing woman and on being asked, said that she had learned her French when younger, in Takoradi where she had been the mistress (*l'amie*) for many years of a certain Monsieur 'X' who later became General Manager of the French Company. (Geoffrey Gorer, author of the anthropological masterpiece 'Africa Dances' encountered in the Thirties a Senegalese woman who had been housekeeper for many years to a Catholic White Father. Her comprehension of French amounted to no more than "*Frottez plus fort!*")

When Monsieur 'X' later married a French wife, he had pensioned off his '*amie*' with a lump sum. She had gone back to her home village some years ago where she set up as a trader, had lost her money and had now fallen on hard times. She was fatalistic about her lot and bore no grudge against Monsieur 'X' of whom she spoke fondly, asking us to greet him for her if we saw him. Richard, who knew 'X' and was then in trouble with him over unpaid instalments for his timber lorries said later that he had toyed with the idea, but decided that it would only, in his case, make a bad situation worse if he did so.

As with my mostly unwritten chapters 'Sex and the Single Schoolboy,' Sex and the Single Airman,' 'Sex and the Single Banker' in this series of memoirs - I too have the same concern as the Victorian Sir Richard Burton for the sensitive feelings of the modern day Mrs. Grundy. I do not wish to bring down around my ears the calumny and odium of the feminist persuasion compounded with accusations either of racism or of male chauvinist swinishness.

All I will say is that it was not 'like that.' Any Old Coaster knows 'how it was' and if the reader wasn't there then whatever else I may say now will almost certainly be misconstrued. For that reason this chapter will be highly selective and at the same time short and sweet - rather like the diner who on being asked by the waiter how he liked his coffee, answered. "Hot, sweet and strong - the way I like my women!" Replied the waiter. "Certainly Sir, black or white?" If what follows appears to rely heavily on other peoples' experiences as recounted to me - and to other authors' writings - then I make no apologies. My own memory is notoriously unreliable on this subject.

There was a bachelor's song in the Gold Coast, which went something like this:

> *"I love a lassie,*
> *A lassie from Kumasi.*
> *She's black as the Ace of Spades as well!*
> *She chops kenke and cassava*
> *And she savvies my palaver!*
> *Oh Comfort -- my Kingsway* Belle!"*

There was another verse, possibly from another ballad, that begins: *"My girl's from Bolgatanga"* but whatever particular attributes the lady in question possessed that inspired the anonymous author to song have long since escaped me.**

My friend Thaddeus Plinge, a timber buyer in Takoradi returned home one day to his flat in Prince of Wales Road from a trip up-country to find his steward, Kofi, deeply distressed and wringing his hands. During Thaddeus' absence, one of his more permanent lady friends, a certain Patience N'kansah - (sometimes known as *Nana Ikor* -'Queen of the Whores') had learned of her lover's irregular dalliance with an aquaintance of hers. Patience came to the flat, found Thaddeus absent, she consumed most of his liquor supply on the spot, and then, her rage fuelled by drink - proceeded to 'trash' the flat. Kofi fled in fear of his life. Patience was not only strong (as her name implied) - she was also one of those ladies who habitually removed beer bottle caps with her teeth - she was definitely not to be trifled with. Patience threw out over the verandah into the compound below, all Thaddeus' clothes, most of his furniture and crockery, but foiled by and unable to move the heavier items such as the bed she departed, vowing further vengeance when Thaddeus returned. (If anyone infers too much significance that in this narrative perhaps too many stewards and houseboys are named Kofi, then they should know that it is a day name only, meaning born on a Friday. In Fanti and Akan society a male child has therefore a one-in-seven chance of receiving this name. I employ it here as a simple literary convenience).

---

* Kingsway Stores were the larger retail outlets of the United Africa Company.

** British servicemen in India similarly used to sing "I love a lassie - a bonny black Madrassi."

Thaddeus was furious at the damage to his property - and also a little frightened for Patience was renowned for her temper. He sent Kofi for the Police, who shortly arrived in the person of the very attractive lady corporal then in charge of the Takoradi Vice Squad. Beatrice wore a crisp light-blue blouse with her rank badges on the sleeve of her starched khaki skirt and neat white ankle socks set off her slim legs. From beneath her uniform cap there projected tight little braided plaits of hair. While sitting on Thaddeus' bed (the chairs were now mostly broken) she sipped a soft drink proffered by Kofi. She listened sympathetically as Thaddeus recounted his tale of woe.

"Mr. Plinge," Beatrice said gently, fixing Thaddeus with her melting, limpid brown eyes and placing her hand on his thigh, "this girl Patience, I know her well - she is truly bad! All this palaver and humbug she has brought down on you - she is likely to do it again. She is not good for you. She drink too-too much all de time, she go with too many men. I think the best thing to stop her making palaver again is for me to move in with you. From now on I shall be your girl friend and Patience will not dare to trouble you! If she humbug you again - I shall arrest her! I shall move in with you this very night! You will have full Police protection."

Before I first arrived in Accra in 1954 it had been alleged that the then Chief of Police had voiced a complaint to Douglas Medcalf, the District Manager, about the riotous parties held by the expat staff living in their bachelor quarters over the Bank. They had two or three roomy flats on the top floor. The police guard had complained to their Chief of the noise (which presumably prevented them from sleeping at their sentry posts guarding the Treasury). The Police Chief said that it was reported to him *"that more women were traipsing in and out of the Bank on Saturday nights than there were customers during normal weekday business hours."* It had been particularly brought to his attention that the so-called 'toboggan' races whereby scantily dressed young women were perched on tin beer trays and despatched helter-skelter down the Bank staircases were highly dangerous, and not least that the onlookers as well as cheering uproariously were placing illegal bets on the fastest descent. What Duggie Medcalf did about it history does not relate.

Those young men were probably among the last of the immediate post-war generation of ex-servicemen finding employment in the Colonies. They were certainly in part responsible for the hard-living conditions that the post-war Bank provided for its expatriate employees. Pre-war there had been more comfort perhaps, but by 1954 there were very limited soft furnishings, carpets or curtains, linen or crockery

- by 1954 we were expected to provide our own basic comforts out of our meagre kit allowance. Matters had earlier come to a head I believe in Lagos where the residents of the bachelors' Mess above the Bank on the Marina waterfront had held a party. Somehow or other the participants had set fire to the curtains, it probably seemed a good idea at the time to extinguish the threatened blaze by stuffing them inside the piano. The piano caught fire in its turn and the blazing wreck of the instrument was then propelled through the window of the third floor in a spectacular trajectory to the Marina below.

Half a century earlier in 1899 Mary Kingsley had written in a letter to her friend Major Nathan, then Governor of Sierra Leone, of her concerns about *"...the kind of Englishman in West Africa. I grant you they are a little what one might call wild at times - and cause me grave anxiety."* Not much had changed in the intervening fifty years before my own arrival on the Coast.

Interlude:

Scene: a bungalow garden in the outskirts of Kumasi, c.1958.

Time, a Saturday afternoon. 'Old Coaster' reclining comfortably in 'steamer' chair, on shady stoep, cold beer to hand, dressed for coolness in bathtowel around waist. Observes ancient crone approaching through garden from left to right balancing a panful of guinea fowl eggs on her head, she is smoking a stubby pipe and supporting her bent frame with a knobbly stick. In her other hand she clutches the feet of an upside-down, protesting chicken.

Old Coaster: (shouting for his steward).
"KOFI!! KOFI!!! Where are you? Damn you eyes!
Kofi: I hear you Sah, I de-come-oh one-time!
Coaster: Tell that scrubby old mammy to get the hell off my f.....g compound!"
Kofi: (In tone of reproof expressing considerable surprise).
"Echhh! ... Massa! She be your mother-in-law. She come to bring you gift.

In West Africa's earlier days young colonial officers in remote up-country stations were officially encouraged to smoke marijuana for relaxation after a testing day's work. It was intended perhaps to help take their minds off other pressing physical needs.

Still None The Wiser

I recall Colin MacLeod in Sekondi holding forth on one occasion to Jacques and myself about the temptations faced by young single men in remote - and sometimes not so remote – stations, saying. "Many Coasters take to women or drink to ease the strain and tedium of their lives. Fine, (this I hasten to add was not advice addressed specifically to me) you can do so if you wish, but whatever you do, don't take to both at the same time!"

It was wise advice as the following pessimistic extract from Frédéric de Janzé's 'The Vertical Land' (1928) perhaps illustrates.

"*Those who return too often to the bottle, slowly soak, and soaking sink. Soon in the house-boys' huts native women will sit and soak; one more enterprising will speak to the white man. He, with convincing faith, will take an interest in her children; tell them to mend their ways, and one tropical night..... a bodily desire takes shape ..... the weeds will choke the garden, the cactus grows through the verandah floor, boards become disjointed; he'll wear khaki - it shows less stains - the white ants one night in a carelessly opened tin box will eat his evening collars, and so he rots.*"

This of course implies that the moment one ceases to dress for dinner, even when dining alone, moral and physical degeneration is both imminent and inevitable. Quite so.

I can call to mind two instances of young bachelors in remote up-country postings who were definitive case-studies of Colin Macleod's sensible counsel. One who lived alone in a small northern town in a thatched bungalow on the edge of the dusty airstrip had among his limited reading material, a copy of the classic Twenties' 'Universal Compendium of Cocktails' and in his generous leisure hours - his office work being neither time-consuming nor demanding - happily worked his way from A to Z through the recipes, ('Adam's Apple' to 'Zombie'[*]) sampling, tasting, testing for effect and annotating the margins as he progressed, sending frequent orders to the coast towns for fresh supplies of Fernet Branca, Angostura Bitters, of morello cherries and dry and sweet Vermouths and strange liqueurs. Whenever I saw him on the infrequent visits he made from his out-station, apart from a slight tremor of the hands and a pinkish tinge to his eye, he was in good spirits and seemed unaffected by his isolation.

---

[*] An 'Adam's Apple' is composed of 1/8 gill each of Calvados, Italian Vermouth, gin; 2 dashes of Yellow Chartreuse, lemon peel, lemon juice and a cherry. A 'Zombie' comprises equal measures of dark rum, white rum, pineapple juice plus 1 tsp. caster sugar.

My second example had taken the opposite tack, being naturally abstemious by nature and largely abjuring alcohol although by no means teetotal. He had acquired a much-thumbed and somewhat tatty, illustrated copy of the 'Kama Sutra' and was alleged to have taken up the pursuit of sexual athletics as his major recreation, although he subsequently admitted to experiencing some difficulties with the local girls who refused to undertake the more unconventional or bizarre positions in a serious manner.

Both of these gentlemen subsequently went on to enjoy highly successful careers, seemingly psychologically undamaged by these long periods of social isolation in remote and strange surroundings experienced in their youth.

Tragedy however struck another colleague, when too much drink taken in combination with a cross-border 'affair' with the wife of a Lebanese trader in French territory led to physical and nervous exhaustion, neglect of his work - (rather than deal with his official mail he would burn it daily in the Bank compound) - experimenting with hard drugs. These he allegedly obtained with the help of another lady, a former dancer from the Crazy Horse Saloon in Paris with a drug problem of her own, whose husband – a government doctor, was said to have married her to effect a 'cure.' It all ended in tragedy with a badly bodged suicide attempt, a cry for help, that was sadly ignored until too late by the Bank's senior managers who had already been warned by letter from the Branch's African Chief Clerk that matters were going seriously askew.

There was a smattering of confirmed 'bachelors' of all ages a few of whom were also undoubtedly homosexual - or 'queer' as they were known in those days before the fraternity (or sorority) of those with same-sex preferences suborned that once useful and attractive word 'gay.' Most of them kept quiet about it; most were either known or suspected to be so; and as long as they didn't upset any applecarts, cause scandal or 'frighten the horses', nobody seemed to mind. Occasionally - to everyone's surprise, they could even return from leave with a brand-new wife in tow. One such, when his bride complained that her husband still obviously preferred sharing the marriage bed with his cook to herself, was alleged to have been told. "Well, he's been with me for much longer than I've had you." On such matters the average West African was usually unprejudiced, open-minded and even handed.

There was the 'Old Coaster's' apocryphal story of the white 'madam' travelling to join her husband up-country by passenger train - in both pre- and the immediate post-war days there were still many expatriate European railwaymen, engineers, District Supervisors and administrators scattered about the country. Madam's train had broken down and was delayed indefinitely at a station well short of her destination. The white

Superintendent dealing with whatever problem has caused the hold-up notices her melting in the heat of her First Class compartment. He sends her up to his bungalow to wait in more comfort until such time as the train is ready to depart again. "My house-boy will look after you," he said, "I'll send my car for you once everything is fixed."

At the Railway Superintendent's bungalow the steward ushers her in, switches on the ceiling fan, brings her a cool drink and departs. In the distance she hears the sound of running water. After a while the steward returns. "Your bath is ready, Madam." He says. "But I don't want a bath; it's not even lunch time yet." She replies, somewhat taken aback. "Madam must take bath now! Mastah will be home lef-small - he tell me often. 'Every woman 'e send to house must take bath first.' If you no go 'gree, Mastah go vex proper!"

If what I have recounted seems reprehensible and inexcusable, or as we once used to say. "Not at all like the Home Life of our own dear Queen," though in view of the details that the tabloid press has regaled us with in recent years - perhaps this saying is no longer as true as once it undoubtedly was. I well realise that many people who may read this account will say. "Stuff and nonsense! He's pulling our legs trying to make us believe these outlandish tales." In that respect I feel much sympathy for Mary Kingsley, writing privately in 1897 to her old friend Lady MacDonald who was in China after leaving West Africa. She complained that her publishers, MacMillan, had felt obliged to suppress her account of a lively quarrel that took place in her presence on a French river steamer,

"... Between a bishop with a long, red beard and voluminous, white flannel petticoats, and the French Governor of the Ogowé. The captain and Miss Kingsley had to take refuge on the saloon table to keep clear of the two gentlemen who were rolling about on the floor of the tiny cabin 'in close but warlike embrace.' Ignoring all exhortations to peace the fight continued until both parties collapsed with heat and exhaustion."

It is perhaps worthy of mention that over the preceding centuries there was a long history of matters involving such issues of moral standards on the Coast as are touched on above. In 1830 Lieutenant George MacLean, became governor at Cape Coast Castle (against the odds having already survived West Africa since 1826) appointed by the committee of merchants (the British government having once more temporarily abandoned the Gold Coast). In 1838, newly appointed Captain and briefly in England, he married the popular romantic novelist Letitia Elizabeth Landon and thereby precipitated a celebrated scandal. Marriage for L.E.L., as her readers knew her, treated her cruelly and nearly brought about her husband's downfall. Cape Coast was not the exotic, mysterious destination she had imagined, but then a squalid little town of mud buildings backed by thick forest, all surmounted by the damp, disease-ridden castle whose crumbling bastions were crowned with rotting and unfireable cannons. On arriving offshore at Cape Coast her husband first made a night landing alone through the surf (it is supposed) to ensure that his long term 'acknowleged wench' had vacated his apartments in the castle. Thereafter it was said, he made frequent nocturnal visits to the town to see his 'country wife,' who had already borne him children and was a half-sister of James Bannerman of Accra, a member of one of the most powerful trading families on the Gold Coast. All the while his abandoned bride fretted and despaired in her uncomfortable apartments in the castle. Two miserable months after her arrival she committed suicide, a bottle of prussic acid at her bedside. The ensuing outrage and speculation at home nearly brought about Governor MacLean's dismissal although the subsequent inquest absolved him of any blame. It is unknown whether Governor MacLean re-instated his African mistress. In 1843 he was replaced as governor when the British Government resumed control of the forts. Appointed judicial advisor he was instrumental in drawing up the Bond of 1844 which effectively set up the Gold Coast Protectorate as a British colony. MacLean and his wife, Letitia Landon lie buried side by side within the Castle walls.

I have also suppressed a great deal, particularly on such touchy subjects as this chapter deals with, not so much as to protect the innocent - who as always are few and far between - but to save hurt to those who are still living and who may not care to be reminded of events that took place forty and more years ago and so far away. I shall close this vexatious chapter with yet more quotations, the first two from 'The Life and Works of Alfred Aloysius Horn.'

"There's traders too, who have their business in all lonely spots. They couldn't work with a sane mind if they didn't obey Nature and accept what she provides. A man'll breed where he stays, and that's one of Nature's laws you can't dodge. "The Ivory Coast in the Earlies." Jonathan Cape. London (1927).

and:-

"The result of Nature's plans're evident in the half-breeds that're running the Sunlight Soap interests up in Nigeria and so on. More than half the ships that touched on the West Coast had their wives and families there. You'd see the woman, dressed up all in her best, trotting up to see the captain as soon as he was at anchor. Nice respectable blacks, innocent as lambs they were and as proud of the children as if there'd been no bar sinister on 'em that'd been derived from an Englishman. How was she to know there was a head wife back in Liverpool or Birkenhead?" idem. "The Waters of Africa" (1929).

There is no getting away from the fact that Trader Horn's views, freely expressed in his (often far-fetched) reminiscences are not, in present day terms, politically correct, but they afford us an open window to the past - and we must neither judge nor deny the past in the light of what is and what is not acceptable today.

Let the ex-preacher in John Steinbeck's 'Grapes of Wrath' have the last word:

"There ain't no sin and there ain't no virtue. There's just stuff people do. It's all part of the same thing. And some of the things folks do is nice, and some ain't nice, but that's as far as any man got a right to say."

CHAPTER 17

'Ju-Ju'

*'Mumbo Jumbo' - Among certain tribes of the Western Sudan,
a village god or presiding genius, who protects from evil
and terrifies the women and keeps them in submission.
(Mandingo:-'mama dyambo')*
US Dictionary c 1958.

According to Sir Richard Burton,* that flawed 19th Century near-genius, white men after long residence in Africa become 'black' in disposition and come to half-believe in Ju-Ju and magic, because they themselves have seen it at work, in their turn becoming subject to charms and fetish, and attributing death and disaster to poison and witchcraft. After a time lapse of nearly four decades and as seen from my present day viewpoint of a country cottage in an English village it all seems ridiculous - perhaps. One sees things differently as a green young man in the shadows of a lantern-lit bungalow in the African night. Servantless because the cook and the houseboy being 'strangers' from another area have 'gone for bush' because the old Chief has died and everyone knows that he can only be buried in company with a living human sacrifice, trussed and gagged with a *'sepow'* knife through his cheeks and tongue - the drums throbbing out for the past two days from the town below, never ceasing until a victim is found and the funeral rites are completed, (*'closure'* is the more modern politically correct phrase). Then the drums stop as one; the streets are busy once more; the electricity generators come back on and next morning the houseboys are back and serving up breakfast as if nothing had happened.

I knew a well-respected former colonial District Officer in Tamale, Gordon Edwards, then a senior Government Agent, who twenty-five years later committed suicide in retirement in Wales. The Coroner heard evidence from his brother at the inquest that "*... a witch doctor had saved his life in Ghana.*" Following an earlier suicide attempt the deceased had told his brother. "*The only thing he could account for it was that he considered a spell had been cast upon him.*" It is most likely that he '*knew*' he had been cursed - without that knowledge he could not have been harmed. The coroner laid

---

*Sir Richard Francis Burton, (1821 – 1890), explorer, traveller, swordsman, Arabist, prolific author, linguist and anthropologist, and not least, eminent Victorian pornographer, was once described by David Livingstone as "an awful ruffian."

the blame for the suicide partly on *"The fact that he had been in far away places."* (Daily Telegraph 24.12.76 report of inquest on Gordon Edwards.) Whatever spell had been cast on him certainly worked - however long it took.**

But then Gordon Edwards was an unusual man. After Gold Coast Independence in 1957 he stayed on in Ghana for a few more years still employed as a District Officer in his chosen area in the far north-east. It was alleged that he donated his government salary straight into Dr. N'Krumah's Convention Peoples' Party coffers to ensure that he could remain in the job he loved. He was certainly wealthy enough in his own right to do this. It was widely rumoured that he was an heir to 'The HP Sauce Millions' (whatever they might have been). He was a confirmed bachelor, notorious for rarely speaking to any white woman. People conjectured that he was afraid they would attempt to compromise him in some unspecified manner and thus lay claim to his money. On his rare visits to Tamale from his distant out-station in Yendi, he drove into town in his white Rolls-Royce - preceded by his luxurious VW camper van - containing his driver, cook, house-boy and camp kit which included Persian rugs and silver candlesticks. His provisions were supplemented with hampers of 'goodies' shipped out from Fortnum & Mason in London which were duly cleared through Customs by the Bank. I remember him as a disconcertingly quiet and unassuming man who travelled from rest-house to rest-house in his vast 'District' always preceded by his luxurious retinue, presumably settling 'palavers,' listening patiently to endless complaints and demands from the chiefs and their subjects. I don't doubt that his decisions were accepted all the more equably because as a whiteman he was perceived as having no obvious local axes to grind.

Gordon Edwards finally left Ghana when either Dr. N'Krumah's government would no longer employ him as a post-Colonial relic, or perhaps because with economic restrictions and strict exchange control he could no longer freely import his hampers from Fortnums or readily obtain spares for his white Rolls (there was in his District a 'bush' mechanic whose ramshackle premises bore a crude hand-painted sign saying 'Official Rolls-Royce Service Agent.') He finished his career as a colonial government officer in the South Pacific - where there was equally the chance that some disgruntled Melanesian grass-skirted magician might have 'pointed the bones' at him.

** An octogenarian Irishman died in the 1970s having worked in Egypt with Howard Carter at the Tutankhamen dig in 1923. The local paper claimed his death was caused by the 'Pharaoh's Curse.'

Fetish, witchcraft and wizardry, ju-ju, sorcery, voodoo, shamanism, all are deeply rooted in the human psyche, in many societies still remaining only skin deep beneath a veneer of Christianity or Islam. They are older than any of the major established or revealed religions. In the West, as conventional faith declines, their modern manifestations become more and more popular on the fringes of our own society where The Lord of the Rings and the cod philosophy of Star Wars* replace King Arthur's Camelot. Sorcery, fetish or whatever one calls it, gives a structure to everyday life where cause and effect are only dimly understood, where there are no obvious dividing lines between perceived reality and an imagined spirit world where dreams and nightmares rule, where bad things, disease, death, failure of crops, famine, are always just around the corner waiting to happen.

In Africa, the missionary Churches, the Catholics in particular, have always recognised the power of the old religions, as often as not confusing them with Devil Worship and Satanism - which they certainly are not. Many indigenous African religions own the concept of a Supreme Deity - but a 'One' who invariably happens to be supremely disinterested in the fate or destiny of the individual. Occupying the vacuum between the immensity and majesty of the Aristotelian Supreme Sky God and the insignificant mortals is another universe of minor deities and powerful spirits - of the land, of ancestors, of rocks and trees, of animals and rivers. Many of these are malevolent by nature and require placating if their often random and usually unwelcome attentions are to be avoided. The Yoruba pantheon alone includes some three to four hundred gods and minor divinities. The Christian emphasis on a single all-powerful God, with Christ, the Virgin Mary and a whole galaxy of Saints as intercessors, the elements of Sin and of blood and sacrifice (particular concerns of the more fundamentalist sects), are easily understood - and quite welcome as they cut out in theory much of (but by no means all) the intervention that is otherwise necessary to deal with the ever-threatening spirit world. The demands of Islam are even simpler. The problems, if such they are, arise when the 'new' religions simply overlay and absorb and coexist with the old beliefs. West Indian and Brazilian voodoo is a powerful and strange mixture of Christianity and the old African Gods - in the same way that the fetish grove at Elmina in Ghana which used to be, and may still be for all I know, dedicated to the rites of the god Nana Ntona, who centuries before had been Saint Anthony when the Portuguese first built a chapel there.

---

* My local MP in his maiden speech in Parliament claimed to be "...a Jedi Knight."

Still None The Wiser

I have experienced *ju-ju* in action. When I was out hunting one Sunday with Benjamin Ladipo in the Ikorodu bush in 1965, accompanying a group of Yoruba 'hunter-men' and their wooden-belled dogs chasing bush-meat - I noticed a small, untidy bundle - no more than 'a rag, a bone, a hank of hair' plus a few feathers and a cowrie shell or two, hanging from a bush at the edge of a cassava patch.* When I asked Benjamin what this was for, he explained that the small hanging fetish was 'powerful ju-ju' - if anyone was foolish enough to activate it by stealing or damaging the crop, the culprit would swell up and burst. It was very effective he continued, nobody would dare - of whatever religion, to offend against it.

Another day, another time with Benjamin. Before setting off into the forest in the early morning, I had noticed several of our 'hunter-men' plucking leaves from a shrub, muttering to themselves the while they rubbed their persons and the barrels and stocks of their locally made muzzle-loading 'Dane' guns with the greenery. One of them took a small gourd of palm wine from his bag, removed the coco-fibre stopper and poured a few drops on the ground. Once again I asked Benjamin what they were doing. He gave his own shotgun a perfunctory rub with a leaf to demonstrate. "Dey mek offering to Ogun - say prayer to bring plenty meat today! As for me, I be Christian." I knew that Ogun was the Yoruba God of hunters, blacksmiths and farmers. As we were not far from the banks of the Ogun River and about to plunge into the god's own home territory so to speak - as unlike Benjamin I was not an active practitioner of either religion, who quite possibly paid lip service to both - it was perhaps unwise of me not to follow suit.

Gareth Plinge had come with me that day. He had long since disposed of the shotgun with which he used to shoot duck in earlier years (and cinema screens in B****e 'The Arsehole of the Empire') but I had lent him my little .22 rifle. Gareth also had his camera.

All that Sunday morning while the dogs, hunting mute, silent - except for the occasional 'clonk' of their wooden bells and the soft calls of the hunters beating through the forest, Gareth and I followed - from time to time placing ourselves fruitlessly in ambush wherever Benjamin positioned us. In the far distance we began to hear the insistent sound of drumming, rising and falling through the dense forest but seeming always closer and more powerful as the hours passed. As indeed it was. Our fellow

---

* Many years later at my daughter's Art College Final Year Exhibition in England I saw several similar 'soft' sculptures, seemingly random accumulations of bio-degradable, non-representational material, presented as works of art, that could have passed equally as 'fetish' or ju-ju objects if transplanted to the African bush)

hunters were drawn to it like bees to honey. In our hearing Benjamin cursed them and the pounding drums, but it was quite pointless, the throbbing beat became deafening as we finally traipsed in single file down a narrow path, all pretence at following the chase abandoned for the moment. The hunter-men rolled their shoulders and shuffled to the drum-beat. The small dogs with their scarred and bitten muzzles followed, heads down, tongues lolling in the heat.

We emerged into a clearing in the forest to discover an extraordinary scene. At one end of the open space a group of drummers were pounding away, eyes closed, their naked chests glistening with sweat. An elderly man, forehead daubed with white clay, clad in white robes and with one or two women similarly dressed appeared to be conducting the proceedings. A crowd of onlookers who shook and jumped, seemed to be in a trance as the old man - the sole person to appear aware of our presence - glared malevolently at us. There was a crude altar on which lay a still twitching white cockerel in a pool of blood below a large wooden cross. The most extraordinary sight of all was a boy, eleven or twelve years of age, fair-skinned enough to be a mulatto - who capered and writhed in time to the drums on the hard packed earth in front of the altar, his bare feet kicking up spurts of dust. The boy's only garment was a pair of skimpy satin shorts, of such a vivid colour - a virulent, electric blue that it almost hurt. The dancing boy's eyes were rolled back so far into his skull that only the whites showed. Suddenly he fell to the ground, his heels drumming on the hard-packed earth, his whole body shaking and convulsing.

"Holy Holy Moley!" Gareth exclaimed, twitching with excitement and removing the lens cap from his camera. "I must get a shot of this! Are these Shakers or Holy Rollers and Speakers of Tongues? Ain't they just something else?"

Benjamin was becoming agitated and our hunter-men were starting to shake and to jig in time to the insistent roar of the drums, submerging themselves into the scene that was swiftly taking over their senses. Ben roughly shook them, urging them to leave, pushing them off down a track that led away from the all-insistent, all-consuming clamour of the drums. Gareth started to snap picture after picture while the old white-clad priest shot baleful glances at us from in front of the altar. Benjamin grabbed Gareth by the arm, saying "No! No! - I beg you, come away! These are bad people - mek we go now-now!" Saying much the same to me, Benjamin led us off, almost running along the narrow path where he had already shooed off his followers. He was sweating profusely. "They are bad people" he said again and again, "far-far better we lef am be."

Later that afternoon, when we had resumed our hunting - the other hunters had already bagged a brush-tailed porcupine and two small grey forest antelope now being carried as head loads by two tiny boys each dressed in the separate halves of a pair of ragged pajama bottoms - I waited patiently, peering through the shadows of the thin undergrowth. Listening to the far-off dog bells I heard the sudden 'BOOM' of a muzzle-loader softened by the dense forest. All my senses were quickened.

A few short yards away in front of me materialised the clear, motionless outline of a bush-buck, a 'harness' antelope (*Tragelaphus scriptus*). In a patch of sunshine its dark red coat, striped and dotted with white stood out clearly against the dark background. It gazed calmly at me, one forefoot delicately raised. I slowly raised my gun, drawing a bead on the neck and shoulders where my load of buckshot would kill it instantly at such close range. I pulled the trigger.

There was nothing but a sharp little 'Click!' like the snapping of a twig, from my gun. I had already tensed my body, expecting the recoil which never came. I was so surprised that I never thought to use the second barrel. By the time I looked again - the bush-buck had vanished as swiftly and as silently as it had first appeared from the dense greenery.

Opening the breech where the shiny red cartridge with its undented cap lay - it was quite clear that I had a broken firing-pin - for the first and only time in my entire shooting career. Testing the unfired second barrel, that at least remained in working order.

When Ben turned up later, I told him what had happened. He was at first puzzled, and then he said. 'Ah-ha, you see now - dis be de Ogun bush, I tell you for true, dem people be bad people - dat ole man, he put *ju-ju* for you gun!"

Gareth Plinge came to me in the office a few weeks later to show me the photographs of our day's hunting, back from processing in the UK.

"It's very odd," he said, "You remember the dancing boy and the drums? I took six exposures before Ben dragged us off - look; all those frames are totally blank! Nothing at all, not even fogged." All the other exposures on the film were fine, but just those six - nothing. The next time I saw Benjamin Ladipo I forbore to mention the matter of the camera - it might have severely tested his faith.

I still partly believe the old man in the clearing in the bush had fixed Gareth's camera in the same way that he had fixed my gun. But by then I had already been more than twelve years in Africa.

Father Malden, the Irish priest from the White Fathers' seminary at Cape Coast would have understood the tale I have just recounted. Ten years earlier when I first met him in Takoradi he was already an old man. When, as he said, he periodically reached the end of his tether with the po-faced Dutch fathers, his colleagues, he would wheel out his ancient black Norton motor cycle and hitching up his grubby white soutane under the leather belt around his waist, he chugged along the rutted laterite coastal road to Takoradi, to come and stay for a few days 'R and R' with my friend the timber buyer, Diarmidh O'Plinge, in his rented house on the outskirts of town, to yarn and drink Irish whiskey and to smoke the rank local cigars and the twists of 'nigger-head' tobacco that he cut up and stuffed in his old briar pipe.

Diarmidh and I being young, thought Father Malden incredibly old. He once told us for example that he had been 'Pilot No. 12' in the old Royal Flying Corps. After the Great War he said, he had joined the notorious 'Black and Tans' - as a result of which he had later fled Ireland and taken up exile in Australia. He had married Down Under, but at the age of fifty-six, after his wife's death, he had converted, became a priest by special dispensation and came to Africa as a White Father, ending up teaching at the seminary. Father Malden said he would die in Africa. He had been allowed to return to Europe once, as was the custom with his Order. Sailing north as far as the Canaries, where he said he had nearly perished of the cold, he had disembarked and taken the next boat back to the Coast. He was probably no older than his late sixties but in our young eyes already far into his dotage.

One Sunday morning (Father Malden had been to early Mass) Diarmidh and I took him in my car on a picnic to Butre, a small village lying by the sea to the west, some three miles from Dixcove. Here were the ruins of Fort Batenstein, where according to the Dutch historian Bosman writing in 1701 *"On a very high hill lies a tiny ill-designed fort ..... An elongated building divided in two, and strengthened with four useless little bastions, upon which are mounted eleven light cannon."* The attraction for us was the lagoon, a sheltered inlet with a fast flowing narrow channel to the sea, all backed by densely wooded hills where centuries ago the good Dutchmen had maintained a sugar plantation in a swampy valley. Now the fort was inaccessible and partly hidden by thick bush.* By 1956 the only trace of its centuries-old European associations were the crumbling ruins on the hill overlooking the lagoon whose clear tidal waters swirled through a deep, sandy channel. Few Europeans bothered to drive down the miles of rough track to this remote spot. Very few expats that I knew were even aware of its existence.

The villagers, simple fishermen and farmers, were welcoming and would sell us flying fish - caught in their cast-nets in the surf, to grill on sticks over a driftwood fire in a little sheltered bay. Here we could swim in the clear lagoon, loaf, drink our beer and eat whatever else we had in the cool bag. Once we had crossed the few yards of the narrow channel in a shaky, dugout canoe paddled by an ancient blind ferryman with eyes blinkered by either smallpox or cataract - we were also safe from the bothersome village children, for whom the water flowed too fast and deep for them to cross safely. In any case Father Malden spoke Fanti and would soon have sent them packing. We lay on the white sand, drying off in the sun after our swim.

Father Malden in his swimming trunks was scrawny, both his thin legs were heavily scarred from the ankle nearly to the waist, as if he had once been badly burned, but had healed. Diarmidh asked the old priest if the scars were the result of some accident, a crash when he was a pilot perhaps.

---

* The Dutch had first become established here in 1598, building a star-shaped stone fort in 1640. In 1863, Richard Burton, visiting Dixcove wrote that Butre "still showed the Dutch flag occasionally" while noting that in 1837 the Dutch commandant and his assistant were killed by Chief Bonsu of the Ahanta at Takoradi. After the British bought it in 1872 it was all abandoned.

"No," said Father Malden, "a few years ago, I became very ill with some strange tropical disease, the flesh of my legs was being eaten away with open sores and ulcers. The doctors didn't know what was wrong with me; nothing they did was of any help. I became weaker and weaker and at the last they sent me to the hospital at Accra to die." He paused and cut a lump of black tobacco from a length of tar-like twist. When he lit his pipe it smelled of burning rubber tyres.

"As I lay dying," he continued," wasting away, one of my parishioners from Cape Coast, a recent convert - a carpenter - came to visit me, I thought at first he had come to measure me for my coffin. But he said he could help me to cure my sickness. If I would agree, he said he would bring me some 'special medicine.' He said my disease was known to his people and that they had a cure. I was so sick that I was prepared to try anything and agreed. Within days he was back again with a small pot of ointment, a black, foul-smelling paste. He told me to rub a little at a time on my great weeping ulcers, and it would heal them." Father Malden puffed a poisonous cloud from his stubby pipe, keeping the seaweed flies at bay.

"I didn't tell the doctors." Father Malden said. "That night I tried out a small patch of the ointment at the back of my knee, on an open sore. The pain was frightful, I couldn't stand it, I couldn't sleep, I wept with the pain. I tried to wipe away the ointment, but it was as sticky and as black as melted tar and I couldn't shift it. By the next morning, the pain had worn off, the paste had dried to a crust - and when I scraped it off, where it had been was a small patch where new skin was forming!"

Father Malden sent for the carpenter, asking him for more details. It soon became clear that the 'medicine' was a speciality known only to the fetish priest who ministered to a shrine in a distant bush village. "First" he said to the carpenter, "Could the 'doctor' make up a weaker mixture of the medicine - he was eager to try it again - but not to suffer the terrible pain from the first attempt." Also, thought Father Malden, he had better confess to the hospital doctors what he planned - and not least, to ask his own Bishop's permission before meddling with anything so obviously involved with ju-ju. Both hospital and Bishop agreed, the former agreeing that they could do nothing more, the latter saying he would 'bless' the medicine when it came, to remove any taint of magic.

Within a month, carefully applying the ointment, inch by painful inch on his legs, Father Malden was healed. Questioning the carpenter elicited nothing more than that the fetish priest "Collected leaves from some rare, special tree, at a special time of the year, deep in the forest, known only to him. Mixed them with more special ingredients, made offerings to his own special fetish - and that was that!" No more information could he get than these few facts. The last remains of the unguent, as a special request from the amazed medical staff, were sent off for laboratory analysis in Europe. "But alas," said Father Malden, "the results were totally inconclusive; the report simply said the pot's contents were a composition of decayed vegetable matter, of unknown origin." Father Malden sighed. "The carpenter then died a few months later and without him we no longer had any contacts. Another miracle drug lost to science!"

Father Malden was interested in Ju-Ju. He told us of the African seminarian, nearing ordination as a priest - "one of our very best students" he said - seven years after first coming from the far north, as a convert. The week before ordination, the seminary received an urgent telegram from the Bishop in Upper Volta, saying that whatever else happened the postulant must be denied ordination. A letter followed in which all was revealed. The would-be-priest was the undercover nominee of a fetish cult, who desiring the extra powers an ordained priest would bring them, had despatched their man to the Fathers on the coast. Word had reached the Bishop that the fetish cult, jubilant that their goal was near, had in their over-confidence begun preparations for the ceremonies that would mark his triumphant return to the fold. When confronted, the man had confessed all, not ashamed but in despair that he had been so close to success, for once ordained a Catholic priest, even if subsequently unfrocked, as he would have been, the 'power' would have remained with him to serve the fetish and make it ever stronger.

Father Malden told us of the remarkable similarities between the old superstitions of Europe and those of Africa. For example that it was well known that witches could not cross running water, that empty eggshells must be crushed and not left whole when evil spirits might use them as boats. He told us of the widely held belief in the Cape Coast region, that a race of magical dwarfs, the 'old people' still lived deep in the forest - a folk memory perhaps of ancient pygmy tribes. (The Cape Coast local football team boasted the name 'The Mysterious Dwarfs!") He told us of another parishioner, a lorry driver who had taken another man's wife. The vengeful husband had a spell cast upon the man - making sure that the victim was informed of the same, the *ju-ju* being that if the lorry driver travelled more than a certain distance from his home, he would die. This was bad news for the lorry driver for it meant that he was ruined, unable to ply his trade or to prosper. He came to Father Malden who mistakenly perhaps, told him that as a good Catholic he should confess all, be shriven and blessed and all would be well. The good lorry driver was later found dead on the roadside, at the wheel of his motionless truck (all his passengers had fled) a few yards past the specified milestone of the curse. The Catholic Church, said Father Malden, believed fully in the 'Powers of Evil.'

The Bank was not immune from witchcraft. At Tamale one of the cashiers ended the day with a £25 shortage in his till - a serious matter for him, for it would be charged either to his bondsmen or to his own 'Efficiency Account.' In either case he would end up out of pocket. By carrying out the somewhat esoteric operation known as a 'Cash Analysis' it was sometimes possible to recreate the day's transactions in enough detail to lead to a good indication of which customer had either paid in too little - or been paid out too much. In this instance the results were conclusive. The culprit was almost certainly a private soldier from the garrison who had received the extra money in error, from his savings account. The following day after making a phone call to the British adjutant, the soldier was confronted with the facts. In the face of his absolute denial there was little more that could be done, the likelihood was not one hundred percent, the mechanics of the proof we had, beyond a layman's understanding. The Adjutant said he would refer the matter to the Colonel, in front of whom the Bank manager, the cashier and the soldier again made their accusations and denials. Once more the soldier denied having received the extra money. The Colonel pronounced. "Did anyone object to referring the matter to the Battalion 'Mallam'? (The Mallam was the senior Mohammedan NCO who had a reputation for being able to get to the bottom line in such matters of truth or falsehood.) The private reluctantly agreed, the Mallam was summoned to the Colonel's office and the problem was explained.

Asking the soldier whether he still denied the charge, which he did, as obstinately as before, the Mallam produced two short lengths of stick, each several inches long which he instructed the private to hold apart, one in each hand in front of him. He then put the question to the test.

"If you tell de truth, den mek you hold de sticks apart, like for now. But if you lie, den de sticks will come together. No-ting you fit do can stop dem."

As the onlookers gazed at the soldier, sweat started to spring from his face, coursing down his trembling cheeks, his outstretched arms shook and quivered with the effort of keeping the sticks apart. Slowly, inexorably, the soldier's arms came together - the last few inches suddenly snapping them together.

The soldier, his eyes popping, shouted "Dis be Ju-Ju palaver, I never take de money! I no 'gree for dis humbug - I BE PROPAH CHRISTIAN!!" Flinging the two sticks at the feet of the Battalion Mallam, he fled from the Colonel's office in fright and terror.

Without the soldier's confession nothing more could be done.

Matters could sometimes be solved more simply. Several years later in Lagos, O. remarked one day that Oliver Eke, our 'small boy' was not well. His complexion was yellowish and his eyes were bloodshot. He was jaded, nervous and distracted. O. spoke first to Jonathan Njoku our cook to see if he knew what troubled Oliver. "Was he sick?" she asked.

"'E no be sick," said Jonathan, "but I tink dere be some palaver for dat nanny from nex' door, Oliver say she be witch an' she done put some ju-ju for him. You savvy Madam dat dis woman she come from .... (here he named some village we had never heard of). ALL dem people dere be witches!" Jonathan did not live on the compound then, but Oliver had a quarter adjoining that of our neighbour's nanny.

When O. taxed Oliver direct, he was at first evasive and denied being sick even when she offered him pills, a suggestion normally welcomed for whatever purpose. Eventually he confessed all. He was convinced the nanny had put a spell on him. Pressed further, he said the nanny came into his room at night, having taken the form of a lizard looking to take a piece of his soul while he slept. The natural consequence of this being that he didn't dare to sleep at night - hence his extreme lassitude, and afraid she would poison his food - his lack of appetite. O. was perplexed, whatever she said to Oliver about all this being nonsense he refused to believe her, merely stating that he knew the nanny, or the lizard as she became at night, was out to get him. O. became convinced a few days later that stronger remedies were needed when she saw Oliver and the nanny passing each other on the outside staircase. The nanny glared at Oliver, who flattened himself against the wall, visibly grey in the face, as if confronted by a spitting cobra.

O. had a brainwave. In her jewellery box she found a small silver crucifix on a chain given to her as a child by her own father. Calling Oliver, she said she had found some special magic for his problem. When Europeans were troubled by evil spells or witches she said, all that was necessary was always to carry the little cross around his neck, particularly while he slept which would protect him. If the lizard appeared he was to grip the little silver cross, displaying it boldly while advancing on the creature - and it would flee, helpless in the face of superior power. O. fastened the cross around Oliver's neck and he cheered up a little.

The next day Oliver was jubilant, the 'special' magic had worked brilliantly. He had awaited the lizard's arrival and transfixed it with the crucifix - whereupon it had fallen to the floor with a 'PLOP!', vanishing swiftly through a crack in the door. He had slept soundly, secure in the knowledge that he now possessed a superior magic. O. never had the heart to ask him for the return of the cross.

Our own two children often played in the compound and in later years they told us the neighbours' nanny would give them sweet local bread and biscuits and play with them. Once they said, they saw inside her room where at one side stood a dark wooden mirror-stand, with candlesticks - "Just like that one that witch had in the book of fairy tales!"

I would like to think that somewhere Oliver is still alive, still wearing the cross around his neck. When we left Africa the next year, Oliver returned to Iboland, to go back to school to resume his studies with the money he had saved. The Biafran War broke out just in time to swallow him up, at the age of fourteen or fifteen. He was I fear, naught but cannon fodder in the terrible times that were to come.

Note: re: Diarmidh O'Plinge: Diarmidh had been a Forest Officer in Nigeria with the Colonial Service before going into the commercial timber trade. He was stationed in the Rivers Division in the distant south, in the creek country of the Niger Delta. There was a sudden outbreak in his area of what was feared to be a resurgence of 'Leopard Cult' killings. Several Africans were found dead in very suspicious circumstances, their corpses mauled, some of them disembowelled and bearing the characteristic marks of a leopard kill. The only trouble with this theory was that it was well known that there were no leopards left in that region as they had all been trapped and hunted to extinction years before. The District Officer became convinced that the killings were the work of 'Leopard Men' re-surfacing once again. Several years earlier the local Leopard cult had been finally and successfully put down and many of its followers imprisoned and proscribed. Diarmidh's boss, the senior Forester thought perhaps not, and persuaded the District Officer to agree to an organised hunt through various forest blocks, surrounding the area and beating through towards nets and waiting guns. To everyone's surprise and to the relief of the District Officer, several fine leopards were flushed out and killed, also proving the extremely secretive nature of leopards - and the fact that when other game is scarce, they will attack man quite freely.

CHAPTER 18

'Of Cats, Dogs and Apes'

"What's time? Leave 'Now' for dogs and apes.
Man has forever."
(Robert Browning)

I kept a nondescript tabby cat at Sekondi. I can't remember now what I called her or who gave her to me. Eventually, as cats are wont to do, she adopted my neighbour, the pharmacist Norman Welch. Later I was given a beautiful, charming and affectionate pure Siamese kitten by some generous soul and when I went on my first leave in 1955 I left her with an Italian friend in Takoradi. On my return he refused point-blank to give her back to me, but later relented and when she produced a litter of kittens, he generously presented me with a pure white female. She was as fine a cat as her mother and when I went again on leave from Takoradi at the end of 1957 I left her with Louis Pugnet, who by then had also moved from Sekondi and lived in the adjoining compound. In 1958 I came back, married, with O. this time to Accra - where Louis eventually reappeared on the scene. He declined to return my cat, but she in her turn, snow-white as she was, then produced a pure coal-black kitten which we named 'Sheba.' Sheba came with us to Tamale at the end of that year, nearly dying en route from the heat, distressed, quivering and obviously in big trouble (crossing the Volta on the ferry at Yeji, the thermometer in our car stuck at about 150 degrees. F) We had exhausted all our drinking water by the time we reached the small town of Salaga and O. took our last bottle of beer from the cold-box (by now a hot-box) and poured it over Sheba lying in a towel on her lap. This revived her and when we finally reached Tamale in the late afternoon, although damp and sticky with beer she had survived.

In Tamale Sheba in her turn gave birth to a litter of four stripey kittens, two of which we drowned - I had foolishly and faint-heartedly asked Charles our steward, to do this for me. Hearing a furious mewing from the kitchen I found Charles holding the two kittens under a running tap. I was obliged, to my distress then to do the job properly in a bucket. I fear Charles was totally nonplussed by the whole procedure, as I am now - with hindsight - as to why this was necessary at all. To Charles it would have been quite logical to rear the kittens and either keep them as 'mousers' around the house, or as and when they became large and succulent enough, to knock them on the head and pop them in the stew pot. O.'s and my reasoning was that two kittens would thrive better with Sheba than four and that it would be difficult to find homes for them all. In the end the two surviving kittens went off to friends' homes, and poor Sheba alas, disappeared while in her next pregnancy. It had already been pointed out to us that Sheba, being jet-black, was probably powerful ju-ju, (for the same reason it was well known that black Labrador dogs were difficult pets to keep in the north) - and being pregnant, doubly so. O. always suspected that the garden boy had made off with Sheba, although with no good reason to think so. Sheba might simply have been taken by a snake or by some predator larger than herself during her nightly peregrinations.

Dogs are really not good news in tropical Third World countries. For obvious reasons they are not easily transportable across national borders because of vaccination requirements. They are prone to parasites and worms, they become mangy and tick-ridden, and of course there is the ever present danger of rabies. I love dogs - but they do have their drawbacks. They can be long-lived and one develops strong attachments to them (one does not 'own' a cat) and the emotional ties can become unbearably stressful. Reading the old accounts of the archetypal District Officers one has the image of the pipe-smoking Sahib or B'wana with a long-legged fox terrier at his heels, but reading between the lines one realises how short-lived these relationships must have been. Accident, disease and predators - human and animal - brought many to swift termination before their time.

In Accra on the coast Paul and June Foot (the 'Feet' as we then knew them), had brought out Ludo, their champion black Labrador. He was a paragon among dogs, sleek, good natured, well-trained and clever, but he suffered dreadfully from the heat. For this reason he was normally walked by June in the early morning or late afternoon along Labadi beach or over the golf course at the Accra Club. At that time O. and I had already discovered the Shai Hills, now I believe a game reserve, but then although only some twenty miles or so east of Accra across the plains - it was still a wilderness area of baboon-haunted cliffs and rocky outcrops, with the *Bateleur* eagles soaring high above. Bird life and small game were plentiful - green pigeon, bush fowl and duiker (once in broad daylight we spotted a large spotted civet cat) that I could hunt with my shotgun 'for the pot.'

The 'Feet' said that Ludo had been part-trained as a gundog and that they would bring him with us one day. They did so one hot Sunday morning when we drove out to the Shai Hills, watching the baboons fossicking in the sparse fields of maize and yams that lay below the rocky slopes and in the distance the long ridge of the Aburi escarpment looming far to the north across the plains. We parked the car after driving as far as we could up a rough track, gathered our kit; intending to picnic as well as hunt and we set off with Ludo up a sandy path leading into a sparsely wooded valley, looking for francolin. Within twenty minutes Ludo was in distress. Tongue lolling and dripping in the heat, reluctant to put one overheated paw in front of another on the baking earth, battered by the mid-morning heat of the blazing sun, Ludo gave up. He found a boulder that gave a little shade, summoned up what little energy remained and within a few moments he had dug a shallow pit in the soft damp soil under the rock and lay there panting and groaning, eyes glazed and rolling. Ludo had shot his bolt. We had a canvas water bag with us and sacrificed a pint or so in giving him a drink and pouring enough over his head and body to revive him a little. Thereafter by dint of part carrying, part pushing and part dragging him we reached our chosen picnic site where he collapsed again in the shade until the late afternoon when the blazing heat declined. So much for the gun dog! He failed to move a muscle when later as we lunched, a thrashing and crashing in the bushes on the slope above us suddenly revealed the only other person I ever saw in the Shai Hills apart from ourselves. A young Englishman, trilby-hatted, bespectacled, slung about with field glasses and camera, once crisp white shirt stained with sweat and torn by thorns, emerged from a thicket. "I say," he said, (without introducing himself), "how lucky to find you here! Do you know where the game trails are?"

Then a year or two later there was Ferdie, bequeathed to us in Tamale by Tony Whiting and his wife Jill when they left the Coast for Canada. Ferdie was what in my later Lake District days I would come to know as a 'cur-dog,' three parts collie-type sheepdog and perhaps a bit of something else. Friendly, clever - but obviously missing Tony who had owned him since a pup, long before he married Jill and the baby came along. In other words Ferdie boarded with us and we fed him and we loved him - but we obviously fell short in other respects.

Ferdie was a companion for O. during the days alone in the bungalow, but his loyalties were somewhat divided. I suspect that in the dim recesses of his mind he always expected his old master to return one day - as he always had in the past. Ferdie also had an incorrigible fault in that he chased the cars and lorries that infrequently came along our little by-road leading along to the Ridge and the airfield. With his old master he had passed his days in town, lying quietly beneath Tony's desk at the UAC office, which he reached by chasing his master's car all the mile or so down the dusty road. Ferdie as a result spent quite a bit of his day mooching across the road from us visiting his old home - just to check up on things - just in case.

One takes on a dog without really being fully aware of all the consequences or of the responsibilities. Before agreeing to look after Tony's dog I doubt if O. or I had given more than a moment's thought to what would happen to Ferdie when we in our turn came to leave as we inevitably would. In the final event fate stepped in. Otherwise looking after Ferdie posed few problems. He was gentle and obedient - when around the house. Charles, our cook and steward, prepared his food - 'gari,' which is dried and grated cassava, with a little boiled fillet steak and gravy. This diet sounds luxurious until one realises that in the market down in the town all beef was the much the same price per pound, joints, chops, liver, heart, lungs, hide and bones, tough and stringy fillet - it was all the same. Mutton or goat was dearer - but again all the same price regardless of the cut, so in the end having inspected the disgusting offal which was initially boiled up in our kitchen as dog meat - we decided that fillet it should be!

Ferdie had a sly streak to his easy-going nature like so many dogs with a touch of shepherding in their genes. Also to put not to fine a point on it, Ferdie was a thief. Had there been to hand a traditional butcher's shop - Ferdie would have been the model for the cartoon dog slinking off with the stolen string of sausages.

Our neighbour, T., who now lived in Ferdie's former residence across the road invited us to dinner one evening. While T. was in his shower prior to changing, Kofi, his steward burst into the bathroom, unceremoniously sweeping aside the shower curtains, brandishing in the other hand a covered oval meat dish from which he dramatically removed the lid to reveal a total absence of anything. T. standing naked and dripping in his shower was totally nonplussed by Kofi's obvious agitation. "Eccchh! Mastah!" Said Kofi aggrievedly. "Some ting done tief dem meat - lookum - no ting dey!" Kofi had been laying the dining table, hearing a sudden scrabble and clatter in his kitchen had rushed back to find the empty dish still spinning on the floor, no other trace of the leg of lamb to be seen. Instead of roasted mutton that evening we dined on freshly opened corned beef. No-one had seen Ferdie that evening and he did not re-appear in our house until the following morning, looking suitably sheeplike with ill-concealed guilt, rolling the whites of his eyes and uncomfortably distended around the middle.

During Ferdie's residence in our household we also, by default rather than by design, became hosts to Sid. I dislike monkeys as pets, but Sid was neither true monkey nor ape - rather a cross between the two, he was - when he came to us - a tiny scrap of life, a newly orphaned baboon who could have been no more than a few weeks old. His origins were unknown - he literally 'fell off the back of a lorry' one day in Bartholemew's motor workshop in the town. A laden 'Mammy' lorry briefly in for repair, careered out of the yard and as it left out flew Sid, propelled whether by accident or by intent no-one will ever know, landing 'Plop!' in a puddle of oil at the feet of R's most trusted mechanic - one Issah 'The Greaser.' Issah then handed the oil-stained mite to R. who with a sudden flash of inspiration, jumped in his car and drove swiftly to our bungalow - knowing that O. was pregnant with our first child. "Here you are -" he said, handing over the pathetic little bundle, "- get some practice in!"

The young of many mammals strike a sympathetic chord in the human breast. Baboons, with their appealing eyes, near-human expressions and reactions particularly so (until rude maleness intervenes, particularly 'rude' in the case of the young adolescent of the species *Papio papio* as to the casual, but perceptive observer, the young male baboon appears gifted with a more or less permanent erection.) Within the hour of his arrival, Sid had been bathed in warm water, de-greased and powdered, his shrill screams and wild chitterings soothed by lying on O's lap, wrapped in a towel, sucking contentedly on the little finger of a pink rubber glove dribbling a mixture of sugared water and warm tinned milk.

Sid was so named in short order because of his startling resemblance to R's eponymous company auditor, who had recently left town after having given R. a hard time. I suppose it was a suitable revenge on the part of R, though jests of this kind have the habit of rebounding if the butt of the joke later discovers the liberties taken.

Easy-going Ferdie became invaluable as Sid rapidly grew and became more active. Sid would lie asleep alongside Ferdie, nestling in his fur. When awake Sid would groom him endlessly - to the great pleasure of Ferdie who enjoyed the active little fingers parting his fur for scraps of skin - grooming in baboons must be inborn for poor Sid's tragically brief acquaintance with his natural mother would hardly have given him time to learn it. Ferdie became Sid's security blanket, Sid could pester him, ride on his back - the two of them living in a sort of symbiosis for Ferdie would also, to our advantage, mop up with gusto Sid's firm little motions which he occasionally deposited on our red painted cement floors. Once weaned, which did not take long, Sid thrived mightily on a diet of fruit, scraps of this and that and unshelled groundnuts.

Sid would follow O. around the garden, out into the road, always busy and inquisitive - but at the first sign of danger rushing screaming either to Ferdie or to O. He grew to tolerate Charles, but at the sight of the garden boy or any other African who passed by or visited the house he would shriek in fear, leaping for safety, clutching at O's bare ankle with all the adhesive power of a limpet while simultaneously widdling copious warm streams over her feet and sandals. While young he was an extraordinarily tactile creature, inviting attention with his prematurely wise brown eyes and mournful expression belying his mischievous intentions. I still recall with pleasure the feel of the velvety warm, smooth patches of skin on his haunches - smoother than a baby's bottom, like stroking the sleek and shiny coat of a dachshund.

Poor Sid, he grew apace and eventually for much of the time if we were not around he had to be confined in a wired-off enclosure in the garden where he idled away much of the day. R. had been on leave during much of Sid's infancy and now he had returned, and with the imminent arrival of our daughter, R. reclaimed Sid for his own. One day Chadwick the game warden from Damongo came to town bearing another orphan baboon, a young female (immediately named Ethel - after the wife of a family friend of O's father). Ethel had been rescued by Chadwick who found her marooned up a tree while nearby a leopard had recently dined off the fresh carcass of her mother.

There was no way either Sid or Ethel could have been returned to the wild. Unable to provide for themselves in the bush they could hardly have survived more than a few days and would have fallen easy prey either to starvation or to a marauding hyaena or leopard. Instantaneous rejection would be the certain reaction of any troop of wild baboons they might encounter. They were doomed to the fickle care of whoever might take them on. The last time O. and I saw them shortly before we ourselves left Tamale to return to Europe, Sid was approaching adulthood, growing the ruff-like mane of the male baboon, his canine fangs projecting alarmingly when he wrinkled back his lips to greet us. He was sitting on the ground, mournfully nursing a poorly healed broken arm from some recent accident, his fur matted and thick with burrs - a chain around his waist, being groomed by patient, sad-eyed, loyal Ethel sitting by his side. I feared for their future.

Alas too poor Ferdie, he too bit the dust soon after Sid left us. One day Kofi came across the road to tell O. that he had found Ferdie lying 'plenty sick' in the garage of his old master's house. O. rushed over and found him stretched out on the ground, outwardly unmarked but unable to move, barely conscious. She fetched water and cupping her palm dribbled a little into his mouth. Ferdie feebly licked her hand and died. Whatever had happened to him, *in extremis* he had obviously dragged himself back to his old home rather than to us.

In the early afternoon R. came up to the bungalow, I could not get away from town because of the need to close up the Bank. We needed to know, or so we thought then, what had caused Ferdie's demise - disease, (almost certainly *not* rabies, but maybe something else), injury, perhaps snakebite or even a scorpion sting, maybe he had been poisoned? R. put Ferdie's now stiffening corpse into the boot of his car and drove north to the Government Veterinary Station at Pong Tamale to see if Hans

Jessen, the polo-playing, cigar-smoking Danish vet. would do a post-mortem for us. I drove up later that afternoon the fifteen or twenty miles to find that Hans being away R. had left Ferdie with the Ghanaian vet. whom I knew well, a quietly spoken, shy man - who also rode at the Polo Club occasionally. He was in his white coat and he took me into a wire-screened room where Ferdie's corpse lay on a slab, half-flayed, the skin peeled off his hindquarters to reveal the unmistakable cause of his death. His spine was almost certainly broken beneath the massive area of sub-cutaneous bruising along the lower back. "Did he chase cars?" Asked the vet. "Yes." I answered. "Well, he won't do it again." Said the vet.

Rabies was common and a real risk, even with pet dogs that had supposedly been vaccinated - I believe there was a less than totally effective vaccine for domestic animals at that time. In Kano I once asked 'Doc' McGregor if there were human cases from time to time. "Frequently!" he replied, "in the local hospitals in Northern Nigeria." I asked him how such patients were treated. "Very simple - once they are positively diagnosed, they get a massive dose of morphine - and that's that." It was I suppose a more humane method than the '*Olde Englysshe*' recipe for hydrophobia which required nothing more than two feather mattresses between which the patient was placed like a sandwich filling, plus ten strong men to sit on top until the 'cure' was complete.

Sputnik's name gives away the date of his birth and the period of his short life. Sputnik was a fox terrier who belonged to the Officers' Mess of the 3rd Battalion in Tamale. Whether he acknowledged any one particular subaltern as his master I can't remember. He was a jolly dog like many of his breed - and a great source of amusement on the Sunday mornings when the Regimental band played for an hour or so while we sat on the shady mess stoep drinking our beer and building up an appetite for the coming curry lunch. There were certain tunes, light opera or themes from popular musical shows which inspired in Sputnik a peak of emotion that I have never seen before or since in any dog. Spurred into action by some peculiar harmonic combination of the brass section, Sputnik would emerge from under a table where he had been snoozing and snacking on 'small chop' - and would place himself immediately behind the bandmaster - who totally unaware of his presence for the moment would continue to flourish his baton.

As the band's brass section struck up the opening bars of a medley from 'South Pacific' or some such piece Sputnik would lay his ears flat, turn up his eyes until only the whites showed, place his head on the ground, he would then slowly roll over onto his back with all four legs in the air. His black and rubbery nose would quiver in anticipation, his mouth would open wide and to the delight of all, he would become, to put not too fine a point on it, sexually stimulated. Perspiring bandsmen peering over their slides and pistons endeavoured to maintain their concentration and composure - all except the bandmaster who continued waving his baton, still oblivious to the presence of Sputnik, now the sole object of attention.

The noise that Sputnik emitted when he started to sing his solo accompaniment was both indescribable as well as unstoppable. He put his entire heart and soul into his performances. The bandmaster would jump convulsively, as the musicians' bell-like tones helplessly subsided into wavering discords along with Sputnik's matchless high-pitched, ecstatic singing. The audience would collapse in fits of laughter and the Colonel or one of the Majors would shout "Someone get that damned dog away from here!" One of the subalterns would grab Sputnik by the scruff and take him forcibly away, still in mid-song and lock him away in the dark in someone's rondavel bathroom until normality returned. "Carry on, Bandmaster" would say the Colonel. "Sah!" Would come the response, and order and harmony was once more restored.

Alas too, for poor Sputnik. His behaviour and mood one day became erratic. He started to lurch and stagger with a strange look in his eyes. The Medical Officer wisely insisted that he be locked away in an empty hut, fed and watered and kept under observation. One morning a day or two later the MO was called to observe Sputnik through the wire mesh of the window.

There was now no doubt, whining, terrified, with foam flecked jaws - there could be no further delay. Sputnik was shot through the window, his corpse dragged onto a sack and burned to ashes. The grass roofed rondavel was hosed out, scrubbed and disinfected - and on the MO's orders, left vacant.

There was no point in removing Sputnik's head and sending it to the Government Veterinary Laboratory for a final verdict, for as I was once told any such specimen received for examination of the brain and spinal tissue involving bio-culture under laboratory conditions was swiftly despatched into the nearest incinerator with a long set of tongs any subsequent enquiry always being responded to formally as 'Positive!' The reason was that if the proper tests were conducted and then found to be confirmed, the laboratory technicians who had handled the specimen were required to undergo a series of painful injections into the abdomen over the next twenty-eight days. It was far simpler to pre-empt what was almost always a positive result.

In Lagos in 1965 or 1966 O was driving to work one morning through Ikoyi en route to Victoria Island when she noticed an obviously rabid dog wandering in the road. Classic foaming hydrophobia. Whining, foam-flecked muzzle, staggering backwards and shaking its head, alarmed cyclists wobbling past and cars swerving to avoid it. Arriving at her office she thought it was probably wise to report it to some authority to take urgent action. Alas, no-one wanted to know, neither Police, nor the Town Council, the Health Department, shunted from pillar to post by each contact. All denied responsibility and after several futile telephone calls which took up most of the morning, she gave up.

'Companion' animals (as is now the politically correct designation) came in many shapes and sizes, allowing those expats so inclined to give free rein to their eccentricities. Werner, the Swiss builder and his wife Ellie, had turned their large garden in Tamale into a haven for orphaned antelope, various duikers, oribi and even a young waterbuck which the African huntermen, having killed game with their young at foot and knowing of Ellie's tender heart, had sold to her rather than pop them into their cooking pots. These motherless and delicate fawns hopped and grazed and browsed her shrubs amid the tame guinea fowl and pet rabbits of her small son, André. (Note: There is a secret recipe to successfully rear young, unweaned antelope which is absolutely vital to prevent them from expiring of acute constipation within a few days. In the wild, as they suckle – the mothers lick the rear end of their young, who deprived of this trigger, will not have a bowel movement. Fortunately much the same effect can be achieved with a wipe of damp cotton wool as they tug at the teat of a bottle.) Whatever in the end became of them I never knew.

One of the army MOs in Tamale collected snakes, not as 'pets' but to despatch to the Government snake farm at Accra where they were milked for their venom. I remember O and I called in at his bungalow one afternoon for tea and hearing a rustling noise from an enamel lidded bucket in the kitchen. He proudly displayed its contents - a small puff adder. On another memorable occasion this same MO had been given a pair of carpet vipers (*Echis carinatus*), small but deadly, which had been caught by one of the barrack's grass-cutters who knew they would generate a suitable 'dash' from the MO and refrained from killing them on the spot. Our medical friend popped them in their temporary cardboard box into the boot of his car to take home to more secure housing. Arriving at his bungalow, on opening the boot, the box lay on its side, empty. There was no sign of its venomous occupants. A cautious and thorough search revealed one viper which was carefully removed from beneath the back seat. The second had seemingly completely vanished and it was hoped (but without certainty) to have somehow or other wriggled out of the car. Some two weeks later, the by now somewhat hypersensitive and paranoid MO, sitting in the driving seat, through the fabric thought he detected a slight and unusual movement beneath his left buttock. Executing a 'crash' stop, he leaped from the car - later to find the missing reptile entwined among the springs and upholstery of the seat he had so lately occupied.

Then there was Hans, the Danish vet. who shared his bachelor quarters with a young male chimpanzee. A friend called in one late afternoon to find Hans (in a not unusual semi-stupor), and the chimp, each comfortably esconced in their respective chairs facing the fridge, both smoking the short, fat Danish cigars favoured by the vet. Each had a pint pot of Star beer in his hands and several empty bottles lay at their feet. The chimp wore nothing but a crumpled baseball cap and was the better host - seeing my friend at the door he strolled over, guided the visitor by the hand to another chair, went to the fridge to take out another bottle - removing the cap with his teeth, fetched a clean glass from the sideboard and sat down again before leaning over to alert Hans to the presence of their guest.

CHAPTER 19

"A Bit More Tether"

"You may take it from me Ma'am, that a man who's spent his life in building up commerce and Empire in secluded spots ... is allowed by Providence a bit more tether than the chap who's living at home next to the Sunday School doing nothing beyond a bit of insurance agency or selling ladies' stockings."
(Alfred Aloysius Horn aka 'Trader Horn' "The Ivory Coast in the Earlies" Cape 1927)

In the Gold Coast - and Ghana - the nickname 'Iron Man' was bestowed on certain Europeans. It was a 'pidgin' term that implied both amusement and a degree of grudging respect, often misunderstood and sometimes the cause of embarrassment. The Africans often gave Europeans and other expatriates nicknames based on close observation of their quirks and foibles - which as I have observed before were often exaggerated, being given free rein in the frequently bizarre circumstances of life in West Africa.

In Tamale, in the immediate years after Independence one of the few remaining expatriate employees of the Town Council was the vehicle inspector, kept on no doubt as much for his resistance (theoretical) to corruption and bribery as for his mechanical knowledge. He was known universally to the local transport owners and drivers of the Mammy lorries and taxis as 'Shaky-Shaky' by reason of his practice of grabbing and vigorously shaking the front wheels of a truck to see how rocky and worn the suspension had become. It was alleged that this was the only test that he ever applied to determine the mechanical fitness of any vehicle plying for hire.

The old Spanish trader in the town - Señor Hurtado - was known to African and European alike as 'Langa-Langa' - in the vernacular meaning something like 'Penny-penny' or 'Cheap-cheap.' As a young bricklayer fleeing Spain during the Great Depression he had come to the Gold Coast in the late 1920s and had worked in Accra as a builder, labouring for the same rate of pay as the Africans he worked alongside. By saving every penny from his meagre wages he had at last set himself up as a market trader, coming north to Tamale in the years before the war. By the time I came to know him he was well over seventy, shrewd, sharp as a razor and as tough as a piece of old wrinkled Spanish saddle leather. 'Langa-Langa' still knew little English and his pidgin was so pure that it was virtually incomprehensible to any European, but he spoke all the local languages. He had a finger in every slice of business pie, trading in everything from shea nuts to Manchester cottons to motor parts and goat hides - and he still served behind the counter of his stores with his daughter and his son-in-law, Garcia. 'Langa-Langa' once gave me a raw, salted leopard skin (which I later had cured and tanned by Rowland Ward's in London) rather than pay me the fee of three guineas I was due for handling an insurance claim for him.* (The Bank's managers in remote areas acted as agents for Lloyds of London assessing minor claims - for which we were paid a standard fee of three guineas). In Tamale I was quite often called into the market to inspect bales of cotton damaged in transit, perhaps having been dropped in the sea on landing, drying out en route up-country. Sometimes a market 'mammy' would ask me to have a look at one of her newly arrived wooden casks of Danish 'pigs parts' (masks, ears, snouts, tails and other unmentionables, all pickled in brine for export and much relished as a local delicacy). The barrels were sometimes stove-in en route, the brine draining off and the resulting gagging stench could be detected at fifty paces. I always agreed these claims from a distance, trusting only the evidence of my nose.

There was a Lebanese trader in Tamale known to all and sundry as 'No Fit' and sometimes as 'Mumu' - I never discovered the real reason for this first nickname but assumed that it referred either to his generous girth and somewhat wobbly appearance or perhaps to his large and notoriously ramshackle fleet of mammy trucks on which his precarious fortunes were so unsoundly based. He was a genial and generous man, but unlike so many Lebanese his business acumen was not as acute as my predecessor in the Bank had imagined. 'No Fit' had been loaned so much money that he over-reached himself. He built up a transport empire of dodgy and ill-maintained trucks bought on expensive credit, opened stores and cinemas in remote villages - where no-one had any money or knew how to maintain a generator. Just before his whole creaking financial edifice crumbled to dust and ashes my predecessor realised that disaster was imminent and about to overtake them all. He managed to persuade 'No Fit' to transfer his accounts, lock, stock, dodgy loans and dodgy security, overdraft included, to Barclays DCO (the only other Bank in town) down the road - who for a week or so at least were convinced they had pulled off the financial 'coup' of the year! Subterfuge, rumour and deceit ruled. It saved John Plinge, my predecessor, a lot of explaining to Head Office. The fact that John Plinge was alleged to be in a poker school with several of the Lebanese in town was more than relevant - all gamblers to a man – who may have given him the advance information that it was time to dump 'No Fit' onto his more innocent competitor.

---

* In his old age I hope he survived to enjoy the castle in Spain he had already bought for his retirement.

Then there was Werner Solenthaler, (known also as 'Tarantula') the middle-aged Swiss building contractor who lived with his wife Ellie and their young son André, plus a menagerie of 'rescued' wildlife in a large, comfortable bungalow near us on the Agriculture Ridge. Werner's nickname was 'Don't-trouble-me!' This derived from his habitual response to his workers if they approached him when he was otherwise pre-occupied.

Werner was notoriously famous for his fractured English and for his widely quoted reply when once asked by a caller "Where's Ellie?" Replied "Ellie no dey for house, she go for trek mit dem piccin in der pushing-cart!" A loose translation is, "Ellie's not at home, she has gone for a walk with the child in the pram."

He often worked from his bungalow, inside a giant wooden playpen which enclosed his desk. When first seen, one thought how fortunate the child it was obviously designed to protect - until one realised its principal purpose was to exclude both their collection of free-roaming pets and their child. Werner was sometimes to be found fast asleep on the floor inside his playpen - safe from all intrusion.

When one met Werner on the bone-shaking washboard laterite roads around Tamale, invariably his car was proceeding at break-neck speed, fishtailing wildly around the bends over the loose and gravelly corrugated surfaces. As he passed and before one was enveloped in the cloud of fine choking dust that boiled up behind him, he could be seen grinning widely, his free right hand punching the air and tugging at some imagined ghostly lavatory chain.

We can no longer avoid an explanation of 'Iron Man.' Those who earned such fame did not achieve notoriety without a degree of dedicated application. To put not too fine a point on it, the term 'Iron Man' was reserved for those whose sexual stamina and prowess - compounded with, one supposes, generosity as well as a liberal dash of promiscuity - duly achieved celebrity and popularity among the ladies of the town. In such small communities the prattle of the close-knit league of bar girls would soon spread into general knowledge. Indeed most expatriates would have been surprised to learn how much the local Africans knew about their goings-on. Houseboys and cooks exchanged gossip in the market and the 'whitemen' in their midst were the subject of close and interested scrutiny. Such an 'Iron Man' in such times (AIDS was still a quarter of a century in the future and penicillin remained the 'magic bullet' for the rest) was likely after a while to find himself famous to the point where his daytime excursions in the town would result in cheers and stiff-arm salutes from passers-by while the young girls and market mammies would giggle and wave - all shouting 'Iron Man! Iron Man!" in exuberant greeting.

One such 'Iron Man' was 'H' who for many years had been a produce buyer and agent for one of the big trading companies on the Coast. In the small town of Hohoe across the Volta River which was his base, H. was well known and popular with the locals. My friend T. knew him well and told me that when H. was in town, in the early mornings the young doe-eyed blue-clad schoolgirls and the bare-foot, khaki-shorted boys would queue up on their way to class, passing through his office where he kept a large jar of boiled sweets to give one to each smiling child as they curtseyed and bobbed past. It goes without saying that H. was a bachelor. In the same way that the 'Old Coasters' paid their cooks and stewards a 'leave allowance' as a retainer when they went on their periodic furloughs - H. was also reputed to pay his current mistress an 'acting yam allowance' as a retainer whenever he was away on leave or even on extended trek.

T. told me that one morning when he drove in earlier than usual to his own office he noticed H. sitting glumly in the cab of his pick-up truck under the spreading branches of the big Ju-Ju tree that shaded the wide dusty street near the middle of town. The pick-up was surrounded by a crowd of passers-by and children, all jumping up and down, cheering and waving. Somewhat mystified, T. stopped to see what was happening as H agitatedly waved to him. T. got out of his car and walked over to see what was up.

Standing up on the running board to look in the cab, T. saw with some surprise that H. was naked except for a striped pyjama jacket covering his upper body. Below the waist his pink, bare wiry legs and knobbly knees stretched down to his shoeless feet on the pedals. Meanwhile more and more onlookers joined the throng, shouts of "Iron Man! - Iron Man!" rang out as the children skipped and jumped in excitement.

"Thank goodness!" Said H. "I was beginning to be afraid I'd be stuck here all day! Have you got a tow-rope? - I've stalled, as you see, run out of petrol, can't move an inch from here without help, old boy."

Fortunately T. had a spare can of petrol and saved the situation. It transpired that H. had woken up late that morning, and had agreed to drive his current lady friend back into town. (In certain louche bachelor circles this used to be known as 'the Milk Run'). In a hurry, he had not bothered to dress and just after he had dropped off the girl and turned around to drive back to his bungalow, the pick-up had gently sputtered to a halt under the big, spreading, silk-cotton bombax tree in the middle of town - where not so many years before the grisly relics of ju-ju and fetish would have been displayed, nailed to the trunk.

H. the 'Iron Man' was also renowned for keeping behind his bungalow a hutch of rabbits for his table. When sufficiently plump, the chosen candidate for the pot would be brought around to the front by the garden boy, while H., glass of whisky and pipe to hand, would take up his shotgun and from the vantage point of his cane chair on the verandah, despatch the rabbit at suitable range while it nibbled and hopped around the wiry crab grass. H. maintained that it was much kinder to the poor creature than to have the cook slit its throat with a blunt knife, as would otherwise have happened. There was of course the sporting element to be considered and H. also reckoned it gave the meat a slight gamey flavour. Who is to say that he was wrong?

As to the possibility of embarrassment, there was the young English second lieutenant (a national serviceman) in Tamale who was detailed by his Colonel to escort the wife and teenage daughters of the visiting commanding General around the town and to show them such sights as there were. With the General's lady sitting beside him in an open Land Rover, and her two girls behind, they set off to visit the town's colourful market. As they drove through the dusty streets they passed one of the local bars where a few of the girls were sitting outside in the shade, idling away the time until nightfall. Our unlucky subaltern was promptly spotted. The cry of 'Iron Man!' was raised and as they drove further into town, perforce slowly because of the goats, the scrubby chickens and throngs of Africans going to and from the market - they gathered a retinue of capering children who waved and cheered, as well as the passing pedestrians who took up the cry, giving the customary stiff-arm salute while cries of "Iron Man - Iron Man!" accompanied their progress.

"I *say*, young man - you do seem to be *awfully* popular in the town!" Said the General's lady, as she and her daughters responded to the crowd - smiling and waving graciously in regal fashion. "What does 'Iron Man' mean? Is it some form of traditional greeting?"

"Why - er - er - . Yes indeed Ma'am - that's exactly what it is." Said the profusely sweating subaltern, clutching at straws, deeply distraught and wishing the road in front would open in some giant chasm and swallow him up.

"Er - it's a traditional northern tribal greeting - er, yes - yes!" He blathered. "That's what it is! It's a sort of compliment - but it's not because of me. Oh no! - It's partly because they hardly ever see any European ladies being driven in a car like this." Here inspired genius took over, richly deserving of some future successful career in politics or advertising. "It's because of the Land Rover Ma'am - like the wartime Jeeps - they think they are so powerful and strong and they admire them so much - that's why they call everyone who drives one 'Iron Man!'

CHAPTER 20

'Office Palaver'

Manager: "You should have been here at 9 o'clock!"
Office Boy: "Why? What happened?"
(Music Hall joke)

I went to Lagos with the United Bank for Africa in April 1964 after an eventful six months with the Bank of the North in Kano. My new Italian friend and colleague Guido Plingetti, a year or so later became the manager of the Bank's Kainji branch opened to service the Niger Dam project. Guido after a few months 'on seat' came to pursue a vendetta with the Clerk of the Native District Council over some dispute or other. I don't think it was a 'mammy palaver' but whatever the cause Guido felt so deeply offended, to the extent that he refused to allow the Clerk into the Bank on any pretext whatsoever, or even to cash any cheques on his personal account. I had it on good authority that Guido, one morning in his office overheard the Clerk trying to persuade one of the bank cashiers to cash a cheque for him. The fiery Italian burst out from his office inflamed with incandescent Neapolitan rage and chased the Clerk (long blue robes flowing) out and down the street all the way back to the Council Offices - shouting "GET OUT! GET OUT!! --- BASTARD! BASTAARD!! BASTAAARD!!!" (This might just conceivably have been "*Bastante!*" misheard, which I believe is Italian for "enough!"), for Guido's command of English always tended to fail him in moments of stress. It took a visit from the Bank's Chief Inspector to make an uneasy truce between them. This was all part of the art of 'Coarse Banking' - long since replaced in our own more temperate High Streets by computers, wimpish Customer Relations managers and New Business Consultants - that is assuming that our Banks today still provide any personalised services at all to their non-corporate customers.

One of my predecessors in Tamale was supposed to have leaped the counter in one bound and felled a customer to the floor with his fist, when having just refused him a loan and shown the supplicant the door, he then overheard him holding forth to the public at large and to the bank staff, pouring scorn and insult on the manager's personality.

In Tamale on more than one occasion I myself became so incensed that I behaved in an equally irrational manner. I had made a bad loan of a few hundred pounds to a plausible carpenter in the town, one Kofi Mankwah who falsely claimed to have a small PWD contract. One morning when I was obliged to bounce two more of the mendacious carpenter's cheques and it was obvious that he was not going to repay a penny of the advance I had already made, I jumped into my car and accompanied by the two Bank messengers, Peter and Winfriend, raced round to his scruffy premises on the edge of the market. There was no answer to my furious hammering on the rough plank door. A helpful bystander offered the information that Kofi had just wriggled out of the back window. The two messengers hared round the back of the shack and seized the poor man - dragging him bodily back to me at the front. I grabbed him by the neck and was about to give him a savage shaking, sorely tempted to thump him as well, when the two messengers intervened, justifiably afraid that my behaviour would certainly bring a charge of assault down on the three of us. I had to be satisfied with delivering a furious tirade of abuse at the somewhat shaken Kofi before retreating back to the Bank. Of course he never paid back one penny, but I felt a little better in myself despite having to appease Duggie Medcalf, the District Manager in my monthly, always troublesome, 'Bad Debt' returns.

I was also afflicted sporadically with staff 'palaver' in the Bank, often involving the personal debts and general peccadilloes of the African clerks in their relationships with the clients of the Bank - outside of their clerical duties. This was in addition to frequent domestic 'palaver' - involving one's house servants in their conflicts with each other and one's neighbours. This was accepted as part and parcel of running an African household. King Solomon would have been sorely tried by many of these disputes.

I found the 'palavers' involving the Bank staff particularly trying at times. Europeans in these situations after extended residence in West Africa, especially when approaching the end of a long tour become more than usually 'tetchy' - perhaps better described as a mild form of paranoid megalomania. The particular instance that I describe is typical.

One quiet mid-morning, sitting in my office doing nothing in particular, Peter the messenger entered and said. "*Someone* to see you, Manager." Wearily I said, "Who is it?" "Sah," said Peter, "…. it is …." He hesitated "… *Somebody!*"

"Go outside. Find out who it is. Come back and tell me!" I began to feel my blood pressure surging. The messenger came back in and stood in front of me. "Well?" I said, "Who is it? "Manager, I de-tell you for true. It is a *certain* man." From outside my office I could now hear the increasing buzz of angry voices. I managed to restrain my rising temper, realising that I had reached an impasse, the usual sort of checkmate position that in the everyday African context was best resolved by unconditional surrender. "OK" I said, "…. show in this *certain* man."

Preceded by a strong smell of iodine and liniment, a strange apparition entered. Beneath a layer of bits of white lint, gauze and strips of pink sticking plaster I recognised the black and homely features of the town's postmaster. He was limping heavily, supporting one bandaged ankle with a walking cane. Concerned at his appearance, I urged him to sit down. As a customer I already knew him as only the week before I had turned down his request for a larger overdraft considering that he already owed the Bank more than he could easily repay.

"Have you had some sort of accident?" I began cautiously.

"Manager," he said. "I have come to complain about your clerk, one Francis, to beg you to sack him now-now for what he do to me!"

I was shocked. "Francis did this to you? He attacked you? Why should he do such a thing?" Francis was one of the best of my clerks, quietly efficient, unassuming.

"Francis has been disclosing secrets about my money to my Sweetie. He tell my Sweetie that I have plenty-plenty money in the Bank - when all the time I tell her I have nothing to give my Sweetie - you know that be true, no be so, Manager? Francis want to take my Sweetie away from me and make ****** (here he used an expression I shall not repeat) with her." The postmaster removed his dark glasses revealing heavily bloodshot eyes and wiped away a tear. In the close atmosphere of the office the reek of iodine was now overpowering.

I was nonplussed. "Then Francis go beat you?" I asked, to my own annoyance slipping into pidgin, which I rarely used in the office.

"No, *my Sweetie*, she done beat me - she beat me plenty, she very angry - she humbug me proper! She rubbish me too much. She say, 'Why you lie and tell me you no have money when my Francis tell me you have plenty for you savings book?' And then she beat me again. My Sweetie she very strong too-too much! ... Then she go off and stay with Francis." He dabbed away another tear.

"Boo-Hoo ..." he wept.

I noticed that from behind his tear and iodine-stained handkerchief he was watching me closely for my reaction. There was a knock at the door. Seeking momentary respite from a situation that I felt increasingly unable to deal with, I foolishly said "Come in." The door burst open and in rushed Francis, the doorway behind him framed with the wide-eyed faces of the other clerks. The normally quiet and well-mannered Francis was frothing with rage. I stood up and placed myself between him and the postmaster who had now backed into a corner looking alarmed, raising his walking stick in a defensive gesture.

Francis was shouting. "You lie! YOU LIE!! - Why you tell such lies to my Manager? You think you get me the sack and then your Sweetie go lef me and go back with you! She my girl - she never yours, she beat you because she know you lie to her! She never hurt you bad, you stick on dem bandage yo'-self - so you tink my Manager get sorry for you?" Francis then stretched out his arm over my shoulder and grabbed the end of a sticking plaster on the postmaster's cheek - he yanked it off to a roar of pain from the latter, exposing quite a nasty and obviously genuine cut.

At this stage, Mr Appiah my Chief Clerk intervened, grabbing Francis by the arms and pulled him out of my office. The two messengers, pre-empting any further instructions from myself also grabbed the postmaster and bundled him out into the banking hall. They hustled him out of the door and into the road before the interested gaze of the mid-morning customers. The postmaster was shouting and waving his stick as he hobbled away.

Later that afternoon the telephone went dead when I was in the middle of a call. Cranking the wind-up handle on the handset drew no response whatsoever from the local exchange situated behind the Post Office. I though no more of it, it was time to go home anyway.

The next morning, the telephone was still out of order. A messenger was just about to leave the Bank to despatch a few telegrams and to buy stamps from the Post Office. I said he should go into the Telephone Exchange and report the faulty line to the operator.

Ten minutes later the messenger was back. "No stamp" said Winfriend, waving the undespatched telegram forms. "No service, de Postmaster he tell de Telephone Exchange to cut de line, he not do any business no more for de Bank! No stamps, no letters, no telegram, no telephone ... no-ting at all, at all!" He finished triumphantly, looking pleased with himself for imparting this information.

It was most unfortunate that at that moment I was holding in my hand a very fine Parker fountain pen (the expensive gift of a Lebanese client to whom I felt totally uncommitted and therefore able to accept such a present without appearing ungracious). As the implications of this situation sunk in, I became on the instant consumed with such rage that I flung my precious pen at the office wall where it shattered into a dozen or more bakelite shards while a great splodge of Permanent Royal Blue Quink from the pen's ample reservoir slowly dribbled down the white painted plaster.

You may ask how the situation was resolved. (**Also see Note :**) It was quite simple - I sent a covert message under a flag of truce to tell the Postmaster that the overdraft he required was now at his disposal. All normal postal services were swiftly resumed. What became of the shared services of *'Sweetie'* I never knew. When I went on leave a few months later the ink stain was still on the wall as a dumb witness to my intemperance.

I wonder if today's average MBA or Business College syllabus includes the solution of such problems.

By the mid-Sixties I had heard that the latest re-incarnation of the old and much lamented Bank of British West Africa (shortly before it passed away into history under the all-smothering blanket of the Standard Chartered Bank) had introduced psychological profiling of its new recruits to try to reduce the number of eccentrics who blossomed into full flower while in their employ on the Coast. I suspect that in many cases it was the effect of the often bizarre living and working conditions that triggered off the already underlying tendencies in those who with hindsight were already sufficiently unhinged even to contemplate a career in West Africa. In the case of our former Prime Minister John Major for example, who soon realised he had arrived in a career backwater, he spent less than six months working for the Standard Bank at Jos in Nigeria before suffering the car crash and the injuries that enabled him to evacuate himself swiftly back to Blighty.

Shortly before my day there was the classic case of the up-country Branch Manager who, as so often at that time, was sweating out an over-extended tour in a small West African town. As the sole European in such a branch he had little contact with his colleagues except by letter and the mostly unreliable telephone, and a degree of paranoia always ruled in one's long distance dealings with the Bank as employer as neither conditions nor pay were good. In my memory, whenever one did meet up with a few colleagues, in our cups we all invariably ended up pounding the table and railing at the iniquities and injustices to which we thought we were subjected. Indeed the manner in which we thought our distant Head Office disregarded us is well illustrated by the case of a major air disaster in Morocco. All Branches received an urgent cable in cipher from London advising us to 'exercise caution' as a copy of the Bank's private Code Book had been on board and had not been recovered from the crash site. No mention was made of our colleague (killed in the crash) in whose charge the book had been. In later years matters did improve, but only because the Bank realised they could not otherwise retain the experienced staff they needed to successfully run their business.

Our up-country 'hero' mentioned above, won £5,000 on the Football Pools when the maximum possible £75,000 jackpot was beyond all dreams of avarice. A small fortune in those post-war days - £5,000 represented at least five years' salary.

(As a Branch manager at Takoradi's Market Circle office I didn't achieve the magical threshold of £1,000 per annum until 1956 - thus becoming in John Betjeman's immortal words "A Thousand-a-Year Man."). As soon as the Pools cheque arrived and was safely cleared he locked up the Bank one afternoon, telling the clerks not to bother coming in the next day. He left the strongroom keys for safe keeping with the United Africa Company manager and before departing for the nearest airfield - never to be seen or heard of again - despatched a cable to London, painstakingly encoded in the Bank's own private five-letter ciphers. When de-coded at Head Office - the cable was alleged to have spelled out: "FUCK OFF (STOP) HAVE RESIGNED (STOP) ABUSIVE LETTER FOLLOWS (STOP)"

There were others we appreciated whose originality and determination set them far beyond the confines of conventional employment in a respectable City of London bank. Distance loosed the chains that bound them to the office desk.

In northern Nigeria until the mid-Fifties many areas had no effective telephone services (even less so today) - telegrams being despatched by post or special messenger. At the dusty town of Maiduguri near Lake Chad, the Bank's Inspector arrived one Wednesday afternoon, after a long and tiring journey over rough roads from Kano. The telegram he had sent two days earlier to warn of his imminent arrival had obviously not been received. The Bank was locked; the notice pinned to the door bore the message. "GONE SHOOTING, BACK ON FRIDAY."

One learned with admiration of the two up-country managers of the BBWA and Barclays DCO who having decided that competition was both unnecessary and ungentlemanly, arranged to open on alternate days, each agreeing to conduct such business as there was on behalf of the other thus maximising their spare time to pursue their personal interests.

In Takoradi we had an enterprising and frustrated young banker who met the skipper of a yacht who came into the bank one morning as his last port of call before sailing across the Atlantic. Learning that the skipper needed an extra hand - he said, "Give me a few minutes to pack, I'll come with you." He was last seen waving cheerfully from the yacht as it passed out beyond the breakwater.

There was a breadth of interest and expertise among the expatriate staff which I suppose drove many of them to pursue a career in West Africa in the first place, banking was a simple and relatively painless path to free them from the humdrum life of a City clerk. *'Carpe diem'* became the motto of many an enterprising bachelor expatriate banker.

A one-time Curator of Reptiles at the London Zoo (Jack Lester) in the 1950s had earlier been a BBWA banker in Sierra Leone and had (very sensibly in my opinion) spent more time collecting wildlife than minding the books. Sadly he was to die after contracting a serious illness while on an expedition to Guyana with David Attenborough in 1955. One can be reasonably certain that it was not a driving ambition to be a successful banker that had first taken him to the West Coast of Africa.

There was a manager in a remote Nigerian up-country branch who received a brief cable from Head Office instructing him to hand over the Bank to a relief who would arrive within a few days and then to fly back to London immediately. No reason was given. Fearing that he was to be sacked - long periods of solitude in remote, difficult places frequently induce bouts of paranoia - and a guilty conscience. He sat up all that night with a bottle of whisky brooding over his fate. The next morning having sent for a gang of labourers, he removed all of the Bank's furniture from his bungalow, had it piled into a heap in his compound and set fire to it. Going into the office, intending to do the same with the furniture, all the files and anything else he could easily shift - he glanced at the morning's mail lying on his desk. He opened a letter from London addressed to him marked 'Confidential.' In it the General Manager congratulated him on his new promotion to a senior position in Head Office. Such were the elements of low farce that lightened our days. The departing manager subsequently explained the total lack of furniture to his relief by saying airily "It was all totally rotten old boy, riddled with termites, a danger to life and limb. Write it off and buy some more from the PWD - I'll explain it all to Head Office when I get to London!"

I suppose the ultimate example of 'Office Palaver' occurred when the Bank of British West Africa* was driven to close down its sole Liberian Branch in Monrovia in the late 1930s allegedly because of the intransigence of the Firestone Rubber Company. The Bank (from 1931 on) had administered the 'Liberian Loan Account' under the auspices of the League of Nations thus exciting the ire of Firestone who otherwise more or less controlled Liberia's economy and still exerted much influence in the 1950s and 60s up until the violent end of President Tubman's rule. Firestone managed to bring the Bank to a virtual standstill by drawing an incredible number of cheques on their account for small amounts of cash, often only a few pence (Liberian currency

---

* According to Graham Greene in his Liberian travel memoir 'Journey Without Maps' (Heinemann 1936) the British Bank finally withdrew from Monrovia when the manager died of yellow fever – one Liberian authority claiming that as 'there was no indigenous yellow fever in Liberia' the deceased therefore must have contracted his final fatal illness in Lagos, the Liberian view being that any local cases were transmitted by preventative innoculation.

was then both the US dollar and sterling) in an endless queue of people either cashing a Firestone cheque or re-depositing the same small amount when they reached the head of the queue again. I was told that (almost) the last straw as far as the Bank was concerned was when the Manager was arrested early one morning by the police who had been lurking in his garden shrubbery. He was charged with 'Indecent Exposure' and heavily fined - his crime was that he had gone on to his verandah in the early morning, yawning and scratching while still dressed in his pyjamas – this being deemed sufficient evidence for the Court.

NOTE: copies of letter to accompany 'Office Palavers.' This is but one of several letters I received from Kofi Mankwah, which helped to spark off my reluctantly aborted assault on his person.

"*Tamale, July 1 1959.*

Dear Manager,

This is to explain the reason why I send you that amount ten pounds (£10)*. It is just for your coca-colla. As a matter of fact what you have done and still doing to me is really worth more than the amount mentioned but just take that for the mean time. Through your help I have developed my work. One thing I should like to tell you is this, that you should not be afraid of any private thing we talk about. Nothing will ever be exposed.   *(Sent to me by way of a 'dash'.)

Please do not mind the Quarter Master of the Army Camp whether they sign the order or not I have work to do to cover the amount I borrow from you, therefore kindly let me have my balance of loan. Through your help my workshop is nicely furnished; now I need a capital to be paying my workmen regularly and so that I am ready to do the monthly payment of hundred pounds (£100) without failing.

Therefore I humbly supplicate your pardon to give me the balance of my loan as early as possible otherwise my business will be damaged and that will mean break of promise which is bad.

I hope this explanation and sympathetic request will meet your favourable consideration.

I have the honour to be Sir,   Yours obediently,   signed   KOFI MANKWAH"

The incident involving the clerk Francis, myself and the fracas with the postmaster had commenced with the following anonymous letter I received but had not as yet formulated any satisfactory course of action.

"Dear Sir,

I have the honour to inform you that an employee of yours, by name Mister Francis ******* according to him, in your department has grossly revealed my savings account to my fiancee and as a result quarrels have been ensued.

For your information the said Mister ****** has taken the advantage of his post, best known to himself and has been flirting with people's wife/wives.

I should therefore be grateful if you would be kind enough to ask Mr. ****** to stop revealing savings account to people; either directly or indirectly.

I have the honour to be, Sir,

Yours sincerely, signed 'A Well Wisher'

After the confrontation in my office between the sorely wounded postmaster and Francis - followed by the withdrawal of all postal services from the Bank - I asked Francis to give me his written report on the matter, preparatory to some sort of disciplinary action - or not, as the case might be. (This must have been the sort of dispute that would have driven King Solomon quite mad.) This is what Francis then wrote for me:-

c/o Bank of West Africa Ltd.,
Tamale, **th June, 196*.

"Dear Sir,

On the **th June 196*, about 11.55 a.m. a certain man who claimed to be on the staff of Post Office, Tamale entered into the Bank and threatened me at the top of his voice. The following is an extract of what he said.

"Any surplus cash, You are a thief, You are a thief, You will see. If you do not want trouble, bring the money. We put on tie when it is hot. When you put on tie it does not mean you are a gentleman, I am from the Post Office and we are all responsible." The following clerks on our staff were in the office, Messrs. (here followed the names of four of the clerks who witnessed the scene).

I am asking for your permission to report this fabricated accusation to Police for immediate investigations today **th June 196*; in that I was threatened in the Bank while on duty, or else I would have got in touch with the Police early enough without any reference to you when I became uneasy over this matter. I want to make a point amply clear here. I am taking anything for granted. Until this matter is investigated by Police I will neither be satisfied nor drop it. It is only the findings of the Police will enable him to determine what further legal courses are open to me.

Yours faithfully, signed FRANCIS *******"

I cannot remember what action I took in the end, if any, I think I probably spoke reasonably sternly to Francis, and apart from giving the postmaster the overdraft he wanted I merely adopted that invaluable tactic, indispensable to the indecisive (or merely idle) throughout the ages - masterly inactivity.

A colleague in another Bank received the following touching missive from a member of his staff:-

"The Manager,

******* Bank, Accra.

"APPLICATION FOR LOAN"

Dear Sir,

I have the honour to tender this my humble application for your candid consideration and prompt approval.

I have accidentally taken seed with a young girl, who is an apprentice to a seamstress at Aburi. According to the Akan custom, the father of the girl on knowing the present condition of his daughter, called the mother and her relatives and asked of the man who conceived the daughter.

The girl, by name **** ***** mentioned my name to the parents. Truly, I am the sole doer of the action - "Conception." The relatives therefore called at my house and according to the Akan custom, informed me that I have incurred a debt of (£32.14s.6d.) Thirty two pounds fourteen shillings and sixpence.

This debt runs as follows: I am to refund (£25) Twenty five pounds for the cost of the Sewing Machine the father bought for the girl in connection with her apprenticeship as a Seamstress. Secondly I am to pacify the father with One Bottle Whisky and a cash of (£4.4s.0d.) Four pounds four shillings. Thirdly I am to give the mother of the girl and her relatives (£2.2s.0d.) Two pounds two shillings known as a pacification fee. After all these expenses I am also bound to take care of the pregnant girl until she delivers. This is treated customarily according to the Akan Laws. If after the girl's delivery, and I have the love to marry her, then I have to prepare and approach the parents in our own customary way of marriage. In fact to be frank and sincere I have no savings to relieve me from this trouble of indebtedness.

I am therefore soliciting your kind favour to tender this my application for a loan of (£25) Twenty Five pounds, which if granted, I promise faithfully to pay (£3) Three pounds monthly, by the debit of my account.

Hoping this will meet your candid consideration and approval; as I am to settle this case by the month ending.

I have the honour to be Sir, your obedient servant, signed *****

I asked my friend whether he had in fact granted his clerk's request, couched as it was in such courteous, detailed and desperate terms. "No" - he said, "I couldn't see my way clear to explaining it away to Head Office. But I did lend him the money from my own pocket."

'Office Palaver' could also take on a political tint as it did in Tamale in 1960 when Paul Gautier was manager of the French trading company with his office in the low-roofed store next to the Bank. The French were not popular in most of the sub-Saharan countries of Africa at that time as they were planning a series of atomic bomb tests at Reggane in the Algerian desert which was only a matter of a few hundred miles to the north of Ghana's borders. These tests were believed to be scheduled to coincide with the prevailing Harmattan wind which would almost certainly deposit radioactive Saharan dust over vast (non-French) areas of West Africa. In all the local markets entrepreneurs were selling a popular line in 'anti-radiation' protective cotton skull caps.

Much publicity was given both locally and internationally to a large group of 'Bomb Marchers' made up of protesters (mostly wearing sandals) from the CND, pacifist clergymen from assorted religious sects, environmentalists, protesters from 'non-aligned' nations - including a party of belled and bangled traditional dancers from India. These having assembled at Accra were intending to process on foot, accompanied by local ruling party activists, demonstrating as they went until such time as they arrived at the French Atomic Test Site in the desert - ready to immolate themselves in the cause of universal Peace and Brotherhood. In Ghana popular feeling was being whipped-up into political frenzy by Dr. Kwame N'Krumah's left wing anti-colonialist government, who at the same time were urging a boycott on French goods and French trading companies. Anything at all to do with France in Ghana was rapidly becoming anathema as the 'Bomb Marcher's' circus slowly progressed northwards towards Ghana's borders with Upper Volta (now Burkina Faso).

The 'Bomb Marchers' arrived in Tamale after several weeks on the road from the coast and soon made their presence felt with a series of rallies culminating with a mass 'popular' demonstration outside Paul Gautier's store. From the Bank next door I popped my head out occasionally to see what was going on as the banners and the chanting crowds multiplied. Being the pragmatist that he was I was confident that Gautier would take it in his stride - and by midday he had ordered his staff to close the store (no customers were foolish enough to brave the mob), to put the shutters down and for their own safety leave by the back door. By the early afternoon Gautier was fed up with all the noise so he departed himself by the same route - all the action being at the front of the building facing the market and the road. He drove home, had some lunch and a while later after a short siesta decided he might as well go and play tennis at the Tamale Gymkhana Club. Having changed into his sports kit he drove back down into town. It was mid-afternoon and if anything by now the crowd was even bigger and noisier and the police were conspicuous by their absence. Gautier stopped his car nearby.

Clad in white shorts and shirt and clutching his racket, he mingled with the rear of the mob. He was soon noticed and a space cleared around him. Most of the Tamale crowd at that time would have known him by sight. The throng grew silent, watching him expectantly.

They were not disappointed, realising that something was required of him, he reacted. Brandishing his tennis racket above his head he shouted. "What are you waiting for? BURN ZE PLACE DOWN! See if I care - I've got better things to do than hang around here - I'm off to play tennis!"

The reaction of the crowd was instantaneous and typically Ghanaian. A few minutes earlier and left to them the crowd might have done anything in the critical state the chanting and the slogans had inspired. As it was they all fell about laughing uproariously, slapping each other on the back, pointing at Gautier with tears running down their faces. It was all over, the crowd dispersed laughing and shouting, all their pent-up anger vanished in hilarity and amusement. The 'Bomb Marchers' folded up their banners and took themselves off as well, probably heartily relieved that their demonstration had ended without violence.

It was to be another thirty-eight years before I heard the sequel to that story. All that time Gautier kept his own counsel, during the many hunting trips we made together in the West African bush, his subsequent visits to London, plus the delivery of a new dog (and Orkney lobsters) to our new Lake District home in 1969. In late 1997 we called in at his home near La Rochelle to see him for what we already feared was almost certainly the last time. Poor Paul, only two years older than I, was now reduced to a pale shadow of his former self. No longer the strutting, stocky, dark little Napoleon of a man that I had known in our youth. Nevertheless he was as restless as ever, aggressive, arrogant, self-important, amusing and charming - and I warmed to him as always. As his spirits revived with food, drink and company he started to reminisce.

It was O. who reminded him of the 'Bomb Marchers.' "There was much more to it than you knew." he said, "The French government took it all very seriously at the time. There was no way they were going to postpone the Bomb tests because of a bunch of *sandalistas*. The French Embassy in Accra called me to a meeting with the *Deuxième Bureau** who had travelled out from Paris. We agreed a 'code' and I was to keep them informed by telegraph of the marchers' progress and whatever else I could find out. When I knew the protesters had left Tamale en route to the border with Haute Volta I sent a cable to Ouagadougou (the capital of Upper Volta) saying *"Expect your visitors within twenty-four hours."* The border was then closed and kept closed until the 'Bomb Marchers' realised the game was up and they packed up and went home." But that wasn't the end of the story.

A few weeks later one of Gautier's 'trusted' customers had decamped with a truckload of goods on credit from the Tamale store - plus the lorry - the major part of which also belonged to the CFAO** Motors Department. On the grapevine (in West Africa more properly 'the talking drums') Gautier learned the same day that the trader had headed due north for the border with French territory and had declared that he was going to sell off both truck and cargo in Ouagadougou the capital of Upper Volta (now Burkina Faso) and that CFAO and Gautier could both 'go take a running jump' or words to that effect. By late afternoon that same day Gautier was roaring northwards in his big Morris kit-car up the Bolgatanga road making for the frontier - a total journey not far short of three hundred miles. Determined to recover the stolen goods he drove on through the night, barely slowing his breakneck speed as he passed through the occasional villages - where the goats and sheep slept on or wandered across the laterite and pot-holed tarmac. By midnight, tired and dusty, he was in Ouagadougou and screeched to a stop outside the Gendarmerie. All was in darkness as he mounted the steps and hammered on the doors. After a few minutes the door creaked cautiously open, a Frenchman wearing a stained singlet, shorts and his uniform képi peered out. Holding a torch to see who was disturbing the peace at that time of night the gendarme said. "Who are you? What do you want?"

"Je m'appelle Gautier. Gautier de Tamalé, je viens pour ....." He was not allowed to finish, the gendarme grabbed him by the arm and pulled him inside shaking him vigorously by the hand. *"Monsieur Gautier? - de Tamalé vraiment!* Welcome *mon ami*, we have much to thank you for." Inside the gendarmerie Gautier said it was a hive of

---

* The French Intelligence/Security Service, rather like MI5.
** Compagnie Francaise de l'Afrique Occidentale

activity. There were banks of humming radios and monitoring equipment manned by French technicians, the blacked-out exterior of the building belied the bustle inside. There had either been a bomb test that day, or one was expected, in the desert to the north.

While being fed and given cognac and coffee he explained the reason for his mission. He said he believed the fugitive trader and the truck would have arrived in the town earlier that evening. "*Pas de probléme!*" Said the senior gendarme. "You want your lorry and your goods? We will have them for you by daybreak! That is the least we can do to repay you."

Gautier said that the policeman was true to his word. Before dawn the truck with its load still intact was under armed guard outside the gendarmerie, its erstwhile owner nursing a large lump on his head while manacled to the front fender. "What happened to the poor chap?" I asked. "I didn't care - that was no longer my business" replied Gautier, "but I had my truck and my goods back in Tamale before dark that same day."

Whenever I hear or see a French military parade on some television news report - in the distance the band always seems to be playing a version of "*En passant par la Lorraine*" and my memory goes back over the years to the times when careering with him over some dusty bush road in Africa, Gautier would sing his old French marching songs. "*Oh! Oh! Oh! Avec mes sabots.*"

Gautier eventually became General Manager of CFAO in Nigeria. I learned that at his first monthly meeting of the nine directors of his various subsidiaries, he addressed them thus. "Gentlemen, *Messieurs*. Pay attention! When I was in your position we used to call the GM - where I am sitting now, '*Le Vieux Con.*' I have to inform you that I am now 'The Old C***t' and I wish you to understand that I know all the tricks you can play on me - or think you can, because I have tried them all. I warn you now once and for all - I know everything and more than you do - if you try to play silly buggers with me, I will come down on you like a wagon load of horse shit. *Je suis maintenant 'Le Vieux Con' Vraiment!*"

In early 1969 Gautier came to London, and we took him to the National Army Museum. As befitted a former *sous officier* in the French Army, he was totally bemused by what he saw. "What are all these victorious battles against the French? Pah! In France we have *nevair* heard of them, *nevair*! One or two of them perhaps, but only as mere tactical skirmishes. And as for victories - where is *your* history of all the times the French beat the English and sent them packing - I suppose you will tell me they were nothing more than mere forgotten skirmishes too!"

(Monsieur Paul GAUTIER - décédé le 8 Septembre 1998 à 68 ans)

CHAPTER 21

'Bat Palaver'

"Ere the bat hath flown ...

***The shard borne beetle with his drowsy hums
Hath rung night's yawning peal, there shall be done
A deed of dreadful note."*** *(W Shakespeare - Macbeth)*

Forty years on I still have books and papers which carry a strong whiff of Africa on their fusty pages. A smell of ancient, primaeval decay combined with that curious and unmistakable aroma reminiscent of mildewed mosquito nets, instantly recognisable to anyone who lived in such places before the days of air-conditioning. Prints and books are randomly stained with brown and dirty-black splatters that look like some creeping fungus. These are the indelible traces of ancient bat droppings.

Before ending up in Lagos, at first when alone in the Gold Coast and later with O. we had mostly lived in houses or bungalows which had wooden shutters and windows that were usually wide open to catch the benefit of any cooling breeze. After dark the pools of interior light attracted swarms of moths and insects - and also the myriad bats that found these a tasty snack. In Sekondi in the living room of my bachelor quarters above the Bank I had a large corner lamp made from an empty glass 20 litre Algerian wine jar (in 1954 this cost one shilling and sixpence a litre - jar included). My cat would sit near this in the evenings waiting for the bats to arrive; they would swoop and flit in tight circles in the darker corners, darting over to the light to seize their prey while the cat danced on its hind legs, paws flailing the air in futile pursuit of the elusive *Chiropterae*. Nearby the pale-coloured house lizards would also gather on the walls on the edge of the shadows cast by the lamps waiting for the opportunity to pounce on the insects.

If there had been recent rain the house would sometimes become the focal point of swarms of new-hatched 'sausage' flies - a myriad host of winged termites looking for a new home. Within a few minutes of arrival these inch-long, plump and juicy 'sausage' flies would shed their lacy wings around the lamps, falling to the floor where they then commenced their mating ritual - linking head to tail in an orgiastic conga line, shuffling and swaying in their thousands across the floor like endless moving strings of beads. They were a positive hazard on a polished floor; a careless foot upon a few fat and juicy termites was as dangerous as treading unawares upon an abandoned roller skate or a banana skin. One can eat them. Deep fried and crisp they are supposed to be delicious and easily trapped by simply placing a bowl of water beneath a lamp. The Africans were said to relish them like this - given the opportunity today I would try them too, but I suppose I was then too squeamish. The following morning the piled-up heaps of their corpses would have to be swept up by the houseboy before the waves of scavenging ants arrived.

There were times when I was sufficiently irritated by the bats to join my cat, flailing my arms to try and drive them out of the room. To close the shutters was not an option, to be left to sweat and stew in the steamy heat was worse than the bats. Once I was so annoyed by a swarm of a dozen or more bats squeaking (in those days I could still hear them) and hawking in the dark corners of my living room that I seized my tennis racquet and joined combat with these creatures of the night, like a frenzied rally up against the net at Wimbledon.

I won the game with a classic forehand smash, a satisfying 'Splat!' A tiny scrap of fur and near transparent wings, white chested and flecked with gore, slid down the wall leaving a bloody smear - to be pounced on and carried off in feline glee by Puss. After that I gave up, consumed with anthropomorphic guilt and conceding set and match to my tormentors.

Still None The Wiser

The principal problem with bats lay with their habit of remaining in the house after one had retired to bed. They would hang upside down on the wires from which the mosquito netting was suspended. Their constant crunching of beetles and moths was quite audible - discarded wing cases, inedible legs and carapaces would be left to litter the floor and the top of the mosquito net like the debris from some late-night take-away frequented by drunks and 'clubbers.' That and the fact that while they fed they also squittered out streams of corrosive droppings, green and semi-liquid crap which stained nets and clothing - not to mention books and papers left open anywhere near a bat roosting upside down on picture rail or ceiling light. The stains were more or less permanent. To avoid the fine spray of liquid bat poop which filtered through the net onto the innocent sleeper below it was common practice to spread an old cotton sheet over the canopy to give shelter from the nightly downpour.

The much larger fruit bats with their luminous eyes and large disproportionate heads like a blunt-nosed fox were common, but were no problem in the house as they fed at night over a wide area wherever they could find ripe fruit. The problem with these inoffensive creatures was their daytime habits. If one's house was surrounded by mature shade trees - this was often their chosen roost. Chittering sociably in the topmost branches, with their two foot wingspans wrapped around their suspended bodies like Dracula's cloak they fluttered and flapped for ventilation through the heat of the day while excreting the plentiful bat-squit, as loose as one would expect from their night-long diet of overripe fruit. This meant that it was distinctly unwise to park one's car under the shade of such a tree. Their saving grace, in the north of Ghana at least, was that if in sufficient numbers - they could often be driven off by small boys with their slingshots and catapults who would bombard them to distraction. Those that they felled to the ground were pounced upon and carried off with glee, the flesh of the fruit bat, dried and smoked being a rich addition to anyone's stewpot. Strung up for sale in the market their mummified corpses looked like nothing so much as illustrations of *Homunculae* in some mediaeval treatise on demonology.

It was in Lagos, driving in to work, that I sometimes saw great wispy trails of these fruit bats swirling in their thousands high up in the early morning air, particularly so during any rainy period when the sun was hidden by mist and cloud. I remarked on this phenomenon from time to time to various acquaintances only to be greeted with utter disbelief or to be told that I was seeing spots before my eyes. It served to confirm my long-held conviction that a significant majority of people go through life virtually oblivious to the sights and sounds of the natural world around them, and who are also incapable of seeing many strange and beautiful phenomena that are daily presented before their noses - if it isn't familiar, then it is invisible, *ergo* - it doesn't exist.**

In Tamale I once read in a book about ancient Peru that the Inca nobles wore cloaks made of the fur of vampire bats to ward off the cold of the Andes. This excited my interest. I remembered that while shooting bush fowl one afternoon far out beyond the fringes of the road that led west to the ferry at Yapei I had discovered a stream that meandered across the orchard bush, hidden beneath a shaded canopy of tall overhanging trees. As I had slithered and tripped in the dappled sunshine along the steep banks I disturbed large numbers of fruit bats that flopped and tumbled among the tangle of branches above me. I remembered this and thought I would return to bag one, to see what the pelt was like - and if they would repay the trouble of skinning them.

I think I have noted elsewhere that this narrative is not politically correct, I make no apologies - the term had not been invented in my youth and there were few acquaintances in my world then, of either sex, who could have met the demands of today's strict criteria. (In the same way that 'Political Correctness' is now described by imprudent or foolishly daring souls as the enemy of rational thought – so it is also patronising in the extreme to attribute more modern standards and ideals to people and events in the distant past - my case rests.)

So, one afternoon an hour or two before dusk I put five or six shotgun cartridges in my pocket before setting off, a couple for the specimen bat at most - leaving three or four for any subsequent target of opportunity - perhaps a green pigeon, plump and juicy from the wild fig trees, or if luckier then a guinea fowl for the pot. I found the stream again and the bats with no trouble. In the shady tangle of branches above the stream the bats still flopped and flitted like shadows as they became agitated at my approach. With some difficulty in the confined space I fired a shot - a clean miss, then another clean miss. Nothing.

More fruit bats came out, disturbed by the shooting. I looked more closely at my quarry to study their pattern of flight - their wingspread was close to two feet - but the wings were mere transparent membranes of skin stretched on a fragile skeleton through which the diffused afternoon sunshine could be seen. Their bodies were much smaller than I had supposed and in proportion the heads much larger. But what

---

* In 1521 Fernando Magellan, the Spanish navigator made the observation that in unexplored Pacific and South American waters, the local natives appeared totally unable to see his ships until the crew's features could be distinguished. As the ships were so strange and unknown, therefore they could not exist.

was most significant was that unlike a bird their flight was definitely irregular, up and down - a ragged, tumbling flight almost as if the wingtips remained fixed and the body bobbed up and down between - like a model studio vampire bat flying on wires in some ancient horror film.

In rapid succession I fired another two shots, again both clean misses. The problem was that in the confines of the trees the range of any clearly visible target was too short to allow a spread of pellets. It was like trying to shoot a sparrow on the wing with an airgun - inside a woodshed. My fifth shot finally connected and a wounded bat tumbled down, but as it fell it clutched at a branch over the water and it hung there upside down several feet above me. I could not reach the bat with a stick and it hung there glaring mournfully at its now reluctant persecutor. What to do? I had but one cartridge remaining - if I backed off far enough perhaps I could bring the whole unfortunate affair to an end, to get a clear view of the bat from the required twenty yards was virtually impossible. Still, I had to try.

I took out the last cartridge and looked at it. Disaster! It was not bird shot at all - it was a single, solid twelve-bore bullet, meant for crocodile or larger game that I always carried in case of need. Damn! I could not leave the bat to suffer - to be certain of hitting such a small target with a single ball I needed to be no more than a few feet distant. Drawing a careful bead from about ten feet away I fired. I suppose the nearest equivalent would be that of a battleship engaging a rowing boat with a sixteen-inch gun at point-blank range.

I managed to fish out a few shreds of skin and bone from the water still attached to part of the fox-like head with its needle-sharp, grinning teeth. As for the fur, it was sparse and gingery in appearance, quite useless - except of course to a bat. As I left, the surface of the muddy stream rippled and quivered as the black and whiskery mudfish fought for the scraps of flesh. Walking back with my empty gun the mile or so to the road where I had left the car I flushed a bunch of guinea fowl.

CHAPTER 22

'The Crocodile'

*"It is shaped, sir, like itself, and it is as broad
as it has breadth; it is just as high as it is,
and moves with its own organs:
it lives by that which nourisheth it;
and the elements once out of it, it transmigrates."*
('Antony and Cleopatra' - Wm. Shakespeare)

Everything around me is pitch black except for a few stars among thickening clouds in a moonless African night. The only other light comes from a dim electric head-torch constricting my brow, strapped round my head above my ears. As I turn my head the furthest feeble rays of the torch illuminate a circle of twinkling ruby-red, fiery sparks on the surface of the water in which I find myself standing waist-deep. Some of these menacing sparks are set in pairs, slowly moving closer, some appear single - unwinking and unmoving. From somewhere close by in the darkness there erupts the blood-curdling, high pitched scream of a tree hyrax, which as it reaches its bubbling crescendo is suddenly cut short, as if a dagger had been plunged into its heart. The gun I am clutching to my chest with a vice like grip suddenly seems heavy and useless. The high pitched whine of mosquitoes sings in my ears - mingling with the cacaphonic chirruping, croaking, whistling and groaning cries of a multitude of frogs. Am I now truly *mad*? Is this some sort of waking nightmare I was trapped in forever?

"*Psst!*" Hissed my companion, virtually invisible a few yards away except for his own dim head-torch - only his torso above the dark water. "There's a big one over there to the right - must be an six-footer at least! Look at the space between his eyes - *Wow!*"

'Psst' indeed! I thought to myself, I should be so lucky! It would help make more sense of the ludicrous - and perhaps dangerous situation in which I now found myself.

Ian Wright,[*] the BAT tobacco buyer, had persuaded me (much against O.'s better judgement) to go crocodile shooting with him - at night - wading out into the murky waters of the Tamale reservoir. This comprised several acres of reed-fringed

---

[*] (Born 2 Jan 1928 - dec'd 6 Aug. 2001 R.I.P)

liquid mud infested with shoals of crocodiles of all sizes that in daylight could be seen either basking on the muddy banks behind the dam, or slowly cruising - bulbous eyes and snouts awash, with only the slightest of swirls from their barely moving tails. One moment they were there on the surface, the next - a tiny ripple and they were gone. The beached saurians, if disturbed could move with astonishing rapidity, lashing their tails and racing for the safety of the water, where they just as swiftly vanished.

Ian had said that he had done this before - the trick, he said, was to wait for a moonless night - the better to see the crocs, and so that they could not see us. This seemed fine, although I had less faith in his assertion about the crocodiles' defective night vision than he did.

Ian with his little .22 bolt-action rifle seemed a teensy-weensy bit undergunned to me, but he was quite adamant as to his ability to nail a crocodile in the dark - between the eyes - with such a puny weapon and a tiny crumb of lead. I was as usual to use my twelve-bore single-barrelled shotgun loaded with heavy buckshot - there was less danger with this of ricochets bouncing off the water and ending up in the now darkened huts fringing the outskirts of town, beyond the far end of the dam half-a-mile and more distant.

"Fine! OK!" I said, "Sounds like a good idea to me." Ian said he would fix it with the PWD waterworks watchman who would collect the carcasses when they floated to the surface the next morning, to take them to the skinners in the market. The hides would be dry-salted for us in exchange for the meat. Ian made it sound like a jolly good idea indeed - particularly when the plan was hatched over a couple of beers in broad daylight!

At ten o'clock at night, waist-deep in water in near pitch darkness - warily watching the fiery eyes of the alleged 'six-footer' fixing his unwinking glare upon us - to me he seemed to have the potential to be much larger as the distance between his glinting red eyes widened as he changed position. I was now deciding quite definitely that it was *not* 'a good idea' - the immediacy of 'practice' was rapidly replacing airy-fairy 'theory!' I was beginning to become concerned that in the darkness behind us perhaps an unseen 'eight-footer' was coming even closer. "Aim right between the eyes - and we'll fire together on the count of three." Whispered Ian. "One - Two - THREE!"

"Splat!" Went his pipsqueak .22 rifle - immediately followed by a great gout of flame and "BLAMMM!!" as my shotgun discharged its load of buckshot. When my eyes had recovered sufficiently from the glare of the muzzle-blast to direct my dim headtorch over the surrounding expanse of water - there was nothing to be seen. No fiery eyes, no thrashing, dying crocodile - nothing, barely a ripple. Even the booming of the frogs was shocked into silence.

We waded back to shore, to smoke a quiet cigarette to discourage the mosquitoes which now whined about us in clouds - and to plan the next attack. After allowing the uproar caused by our earlier assault to subside for about ten minutes we moved down the bank and once again entered the water, quietly wading out and waiting until we were again ringed by the unblinking stare of some twenty or so assorted crocodiles. "*Pop*-Splat! Went the pip-squeak .22 rifle. ***BLAMM!!***"went my 12 bore, again on the count of three. I was getting used to the system now, but still experiencing a definite feeling of over-exposure in my fully clothed, submerged (and rapidly shrinking) nether parts.

We repeated the exercise another couple of times with as little apparent result as the first - and then went home to bed. O. was I think, quite as relieved to see me as I was to be intact, in one piece and on dry land. She had heard the shooting from the stoep of our bungalow which lay about a mile away up the wooded slopes to the north.

Ian came into the Bank mid-morning to report the score. "Zero - bloody ZERO! That idiot nightwatch - he said to me - 'No-ting Massah, too-too much crocodile dey for water dis time - if you go kill-am - they go chop-um one time! You plenty lucky dey no chop you!!'" Ian continued - "I bet that bloody nightwatch was down there at first light - he's fished them out and by now they're skins and meat in the market - and cash in his pocket!"

The truth of the matter will never be known. The general belief was that a dead croc did sink and would only surface much later for an hour or two when its stomach gases had expanded sufficiently to overcome the reptile's slight negative buoyancy. But it was the dry season and any stretch of permanent water acted like a magnet to the displaced and hungry crocodiles that one frequently saw wandering over the countryside by night - scuttling bow-legged in the car headlights across the bush roads, some of them considerably larger than the 'six-footer' that had first drawn our fire. I am certain they would have had no qualms about eating each other (or us) in the right circumstances.

There were various myths about crocs - how true these tales were I never knew, but certain of them we accepted as gospel. First and most relevant was the belief that certain areas or stretches of water were safe - the resident crocodiles would not attack humans. Still water was reckoned to be 'safe' in general (until proven otherwise), but then in certain areas of the north the crocodiles themselves were also safe from persecution - being 'fetish' inasmuch as they were the living repositories of the spirits of tribal ancestors.

In running water crocs were never 'ju-ju' as far as I could discover, and it was always advisable to enquire at the nearest local settlement or of passing fishermen whether or not they were 'safe' before wading in to recover a shot duck perhaps or pushing our boat across shallows. A good indicator in riverside villages was to look out for one-legged or one-armed inhabitants and to enquire as to the reason for their present disability. When in my second year in the north we first trial-launched our newly constructed boat on a small tributary of the Volta - we very soon ran into a tangle of nets and fishing lines stretched across the river hard by a village, blocking any further progress upstream. Someone had to get out into the water and unwind the bird's-nest of net and line from the jammed outboard propeller. "Crocodile de-deh?" Shouted R. to a small crowd of villagers who had gathered. "Yes - big one 'e deyoh but 'e no fit chop any whiteman!" Came the equivocal answer from a one-legged onlooker leaning on a rough hewn crutch. We sensibly cut the tangle free with a sharp knife from inside the boat and made our retreat downstream into less obstructed waters.

Shooting crocodiles is a poor sport from the point of view of recovering the quarry. I never really cracked the problem - nor knew any whiteman apart from the army subalterns in Tamale who managed this - their limited successes I shall recount later.

There are three resident species of crocodile in West Africa. There is the small 'Broad-Fronted' variety (*Osteolaemus tetraspis*), quite rare, mostly solitary and living in dense forest habitat - I once wasted an hour or so in the Ikorodu bush in Southern Nigeria while Ben Ladipo and his fellow hunters poked around with sticks and waded and thrashed about in a large muddy puddle - sticking their arms shoulder-deep into tangles of water-logged roots searching for the creature they insisted was there. As this incident indicates, it is relatively harmless, a solitary forest dweller that rarely grows more than three or at the most four feet in size - and it is of course mainly constructed of meat, which is why Ben and his merry men were after it. They didn't catch it on this occasion.

Then there is the much bigger 'gharial' (*Crocodylus cataphractus*) also quite uncommon, said to reach as much as eighteen feet in length, a crocodile with a long, narrow snout, which lives almost entirely on fish - except when the water dries up (the fish bury themselves in the mud until it rains again) when it will roam on dry land and attack small mammals and antelope, lying in wait for them at night. I saw these at the

Mole Game Reserve in the north of Ghana - where Chadwick the Head Warden and his Game Scouts had killed several that were decimating the smaller varieties of game in the dry bush near the almost waterless river. Their desiccated corpses, long jaws with needle-sharp teeth propped open with sticks formed a macabre decoration to the approaches to the main camp.

The 'Nile' crocodile (C. Niloticus) is the common or garden variety and the real villain of the piece. This is the creature that Ian Wright and I were after on our nighttime venture - the croc that we all know and visualise when his ugly snout pops into mind. In my time in the 1950s and 1960s they were still generally plentiful - although heavily persecuted in many places. Around Lagos in the extensive creeks and lagoons that stretched west to Dahomey (now Benin) and (confusingly) east to Benin City and the Niger Delta, they were uncommon. In 1964 or 1965 I did see one monster in a mangrove-fringed lagoon several miles up Badagry Creek - Jacques and I had gone out in his fast boat very early one Sunday morning specifically to look for them. I only saw the great ugly flat head rear out of the water a split second before we ran over it, fortunately without making contact. It was a huge head that must have been attached to a twelve or fourteen-foot body, no doubt fattened on the big, black, spiny catfish that lived up the brackish waters of the creeks. Even had there been time, I would have definitely hesitated before trying to shoot a monster like this! At that time I used to hunt with Ben Ladipo and his Yoruba followers up the Ogun River to the west of Ikorodu and although it was typical habitat - Ben said there were none of these left, except for one big one "'E clever too much, 'e go tief de fish from de hook at night, once I see his track - 'e plenty big-oh!" This croc was apparently clever enough to evade the traps and baited lines that were laid for it.

The Nile crocodile was common forty years ago in Ghana - but I believe now that in places they may have been persecuted to the point where they could be endangered although the vast flooded area of the Volta dam must provide ideal habitat. I came across them right from the coast up into the far north in the savannah. In the water supply dam at Inchaban to the east of Sekondi Richard Steimann and I used to fish using as our canoe an old wingtip float from a Sunderland flying boat that had crashed at Takoradi. Here the waters were backed up for two or three miles into thick forest and Patterson the dour, Scots PWD Engineer (who lived a solitary existence in the bungalow on the hill above the pumping station) told us there were no crocs left, that he had shot them all out. This was patently untrue, I think that they had just become extremely wary - we never caught a glimpse of one, but frequently found their tracks on muddy patches of bank, some quite large with footprints bigger than a human hand, and their distinctive hard, white droppings - with traces of indigestible bones and catfish spines, left on grassy spits of land at the waters edge. They would have had quite a fat living with the shy forest antelope whose dainty tracks marked the shore along the forest edge plus the plentiful catfish that grew large on the ripe flesh of palm nuts that fell from the oil palms that overhung the water. Some of these catfish were themselves so plump that they could be fried in their own yellowy-red strips of fat that lay inside their abdominal cavities. Some were also so large that they proved impossible to land using the fairly light spinning rods and tackle that we customarily used. We never saw any other people there for the very good reason that I think it was both a Forest Reserve and a prohibited area for several miles around to avoid pollution of its waters from human habitation. There was evidence of local fishing activity when we sometimes came across 'trot' lines baited with ripe palm nuts or cubes of bar soap (made from palm oil) suspended across narrow inlets and once a dead catfish floating nearby that must have weighed more than sixty pounds.

Inchaban was a magical, lonely stretch of water, surrounded by high forest where troops of showy and colourful Diana monkeys hurled themselves noisily through the treetops. There were flocks of wild grey parrots that would whoop and whistle around our heads when we called to them from our boat out on the water. A pair of River Eagles - African Fishing Eagles - were often to be seen, the high pitched screams of *Cuncumer vocifer* carrying for miles across the water from the sandy shallows to the north where the clear black waters of a forest stream fed the lake, to the southern dam above the filter beds and the huge wood-gas fuelled pumping engine. African darters dived and fished, only their head and necks above water as they swam looking like the 'snake birds' they were sometimes called, they perched with ragged wings outstretched to dry on branches over the water or stood glumly on the bank resembling the traditional 'dying duck in a thunderstorm.' Richard and I had many adventures at Inchaban during the years I lived in Sekondi and Takoradi and we caught many strange fish, some of which were identified only with difficulty from the descriptions in his old, mud-and-water-stained copy of 'Fishes of the Gold Coast.'

The lake at Brimsu (another reservoir behind a dam) to the west of Cape Coast where Richard and I also fished (this was in 1955) was much larger than Inchaban - and definitely held many crocodile, elephant were not unknown in the area which lay on their ancient migratory route that came from Sunyani in Western Ashanti. Around the fringes, along the edges of the reed beds the local fishermen had constructed a few stout timber stockades driven hard into the muddy bottom. These had a weighted sliding door tripped by a stout line to which was attached a lump of bait lashed along a double pointed stick, the latter presumably intended to wedge in the croc's gullet or stomach and act as a hook. Do not ask me how the crocodile once trapped was then subdued and extricated from the stockade. I do not know, but the process must have been exciting.

The fish we caught at Brimsu were mostly various species of *tilapia* and were small compared with those at Inchaban. Whether this was to do with the different crocodile populations, again I do not know. When our fishing palled we sometimes gently cruised the reed-fringed inlets along the shore, trying to surprise an unsuspecting croc at close quarters from our tiny dinghy. One day we did just this with unexpected results. Richard and I had taken along Peter, a stoutish, somewhat plump young Belgian, and our guest out of simple curiosity on his part. Peter was rowing (partly the reason we had brought him), very slowly, as quietly as possible from the centre of our ten foot plastic cockleshell, facing Richard sitting in the stern, his camera at the ready. I was kneeling in the bows - alert as a pointer, holding a 38-inch razor-sharp hunting arrow firmly notched in my 60 pound draw-weight steel bow (I was a keen archer in those days).

As we inched round a reedbed I suddenly saw a crocodile, about six-feet long, eyes apparently closed, with its full length exposed and resting quietly on the surface. It was dead ahead of us and no more than a few feet distant. Without thinking, for none of us had really thought this thing through - I drew the bow to full stretch and loosed the steel barbed arrow at point-blank range, aiming for the soft angle behind and just below the croc's right shoulder, on the waterline. If a crocodile has a heart, this I deduced was where it would be most vulnerable.

The results were as startling and immediate as they were unexpected. Richard managed one exposure as the crocodile launched itself forward like a supercharged torpedo in a great "WHOOSHH!" We were immediately drenched with a shower of muddy water thrown up by the lashing tail as at the same time we drifted on top of the maelstrom. Peter, who had received no forewarning of what I had done, at once dropped the oars into the water in a panic and crouched in the bottom of the boat, hands clasped to his head, wailing and shrieking as the croc twisted and thrashed beneath us, loudly banging and thumping the thin dinghy shell with its tail. As for Richard and myself, there was nothing that we could do except hold fast to the gunwales in the rocking boat. After a few moments the commotion subsided and we drifted (or were driven) away from the swirling centre of the disturbance. Peter, his equanimity now partly restored, roundly cursed Richard and myself in French, English and German - for being a pair of silly, feckless bastards giving him such a severe fright. I think, with hindsight, that he was entirely justified.

Paddling cautiously with a loose floorboard, we recovered the oars from the water. There was no sign of the crocodile. A few bubbles of gas dimpled the surface. Several minutes later as we still watched, the turbid water suddenly swirled once more from the depths and my bright-yellow arrow shaft floated to the surface. I recovered it and examined it closely. The long flight feathers had been stripped off, the yellow paint was scratched but the shaft itself was still intact. The three-inch steel V-shaped head was missing - but the ferrule that had held it to the shaft was neatly snapped in two, leaving behind a half-inch of steel tube still firmly attached to the arrow. This was the strongest part of the arrow, presumably broken and dislodged by the croc rolling and flexing its muscular body. We saw no further trace of anything before the darkening afternoon drove us off the water.

Peter declined any further offers to accompany Richard and me on our fishing trips.

In Tamale the young British subalterns, doing their National Service in 1960 with the Ghana Army (the successor to the Gold Coast Regiment of the old and much-honoured West Africa Frontier Force, still had a proportion of British officers) and they made use of the small sporting armoury that belonged to their Mess.

Using .22 rifles the more bloodthirsty of these 'sportsmen' would of a late, sunny afternoon, creep up behind the waterworks dam, and carefully parting the grass overlaying the bund would peer down on anything up to a dozen or more crocodiles that lay on the shore, basking in the warmth, twenty-five yards or so distant. With such a small-calibre rifle it was essential to go for a brain shot, nothing less would have any effect. To do this, avoiding the thick and bony skull and the armour plated hide, meant placing the first tiny bullet through the eye-socket into the brain pan. Do this properly and with luck you have a dead crocodile that has expired before it reaches the water. Otherwise you have to rely on the uncertain services of the night-watchman, as Ian Wright and I had found out to our disadvantage.

The subalterns valued the skins and skulls as trophies. One afternoon 2nd Lt. B. pulled off the feat of marksmanship that was necessary. The five-foot croc barely flinched at the shot while its companions skittered and raced full pelt for the safety of the water. Taking a long stick to prod the 'dead' reptile before approaching any closer, it still didn't stir - B. then deliberately placed another five pip-squeak .22 bullets into the top of its head at point blank, just to make sure.

Pressing a shilling into the watchman's hand he enlisted the latter's aid in lashing the corpse to a pole, loading it into the back of his borrowed Land Rover. B. proudly drove his prey back to the Officers' Mess as darkness fell. With the help of the Mess corporal B. dragged the reptile by its tail into the ante-room where he laid it out, now freed from its pole and lashings, on the floor by the bar, gaping jaws propped open with a pineapple from the fruit bowl. Pot of beer in hand, elbow on the bar, one foot nonchalantly placed on the ridged back of the deceased, B. awaited the arrival - and the plaudits - of his fellow officers.

"Well done, B!" Rang out the congratulations as they gathered round, toasting B's prowess. The beer flowed for the next half-hour while they urged B. to recount his epic. The supine croc was prodded, measured, admired despite its stench and the disgusting state of its large green-slimed teeth.

"I say, B," said one of his fellow subalterns - kneeling down and looking at its impressive jaws, "- are you quite sure, positive I mean, that it's really, *really* dead? I thought its eyes were closed before - they're open now."

The cheerful conversation hushed. The throng around the reptile drew back. "Look!" Said another, "It *winked!*"

Suddenly the crocodile came to life, drawing itself up off the floor on its stumpy legs which up until now had lain limply alongside its supposed 'corpse.' Lashing its tail it sent a bar stool flying, its jaws went "CHOMP!" The pineapple became pulp - "WHo-OOO-00-ooayyy!!" shouted B, jumping onto the bar - "GERRAWAYY!" The gallant officers scattered wildly sending drinks and chairs crashing to the floor. The Mess corporal fled into the kitchen causing panic among the cooks who ran out into the dark while pots and pans crashed to the ground.

Before the gaze of the highly alarmed onlookers, peering from their safer vantage points, their lines of retreat now secured in proper military fashion - the crocodile made a stately and dignified exit threading its way past the scattering of chairs and broken glass until it reached the top of the steps that led out to the African darkness. From where, pursued by a hail of cushions and cane chairs it went into top gear and vanished like a demon of the night.

"Bloody fool, B!" Said the adjutant when he heard about it. "Who's going to pay for all the damage?"

It may seem sometimes from these accounts that I spent the greater part of my spare time in Africa either harrying the more or less inoffensive and vanishing wildlife or fishing or thinking about food. Both as a bachelor and also later when married perhaps I did these things, but only when and as the opportunity offered.

The office work involved in banking was generally tedious and not to my taste (as noted before I was always generally unsuited to the demands of corporate life) but in postings like Sekondi or Tamale in Ghana, or even Kano in Northern Nigeria where the hours of work were not onerous or unduly irksome - unlike in Lagos or Accra, it was always my pleasure to take whatever opportunities arose to roam the fringes of whatever wild places were still to be found. This was not as impossible as it might seem. The days when the men in suits, the 'experts,' the 'number-crunching bean-counters' and the 'men from out of town' would take over everything from their air-conditioned offices in the cities still lay in the future and a 'Mission Statement'* still something an evangelist declared from his soapbox.

---

* In today's business environment your friendly corner shop may well display a notice that states. "We are an equal opportunities employer. We aim to serve our customers swiftly and efficiently with newspapers, pornography, cigarettes and alcohol regardless of age or gender or sexual preference, disability (mental or physical) or religion etc. etc." It was refreshing once upon a time when Alan Sugar, the enterprising founder of Amstrad was asked if his company had a 'Mission Statement." Pondering a moment, he replied. "No. But if we had it would be "We Want Your Money."

It was altogether a more leisurely and less-pressured existence in the fifties and sixties; the dictatorship of the computer was still lurking well below our horizon and the 'perceived' need for ever-longer office hours to prove one's loyalty, for employee/employer 'appraisals' - which much later would come to overshadow personal relations with one's colleagues - all lay in the future. Most upcountry stations were still free of the tyranny of instant communication which now bedevils the world of commerce. In many of these places the 'Executive Washroom' was still no more than a galvanised bucket in a rickety spider and scorpion haunted shed - to which I held the sole key. For me a fishing rod or a gun were not ends in themselves but open windows to escape into what was a much more fascinating world. Neither tennis, nor golf nor organised games, nor drinking endless pints of beer at the Club over interminable games of snooker were recreations that ever entered other than marginally into my conception of what made 'Life' interesting.

The hunting instinct is hard-wired into the human brain and a young man's interest in Nature is much sharpened by this urge to hunt or fish, indeed to achieve any degree of success in these pursuits it is vital to understand - or to seek to understand Nature's first principles. By the time that a keenness for the chase has abated either with satiety or simply the passing of time, as it inevitably will, the pleasures of merely observing wildlife are enhanced to the point where they may well exceed the former. If hunting is properly described as an intellectually honest way of being a carnivore then I thank God that I had the chances to hunt and to fish as and when I did. I *would* not - indeed could not, do it all again. But I still have the pleasure - and the guilt, of my youthful memories even though my appetite for the chase has long since diminished.

In Tamale in the late afternoons, towards the start of the rainy season in June and July before there was water everywhere and the wild duck began to disperse, I would sometimes drive out a few miles on the Damongo road. During the hour or two before dusk I would walk in to Langa-Langa's plantations of mango and kapok trees which the old Spanish trader still tended with his own hands. He had planted them many years before, more perhaps as a hobby than as a commercial venture for there was no real market for the fruit - and in any case the dense, dark-green leafed mango trees although well-grown never seemed to bear much of a crop. As for the kapok or silk-cotton trees, these were now thirty and forty feet high with their straight, grey trunks covered in spikes like giant rose thorns. The kapok fibre is contained within the large bean-like seed pods. It was formerly used for stuffing things like Teddy Bears and the old Board of Trade ships' life jackets. (Kapok was more yielding and much less likely to break one's neck than the alternative rock-hard cubes of granulated cork if you had to jump overboard in a hurry). In our Tamale bungalow we had chair cushions and 'morocco' leather footrests filled with the locally picked kapok, it was incredibly heavy and still full of small black seeds, like rabbit droppings, which gradually settled into the bottom - when the stitches or the material split, as frequently happened - then the seeds would rattle out under the chair onto the polished floor, startling the sitter - particularly if asleep.

The reason I went to Langa-Langa's 'farm' was not to pick his fruit but to wait for the flighting wild duck which used to circle low over the trees before dropping in to roost on the waters of the area's many little dams, one of which lay in amongst the mangoes not far from the road - and one or two more further out in the bush. These were fed either by streams or by rainwater which would otherwise have run off.

I still retain a great affection for those plump little duck. In West Africa we knew them as 'Whistling Teal' but more correctly they are the White-Faced Tree Duck, *Dendrocygna Viduata*. Their name in Hausa is 'Wishi-Wishi' because of their piercing call, not unlike the whistling cry of a European Widgeon. They are a distinctive, smallish duck (one will make a dinner for two persons of modest appetite, but two are better) with a very characteristic alert, upright stance when seen on the water or on the banks of some tropical stream. Their plumage is barred black and white, black belly and tail with a rufous chestnut breast and a bold white patch on the black-billed face. In later years I used to pursue them in Nigeria, in the flooded 'fadama' areas north of Kano. It gave me a sudden jolt of pleasurable recognition to encounter them in large numbers some twenty-five years later in the Venezuelan flood plains of the Orinoco (there the duck is known as '*El Yaguaso Cariblanco*) and even more recently to see a few captive birds in the Jurong Bird Park in Singapore. When I first met them I knew little enough of their natural history, but only that they were a welcome addition to our limited African diet, along with the Green Fruit pigeon, the wild guinea fowl and the francolin that made up my usual quarry. I have to say here that if there is any finer tasting wild game bird than the African guinea fowl taken from its natural habitat – then I have yet to savour it – and I have in my time eaten most things from rook-pie to bustard to moorhen and capercailzie and back again with many diversions in between.

This however is about crocodile rather than duck, - for in this instance they are not unconnected. Standing under the cover of Langa-Langa's mango trees one evening, listening to the distant cries of the duck, I was also whistling their three-note call in reply to lure the birds closer. Two or three circled nearby, dropping down towards the water of the little dam in answer to my call. I fired and a duck spiralled down, flopping into the water where it fluttered briefly on the surface and expired. It was only a few feet from the bank; the expanse of water was no larger than the size of a tennis court. I went to find a long stick to draw the duck in towards me.

Earlier I had noticed the nostrils and bulbous eyes of a four or five-foot croc dimpling the surface - a common enough sight in many of the shrinking patches of standing water before the dry season began to break - the croc wasn't the reason I was reluctant to wade in and retrieve my duck, I simply didn't want to get wet up to the knees - or further, if I could avoid it. I had picked up a longish stick from a heap of Langa-Langa's mango prunings and was leaning out to try and draw the duck in - when there was a sudden swirl in the muddy water in front of me, a brief vision of a wide-open jaws, lined with a yellow slimed set of teeth chomping on the dinner intended for O. and myself - and the duck was gone, leaving nothing but a chestnut-barred feather or two floating on the blank surface. It was getting dark, the stars were beginning to show so I walked back to the road and drove home to Tamale.

A few evenings later O. came with me to the same spot, but this time I also had a few heavy buckshot cartridges in my pocket. We sat a while under the mango trees as the late afternoon drew on with lengthening shadows. Both of us listening intently for the whistling cry of the duck in answer to our own efforts. Nothing but the distant 'Hoo-Hoo' of a hornbill and the sad and plaintive murmurings of tiny doves in the mango trees responded to our call.

The calm surface of the dam dimpled from time to time with small bubbles and disturbances, probably caused by mudfish fossicking in the murky depths. Suddenly, without so much as a ripple on the glassy surface, there was the crocodile, sideways on, about five yards off - half-awash, head clearly exposed, the ridges on his back and tail plainly visible. He was larger than I had previously thought. I was still aggrieved about my duck that the croc had filched from beneath my nose on my last visit. I quietly removed the small-shot cartridge from the breech of my single-barrelled Greener and slipped in a buckshot load. O. sat quietly watching the croc as I aimed carefully at the exposed head - and pulled the trigger.

I have said before that this narrative is not about what is right nor what is wrong, and neither is it, but this is the way things were and although with God's gift of twenty/twenty hindsight one sometimes has regrets - there is absolutely nothing to be done about it. I suppose that I thought I would have the croc's hide in exchange for the duck. I can no longer recall a young man's reasoning on such matters as this with any clarity. Suffice it to say that it was done - and there's an end to it.

O. jumped about three feet in the air; she was not expecting me to shoot. The close pattern of heavy buckshot enveloped the croc's head in a slather of foam as the reptile reared and plunged before diving - only to surface a few moments later to commence churning up and down the length of the pool like a torpedo boat. It was so fast I could not get a steady enough aim to be certain of an effective second shot. I quickly realised that the poor creature's fleshy valve-flap at the opening to the gullet (that permits a croc to submerge without drowning) must be damaged. The croc continued to plough up and down the pool without any sign of flagging. Then suddenly changing direction it headed straight for the shore where O. and I now stood. It came full-length out of the water and lay almost at my feet, quite still. O. by this time wisely retreated several feet away. I thought the crocodile was now at least moribund, if not dead.

O. says that at this point I brusquely ordered her to fetch me a long stick. I may well have done so as it made an eminently sensible next move to prod the croc for signs of life before taking measures to secure it - such as binding up its jaws with the ubiquitous piece of stout string I invariably carried with me in the bush. (O. says that she always thought this was for applying a tourniquet in case of snakebite - whereas in reality it was for nothing more practical than making it easier to carry dead game).

O. didn't move. She says today that she was rooted to the spot with fright and her most vivid recollection is of the rancid, musky smell emanating from either the croc or the stirred-up mud and water. I confess to remembering being mildy irritated at her lack of action at the time. Thinking that I detected a faint movement in the croc which now lay at my feet, I pressed the muzzle of the gun to the middle of the skull behind the eyes - and put another load of heavy buckshot into its armour-plated brainpan at point blank range.

What happened next came as a complete surprise and illustrates, if such is necessary bearing in mind what I have written earlier, that if not immortal, then crocodiles have a strong streak of indestructibility in their physical make-up. The croc opened its jaws wide, gave a bellow, and whisking round - its heavy ridged tail just missing my legs as I did a standing jump backwards, surged back into the water in a welter of foam. It did one or two more furious lengths of the pool and then porpoising out of the water made a crash dive into the depths. (O. says with hindsight that she was amazed the creature did not at the least break my leg. Attributing my escape both to my lightning-fast reactions and the fact that in those days I was also 'quick on my feet,' she merely snorted.)

That was the last we saw of the poor croc. I fished about from the shore with a long stick, prodding the shallows ineffectually as I now felt strongly disinclined to wade in and poke about looking for what must now have been a carcass. An African had now joined us, a farmer with a hoe and a cutlass over his shoulder - returning to the small compound of huts about a mile away, beyond the kapok trees. I managed to explain to him that there was a dead croc in the dam and it would probably surface by the morning - and that I would 'dash him plenty' if he recovered it for me. It was nearly dark by now and O. and I drove back to Tamale and home.

The next afternoon I went to the farmer's little hutted compound and finding him at home asked about my croc. Alas, venality probably ruled. The value of the belly skin and the meat greatly exceeded any 'dash' I was likely to give, and that was that! But we parted friends, he 'dashed' me some guinea fowl eggs (most of them addled as usual) and I gave him some cigarettes in return. I think he had the better bargain.

Late one afternoon the following year Ralph and I drove up from Tamale to the river at Nabogo where at that time we kept our boat in the pool below the pumping station which piped river water south to the town in the dry season. I think we had gone to check that the moorings were holding, having previously dumped an old engine block into the water for this purpose. Usually the pumping house was deserted, but now there were two Africans sitting on the ladder that led up to the door of the engine room - above the floodwater level. They greeted us and pointed out that lying on the opposite bank of the pool was the largest croc we had yet seen in that little river. It was at least eight or nine feet in length, less than thirty yards distant and several feet away from the water's edge. In the back of the car I had an ancient Lee Metford .303 rifle which 'Mumu' Moutrage (sometimes also known as 'No Fit') the Lebanese trader had lent me, plus a few rounds of equally ancient fifty year-old ammunition, pretty unreliable hit-or-miss stuff.

Before I could stop him, Ralph had picked up the rifle - jacked a round into the breech and was drawing a bead on the creature. I started to say - "The only way to be sure of it is ...." BANNGG! ".... to go for a brain shot!" By which time it was too late. At the shot, which was clearly a palpable hit to judge from the unmistakeable solid thump of a bullet strike - the croc opened its jaws wide, gave vent to a gasping bellow and scuttled full tilt into the river.

"You silly bugger!" I said. "*What* have you gone and done now? I tried to tell you to go for a head shot!!"

"When *I* shoot crocodile," said Ralph, very self-assured as always, "I *always* go for the heart! Never fails."

"Well, its bloody well failed this time you silly twat. I bet you don't even know where its heart is?"

By this time the two Africans had come down to the river bank and were jumping up and down with excitement and pointing to a reedbed some yards below where the croc had plunged in, where there was now a considerable commotion going on. The long reeds waving and flexing as the croc rolled and thrashed about, totally invisible to us except for the agitation of the high rushes.

"It's only a matter of time now." Said Ralph several minutes later, "... Slow but sure, the heart shot is - never fails!"

It was beginning to get dark, the first stars were beginning to show and the commotion was still continuing in the reed bed over the other side of the river. There was nothing we could do further; we had no torch and no oars for the boat, so we drove back the twenty miles to Tamale. The two Africans at the pumping station said the croc would soon be dead - "... For true - lef small 'e go die-oh." They agreed that they would recover it next morning for us. 'Dash' was promised.

The next day Ralph and I drove back north to Nabogo to find the pumping station was now deserted - the engine silent. Our two Africans and our crocodile had vanished without trace. Ralph promised that the next time it was definitely 'the brain shot.' I don't think we ever had such a chance again.

The river at Nabogo contained quite a few crocodile, many of a fair size. One evening Paul Gautier and I were out shooting duck in the extensive area of the river's flood plain (I think the river was named the 'Nyakpuni' - one of the many little tributaries of the White Volta that lace the Northern Territories). The surrounding area was now relatively dry except for isolated pools which sometimes held duck or perhaps a pair of fast flying multi-coloured Pygmy Geese. When we returned to the steep river bank to walk back to the car left as usual at the pump house - there was a large croc awash in mid-stream, head and body fully exposed, slowly drifting down with the sluggish current. Gautier for some reason had a .22 rifle with him as well as his shotgun. Putting down the latter he began to 'Ping!' away at the croc with the puny rifle, now no more than thirty yards off. Gautier later claimed that the ammunition was faulty - damp most likely as the first shot splashed down a good few feet short. The croc continued to drift with the current. Gautier overcompensated and the second bullet (now back to full speed again) hit the water several feet beyond. The croc still took no notice. It may have been asleep. The third tiny bullet hit the croc 'twixt wind and water,' amidships. This woke it up and with an oily surging swirl in the water it was gone, doubtless with no more injury than a flattened crumb of lead stuck in its armoured hide.

Gautier and I did have a more alarming experience one Sunday morning when we left Tamale at first light to pursue whatever quarry was fit for the pot. In his big Morris Isis station wagon we went bucketing along a rough dirt track about 30 miles to the north at Pigu off the Bolgatanga road. This then led off to the east in a long sweeping route back to the village of Zawire a few miles out of Tamale. We had trundled along over the rough laterite on which recent rain had laid the dust, stopping once or twice when we saw francolin and guinea fowl on the track, chasing them off into the long grass and each time bagging one or two. By mid-morning we were bounding along intending to get back to Tamale in time for a Sunday curry lunch. Gautier singing at full blast his old French army (mostly scatological) marching songs. The only one I can recall goes like this:- (though I doubt that it was these words that he sang to the traditional melody.)

'En passant par la Lorraine, avec mes sabots,
Rencontrai trois capitaines. Avec mes sabots, dondaine,
Oh! O-Oh! O-O-Oh! Avec mes sabots!'

Where the narrow dirt road crossed a dammed-up stream, we saw a small bunch of 'Wishi-Wishi' duck sitting on the pool behind the dam. As we stopped they rose off the water and began to fly directly towards us. We took cover, concealing ourselves behind the car and they flew almost overhead. We both fired, dropping two birds into a high bed of reeds that lay below the dam where the stream meandered onwards. We heard the birds splash down, both seemingly dead. The reeds were quite extensive but we had closely marked the spot where they had fallen and we started to wade in to recover the duck. The water was rather deeper than we had thought.

I think both of us stopped in our tracks at the same moment. From the banks of the stream - which was several yards wide at this point with the sloping banks obscured by the tall grasses - we heard a succession of loud 'Splosh-*Splosh*-Splash!' noises. Looking to the edge of the reed bed in which we now stood thigh-deep in the warm muddy water, we saw the tops of the reeds beginning to wave to and fro. There were several separate centres of commotion - and they were all heading in our direction! There was no discussion - Gautier and I made it back to the dam, just short of walking on the water, in record time, sodden to the waist and considerably relieved to be on solid, dry ground once more. In the reed bed below us, where the two duck had fallen, the shoulder-high stalks of the reeds waved furiously and above the splashing and wallowing noises could be heard the soggy 'Chomp' of large reptilian jaws as our two 'Wishi-Wishi' were swiftly metamorphosed into Duck *paté*.

No. 3986

CC.

WILD ANIMALS PRESERVATION ORDINANCE
(Cap. 203—Applied to Ashanti and Northern Territories)

QUALIFIED GENERAL LICENCE
Available for Colony/Ashanti/N.T.

LICENCE is hereby granted to *Paul M. Adamson* of *Accra* to hunt any wild animals except elephants, rhinoceroses and hippopotami until the 31st day of December ~~next following~~ 1959.

Dated at *Accra* this 13 day of *January*, 1959.

Fee: £1

District Commissioner

This Licence is not transferable and only entitles the holder to hunt within the Colony/Ashanti/N.T.

CHAPTER 23

'Snake Palaver'

"I wants to make your flesh creep ….."
(*The Fat Boy in Charles Dickens' Pickwick Papers*)

"Latet anguis in herba"
(*"There's a snake hidden in the grass"*)
(*Virgil, 70 - 19 BC*)

"There are well over a hundred kinds of snakes in West Africa" wrote George Cansdale in his 'Reptiles of West Africa,' *(Penguin 1955)* and as we have already discussed crocodiles, I might as well deal now with snakes and have done with it. (NB those who are at all squeamish are advised to skip the next several pages.)

Snakes are equally both fascinating and repellent. There are those who are convinced that Africa is a dangerous hotbed of poisonous serpents and I have known expatriates who have spent their entire time in Africa avoiding even grass lawns, having convinced themselves that once out of the house and away from concrete or tarmac, they were in grave danger.. In fact anyone coming to any harm would generally be both extremely unlucky and would usually have themselves to blame for their misfortune. Snakes are quite common, but rarely seen - being shy and secretive creatures. Many of them are not venomous and those that are certainly have no hidden agenda as far as humans are concerned. Almost all snake bites are accidental, very few species are aggressive unless cornered or trodden on unwittingly. Like all generalities this last statement is not entirely true. There *are* some notable exceptions.

My old friend (and now sadly the late) Richard Steimann, the Swiss timber trader who I first met in Sekondi in 1954 was fascinated by snakes. He simply could not leave well alone. He never actually came to harm (by good luck and the skin of his teeth) but he had one or two close calls that I knew of and from which he had obviously learned little or nothing.

When Richard first came to the Gold Coast as a young man in his early twenties just after the War he worked in the high forest country of the Western Nzima region, employed there by his Swiss Uncle Ümeger who owned several timber concessions in that area. One day Richard was following a narrow path through the forest with a few African labourers, 'looking for trees,' that is, trees of specific commercial species suitable for felling. His companions were required to clear the path and to mark the trees when found. Richard's headman was in the lead, Richard and the other 'tree lookers' following in single file.

The headman suddenly came up all standing, gesturing urgently to the others to stop. A yard or two ahead, clearly visible and lying motionless across the sandy track was a large Rhinoceros Viper (*Bitis nasicornis*). This is a large, thick-bodied member of the same family as the Puff Adder and the Gaboon Viper - and notoriously the least placid of the three. It is unmistakable both from its handsome colouring and the two small but quite prominent rough horns on the tip of its snout. Richard's headman indicated that they should give it a wide berth and rejoin the path once safely past.

Richard, with a young man's confidence born both of ignorance and a close study of too many boys' adventure stories - thought otherwise. He decided that he would impress his own 'boys' with his superior 'whiteman's' daring and skill.

Ignoring the headman's protestations Richard persuaded him to distract the snake with a stick while he manoeuvred himself into position behind it. Richard's intention was to grasp the snake firmly behind the head and then to display it safely for his - and the admiring onlookers - gratification. I have noted that when people hatch such wildcat schemes on the spur of the moment it is a not uncommon failing for them to disregard either the possible consequences of failure - or having initially succeeded, to have then considered a practical method of bringing such an exercise to a safe conclusion, sometimes known today as 'an *exit* strategy.' (This observation applies particularly to politicians throughout the ages.)

In one respect Richard certainly achieved his objective, as he bent down and grasped the large and quite unwieldy snake behind the neck and lifted it triumphantly at arms' length. There was a unanimous gasp from the onlookers, but of alarm rather than admiration. Richard's followers fled as one man and peered out wide-eyed from behind the cover of the headman who had bravely stood his ground.

It didn't take Richard long to realise he was in trouble. The viper was both heavy and active. If he dropped it the snake was more than likely to strike at him and he was bare-legged, wearing only shorts and tennis shoes. What was worse, he had grasped the viper too far back, mis-judging his grip - and the snake was vigorously twisting and turning its head attempting to bite Richard's forearm. He was in something of a quandary, unable to drop it - and unable to hold it much longer at arm's length as his nerve and muscle flagged - neither could he change hands.

The headman provided the solution. "Hold still Massah!" He cried, wielding his cutlass, feeling its edge with his thumb. "Hold still, mek you turn your head!" In desperation Richard obeyed him, not only turning his head but closing his eyes while he held the wriggling and potentially fatal burden as steadily as he could in his present state of high alarm.

"SWISH! THUNKK! THUD!" The headman had sliced off the viper's head with one swift and deadly swipe of his blade, like taking the top off a hard-boiled egg. The boys of course took the snake for 'chop.'

One would have thought that would have cured Richard of further experimentation, but he was undeterred. Whenever he and I were off fishing or in the bush, we did occasionally see a snake. Usually as it retreated at our approach. Sometimes we saw water snakes swimming and Richard would always make some futile and hazardous attempt to follow and catch one before it vanished. As often as not to my eye these, on dry land and in the water, looked suspiciously like black forest cobras - which also spit!

Richard told me of one occasion when he had called on the owner of a timber concession who kept a tame, or rather semi-domesticated, Royal Python (*Python regius*) in his bungalow as a rat-catcher. These snakes are quite easy to keep and once one becomes accustomed to their presence around the house, they are both handsome and easily handled. Usually they are no more than three or four feet long, but they are quite stoutly built for a constrictor, the body narrowing only at the tail and behind the rather distinct head.

Richard was much taken with the creature and having a camera with him, asked his host to take a picture of him with the python draped across his shoulders. Richard picked up the python and draped it round his neck like a scarf. His host beckoned him to come forward on the verandah, more into the light. As Richard moved, the Royal Python suddenly tightened its grip, lashing a thick, single coil fast around his neck. Before he could speak, to alert the cameraman now peering through the viewfinder, Richard was first gasping for breath and then rapidly choking as he vainly attempted to tear loose the iron grip of the constricting coil which grew ever tighter.

"Just stand still for a moment, will you! How do you expect me to take a picture with you messing about like that? For Christ's sake *Richard*! Stop playing silly buggers! - Stop rolling about on the floor!"

By the time his host realised something was wrong and that he was not just acting the goat, Richard's face had gone purple and his eyes were popping out on stalks. It took the combined strength of the owner and the hastily summoned houseboy to free Richard, by which time as he later said to me "I vos nearly a f.....g goner! Und der f.....g bastard never got vun shot of me f.....g croaking before his f.....g eyes!!" (Richard's English learned in the timber camps was rarely fit for normally polite society).

In Takoradi there was Herman Hottinger, another Swiss who had snake palaver. Herman was the manager of the FPH Rest House (named after the Finsbury Pavement House Head Offices of the mining companies) for the up-country gold miners either passing through or having a short break. Herman was very proud of the small flock of much-prized chickens he kept in the compound. The trouble was that his chickens kept on vanishing from his hen-house. Every few nights or so another one would disappear. Herman was very upset and directed his suspicions at the night-watchman - who vehemently denied any involvement.

Just as Herman was preparing for bed one night he heard the night-watch shouting "Massah - come QUICK! Now-now! Some-ting go tief yo' chicken!!"

Swiftly girding his loins with a towel Herman leapt into action, pounding down the steps and into the compound where in the light of the watchnight's lantern he saw a python, several feet in length, making heavy weather across the smooth gravel with one of Herman's last remaining prize fowl in its jaws, the hen was still fluttering. The python soon had got its head, plus chicken, firmly inserted into a pile of rock on the edge of the compound. The watchnight was capering excitedly as Herman now incensed beyond all measure at the fate of his beloved chicken grabbed the snake by the tail as it endeavoured to wriggle further into the rock pile. As Herman engaged in a tug-of-war with the python, his towel now abandoned on the ground, cussing and swearing mightily, lights began to come on in the Rest House. Before the eyes of the fascinated onlookers the *tableau-vivant* progressed. The stark-naked Herman, like some *Laocöon* come to life, dimly lit by the watchman's flickering lantern in his primeval struggle with the serpent, was a stirring sight.

Herman had reached stalemate as in spite of his strenuous efforts the snake was now wedged tight, immovable. If he relaxed his grip the python would escape further into the rock pile. His bare heels were dug fast into the gravel and beginning to hurt. He called upon the nightwatch to put down his lantern and to add his weight to the battle. Shouts of "Yo-Ho - HEAVE HOH!" came from the spectators watching from the windows.

The watchman was unwilling to grasp the nettle as it were. Herman's grip was tiring and his hold on the python's tail was slipping towards the extremity. The nightwatch took up his cutlass from the ground and stepping forward, with one swift blow sliced the hapless serpent into two pieces. Caught unawares, Herman did a backward somersault still grasping a yard of tail in his hands. The nightwatch did a little dance of victory, the onlookers cheered, and the front section of the python disappeared, complete with chicken into the rock pile. Herman gathered up his towel, mopped his sweating brow - and swept a deep bow to the wild applause of his audience.

I sorely wounded and certainly killed a python once, a fact of which I am now truly ashamed, but there is nothing to be done about it. Python skins were commonly offered for sale by the Hausa traders who sold curios and native trinkets to the Europeans in their bungalows. Some of these skins were as much as fifteen feet and more in length, but were often badly stretched in the process of tanning. Forty years ago they were not expensive, a pound or thirty shillings would buy the largest skin. The trade in them is now banned, and quite rightly so by CITES, but the skins were formerly made into expensive belts and handbags. Like many of the natural products of West Africa, snakeskins were often unintentionally spoiled before they reached the skin and hide buyers who shipped them in bulk to Europe.

Snakeskins and also crocodile belly-hides were sold by length, or in the case of the latter, by the square inch. Cattle hides were sold by weight, as was also the wild rubber, gathered from the forest and smoked around a stout stick into fifty-pound balls. The native African producer therefore habitually overstretched the snake and crocodile skins - to gain a better price, but in fact because the quality was thereby lessened, they brought a lower price. Cowhides were similarly soaked in water, thereby spoiling the quality, but in the vain hope of bringing a better price for the extra weight. The traders who dealt in the wild rubber, also buying by weight - always needed to check carefully that the core of the smoked balls of latex was free of rocks and stones. Copal gum and beeswax were also cleverly adulterated. It was always a case of *'caveat emptor'* when trading on the Coast.

From Tamale I made weekly visits to a small branch of the bank at Yendi for which I was responsible. I always took my shotgun on the back seat of the car for the sixty miles drive along the dusty laterite road out to the borders of Togo. With any bags of cash left securely locked in the boot, I was then free to chase after the odd francolin or guinea-fowl for the pot. To travel on the corrugated washboard surface of a laterite road* one has to reach an optimum speed to iron out the humps and bumps and other irregularities - while keeping a watchful eye for the occasional hazardous mound of a culvert which could spell disaster if taken at too high a speed. These 'danger spots' were often marked by the wrecks of mammy trucks or clapped-out cars which had careered off the road and into the bush when they had become airborne after striking such a hump at too high a speed - often the best manner in which to smooth out one's otherwise bone-jarring progress. Mammy lorries would often crash simply because the driver either fell out or was thrown out of the doorless cab by hitting a pothole - due to adopting a curious sideways driving position with the aim of being able to bale out quickly and to avoid being crushed whenever a head-on collision seemed likely.

My friend T. told me that once when he was endeavouring to overtake a mammy lorry on a bush road near Hohoe, he noticed the young driver's mate perched up behind the cab holding a long pole through the open rear window with which it soon became obvious he was operating the accelerator pedal, while the driver - in the usual position of half-in, half-out of the open-sided cab - was doing nothing more than steer the vehicle. As T. said "the 'mate' was probably under tuition." The lorry then hit a deep pothole at too high a speed and the driver flew out sideways, landing

---

* The PWD invariably 'graded' these roads by dragging an iron girder or length of rail track over the surface behind a tractor. This got rid of the worst bumps, but accentuated the washboard-like ridges.

on his backside in the road while the lorry careered off into the bush shedding in turn the driver's mate (and his pole), various passengers and cargo until it struck a tree and came to a timely halt. T. said he stopped to help, expecting to find several badly injured passengers and crew, but no-one had had suffered more than a few bruises and T. went on his way leaving behind a furious altercation in progress with most of the blame being directed at the hapless driver's mate. Such hazards as these were usually made worse by the blinding clouds of red and choking dust which on windless days trailed for miles behind every vehicle - few as these were on such a road as that out to Yendi from Tamale. Often I encountered no more than three or four other vehicles in the entire journey of sixty miles or so each way.

There were only two small villages on this road, Jimle, not far from Mile 28 - and Sang about ten miles before Yendi, in the entire distance. The road was mostly straight, through orchard bush and savannah, except for some low hills near Milestone 30 which the road curved to the north to avoid. One often saw antelope or baboons and sometimes the occasional family of the red Patas savannah monkeys (*Erythocebus patas*) loping across the road. It was near Mile 28, beyond the low range of hills to the south that Dick Chadwick, the Game Warden, had shot the bush-cow whose black-buttressed horns and whitened skull lay on his stoep at Damongo. It was also near here that British and German patrols from Tamale and Yendi respectively had clashed on 6th August 1914, Sergeant Alhaji Grunshi DCM, MM, of the Gold Coast Regiment being credited with the distinction of firing the opening shots of the Great War on behalf of the British.*

It was on the Yendi road that I once became 'bushed.' Having hurriedly left the car, taking the gun I chased off into the orchard-bush after a flock of guinea fowl that I had seen at the roadside - they ran ahead of me just out of range while I followed at a matching pace through the tall grass and scrubby trees, for what might have been ten or fifteen minutes before I realised that they had vanished without trace. I began to follow my tracks back to the road - but there was no sign of which way I had come,

---

* The story I was told was that on 4th August 1914 a training patrol of the WAFF two days out from Tamale was fired on by a German fighting patrol of schütztruppen already pushing west along the Yendi road. The Germans had a powerful wireless station at Kamina in Togo and knew the war had begun, the British didn't. "Oy Fritz! Shouted the English lieutenant. "What's the Hell's going on? It's me, your friend Harry." "Sorry Harry" replied Fritz, "ve are now at war." Harry. "But Fritz, I've got no ammunition – it's all back in Tamale." Fritz. "OK Harry – ve vait for you here for two days only, go get it quick!" Harry returned with major reinforcements on the 6th. Alas the 'Gentleman's War' was soon over and the rest is history.

in every direction lay nothing but more long grass and scrubby trees. I knew I had gone south when I left the dead-straight road - but where now was north? There was a hazy, cloudy sky with the sun almost directly overhead – no help at all. I wandered for half-an-hour and more becoming sorely confused. Eventually I attempted to mark the way I had come with sticks, thinking that I had passed one particular clump of trees more than once. Perhaps I was moving in a circle? After an hour by my watch I knew I was properly lost. I wasn't unduly worried. By late afternoon when the sun started to sink to the west I knew I would easily find my way back to the road which lay due north - wherever I was now. It was important that I didn't panic, and that it didn't get dark on me before I found the road again. It was a nuisance, I had no water, that was in the car and O. would worry when I wasn't back in Tamale by late afternoon. The car would be safe enough (with the money bags locked in the boot) at the roadside. I sat down on a large lump of laterite rock and lit a cigarette - at least I had those with me. Another ten minutes passed while I pondered my situation. Apart from being lost (and as I knew where I was it was just that I was totally disoriented) I was otherwise comfortable with the landscape and my surroundings. The things around me were all familiar - and if I was unaware of some of their names at least the birds, the trees and the sounds of the bush, they were all part of my everyday African environment. There would be no sudden surprises. From somewhere far away came the soft, mournful 'hoo-hoo' call of a hornbill. Tiny stingless sweat bees began to gather irritatingly now that I was no longer moving. I could feel them against the palm of my hand as I futilely tried swatting them away from my face. Sitting in the shade, the occasional tsetse fly homed in on me, seeking bare flesh - their presence was an indication of the wild game that still inhabited the area.

    Time passed and then at last I heard a welcome sound, a lorry engine far away in the distance. I tried to pinpoint the remote droning as it grew louder. To my great relief I heard the truck rattling and banging along the washboard laterite road less than a hundred yards away while a great plume of red dust rose to tree-top level. I was safe again! Within a few minutes I was back on the roadside wondering where the hell my car was - until I spotted it at last, a tiny speck where the road vanished in the distant trees of the savannah. I must have wandered parallel to the road for some time. It was a salutary lesson. After that incident I took considerably more note of where I was going when in the bush and as soon as I could, which was not until several months later while on leave in Switzerland, I bought a pocket-compass. I later realised that like many people who wander off into a flat and almost featureless landcape - that without landmarks one does not walk in a straight line. T. and I tested ouselves on more than one occasion, using a compass, both of us to a greater or lesser degree wandered off in an ever tightening anti-clockwise direction.

On another day when returning from Yendi I had stopped the car near a culvert where a rainy season stream went under the road, shaded by trees that were lush from the then plentiful water. I hoped maybe to bag a green fruit pigeon. It was a likely spot. Looking over the low parapet at the fast-flowing water my eye was drawn to an odd shape on a sun-dappled patch of vegetation in mid-stream. It was a diffuse heap of something or other, a log perhaps - or a tangle of branches. It did not look quite right.

I suddenly realised that what I was looking at but *not seeing* until then, only a few yards off, was a very large python, resting in a mound of its own brown and yellow patterned coils. I thought I could pick out its head somewhere near the middle of the heap. It didn't move.

On looking back, I don't think I would have done anything more had not an African farmer passed by, wobbling unsteadily and squeaking along the ridged and dusty road on a rusty bicycle. He toppled off his machine to see what I was looking at. I had my shotgun in my hand.

"Dat be big sshnake Massah. 'E be big-oh pass all. 'E be bad sshnake." (This last statement a patent untruth - unless I suppose you happened to be an unfortunate duiker or some poor villager's goat). "Why you no kill-am? He continued, "Plenty meat dey for chop."

Being young and foolish and needing little encouragement to make me more so, I aimed carefully at what I thought was the python's head about fifteen feet away in the middle of the heap in the shallow stream and fired.

It was a *very* large python indeed. It leaped up in the air uncoiling like a giant spring, vanishing swiftly into the water and swirling off downstream with its head held high. The African who had been closely watching the proceedings, suddenly jumped over the low wall of the culvert into the knee-deep rushing water and fished about with his hands, coming up after a few moments with about three feet of the poor creature's tail, severed by my shot. I was very upset by all this, the African was delighted and before wobbling off again along the road he lashed the still quivering snake tail to his bicycle crossbar with a piece of the ubiquitous string I always carried with me.

It is a sad fact of life that snakes are almost universally persecuted, it being a natural human reaction on coming across one to kill it. Africans do so just as much as Europeans, but at least the former have a better excuse, the larger species like the pythons and the big vipers being often killed for food, though most snakes are just killed and thrown away. I have never felt threatened by any snake, although I have felt the need to observe caution - unlike my friend Richard.

Late one night in 1956 I drove home to my house in Takoradi and in the headlights observed both the sleeping watchnight enjoying a sound night's work as usual - and also a large black cobra slithering into the garage ahead of me. These ring-necked spitting cobras (*Naja nigricollis*) were quite common in the area, and potentially they could be very dangerous. I had no wish to let it take up residence among my stack of wooden boxes piled up against the back wall. Waking up the nightwatch with some difficulty (he pretended that he had not been sleeping but engrossed in saying his prayers), I told him there was a snake in the garage. Between the two of us we traced it to the rear of one box, carefully moving the others aside. As the nightwatch stood ready with his cudgel I jammed the box against the wall, the snake popped its head out, and BOP! The deed was done. The nightwatch bore it off in triumph, no doubt to lend its corpse to his fellows (in exchange for some small sum) to display to their respective employers in turn the visual evidence of their nightlong vigilance - until the snake finally decomposed and became useless for further commercial exploitation.

In Tamale O. was discommoded by a thin, bright green snake which came into our bungalow one morning, probably via the screen of vines which grew along the wire mesh along the covered way at the rear of our bungalow. One should always be slightly cautious about green snakes in Africa as any such reptile over three or four feet in length has a better than even chance of being a green mamba. What upset O. was that it was wriggling across the carpet between her and our baby daughter also lying wriggling on the carpet inside her playpen. Rapidly leaping over the snake, shouting for Charles the steward to come quickly - she snatched up her infant into safety and watched while Charles swept the snake out onto the stoep with a broom. Then, taking the broom from Charles she walloped the snake into a pulp with the brush shank, shaking with rage as she did so. That is what people do to snakes. When I came home in the late afternoon it was beyond identification what with the walloping it had taken and the ants having got at it where it lay in the garden.

The only big, fat viper I ever came across in the wild, alive, was a Gaboon Viper (*Bitis Gabonica*) - the largest and most poisonous of its species. By nature sluggish and lethargic - it often reaches a size that can only be described as 'frightening' (q.v. G. Cansdale), up to six feet in length, four or five inches thick and weighing twenty pounds or more. It lies in wait for its prey on the forest floor, wherein lies its danger. It does not move out of the way and being trodden on by the unwary farmer or hunter, it may cause more actual deaths than any other of the vipers. Its venom causes both massive tissue damage and internal bleeding, its dual purpose venom is also like that of the cobra, in that the victim's vital nervous system is affected.

Sometimes at night, driving out from Tamale - along the narrow bush roads, we were usually seeking hares to shoot, picking them out in the car headlights or in the powerful beam of a torch. These made very good eating having a light and succulent flesh. They were quite large, with pale grey fur and enormous ears. I never saw one in daylight as they seemed solely nocturnal in habit. The Africans, some tribes anyway, endow them with the same magical quality that the European hare possesses and regarded them as 'Ju-Ju.'* My car at that time was ideal for this purpose, a VW 'Beetle' but with a sliding sun-roof that served as a gun turret when the front passenger seat was positioned right forward. A moonless night was best for this purpose.

The bush roads at night could reveal a fascinating wealth of wildlife, from nocturnal birds and small creatures to the occasional crocodile migrating from one patch of water to another. Large black scorpions of frightening size could be seen scuttling in the dust like landlocked lobsters. There were the nightjars with glowing ruby-red eyes who would sit tight in the headlights until fluttering up at the very last moment. Sometimes the rarer pennant-winged species (*Cosmetornis vexillarius*) trailing eighteen-inch streamers would spring up into the beams of light. Always there was a plethora of owls, sitting large-eyed and swivel-headed in the track, stubbornly refusing to move to let us past.

Tom, Michel and I drove out one moonless night, we had already shot one or two hares and we were driving slowly along a narrow and sandy bush track that led to a remote village. We had just passed three or four men wheeling their bicycles on foot making their way home from the main road a mile or two back, the soft sand making it difficult for them to ride in the dark, with only a dim hurricane lantern between them. Across the track ahead lay what first I took to be a length of tree trunk, I clearly recall taking it for a chunk of paw-paw tree - the pattern on it was so distinctive. I stopped the car, the 'log' was too thick to drive over and I could not go around because of the undergrowth. Michel got out to shift it. He approached the obstacle and giving an audible yelp made a standing backwards jump for safety.

---

* Note: These were of the genus Lepus capensis zechi, the Togo Hare - probably the original of the 'Brer Rabbit' of the American folk-tales.)

The Gaboon Viper was impressive in the headlights; totally unmoving it stretched most of the way across the track. The pale white head-markings identified it without any doubt. The diamond 'dazzle' pattern of buff, brown and purple spreading out from the central line along its back explained why I had taken it for a lump of paw-paw stem. It was quite beautiful - and deadly.

Michel took his gun and at (a safe) almost point-blank range shattered its head to pulp. In the distance we heard the chatter of the approaching Africans who would almost certainly have stumbled over it in the dark. Michel dragged the carcass to the side of the track and we drove on. I suppose we were justified, but given the chance again I would have perhaps tried to prod it out of the way. But then had the approaching Africans stumbled over it in the dark it could well have killed one of them - or had they seen it in time, they would have almost certainly killed it themselves in their turn with the cutlasses they carried.

A mile or two further on we spotted another hare on the edge of the track, transfixed by our lights. Michel shot at it and somehow missed, the hare lolloped off, its huge ears erect - and then we heard the pellets rattling down against what sounded like corrugated iron. Voices were raised high in alarm, matches flared twenty yards off as hurricane lanterns were lit. Michel now shone his powerful torch around - we were right on the edge of the village at the end of the track. Time to go! I swiftly turned the car and drove back the way we had come. We passed the men with the bicycles; they had the Gaboon Viper draped in an ungainly fashion over the handlebars. "Plenty fine chop!" They shouted to us.

Michel figures in another snake 'palaver' worthy of record. He had succeeded Paul Gautier as manager of CFAO in Tamale. Before the Gautiers had departed on leave they had been troubled by the presence of a large spitting cobra which had taken up residence in the garden of their compound. The 'watchnight' had reported its presence and from time to time in the dark, with the help of the nightwatch and his lantern Paul had attempted to dispose of it, each time only succeeding in losing it in the grass, but from its tracks across the patches of dust, it had clearly taken up residence inside their concrete septic tank, gaining entry through a large crack near the top. As was only fair, before Paul and Juliette left Tamale they warned Michel of the cobra's presence. Michel was a Frenchman of a highly-strung and nervous disposition, possessing an over-active imagination in such matters. He brooded over the problem for several days, marooned each evening in his bungalow and further alarmed by the watchman's nightly up-dated situation reports. He decided to put paid to the problem once and for all. Returning home one afternoon with a bag of cement from the store he swiftly mixed up a batch of mortar. He then proceeded to plaster over every nook, crevice, crack and cranny that he could find in the fabric of the septic tank behind the bungalow.

As a solution to the problem it had one major flaw. Having blocked up every external entrance - or exit to or from the tank, if the cobra was already inside its sole way out was now via the waste-pipe up into Michel's bathroom. This had not occurred to Michel until one morning a few days later he lifted the lid of the lavatory pan and to his horror saw the business-end of the cobra poking out from around the U-bend - enough to make a chap severely constipated. The snake had swiftly backed off down the waste pipe - and was not seen again for a while. Michel used the lavatory infrequently from then on and only with extreme caution. He swore that whenever he raised the lid of the lavatory pan the surface of the water always trembled slightly, re-affirming his certainty that the cobra was still lurking round the bend.

Eventually Michel became even more neurotic than usual about this intolerable situation. Standing on the lavatory seat, he took a sledge-hammer and swung a mighty blow at the U-bend, shattering it into pieces.

Out popped a large and angry cobra amongst the shards of china and the spreading pool of water. Michel in a panic then dropped the sledge-hammer down the lavatory pan which broke in its turn adding a further flood of water to the chaos. Michel, along with the snake, exited rapidly into his living room, taking refuge on the dining table - the snake by this time probably even more alarmed than its persecutor, slithered across the polished cement floor and out on to the stoep where it vanished down the steps once more into the garden. Michel once more was left with an unusable lavatory and the sneaking suspicion that the snake was still lurking in the compound waiting for its moment of revenge.

I said earlier that the only big, fat viper that I came across in the wild, was the Gaboon Viper which is not entirely true, I should have added – *alive*. Early one Sunday morning before dawn I had left Tamale with T. to go shooting to the east of the dry-season Kintampo road in a remote area across the Volta. On the most recent maps I have seen this still remains a blank space that today fringes the northern extremities of the vast lake behind the Akosombo dam. There was game there, T. and I were once chased on foot for a mile or two back to our car by a very angry troop of baboons seemingly determined to have a go at us. We found plentiful antelope tracks and once we saw a leopard 'pronking' through dew-wet grass like a huge domestic cat. There was at least one village we found a long way down a narrow dusty track - where all the children fled shrieking at our unexpected appearance - but otherwise it seemed totally uninhabited. I believe that some sixty years earlier one of the last raiding columns of the Malian slavers/freedom fighters (which description you prefer depends on one's political viewpoint* **See Note at end of Chapter**) Samori and Babatou had ravaged and de-populated the area. It was in this remote bush area (by now I had a reliable pocket compass) that I shot a francolin that flushed from beneath our feet. I winged it and it hit the ground running hard. I fired a second shot and tumbled it to a dead stop in a cloud of dust. I went forward to pick the bird up but recoiled in some alarm. The bush fowl was lying dead on top of a now moribund and audibly deflating puff adder which had been in the process of ingesting a saucer-sized frog. The frog was also twitching in its final throes, either from the puff-adder's venom or from my shot which had also simultaneously done for both the snake and the francolin. Had I not had a witness I would otherwise forbear from recounting this Munchausen-like tale.

One last tale of 'snake palaver' and then those who suffer from a phobia about such things can re-open their eyes again and read on in safety. I shall not mention them again.

The late Mike Venn once recounted to me an occasion at a party in the Gambia when a lady emerged with a shriek from the 'small room,' and announced to the assembled guests in a trembling voice that there was "A snake in there!"

A fellow guest to whom Mike had been chatting was a well-oiled PWD man. Getting up from his chair with some difficulty - for he was quite smashed - he announced in his turn that he would '*fix*' the snake, 'no problem,' he knew - hic! - how to deal with "*damned* sschnakes!"

The PWD man staggered off into the lavatory, closing the door behind him. He emerged a few minutes later clutching a quite long, thin green snake which he had neatly tied into a couple of half-hitches - almost a 'reef' knot in fact. It was still wriggling. "*Hic* - there you are - I fixed it!" He went back into the lavatory dropped the snake into the bowl and flushed the cistern before coming out again to sit next to Mike. The guests applauded the hero of the moment.

After several more minutes drinking and chatting, Mike noticed the PWD man had a slight film of sweat across his brow and he had gone quite pale and silent. Mike said solicitously "I say, are you sure you're all right? You don't look so hot to me. In fact you look quite green."

"I think the dam' thing bit me" slurred the PWD man, looking even greener. "Here, on my thumb - it was only a tiny thing, I thought it was harmless - maybe it wasn't." Then the PWD man passed out.

Mike and his host dragged the now semi-conscious PWD man to a car and swiftly drove him off to the hospital. The doctor on duty examined the patient, looking at the small twin punctures on the ball of his thumb, shining a light into his shrinking eye-pupils and listening anxiously to his now laboured breathing. "Where is the snake that bit him?" Said the doctor, looking at Mike. "What was it? I need to identify it so that I can administer the correct anti-toxin to neutralise the poison. It's quite dangerous to give him the wrong antivenom you know."

Mike and his host had to confess that the snake had been tied in a sort of granny knot and flushed down the lavatory by its victim and was now probably swilling around in the bungalow's cesspit. "Do you think you can recover it?" asked the doctor - "the sooner the better!" Mike and the host drove back fast to the bungalow where the party was still in full swing. Swiftly mustering several unwilling helpers they prised the lids off the sewage tank in the garden and by the light of several torches and a lantern or two they probed and prodded the pit's noisome contents - eventually fishing out the now defunct snake on the tines of a rake. Popping it into a basket they rushed back to the hospital.

"You might at least have rinsed it off first!" said the aggrieved doctor, wrinkling his nose, "- it doesn't look like a dangerous one to me. By the way, your friend seems OK now - but he's totally pissed - he can stay in hospital overnight and sleep it off. He's going to have a terrible hangover in the morning..... "

Do *crustacea* come under the heading of reptiles you may ask? No, is the usual and correct answer, but I shall make them so to include a brief mention of the huge land crabs that wander the low-lying environs of Lagos and its adjacent lagoons and mangrove swamps. Some are of the size and shape of a squat German 'coal scuttle' steel helmet. Blackish purple in colour they roam about on dry land at night, waving their enormous coconut-cracking claws as they scavenge for scraps and rubbish. They are frequently seen on the roads after nightfall and they will readily enter houses at ground floor level - giving the unwary occupants a nasty shock as the crab skitters over a tiled foor, alarmed by the switching on of a light. On Ikoyi Island where we lived during our time in Lagos, I kept our boat in the garage. Once when I had it propped up and blocked on one side one evening and was applying anti-fouling paint to its underside, working in the light of the single overhead bulb O. came out to see how I was doing. She assumed at first that I was sitting; or rather squatting on a large paint tin while I laid on the last few brush strokes. As she came near she suddenly realised that the 'tin' was a large land crab waving its huge claw at my unprotected rear. "Psst!" She said, "Don't move." The usual result of such well-meaning cautionary advice kicked in as expected, as looking below and behind me and seeing the menacing shape brandishing its huge claw at my nether regions I executed an abrupt standing jump, sending my paint pot flying, while the crab scuttled off into the darkness and O. collapsed with laughter.

My friend Gareth Plinge enhanced his reputation when he dealt with an embarassing domestic crisis for our mutual friends Leslie and Jamie Wetherley who lived nearby. They occupied a two-storey house which had a downstairs cloakroom off their living room. The lavatory had been colonised by a land crab somewhat in the manner of Michel Cordon's cobra in Tamale several years earlier. The crab, although not dangerous in any way was proving impossible to evict and its dietary habits were probably too disgusting to contemplate. Its size and shape allowed it to wedge itself immovably, jamming carapace and claws somewhere down beyond the bend, proof against the Wetherleys' futile and puny attempts to dislodge it with Harpic or flexible rods. By evening time whenever anyone attempted to use the loo, on lifting the lid they were faced with the implacable crab, its beady eyes on stalks, unyielding and obdurate, jammed across the bottom of the bowl while it waved its huge claw in grim greeting. Gareth Plinge having unexpectedly encountered their unwelcome guest one evening, offered to remove it for them. All he needed he said, was for them to go out to the Club or to the cinema whenever it suited them. If they could leave him with a half-case of cold beer ready in their fridge, a ball of string, a small bundle of darning wool and a piece of chicken or fish (preferably a little high), a pair of scissors and a bucket with some sort of lid, he was ready to do the business. Somewhat mystified, they agreed.

One evening a few days later found Gareth Plinge comfortably ensconced in the Wetherley's living room, the contents of the first bottle of Star beer in a dew-frosted glass at his side. On the black and white TV set he was watching an episode of Sergeant Bilko **(See Note)** - then all the rage on the newly installed Lagos transmitters. A length of string stretched from his sensitive grasp across the floor, disappearing through the crack of the door and into the bowl of the downstairs water closet.

An hour and two more bottles later he was dozing quietly in front of 'I Love Lucy' when the string twitched, once, then twice. Instantly he was wide-awake. On tip toe he approached the lavatory door, quietly taking up the slack in the string - until after a few tentative tugs the line met with a firm resistance. Casting caution to the winds he flung open the door, switched on the light and triumphantly hauled out the captive crab, firmly entangled in the snarl of darning wool, a chicken drumstick locked in its massive claw. Lowering the crab into the bucket beside the lavatory - drawing the scissors from his shirt pocket he snipped the string, placed a tin beer tray over the top of the bucket and leaving the crab to enjoy the remains of the chicken leg as best it could in its woolen entanglement, he retired satisfied to his chair to open his fourth bottle of beer. I think the Wetherleys enjoyed both the film and its succesful aftermath. I don't know what they did with the crab.

---

*Note: - Samori, the '*African Vercingetorix*' (c. 1830 - 1900) was an active thorn in the side of the (mainly French) colonial powers in West Africa for more than thirty years. At the height of his power he controlled a vast area of territory extending from the Soudanese hinterland of Sierra Leone across the Ivory Coast and into what is now northern Ghana and Burkina Fasso. His army at times numbered 12,000 men armed with up to 6,000 modern rifles and a modest force of artillery, trained and clothed to mirror the French Marine Colonial Infantry who pursued them fruitlessly for many years.

In 1896-1897 Samori was in Western Gonja (the area I mention above). In 1897 his army destroyed a British column (Henderson's) operating near Wa in the north-west corner of what is now northern Ghana. He was captured by the French in 1898 and died in exile (allegedly poisoned) in Gabon in 1900.

In Tamale in 1960 there died one of the last surviving followers of Samori's principal lieutenant, Babatou. In Lagos in 1964 O. was working for the Ivory Coast Embassy, whose First Secretary, M. Fany Amara, told her that his own grandmother had been captured and taken as a slave by Samori - never to be seen again.

**Note: - The introduction of television in the major towns of the Coast in the early Sixties was in my opinion one of the final nails in the coffin in which was buried once and for all the air of mystery, awe and a measure of respect which formerly the average African had for the 'natural' authority of the whiteman. This came home to me in Lagos with all the sublety of a sledgehammer while watching an early episode of 'Steptoe and Son,' the brilliant comedy series about the cockney scrap dealers. Steptoe senior was esconced in front of the parlour fire sitting in a tin hip-bath, wearing a bowler hat and eating pickled onions from the bathwater around him where they had spilled from the jar. "You *disgustin'* old man" said his son Harold, showing not the least respect to his aged parent. Behind us I heard gasps of amazement from the open kitchen door where our cook and 'small boy' were watching wide-eyed with horror.

Another 'coffin nail' in the same vein was the arrival of the Americans en masse at more or less the same time as we first arrived in Lagos in 1964. It now became a common sight to see the American 'Madams' shopping in the air-conditioned downtown Kingsway Stores and the U.T.C. supermarkets - in full daylight, in garish Bermuda shorts or 'pedal pushers' chewing gum and with their hair in curlers. The day of the white European's innate superiority was fast coming to its close for all to see.

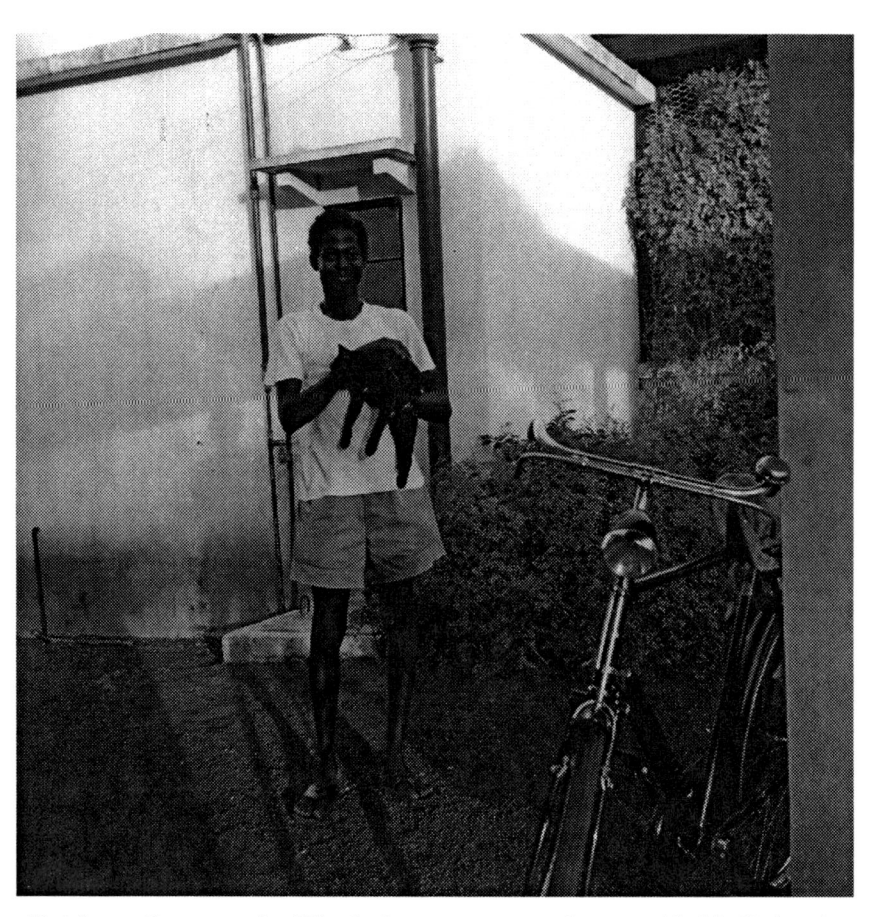

---

19 Adongo Zurungu, aka 'Charles' our paragon cook-steward holds Sheba, the black cat we brought from Accra.

20 O, with Ferdie and Sid the baboon, both of whom we inherited in Tamale.

21 Sunday morning 1959, 7 a.m 'meet' of the Tamale Polo Club at our bungalow starts with brandy and ginger before hacking and return for 9 a.m. breakfast and more brandy. O. on left, Keith Hitchcock on Sindbad and Ralph Little on Tusker.

22 Probably 1960. O, Paul Gautier and I make unsuccessful hunting excursion up the Black Volta near Kintampo. We nearly capsize our tiny canoe, get lost for hours in the bush, all for one francolin which O. is holding.

23 Tom Gardner and I build the first powered boat to be launched on the White Volta above the dry season bridge at Yapei. We later receive note from Tom's UAC storekeeper in nearby village *'Dear Sir, I beg to assure you your boat is totally sunk. I have the honour to be, Kotoku, X, his mark.'*

24 1961. O. with our daughter Isobel born in Tamale, on the stoep of our bungalow.

Still None The Wiser

25 Author with rod and gun on the White Volta at Daboya, 1960..Sporting dress standards have slipped since 1955.

26 1961, staff photo at Tamale. Wonderful N. Storph, then Chief Clerk, left centre. I was so ill I was carried out in my chair by Peter and Winfriend, the two messengers, front.

27 Visiting Yendi Branch 1961, Wonderful N. Storph, centre in tie, now manager.

28 Proper' (i.e. non-sport) Dagomba fisherman on White Volta displays catch.

Still None The Wiser

29 1966 Lagos, Ikoyi, Oliver Eke our 'small boy' shortly before he left to return to the East as the Biafran War flared.

Still None The Wiser

30 1965 Yoruba hunter with 'Dane gun' on banks of River Ogun.

Still None The Wiser

31 1965 Benjamin Ladipo 'dressed to kill' with (dead) monkey near Ikorudu. He holds an antique English duelling pistol for reasons which now escape me.

Still None The Wiser

32 'Fingal O'Plinge' and Ben Ladipo on Ogun River re-tracing Sir Richard Burton's 1860 tracks in same area. Note breakfast beer bottle to hand.

Still None The Wiser

33 Jimoh Babatunde, Yoruba blacksmith holding flintlock musket he made for me in 1964.

Still None The Wiser

34 1965, hunting dogs queuing to have their wooden bells hung around their necks.

35 1966, Paul Gautier and fellow 'Sunday hunters' in Ikorudu forest. Probably the last trip we made together before violence and unrest made such excursions too risky.

CHAPTER 24

'Bee Palaver'

"How doth the little busy bee
Improve each shining hour,
And gather honey all the day
From every opening flower!"
(Isaac Watts 1674 - 1748)
"Ow-wow-ow-OOOWWW! ... Merde!!!"
(Michel Cordon, near Savelugu, 1960)

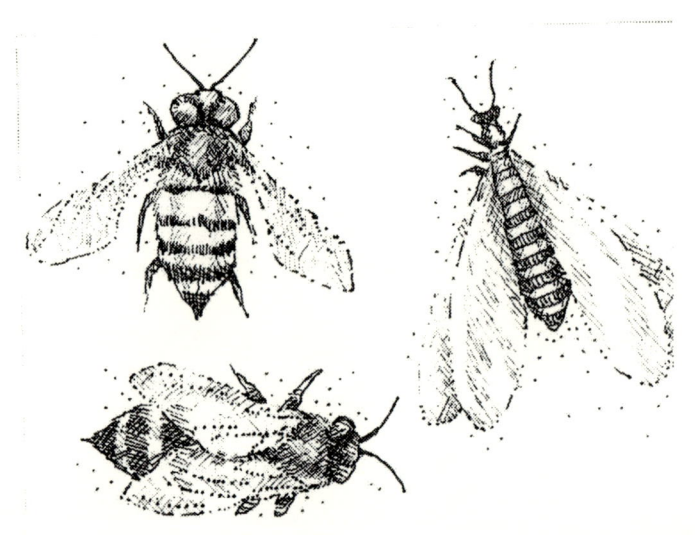

Second Lieutenant 'Poxy'* Plinge from the infantry battalion of the Ghana Army based in Tamale was off in the bush to the north with his platoon on a training exercise, preparing to camp for the night.

---

* (Note: He earned this unfortunate nickname in the Congo when his battalion formed part of Ghana's contribution to the UN so-called 'Peace-Keeping' Forces during the regime of mayhem, anarchy and violence that followed Independence from Belgium in 1960. 2nd Lt. Plinge - because he spoke French became the UN Force's official liaison officer with a provincial Congolese governor, whose mistress was an accommodating lady with whom Plinge forged a close bond in the interests of furthering his official duties. Plinge subsequently suffered an embarrassing attack of 'Cupid's Measles' as a result of this association – which he averred was strictly in the line of duty and its unfortunate side effects as honourable as any battle wound. His brother officers, when they stopped laughing, henceforth knew him as 'Poxy.')

"We shall camp here, Sergeant," said Poxy, indicating the immediate area surrounding a large, isolated baobab tree. It would be dark within the hour.

"I beg you Sah, not here - no be fit." Replied his African platoon sergeant. "More better we no camp for dey - too plenty bees for dis tree."

"They won't trouble us," said Poxy "put up your bivouacs, get a fire going and tell the men to clean their weapons before they start chop." "*Sah*!" Responded the sergeant, he'd offered his advice, it had been rejected. He'd done his duty. Nature could now take its course.

After a while, one of a group of soldiers sitting on the ground cleaning their rifles, let out a piercing yell, slapping the back of his neck. "Bees! Sah - dey trouble me too much!"

"Stand your ground," said Poxy noticing some of the other men beginning to wave their arms about, letting out the occasional yelp, "if you don't bother the bees, they won't bother you! Whatever you do, don't PANIC!!!" He yelled as the men started to jump to their feet, dropping the weapons they were cleaning - starting to run off into the surrounding bush. "STAND STILL! Roared Poxy. "If you stand still and DON'T MOVE - THEY WON'T STING YOU!!!" He shouted after the retreating figure of the platoon sergeant. The men gazed back in admiration from a safe distance, rubbing their stings ruefully - while watching their intrepid leader standing rigidly at attention beneath the baobab tree as the centrepiece of a swirling cloud of bees.

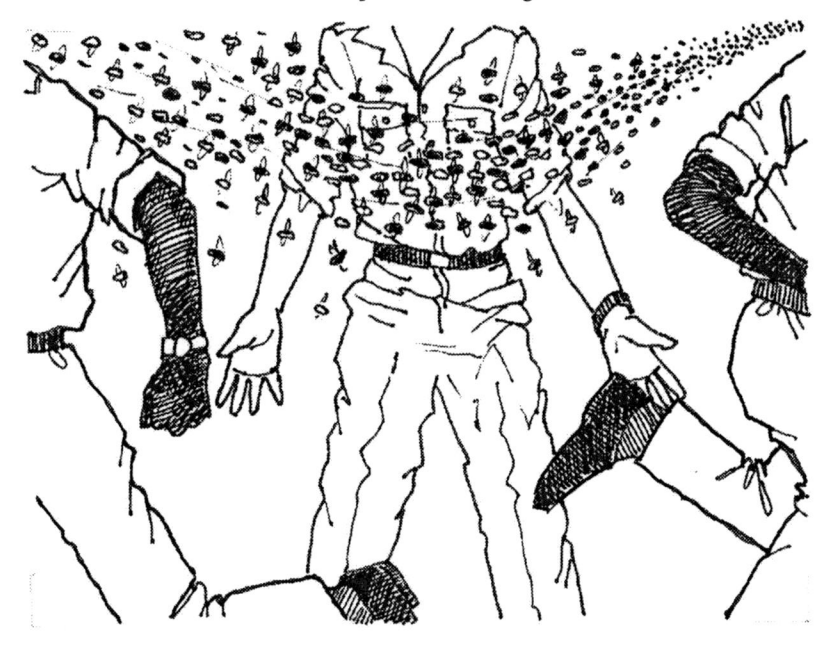

At last, after at least fifteen seconds (which is a long time in such circumstances), the truth became apparent to Poxy Plinge. He had now become the principal target of an ever increasing swarm of agitated bees pouring out of every crack and hollow of the knobbly, grey trunk of the baobab. His composure broken, with wildly flailing arms he fled - trailing an angrily boiling plume of bees behind him as he ran off into the bush - his soldiers scattering at his approach, anxious to protect themselves from Poxy's attendant cloud of venomous harpies.

It took Poxy and his men most of the night, crawling through the dark without a light that would have drawn more bees down to them, to recover their weapons and kit before daylight placed them in danger again. Poxy was the worst stung of them all and became quite feverish - as well as hungry during what was a very long night.

History has a habit of repeating itself in the same manner that Life often imitates Art - or is it the other way around? In *'On the March to Bole - 1917"* another writer, also an officer in the Gold Coast Regiment of the WAFF recounts a similar set of circumstances while putting down a minor insurrection in the Northern Territories. Approaching a rebellious village his entire column is put to flight by a swarm of bees. Carriers, white officers and NCOs, troops abandoning rifles, all bolting wildly to the derisive jeers of the watching villagers. The author is obviously a religious man for he quotes Mahomet's Surah of the Bee, from the Koran - *"If ye make reprisals, then make them to the same extent that ye were injured, but if ye can endure patiently, best will it be for the patiently enduring."* (This advice remains as politically apposite at the end of the 20th century as it was in 1917).

The wild African honey bee is probably the most dangerous creature (excluding man and barring the mosquito) that the average, sensible traveller is likely to encounter in tropical Africa. Of uncertain temper, common almost everywhere - and sometimes in huge colonies, they are not to be trifled with, least of all by the inexperienced. Their honey is dark and sweet and much valued by the African, as is the wax from the combs - but then the locals have had long practice in dealing with them. I personally knew one European in later years who was killed by bees in 1974 while rock-climbing at Jos in Nigeria, and earlier in 1960 I was involved myself when an African was stung to death.

In Tamale our bungalow on the 'Agriculture' Ridge to the north of the town was surrounded by 'bee trees' - where the nearby villagers had lodged hollow lengths of log in the upper branches to encourage the bees to settle there whenever the frequent

---

* 'Our Days on the Gold Coast' Ed. Lady Clifford, John Murray 1918.

swarms passed by. At night, particularly on dark, moonless nights, if we sat out on the stoep for our coffee or for a final nightcap, we would often see and hear the honey-gatherers at work with dim lanterns and glowing, smoking torches, climbing about in the upper branches raiding the hives.

We also had trouble from time to time in the bungalow. Out at the back of the house there were two kitchens, each with its own wood-burning 'Dover' stove. Why we had two I never knew (O. said that the second kitchen was properly for the laundry). Our Cook-Steward, Charles, whose real name was Adongo Zuarungu, but named Charles by a predecessor for some reason, only ever used the one kitchen, as the washing always seemed to be done in one of the bathrooms. The unused kitchen stove attracted a swarm of bees who took up residence in the flue-pipe. Charles said nothing about it and neither O. nor I noticed what was happening in our spare domestic 'office' until Charles observed to O. one day that honey was running out of the wood-stove on to the floor in the unoccupied kitchen and that the bees were beginning to make it difficult for him to cook - or to iron in the adjoining room - except in ever shorter bursts of activity - to the detriment of our normally efficient household.

Events overtook us before any remedy was determined upon. Shortly after dark one evening O. and I were awaiting Charles' usual enquiry. "Pass chop now Madam?" The table was already laid, when Charles ran in from the covered way that led to the kitchens - minus food. He announced that the kitchen was full of bees, that he was getting stung - "Dem bees humbug me too much!" he complained, allowing O. to pick out a couple of stings and apply a little soothing TCP. At that point, the electricity supply failed - as it frequently did. All the lights went out and as we lit the oil lamps and candles that were always kept in a state of readiness, we noticed that more and more bees were now flying about in the room, obviously attracted to what was now the only source of light. The three of us rapidly closed all the windows and the glass-covered doors that led to the outside.

It grew stiflingly hot. We swatted and killed most of the bees that had found their way in. The odd bee bumbled its way in through keyhole or ill-fitting window frame. We noticed that the window and door panes on which our soft, dim lantern lights were reflecting were becoming covered on the outside with a thick veil of bees attempting to force a passage to the light. It was now out of the question for Charles to attempt to retrieve our 'chop' from the kitchen. Charles said after an hour or so with no sign of the bee-siege lifting, that he would make a run for it in the dark, to reach his own quarters on the far edge of the compound. This he did, easing out swiftly through the door that O. and I briefly opened for him, folded newspapers in our hands ready for any bee that slipped by. O. and I sat down by candlelight to a dinner of bread and water, with Worcester Sauce, which was all that Charles had delivered to the table before the bees brought proceedings to a halt.

After our meagre repast we decided we might as well go to bed. O. then exited and safely made it to our bedroom in the dark, feet crunching on dead and dying bees that lay underfoot. I decided that I needed to visit the bathroom and foolishly taking a candle with me I followed O. a moment later down the open passageway at the back and went into the bathroom. This had a clear glass door (I think the original Lebanese builder had cornered the local market for these - they contributed little to one's privacy). I put the candlestick down, closed the bathroom window to keep out any more bees that might be on that side, and attended to my ablutions. These satisfactorily completed, I suddenly realised that both window and glass door were now festooned with bees - on the outside. I was trapped!

I shouted to O. in the adjoining bedroom telling her to extinguish her own candle, to wait five minutes - then at my signal to open the bedroom window to allow me in. I blew out my candle, waited in the dark, then cautiously opened the bathroom window, climbed out and dropped down onto the driveway, tapped on the bedroom window which O. opened then I climbed in like some illicit swain, rapidly closing the window behind me. It was quite ridiculous that we could be brought to such a pass by a mere swarm of bees - except these were potential killers.

The next morning revealed the scale of the assault. All around the house lay a wide carpet of dead bees - the stoep outside the verandah doors to the living room was layered inches thick with their corpses, to the width of a foot or more. There must have been millions of dead bees! Charles and the garden boy gaped in amazement as they swept them up by the bucket load. Our kitchen hive was still active and buzzing so where they had all come from was anyone's guess.

We called in the 'Pest Control Officer' (sic) from the Town Council - I was surprised to discover that such a person still existed, perhaps as a hangover from the old Colonial regime that had finally expired some three years earlier. After all we still had occasional inspections from the Public Health Department to check that we had no obvious mosquito breeding-sites in the garden, or near the house - such as empty tins or bottles, which would hold rainwater - or even Canna Lillies whose funnel-like leaves held water and allowed the mosquito larvae to flourish. The 'Bee Man' was a small and cheerful character (surprisingly so considering his painful trade) who arrived early one morning on a bicycle carrying a large tin of white powder and a 'Flit'-gun. He wore tattered shorts and a singlet as his only form of protection. I was at work that morning so relied on O.'s description of what followed.

Once the bee-hive was pointed out, the 'Bee Man' shinned up onto the kitchen roof clutching his tin, and immediately beset by a multitude of angry bees plunged his arm down the flue-pipe and proceeded to pull out large chunks of wax and comb, dripping with honey. These he then threw out onto the roof, scattering them far and wide. He continued to do this until he could withstand the attentions of the furious bees no longer and messily tipped most of the contents of his tin down the chimney, scattering the remaining white powder on the honeycombs and the honey dripping down the roof into the guttering. He jumped down to the ground and fled. On reflection it seemed a less than satisfactory method of pest control.

O. and Charles took him into the house and helped him to wash off the honey and the dead and dying bees which still clung fast, attached by a wisp of glistening membrane to their barbed stings and pulsating poison-sacs now embedded in the 'Bee Man's' skin. He was badly stung and in considerable pain. O. brought him the bottle of TCP after all the stings had been carefully plucked out - dabbing it plentifully on the welts which covered his head, arms and legs. A beatific smile creased his cheerful face. "Ah! Madam" he said, "dat be plenty powerful medicine, 'e fix dem bee-sting proper, one-time!" O. asked him about his usual *modus operandi* for dealing with domestically entrenched bees and he confessed that what she had just witnessed was more or less his usual practice and that he was always badly stung. The Town Council provided nothing but a small wage and the 'white powder.' O. 'dashed' the 'Bee Man' a few shillings for his pains - plus the remains of the TCP. Away he rode, wobbling precariously on his bicycle, waving cheerfully, brandishing the prized bottle of TCP and a wad of cotton wool.

The brave 'Bee Man's' efforts virtually came to naught for although the resident bees were partially exterminated they were only temporarily discouraged, the scattered comb and honey left on the roof attracted ever more bees from the surrounding colonies and within a month of two the hive was once again flourishing in the kitchen chimney.

Bees were an ever present problem. In November 1960 our daughter Isobel was born in the small Government-run West Hospital near the Army lines. Under the eaves of the roof above the two bed ward where mother and new-born child lay, there was the constant, steady humming of a thriving colony of bees - stilled only at night. A week or two later after O. had brought our infant home to the bungalow, O. had put her down to rest in her cot, in our bedroom which was shaded and airy. The windows were wide open, but because there was a slight breeze that morning O had put the cot underneath the big mosquito net which covered our bed.

O. was sitting in the next room, reading or sewing, when she noticed an all-pervading humming noise, plus the odd bee or two winging its way through the bedroom door. Going to the open doorway she looked in to check that Isobel was safe. To her horror she saw a large globular cluster of bees attached to the mosquito wire which held the net suspended over the bed - and the still quietly sleeping child.

Highly alarmed and sensibly thinking it unwise to rush in and risk both herself and Isobel - she called for Charles, who came running. With great aplomb Charles grabbed hold of a broom (his usual weapon for dealing with hazardous intruders) and O. cautiously following, Charles gently pushed the swarm off the wire with the brush, guiding it through the air to the open window from whence it slowly made its way to the wild-fig tree in the garden, where it attached itself to a limb. O. grabbed Isobel from under the net while Charles hastily slammed shut the windows.

I think it was either that year or the next when the Queen, as Head of the Commonwealth, was due to make an official visit to Ghana - including Tamale. Before her tour was cancelled, owing to her pregnancy with Prince Andrew, the Town Council panicked when they realised quite how many 'bee-trees' were located along her likely route through the town and its environs. The PWD were hurriedly mobilised and in the months before the Queen's intended arrival, carried out a 'Chainsaw Massacre' of all the likely trees around.

One bee-episode ended badly. It occurred one Sunday when Michel Cordon, the French manager of CFAO (who had succeeded Gautier) and I went for an early morning duck-shooting trip north of Tamale. By ten o'clock we were driving homewards down the Bolgatanga road to Tamale for a late breakfast. The morning was hot and overcast. We were bowling along in my VW 'Beetle' with the windows and sun-roof wide open enjoying the breeze when past the village of Savelugu we whizzed by a small group of people on the roadside who waved and shouted, jumping up and down as they gestured wildly, laughing and yelling. Michel and I waved back and drove on. There was nothing unusual in this. Had we stopped, I assumed that one or more of them would have begged a lift into Tamale.

Suddenly, ahead of us, below the huge bulk of a stumpy baobab tree at the roadside, fifty yards and more away we saw what appeared to be a fire burning in the middle of the road. But strangely there was no visible flame, only a column of smoke rising from a jumbled and barely moving bundle of matting on the ground. It was difficult to see clearly because of the haze of smoke which shimmered and shifted, swirling around the weird, upside-down branches of the baobab - more like air-borne roots than limbs.

I had slowed the VW down to a crawl and both Michel and I realised simultaneously that we were now looking at a human body wrapped in a straw mat. With a shock heightened by alarm as the drifts of smoke turned into a cloud of bees that enveloped the car - which was now filling rapidly with angry demons that stung and buzzed and crawled up and around our heads and shoulders. As I rammed the gear lever into reverse and gunned the motor I noticed a human arm limply extending from the loose bundle on the ground.

"MERDE!!! ALLEZ - ALLEZ ALLEZ!! - VITE!!! AAaaaarrrGGHH!! Roared Michel as I reversed back up the road at maximum revs - I must have reached top speed for a VW in reverse gear but we had gone no more than a few yards before it became obvious that the car was already dangerously full of bees that stung us in successive relays, jockeying for position. They were pursuing us and in reverse we could not outpace them.

I braked to a squealing halt, stalled the motor as we flung both doors open wide - 'à la Keystone Cops' and leaving key in the ignition and guns and ducks behind, Michel and I fled. I was luckier than Michel, for he sprinted full pelt up the middle of the road in a haze of furious bees towards the small knot of Africans who were now nervously retreating even further away. I ran off into the bush which fringed the roadside, figuring that if the bees couldn't see me, they would leave off their pursuit. I dragged my shirt over my head for protection and ran - and ran - and ran, twisting and turning through the tall grass and scrubby trees until at last I sensed myself free of my pursuers. I rejoined Michel and the Africans on the road, where we cleared the bees from our clothes and hair and carefully pulled out the stings and their attached poison-sacs. I had received about twenty stings - Michel had forty or so. They were very painful.

The car now lay abandoned sixty or seventy yards away and itself about twenty or thirty yards from the baobab tree. The cloud of bees seemed to grow ever thicker. The matting bundle barely moved. The Africans chattered and laughed - they said the man who lay on the road was a cripple from the village who had been riding his donkey past the baobab tree when it must have been stung by a bee, bolted and thrown its rider from his perch on its rump. We were the first vehicle to pass by for nearly an hour. They said the bees had then attacked the cripple and that by now he was almost certainly dead. This huge baobab was well-known as one great hive from its hollow base to the top of the trunk. As long as the man lay there, dead or alive - or until it became dark, the bees would continue to call on their seemingly endless reserves from the bowels of the giant bee-hive and from the foraging workers returning to base. They would selflessly commit suicide (unlike wasps or hornets who can sting their victim repeatedly - a bee stings but once, fatally disembowelling itself in the process) in defence of the colony, excited to excess by the scent of bee-venom and the angry vibrations of their fellow warriors which acts as a trigger to their aggression.

Neither Michel nor I could get anywhere near the abandoned car. Each time we approached the bees sensed our presence and gathering their cohorts and squadrons swept in to attack, forcing us to flee again. The continual chatter and laughter of the villagers began to annoy us. Michel remonstrated with them, uselessly. I suppose it was no more than a nervous reaction to a situation about which they could do nothing, a way of asserting how fortunate they were to have been spared themselves - or perhaps of placating the spirits who might otherwise bring down misfortune on their own persons. In our more fortunate European homelands we rely on a familiar and well-organised system of rescue and support, ambulances, the fire brigade and police - rarely more than a short telephone call distant. Throughout West Africa, these services are almost entirely non-existent, including the telephone. Disaster and disease for human beings and livestock alike lurk around every corner. When they strike, people count themselves fortunate if they are spared, which is why the children will prod and poke their sticks at the broken-backed dog struck by the passing lorry, laughing at its agony. It is not wanton cruelty but a form of aversion magic that says "Look at me!! I am safe, I am spared once more!" It is why the cripples and beggars outside the big city stores come to the town to hold out their stumps and twisted hands to the European shoppers, ignoring their fellow Africans, most of whom will also ignore them. Charity, compassion and guilt march hand-in-hand with wealth and prosperity. They are luxuries the 'have-nots' do not even dream of possessing. Life, after all, is cheap.

Ten minutes passed, another ten - then in the distance from the north appeared a Land Rover. Michel and I flagged it down. It held a group of Africans from the Veterinary Station at Pong-Tamale driving into town. I persuaded the driver to make room for me in the passenger seat, asking him to stop by our abandoned car and allow me to jump in without attracting too many bees. He grumblingly agreed for the Land Rover was far from bee-proof. As he stopped I jumped across to my VW Beetle, slamming the doors and sliding the open roof shut in double-quick time. As the bees accumulated on the windscreen, futilely trying to force entry, I reversed back to Michel. The Land Rover also gunned its motor, barely slowing as it passed the pathetic bundle of matting on the road. It was none of their business, and anyway the box-body of the Land Rover by now was probably leaking in bees. In Africa, death in all its guises is no stranger.

Michel and I drove up and stopped beneath the baobab tree where the VW became once more covered in bees. There were still clouds of the insects swirling and descending from the bulbous grey trunk of the baobab. Around the bundle of matting on the ground was a thick layer of dead bees, carpeting the road. The bundle did not move, an arm poked out from one side, every inch of skin thickly covered with either crawling insects or the little grey poison sacs torn from the bees' abdomens. There was nothing we could do. Even with hindsight there was nothing we could have done with the resources we had on the spot.

We were back in Tamale at the bungalow within twenty minutes. I telephoned Hans Mees, the Dutch doctor in charge of the Tamale hospital, to alert him in case we could recover the casualty and get him to the hospital. O. and I collected spare mosquito netting, rubber gloves, boots and hats - plus our trusty Flit-gun well-primed with Shelltox - while Michel ran across the road to alert our neighbour T., who had a much larger car than my two-door Beetle. T. drove round and as we hurriedly packed his car with our puny rescue aids O. dabbed at the bee-stings with which Michel and I were still covered. Our small rescue party then tore off again at high speed up the road to the north.

We arrived at the scene to find two more arrivals. John Ramsay, the Forest Officer, a neighbour of ours had been driving north in his car and had stopped, 'Ramjohn' said that a few mammy lorries and cars driven by Africans had passed straight through without stopping.

The other arrival was an American missionary whom I knew as a client of the Bank, the Reverend Mordecai Plinge. He was either a Southern Baptist or from the Assemblies of God Mission at Wale-Wale near Bolgatanga, further to the north. The niceties of distinguishing between the various dogmas of these evangelising churches now escapes me, but dealing as I did with their financial transactions I had a passing interest in the way in which they practised their calling, the American varieties in particular.

I will briefly digress on the subject of American missionaries (our bee-stung casualty will not leave the scene I am describing). Few of them were educators other than in the religious sense; a few more professed an immediate or obviously useful skill, such as medicine or farming or basic engineering - but the principal benefit they mostly afforded their flock was the promise of salvation. Their interest in local culture and religion was prompted by their need to counter what they interpreted as the Work of the Devil. They were usually self-funded in this drive towards their own peculiar vision of Redemption in that whenever they became short of cash, they would return to their home-bases in the United States, often in the Bible Belt of the mid-West, embark on a series of illustrated lecture tours with lantern-slides of the Benighted Heathen and within a period of six months or so would raise ample funds to support themselves and their families in considerable comfort for another couple of years in the 'Wilds' of Africa. Their houses, sometimes built (I must admit) by themselves, were invariably lavishly equipped with diesel generators, air-conditioning, capacious freezers, personal medical stores, servants' quarters (guaranteed employment was reserved for their early converts) and flocks of poultry, goats and whatever other livestock would flourish. In earlier years in Takoradi and Accra I had often overseen the clearance through Customs of their household stores and refrigerated containers in transit to their up-country mission stations. Some owned and flew small planes to ease their transport difficulties in remote areas. Others had lavishly equipped 'safari' wagons to add comfort to their pioneering existence. The fact that most, if not all of them had forsworn the consumption of alcohol in all its forms meant that they rarely socialised with other expatriates. That was their loss, not ours, but it was a pity from the point of view of the sex-starved European bachelors, as many of the missionaries had large families, including some remarkably pretty, nubile daughters. The over-high price for pressing any suit in this direction probably involved a public and personal commitment to salvation as well as to total abstinence.

The Reverend Mordecai Plinge was tall and spare, dressed in standard American missionary garb of Panama hat, steel-rimmed spectacles, short-sleeved check shirt with a breast pocketful of pens, white T-shirt peeping through at the neckline, crisply pressed chinos and sensible shoes. Gaunt and gangling, an Elmer Gantry look-alike - he was also stern and uncommunicative. He already had the situation in hand; he had arrived in his large American station-wagon with his African driver to whom he was now issuing instructions. I'll say this for the Reverend Mordecai, he was a brave and determined man and one could easily visualise him on the deck of a battleship under Kamikaze attack belting out "Praise the Lord - and pass the ammunition!"

He lay on his belly in the back of the station wagon facing the tail gate, which was just barely open. We draped our tatty old net over him, gave him our rubber gloves and pumped the vehicle full of Shelltox from the flit-gun while the Reverend and his driver coughed and spluttered in the fumes.

Still None The Wiser

The driver gunned the motor and reversed the big station wagon back towards the pathetic bundle on the road and as it stopped Mordecai Plinge threw open the tailgate, leaned out, arms extended and grabbed the victim's body dragging it by brute force half onto the vehicle floor - yelling to his driver "GET THE (EXPLETIVES DELETED) OUTTA HERE NOW! NOW!!!-ow-wow-OWWW!" I half expected to see both the Reverend Plinge and the body of the victim spill out onto the road as the driver spun the wheels in a cloud of burning rubber and accelerated madly towards us.

The interior of the station wagon was swirling with bees, but the main body had not pursued the rescuers all the way back. We sprayed and swatted while the Reverend Plinge tried to clear the cripple's mouth and nostrils of bees and wrapped him in our net. There were no signs of life. The Reverend Plinge, his driver and the victim now roared off south down the road making for the hospital at Tamale. Before we drove off ourselves, T. took us up to the bee tree in his now hermetically sealed car. The bees were still pouring out of the baobab and dead bees lay in drifts and swathes across the road. The straw mat, a conical straw hat and a solitary discarded sandal - were the only reminders of the tragedy. We noticed that at the side of the road there was a ditch full of water apparently deep enough to have given the cripple a chance to escape if he had managed to roll the short distance. Maybe he had been stunned when he fell off the donkey.

We were back at the bungalow again by half-past eleven, O. and Charles gave Michel and me a late breakfast - coffee and toast - and honey!

`Later that day, Hans Mees drove up from town bringing back our old mosquito net and other bits and pieces. The victim had died shortly after reaching hospital. Hans said they had scraped a bucketful of bees from his body as they tried to save him, that his mouth and throat had been choked with stings and that he had no detectable blood pressure on arrival. Injections of adrenaline had no effect. Hans said "There was not a square inch of his body that had not been stung several times over!" I asked Hans what he had actually died from. "Total body failure - of every single organ!"

These were the same species of wild African bee that was later introduced into Brazil for experimental purposes in the 1960s - and which then inevitably, escaped into the wild, cross-breeding with and dominating the native honey bees and inexorably spreading north into Central America and the Southern States of the USA - true 'Killer Bees' - the stuff of which nightmares are made.

CHAPTER 25

'Alas poor Yaro – I knew him well'

"*As regards domestic staff, it should be remembered that cooks and stewards are a definite profession in this country, enjoying higher status than their opposite numbers in England. It should be borne in mind that food for the European is quite unlike what the cook is used to himself. This is why the cook is so much more expert with food to which he is accustomed, curries, groundnut and palm oil chop and the like.*"

(From: *'Notes for the Guidance of Europeans in Ghana'*
Chamber of Mines, Tarkwa, 1957.)

As soon as one employs a servant - and by 'servant' I do not mean a part-time cleaning lady - then you take over a measure of responsibility for another person's life. At the same time you divest yourself of an equal measure of your own independence. The pattern of each party's life undergoes radical change. The previously ruling maxim that one's personal life is entirely one's own business flies out of the window. Privacy and freedom are diminished to a considerable degree and one is immediately beset with cares and duties. When the servant is an African then the difficulties of coming to terms with a symbiotic master-servant relationship are liable to be compounded by cultural differences and linguistic incompatibility. Making do without servants for those who make their living in the Third World is seldom a realistic option. Apart from any practical aspect it deprives the host country's inhabitants of both employment and the chances of at least some small proportion of the expatriate's (usually) inflated salary being ploughed back into the local economy. At least two young married couples of my acquaintance tried to do without servants, either on grounds of economy or in a mistaken Fabian belief that one should not have servants as a matter of principle. It was never long before one or both partners cracked and recanted. Without servants they soon found that their social life was restricted and running a household single-handed in the tropics soon becomes an exhausting chore for a young English bride. Far better to endure the petty tyrannies of a cook or house-boy.

One hopes that George Bernard Shaw was wearing his whimsical Irish hat (the cap with the bells on it) when he said. "*When domestic servants are treated as human beings it is not worth the while to keep them.*" Shaw's tongue-in-cheek dictum may however strike a wistful chord with many an old Africa hand recalling the frequent vicissitudes of domestic management in far-off days and places. 'Cook Palaver,' 'Steward Palaver,' 'Garden Boy Palaver,' 'Small Boy Palaver,' 'Nightwatch Palaver' - and if married with children, 'Nanny Palaver.' In West Africa no-one could live there for long without coming under siege. Those who came off the best were invariably the middle-aged bachelor Coasters who had often kept the same 'boy' for years - both becoming accustomed to each other's foibles, like some comfortably long-married couple. Although of East African origin rather than a 'Coast' story I have long relished Margaret Lane's tale of C. J. P. Ionides, the veteran 'Snake Man' (ex-Game Warden and ex-elephant poacher, who like Fred Selous[*], the 'great Nimrod' of the late Victorian era, was educated at Rugby). She recounts her tale of sitting at Ionides' somewhat basic bachelor table when he accuses the cook of failing to fill the pepper pot. The cook, not unreasonably, having served Ionides for nineteen years, pointed out that his employer was trying to shake the pepper out from the wrong end of the pot. Ionides exploded with rage, shouting. "Who are you to tell me from which end I should shake my own pepper pot? YOU ARE SACKED!!! Pack and leave AT ONCE!!" Margaret Lane was interested to note that at breakfast the following morning both Ionides and the cook were present and showing no signs of the previous night's rancour.

That said, I remember most (but certainly not all) of my household retainers with affection and regret that neither can I belatedly apologise to them for my sometimes outrageous and eccentric behaviour nor is there now any way of learning how they fared in their later lives.

Looking back it is difficult to remember what one's expectations about servants might have been when first arriving on the Coast. There was the ideal, as portrayed in 'Boys' Own' safari stories of the loyal gun-bearer type who could track a wounded buffalo (sometimes sacrificing his own life in the process to save his master) while also doing the laundry and cooking roast eland and Yorkshire pudding on the camp fire. There was the real life example I knew of in the Persian Gulf, of the Englishman's Sikh major-domo who faced down a mob of rioters intent on burning and looting his master's bungalow. Bearded and turbanned, Gulab Singh, stood fearless and alone on the verandah, looking down on the noisy rabble while brandishing a gleaming, curved tulwar, declaiming. "Ten men die before the Sahib!" While the said 'Sahib' peered out in a blue funk from behind the shutters. The rioters sensibly withdrew, then went

---

[*] Frederick Courtney Selous, 1853-1917, shot through the head by one of General Paul von Lettow-Vorbeck's formidable askari Schutztruppen, in action in Tanganyika, at the age of sixty-four - possibly the oldest fighting subaltern ever in the British army. Selous National Park in Tanzania is named for him.

next door and burned down the neighbouring bungalow, murdering its occupants. The courageous and faithful Sikh was later rewarded on his master's return to London by being set up as a door-to-door oriental carpet salesman in Knightsbridge.

There is the other side of the coin an example of which occurred during the first massacre of the Ibos in Kano in 1965 (Nigeria became independent in 1961). A Dutchman (Wim de Bonk), about to sit down to lunch, saw a Landrover full of armed Hausa police sweep into his compound. They stormed into his kitchen, seized the Ibo cook and steward and started to drag them off. The bold Dutchman confronted the policemen, demanding they release his servants. "Besides," he said, "I haven't had my lunch yet!" "Don't worry Sah." Came the reply. "*We* were trained by the British." Whereupon they let the two men go, the police sitting idly by in the compound while the Dutchman's meal was served and cleared. When all was finished, including the washing-up, the Hausa police took the two Ibo servants outside again and shot them against the garage wall.

What we all ended up with, both masters and servants, was usually something falling far short of these somewhat extreme examples.

In Joyce Cary's classic tragi-comic novel of West Africa, 'Mister Johnson' there is a scene when the newly arrived bride of Rudbeck, the District Officer, is served a dish prepared by her husband's cook. "What is *this* supposed to be?" she asks Rudbeck, looking at her soup bowl. Rudbeck briefly removes the pipe otherwise permanently clenched between his teeth, gazes in some surprise at his own plate, saying. "Why, my dear? It's groundnut soup, isn't it?" His wife, bursting into tears, wails. "But darling - it's just hot water with some peanuts in it!"

Quite a number of bachelors in British Africa tolerated this style of cuisine without a second thought simply because it was easier to do so than to upset their own - or their cook's equanimity - by demanding something better. The fault did not lie with the cook. But the servants of a bachelor Coaster's household seldom survived with any measure of success their master's transition to the married state.

When I arrived in Sekondi in 1954 I had to establish my domestic arrangements from scratch. All a simple bachelor establishment generally required was a Cook/Steward who could cook basic European meals, shop for food in the market well enough to buy the necessaries, clean, wash and iron. I ended up with Yaro - who stayed with me for the next four years. I suppose in a way we grew up together.

Yaro was a Frafra from the far-off Northern Territories of the then Gold Coast, how old I never knew but I suppose he was of an age a little younger than me, nineteen or perhaps twenty at the most. He had a proper registration card - all domestic servants had to be licensed by the Police - and a reference (of sorts) from a previous employer, a PWD man for whom he had worked as a 'small-boy.' He could speak a certain amount of pidgin and claimed that until his previous 'Master' had retired to the UK he had sometimes doubled as cook. The reference from his previous master simply stated that Yaro had 'worked' for him for six months.

References were sometimes written by previous employers in a sort of ambiguous coded shorthand, and required careful consideration to decipher them. Employees of all types, even if dismissed for stealing would usually request a reference. Phrases such as 'Kofi has carried out his duties entirely to his own satisfaction,' or 'Kofi came to us as he left us, fired with enthusiasm,' or 'It will be a fortunate employer who succeeds in getting Kofi to work for him,' required a second glance. 'Kofi looked after all his master's possessions as if they were his own' was not unknown as was 'As a cook Kofi has always been light-fingered.' Or again 'Kofi has very taking ways and is very good at lifting things and has lifted many things from here.' I even heard of one reference which said; 'My wife and I at all times have found Kofi to be very trying. I truly believe this man to be capable of anything and I can assure you that if you employ him you will find that he will do you as he has done for us.' Alas, poor 'Kofi' - most of the 'Kofis' that I knew were in reality mini-paragons of virtue and honesty, if sometimes a little hazy about the expenditure of the daily marketing money or explaining why one needed to buy so much sugar and tea and matches. Unlike many 'madams' who so distrusted their servants that they kept the key to the store cupboard and doled out the tea and the sugar as needed to the cook, I never felt any need to do so - and neither in later years did my wife. To keep a meticulous check on items like matches, or tea and sugar and rice was demeaning to all parties.

With Yaro I always made the mistake of assuming that he somehow 'knew' how to do things - how to cook, how to clean, what food I needed - in short, taking him at his own face value was not a successful ploy. If I said "Yaro, you savvy how to do dis-ting?" Yaro would invariably reply, "Yes Massah, I savvy." The results could be both disgusting as well as disastrous.

The first morning in my employ Yaro appeared on the scene at a quarter-to-seven (I had given him my alarm clock) with a bad case of 'first day nerves' and the sound of his bare feet padding across the wooden floor and a loud chinking and rattling of tumblers and bottles on a tin beer tray woke me from my sweaty slumbers. Putting the tray down beside the bed he drew aside the mosquito net, gesturing to the tray.

Instead of the expected refreshing 'cup that cheers, never inebriates,' (I had of course neglected any instruction the previous night apart from the time that I wished to arise), the tray contained a glass, a bottle of cold boiled and filtered water, my new bottle of gin and two large bottles of Heineken from the fridge. "Yaro," I said patiently, "what is this - where is my cup of *tea?*" "*Tea*, Master?" Looking genuinely nervous and puzzled, he added. "But Master - all whitemen drink gin and beer for morning time - no be so?" I later gathered that this was how his previous, and only, employer had bump-started each shaky day.

Yaro's pidgin was poor, but as time passed we eventually managed to communicate in a reasonable fashion. Many Africans from the hinterland * unfamiliar with western ways found the Europeans totally incomprehensible - rather I imagine like wayward children needing to be humoured. I fear at times that the depths of our mutual incomprehension were never fully plumbed. Not perhaps to the extent of my colleague, Arthur Ball in Takoradi. Arthur one day sent his cook to the United Africa Company's store, to buy "A packet of plaice and some fresh lettuce." That evening when Arthur bemoaned the lack of fish and salad at his dinner table, and asked the cook what he had bought, the cook produced for Arthur's bemused inspection a packet of Players' cigarettes and a discreetly wrapped 'weekend economy' pack of what were then euphemistically known as 'French Letters.' It is fair to say that Arthur at that time although a smoker was a remarkably celibate bachelor.

There was also of course the bachelor Coaster who one day noticed that his sherry bottle's contents were almost imperceptibly diminishing day by day. Thinking to deter his steward whom he suspected as the culprit, he marked the label (the correct way to do this is to turn the bottle upside down so that the mark on the label is not so obvious). The level continuing to fall, our chap thought to himself. "I'll fix the bastard." He emptied the bottle into another and replaced the contents with urine (his own it must be said). To his amazement the level still continued to fall for the next several days - until unable to stand the suspense any longer, he confronted his steward. "I know it's you - confess now, or you're sacked, you're taking my sherry aren't you?" Came the answer. "Yes Master, each day Cook tell me to put small-small for you soup."

---

* Note: The Africans along the seaboard who had contact with Europeans for the past five hundred years fully understood only too well how the mind of the whiteman functions. Captain Phillips of the 'Hannibal,' he who also reported the 'mammy palaver' at Sekondi involving the Dutch and English factors, wrote in his log in 1693 "The Africans often knew more of the Europeans than the Europeans knew of them ... they know our Troy weights as well as ourselves." In the 1670s the Huguenot Frenchman Jean Barbot wrote: "The Blacks of the Gold Coast ..... having traded with the Europeans since the 14th Century are very well skilled in the nature of all European wares traded there ... they examine everything with as much prudence and ability as any European can do."

As a cook, Yaro was consistent in that if I showed him that I liked some particular dish he would then prepare it day after day until I told him to do something different. If I neglected to tell him what I wanted, or failed to fill in 'the book' for my orders from the UAC's Kingsway Stores where I kept an account or failed to instruct him what to buy in the market, then 'pot luck' could turn up some unwelcome surprises. One day in a fit of exasperation, weary beyond belief of the daily necessity of detailing what I wanted him to buy - I said in effect. "Yaro - you be cook, no be so? You fit go to market? Buy chop, make you cook 'am - then you pass chop for my dinner!"

A somewhat baffled Yaro agreed, a brief smile flickered across his face - which I mistakenly took for enlightenment, and he was gone. That evening Yaro laid my table as usual, I sat down, Yaro said. "Pass chop now Massah?" On my agreeing, he vanished back to the kitchen to re-appear a few moments later with a bowl of plain boiled rice, what next I wondered - a delicious groundnut soup perhaps? Yaro re-appeared with my soup tureen which he set down before me. "Fish soup, Massah." said Yaro.

Yaro's 'fish soup' consisted of the contents of a tin of sardines boiled up in a quart of water.

Time and time again I should have been forewarned that whenever I said to Yaro. "You savvy dis ting, you fit cook 'am?" the fact that he answered "Yes, I savvy" meant no more, no less than that he was willing to have a guess. One Sunday morning down on Sekondi beach as the fishing canoes came in I bought a large, fine crayfish, about two-and-a-half pounds live weight, for a shilling and I took it up the hill to my flat over the Bank, Yaro was outside the kitchen leaning on the open verandah rail, engaged in a long distance conversation with some compatriot in the market that adjoined the Bank compound at the back. "Yaro," I said, "you savvy dis ting, fine chop too much! Make you cook him for lunch today, OK?" Yaro took the spiny, wriggling crayfish from me without hesitation, with all the aplomb of a Billingsgate fishmonger. "Yes Massah!" Said Yaro.

I spent the rest of the morning with my neighbour Jacques chatting and drinking beer, looking forward to my cold crayfish tail, with a mayonnaise dressing (bottled perforce) with a spoonful or two of (tinned) Russian salad. As I passed the kitchen on my way back to the flat for a late lunch - a vile smell assaulted my nostrils and I saw Yaro bending over the wood-fired oven, pushing in more mahogany off-cuts as flame and smoke belched out through the open fire-door. "I wonder what he's doing?" I thought to myself. "He's probably cooking up some disgusting chop for himself."

"Pass chop!" I said to Yaro, having settled myself at the table. The foul smell preceded my triumphant cook as he bustled in, setting down my largest meat dish in front of me. Resting on the dish was the hot, smoking carapace of the crayfish, emitting wisps of evil smelling vapour and oozing a greenish slime from the joints of the shell and its blackened extremities. "YARO!!" I shouted. "How you think I fit eat THIS!!!"

"Ah-hahh!" Said Yaro. "Massah no fit open am." With that astute observation he went over to the sideboard where he took my carving knife and fork from the open canteen, laying them down beside my plate, a dish cloth neatly folded over his forearm. When in desperation to retrieve at least something that might be edible I took the cloth from him, grasping the hot, charred remains of the crayfish, attempting to wrench the tail apart from the body - the liquefied head and body contents discharged themselves in a scalding stream across the table. When I later remonstrated with Yaro over this fiasco, he explained that in the absence of any alternative recipe he had decided to cook the crayfish as he would a tortoise (a local delicacy) - roasting it first in the oven and finishing it off in the flames.

One day Yaro said to me. "Massah like steak and kidley pie?" On my answering in the affirmative he assured me that my neighbour Jacques' cook, Christian, had shown him how to prepare such a treat.

At seven or so in the evening I sat down at the table, it was already dark. Yaro entered and with a flourish put down the pie-dish in front of me. It looked fine, the pastry crust crisp and lightly browned from the oven of the mahogany-fuelled Dover stove. Yaro stood back as I took up knife and spoon. I cut into the crisp pastry, removing a slice to reveal a bloody mess of gobbets of uncooked beef, chunks of raw kidney - complete with protruding segments of pipework and plumbing, all swimming in a greeny-yellowy liquid. I think it was getting on towards the end of my tour and I was more than usually 'tetchy' as over-exasperated Europeans could become. In a sudden fit of rage, I seized the pie dish, and threw it and its contents out of the open first floor window into the darkness. There was a crash and a muffled shout from the compound below. Yaro retreated in confusion to the kitchen while I ate the fried yam cakes and stringy beans that were left.

After a few minutes I heard raised voices along the passageway to the kitchen. Then came a knock at the door. I opened it to reveal the splendid figure of the veteran Escort Police sergeant who commanded the nightly guard on the Bank premises. He was vainly trying to wipe off the plentiful gravy stains and fragments of pastry, raw steak and kidney from his red tarboosh and from his broad scarlet sash that crossed his shoulder over his medal-beribboned blue jersey. He looked at me mournfully, holding out his hands in a gesture of reproach.

"*Ecchhh!!* Massah?" He said.

I apologised profusely to the sergeant and he gracefully accepted my explanation and the generous 'dash' I gave him to have his uniform suitably cleaned. "Thank you Sah! Dat boy Yaro - he be proper bush man!"

From Sekondi I used to go from time to time the few miles to Takoradi and once when I found myself at a party on board a Dutch boat in the harbour, the Chief Steward gave me a parting gift of a stick of celery and a small bundle of smoked eels. The eels posed no problem, but the next day - looking forward to some crisp celery and cheese - how one longed for crisp, fresh, tangy vegetables in such a climate as the Coast - I gave the celery to Yaro - standing in its jug of water where I had kept it overnight in the fridge. Unthinking as ever. "Yaro, you savvy dis be celery, you know what to do with it?" "Yes Massah, I savvy."

Finishing my dinner that evening, I said to Yaro. "Pass cheese and biscuits - and celery."

Enter Yaro, bearing a small bowl containing a sort of watery mush - with a few fibres sticking up, a teaspoon resting on the rim.

"Bloody Hell Yaro! What's this????"

"Dis be your selly Massah, I put am for mincer but I no fit strain all de water."

Soon after my arrival in Sekondi in very short order Yaro did for my expensive white linen dinner jacket I bought at Alkits, the tropical outfitters in Cambridge Circus in London. It was, as the salesman had claimed, washable. What he hadn't fully explained to me - and I totally failed to pass on to Yaro was that before washing it was first necessary to take out the shoulder pads that were held in place by press studs. Yaro put the jacket in the bath as usual with the rest of the washing, rubbing it vigorously with bar soap and left it all to soak for a while before returning to trample it all with his bare feet (as I subsequently discovered). The shoulder pads were stuffed with a sort of flock, unfortunately suffused with a rich blue-ish dye which then seeped out, irredeemably staining the collar and shoulders of the jacket a shade of Imperial purple. Some of my towels and bedsheets bore the same stains until they eventually wore out or were replaced following the burn marks and spark holes that resulted from Yaro's preferred charcoal-fired pressing iron.

In a corner of the room where I write leans a red-leather covered bow with its decorated black and white leather covered quiver - still containing a dozen or so reed arrows, their barbed and blackened iron points caked with the dried remains of what was once a fresh and sticky poison. In late 1954 Yaro came to 'beg' me for a loan of £10. (His monthly wage then was less than £7 and at that time I earned under £70 a month myself). He explained that he wished to return home to his village in the far north where his family had arranged a wife for him. The £10 was part of the bride price intended for the purchase of a cow. I reluctantly agreed, on the condition that Yaro found a replacement cook for me during his absence - as long as it wasn't his 'brother' who had appeared a few months earlier and now shared the boys' quarters in the Bank compound below my flat. The so-called 'cook' who filled in for Yaro during his three weeks wedding trip was possibly part of some deep laid plot on Yaro's part, for he was so incompetent that he made Yaro's ministrations to my household seem like room service at Claridges by comparison.

When Yaro returned with his bride he brought me the bow and its quiver of arrows as a gift. I was quite touched as well as relieved by his return. The child-wife who now took up residence with him in their cramped quarters, also shared with the 'brother,' seemed remarkably young. I asked Yaro how old she was. "I no savvy," was his reply, "she never pass flower yet."

A West African turkey bears scant resemblance to the table-reared birds we know in Europe. The Coast variety is usually a scrawny, moth-eaten fowl in size and temperament resembling a vulture (in fact a Gold Coast euphemism for vulture used to be 'Winneba Turkey'), but built for speedy evasion on the ground like a whippet rather than for the soaring and graceful flight of its more useful cousin. In later years in Tamale when the poultry run in the garden of our bungalow received any of these creatures - as 'dash' from customers, invariably delivered, unknown to me and behind my back when I was in the office and O. was at home to receive them - she negotiated an arrangement with a 'mammy' in the market in town who would take our turkeys on account in return for the much preferred guinea fowl. But back in Sekondi in 1954 or 1955, either Jacques or myself, I forget who, was 'dashed' a turkey. It ended up in my kitchen, tethered by a piece of string around its leg to the wooden table. Yaro fed it on corn and scraps for several days while Jacques and I monitored its progress. It ate voraciously, 'gobbled' noisily day and night, defecated profusely while we vainly prodded its sinewy form and razor-like breast bone for signs of weight gain. Its sex was indeterminate, as was its age.

After several days the turkey was becoming a liability. It gained no weight, its prolonged presence in my kitchen was definitely unhygienic and it was returning no profit on the outlay involved in its keep. The time had come, as for the proverbial Irish pig, when it had 'to pay the rent.' Yaro was complaining that he was always tripping over it in the kitchen and he displayed the scars on his legs where it pecked him whenever in range.

Jacques and I decided that we would eat it one weekend after it had been in residence for several days. We were drinking beer in my flat when we gave Yaro the verbal order to execute the death warrant. Thinking no more of it Jacques and I resumed our refreshment. There was a sudden clatter from the kitchen, pots and pans fell to the floor, voices were raised as the turkey gobbled and squawked in protest. This went on for several minutes until we could stand it no longer and Jacques and I went to the kitchen door to find Yaro, his 'brother' and Christian, Jacques' steward, wrestling ineffectually with the outraged bird on the floor, attempting to position it for Yaro to attempt to saw through the turkey's wiry neck with my very blunt carving knife.

"Stop it - AT ONCE!!" Ordered Jacques, with all the authority of his National Service days as a subaltern in the Dragoon Guards. "After all that hassle the poor bloody bird will be as tough as an old boot if you carry on like that!" I said to Jacques that I had read somewhere that it was best to relax - and tenderise a goose or a turkey - by first giving it a stiff drink to soothe its nerves before despatching it swiftly and humanely by wringing its neck. (Anyone who has ever attempted to wring the neck of a goose tranquillised or not, will know that this is a task comparable to drawing teeth from an enraged Rotweiller). Jacques said, "I've got just the thing! Christian, fetch that bottle of schnapps that Kobina Kwarshie done dash me - one time!"

By the time Christian returned with the square-faced case bottle of cheap schnapps – Jacques had justly claimed that it was undrinkable - we had dragged the protesting, but slightly quieter turkey into my living room. Jacques held the bird between his knees, forced open its beak - while I poured a generous 'treble' from a tumbler down its throat. The fiery spirit disappeared in a single smooth movement of its neck muscles as we massaged its throat to ease its descent. After a moment or two, the turkey, now visibly tranquillised, was released by Jacques. It carefully paced the edge of the carpet, pecked feebly at a peanut or two we placed before it, gave a convulsive shudder, staggered - and collapsed, as dead as the proverbial Dodo before the amazed glances of Yaro and Christian who had keenly followed the entire operation.

"There, you see now, this is how the whitemen kill their meat - no need for all that palaver in the kitchen - no 'hullah-hullah' - no need for 'halal'* with a blunt knife, the meat will be very tender!" Said Jacques triumphantly. It was in fact when we ate it, as tough and as stringy as the proverbial old boot. Jacques later gave the remaining schnapps to Christian as a small bonus.

When I left Sekondi on leave at the end of 1955 I had become more or less reconciled to Yaro. I paid him three months half-pay as a retainer and arranged for him to be temporarily employed by Ron Copeman who took over from me as Accountant

---

*Note: Most domestic fowl and animals in West Africa after purchase 'on the hoof' were butchered in the Muslim style - and wild game also required its throat to be cut symbolically at the point of death. I recall an ancient Malian hunter (whose otherwise fertile garden on the edge of the Sahara was ravaged by rampaging pachyderms) being asked. "How do you 'halal' an elephant?" To which the bold hunter replied. "I shout 'In the Name of Allah' when I shoot it."

while he, as a newly arrived although quite senior man, became familiarised with the Coast. By the time I returned some three months later, Ron's wife and child had arrived and I think he was quite relieved to relinquish Yaro back into my service.

I have a letter that I received while on leave, dictated by Yaro but type-written by one of the licensed letter writers who plied their trade on the steps of the Post Office.

"C/O Mr. R.A. Copyman,
B.B.W.A. Sekondi.
22nd January 1956.
Dear Sir/

I was happy to hear that you have reached home without any harm. I was very sorry when departing from me last-time, I nearly wept.

Please, I have heard that, if you come back you won't stay at Sekondi, but, rather Takoradi, and I would like to know if it is true that you are to stay at Takoradi, state where you are going stay when replying to my letter.

When you were going I told you that you should buy me some fine clothes, such as trouser, coat, shoe and hat, I am waiting for them when coming.

All my brothers extend their greetings to you.

May the Almighty God assist you in all your ways, give you long life and wisdom.

I remain,
greetings to you all
X
Yaro Frafra, his mark."

When I went back to the Coast in early 1956 after my leave, I worked in Takoradi but still lived for the time being in Sekondi. Ron Copeman and his family went off to Accra and my old flat over the Bank was taken by the new Branch Accountant. I lived for a few months in a roomy, but dark, old-style 'keeping in touch with Africa' two-storey house up on the Ridge. It had cool, high-ceilinged rooms and shuttered, moon-flower garlanded verandahs, all shaded by tall, glossy leafed trees - heaving with fruit bats whose tinkling, mechanical, piercing 'ping-ting, ting-ping' monotonous calls vied day and night with the rustling of their leathery wings to disturb my peace. They also voided their copious fruit-generated droppings all over my newly acquired car wherever I tried to park it. I daily commuted to Takoradi the seven or eight miles from

Sekondi. I missed the colour and the noise and my former companions from my old bachelor quarters below Fort Orange next to the clamour of the market. I think that Yaro also felt the isolation of living up in the 'smart' European residential quarter rather than on the wrong side of the tracks, downtown. I later moved to Takoradi where the Bank had built a small group of new houses for the expat staff.

Compared with the old-style colonial residences of the Bank, the new houses, although supposedly designed with the best of intentions by 'innovative' architects, were not a great success. Without air-conditioning the cuboid concrete-block houses seemed cramped, hot and stuffy, the rooms tiny and all more suitable for a London suburban breeding-hutch for City clerks than to a bare, sunbaked laterite surfaced compound on the outskirts of Takoradi. The tiny verandahs had no shade, the gardens had not yet developed and there was nothing apart from hard red gravel and newly planted hedges made from criss-crossed twigs of hibiscus stuck in the soil-less ground. Yaro's box-like two-roomed servants' quarters around the back of my house must have been like a baker's oven for himself, his child-wife and his 'brother.' They did however have the luxury of running water, a solitary standpipe. One had the impression that the architects had given little thought to the realities of tropical living.

Here Yaro ran into the same sort of trouble which in later years I experienced in Accra with another house-servant, Kweku. The majority of the other servants on the compound, living cheek-by-jowl in their concrete shacks were mostly Nigerians, Yoruba and Ibo. Linguistically and temperamentally detached from Yaro by light years of differing culture and tribe, in spite of technically being 'guest workers' from another country, they looked down on Yaro, ganging up on him, mocking his origins as a '*Kaya-Kaya*' boy from the North - more suited to be a labourer than a houseboy. It is a figment of the European or Afro-American politically correct imagination that Africans are democratic and classless by nature, that they disregard shades of colour, that they do not discriminate against one another, that they look upon each other as soul-brothers. They do not. Tribal dislikes and rivalries are intense. There is a West African proverb that sums it up. "Only slaves are equal." Loyalties are personal, first to their extended family, then to village or town, then to tribe - and last of all to country.

In Africa, skin colour does not constitute a common brotherhood as some would have us believe and it is not surprising that Afro-Americans visiting their ethnic roots for the first time can experience a degree of culture shock when they encounter this. I can personally vouch for the following anecdotes. In Lagos, friends of ours periodically hosted the family of an American Baptist missionary newly arrived and based in Abeokuta. As an Afro-American the pastor found considerable difficulty both in obtaining recognition and in coming to terms with local culture. The missionary's pre-teenage daughter confessed that she longed to return to the USA - saying that "Each evening at family prayers Daddy says 'We thank Thee O Lord for Thy manifold blessings vouchsafed to this family by the institution of slavery."

At an official opening ceremony for a US Aid sponsored manufacturing enterprise in the outskirts of (pre-coup) Lagos, in 1965 the US Embassy had several Afro-American officials at that time, one of these being present. A Nigerian Minister, a tall and stately pale-skinned northerner of aristocratic Hausa Fulani breeding, swathed in flowing blue robes and turban, directed his finely featured gaze at the senior white American at his side and asked, witheringly, "Why do you send all these black men back to us? We sold them to you in the first place because we had no further use for them."

In Lagos also, O. who for some time was a personal secretary to the Ivory Coast Ambassador, (a man of considerable charm - not to mention rotundity - and civilised manners, invariably dressed in black jacket and striped trousers, the *epitome* of a French diplomat albeit black), told me that on more than one occasion, exasperated by some fresh *bêtise* on the part of the citizens of his host country, he would refer to them as '*Ces sauvages.*' I always liked the fact that the Embassy staff referred to and adressed His Excellency informally as '*Patron*' (coll. Fr. 'Boss') except in strictly formal situations, when he was of course '*Excellence.*'

As a counterbalance to these anecdotes, I shall mention the incident (which unlike the others I cannot personally vouch for) at Ghana's Independence celebrations in Accra in 1957. Richard Nixon, then Eisenhower's Vice President was representing the USA. At the height of the jollifications he was said to have thrown his arm around the shoulders of a nearby fellow guest who was wearing traditional Ghanaian *kente* cloth, saying in jocular fashion. "Well, boy, how are you enjoying your 'Freedom'?" To which he received the unequivocal reply. "Ah don't know nuthin' much 'bout that, Mister Nixon. Ah'm from Alabama."

Yaro was twice accused of 'assault' by the other servants who lived within the compound of the three Bank houses and both times I had to bail him out of police custody. He may not have been entirely innocent, but he had certainly been provoked.

In early 1956 I became Acting Manager of the Bank's Market Circle branch in Takoradi - I lived for the few months of my exalted position (or so I considered it then - aged twenty-four) in a barn-like, echoing monstrosity of a house – hot and airless, with metal window-frames, square concrete rooms, virtually unshaded and newly constructed in the super-modern style that the Bank had now adopted. Yaro and his menage took up occupancy of the two-roomed boys' quarters across the driveway. I regret to say that I took little notice of his domestic affairs as long as my own household functioned on a more or less even keel. For several days I had noticed that Yaro seemed edgy and pre-occupied. I also half-noticed from my sitting room during my lunch-hours and late afternoons room the presence of an aged crone (I apologise for the use of this 'sexist' and hackneyed word - but none other fits) who, bent and crabbed, seemed to be coming and going from Yaro's quarters, haunting the compound at all hours of the day and night. I thought little of it.

One hot Sunday lunch time, having returned from the Club after a few beers, I came back to my house to find the dining table laid for my 'chop'. There was no sign of Yaro, the kitchen was empty, no food prepared. Outside across the driveway, out of sight behind the boys' quarters there was quite a racket going on, shouting and screaming - what could only be described as 'Hullah-Hullah!' Obviously 'palaver' of some sort - not yet serious enough to warrant my intervention. I opened a bottle of cold Star beer, lit a cigarette and sat down to await the arrival of my lunch.

Suddenly Yaro emerged from round the back of his quarters, running like a hare - in through the door, full pelt across the room - without saying a word to me he opened the cutlery canteen, seized my carving knife and bolted again back to the doorway.

"OY!!!" I shouted. "YARO!!! STOP!!!!" I must confess that the first thought that entered my head was that he was going to murder someone - something to do with the 'palaver' now disturbing the erstwhile peace of the Sunday afternoon. The bare-footed Yaro skidded to a halt, wild-eyed, sweating - my ten-inch carving knife looked very threatening.

"Massah! My wife go born piccan - now-now, my Auntie need de knife to cut de string!"

Feeling considerably relieved at this explanation I sprang into action. Taking the carving knife from him - I had no wish to be permanently reminded of the use my table cutlery would have been put to whenever I carved a joint - I said. "Wait small, Yaro, dis knife no fit." Quite true, it was unusually blunt and had already proved incapable of cutting a turkey's throat, let alone an umbilical cord. Ratching about in the drawer I found a small Norwegian fishing knife that O. had given me when I had been on leave (perhaps formally severing our foundering relationship at that time). Swiftly honing its edge on the steel from the cutlery box, I poured a tumbler of gin and dabbled and stirred the little knife in the hopefully sterilising liquid and gave it to Yaro. Yaro vanished again as swiftly as he had appeared. After a few minutes peace and quiet descended once more.

I went into the kitchen, took some ice and tonic from the fridge for the gin I had already poured, opened a tin of meat from the store cupboard and made myself a Spam and cucumber sandwich.

The baby was a girl. Yaro's wife had obviously 'passed flower.'

When I went on leave again in late 1957 I paid Yaro off, giving him two month's wages, saying that I had no idea where I would be coming back to on my return, which was true. The chap who relieved me took on Yaro and seemed happy enough with him. When I eventually returned some months later, now married to O. and posted to Accra, I phoned Takoradi and while speaking to my colleague asked him about Yaro - I had no intention of employing him again. . In a married household he would have been impossible. "Yaro?" he said, "I had to sack him, he was charged with assault again by the Police - came up in Court after I had bailed him out. He was sent to prison for three months."

Alas, poor Yaro indeed. I still think kindly of him, and hope, unrealistically perhaps, that eventually he prospered.

There were other servants in the years ahead. In Accra when O. and I lived when first married, there was Kweku. An Ashanti, tall and somewhat stooped, mild-mannered and pleasant, he was I suppose in his late twenties. He did very well for us - he was a good cook, O. and he got on well together, not resenting each other's presence in the kitchen. He would market cleverly for us, buying fresh fish and fowls, local vegetables - and other delicacies such as the yellow-bellied and green fruit-pigeons (*Treron waalia* and *Treron australis*), with bright blue eyes rimmed with scarlet, olive green plumage and orange feet. They fed on fruit and wild figs in the bush and were trapped alive with bird-lime and sold in the market 'on the hoof.' One felt desperately sorry for them, but smeared with 'sticky' as they were they would never have flown again. Swiftly knocked on the head, plucked and roasted they were delicious. I always regarded them as much prized quarry when out shooting. Shooting accorded them a much kinder fate than being ensnared in a mess of sticky goo on the twigs of a wild fig tree.

Kweku stayed with us for most of our time in Accra, but like Yaro in Takoradi he fell foul of the other servants in the compound of the small block of flats we lived in at Tesano. The other 'boys' were mostly all Nigerian and plagued Kweku with their 'palaver.' Matters came to a head one night when O. and I, returning from an evening at the cinema, drove into the compound to find a neighbour's steward waiting for us in our garage. He approached me loudly complaining that Kweku had 'assaulted' and 'stabbed' him. I demanded to see the wound, displaying his thumb he revealed a tiny puncture which when squeezed hard by the victim, oozed a tiny pin-prick of blood. "What" I demanded to know, "was the weapon Kweku used?" "*A fountain-pen.*" Came the answer.

I exploded with rage, O. claimed it was the first time she had ever seen me lose my temper. The steward fled, and I calmed down suitably soothed by O. for whom this was one of her first experiences of Coast 'palaver.' Questioning Kweku the following day threw little light on the matter. He quite rightly maintained that he didn't own a fountain pen for the simple reason that he couldn't write. In the event the other steward brought a charge of assault against Kweku and he was fined £2 in the Native Court The persecutions continued eventually leading to a trumped-up charge of attempted rape being brought against Kweku. False witness was borne by the other servants on the compound. Kweku, recognising '*force majeure*,' disappeared, 'going for bush' back to Ashanti to avoid further persecution. He left us a letter, written by a friend, apologising for the situation. He was a good chap, but in the circumstances there was nothing we could do.

By this time it was on the cards that O. and I would be leaving Accra in the near future. In late 1958 Lord Milverton (a former Governor of Nigeria) and Sylvester Gates, both directors of the Bank, were touring West Africa and Duggie Medcalf the District Manager gave one of his very rare parties for the Bank's senior staff, to meet them. O. took the opportunity to corner Duggie Medcalf, bending his ear quite severely about various matters (including the lack of double-beds in staff houses) and asking why married couples were not offered 'bush' postings away from the main centres of Kumasi, Accra or Takoradi. Duggie was quite taken aback. Because of some of the disastrous situations that had arisen when ill-prepared couples had gone off to more remote areas, the Bank had decided to leave married postings to the towns and cities where the so-called trappings of civilisation would supposedly oil the wheels (or was it the bedsprings?) of marital bliss.

Still None The Wiser

Duggie Medcalf was delighted. Our willingness to 'go to bush' had opened up his staffing options and within weeks we had been given the (to us anyway) absolute plum posting of Tamale, provincial headquarters town of the Northern Region of Ghana. This was some three hundred and fifty miles distant from Accra, beyond the forest belt and into the orchard bush country and savannah leading to the fringes of the desert.

By now we had employed Atiah, to replace the much-persecuted Kweku. Atiah was a northerner himself and offered the opportunity to return to his home country, said he was happy to come with us - or at least he was until he actually arrived there and started pining for the sophisticated 'big city' fleshpots of Accra. While Tamale offered O. and me all the trappings and variety we asked of life in West Africa, it soon became obvious that Atiah was less than content and he asked us to let him return south.

All fell into place. In Tamale I relieved Stan Butcher who had been the Branch Accountant in Accra when I first went there five years earlier. He was now been eking out a meagre grass-widower's existence in Tamale, supporting his sorely-missed wife and children and their mortgage back home in England. It was a time when the Bank's expat staff were badly paid - certainly not well enough to support a growing family, a house back in England as well as an adequate bachelor establishment in West Africa. We found Stan half-starved, thin as a rake, still as ever smoking his stubby pipe, living off the local bread and tins of mixed veg. plus the few eggs that the scrubby fowl in the poultry run in the garden provided. By the time he departed en route for his eighteen-monthly visit to his family, we had fattened him up a bit. He left behind a half-case of bottled Guinness that had been the sole luxury he permitted himself and ice-cold from the fridge it was quite palatable.

Stan's most important legacy to us was one Adongo Zuarungu, otherwise known as 'Charles,' having been thus christened by John Brand, an earlier Branch manager at Tamale. Why Charles? We never knew, but probably in keeping with the same delusions of grandeur that had inspired John to name the Bank's bungalow on Agriculture Ridge to the north of the town, 'Lombard Lodge.'

Charles 'went' with the house as it were. Atiah's decision to go back south suited everyone and Charles remained our steward and cook until O. and I left the Coast for the first time – (on a permanent basis, or so we then thought) - some three years later.

Charles was a paragon. If he was ever homesick at all it was for his home a hundred miles further north near Bolgatanga. He was a Frafra, from the same tribe as Yaro, my first house servant and had the large transverse scar across his cheek that in the earlier years of the century and for long before that had served to identify fellow tribesmen to each other when dispersed by the slave trade across the Atlantic or across the wilds of Africa to Morocco, Egypt or far-off Arabia. He was pleased to have a 'Madam' again, and to work for a more active household than Stan had afforded him. It enhanced Charles's status as the Bank Manager's steward.

Charles was the linch-pin of our domestic arrangements for the three years we spent in Tamale. Innately cheerful and well mannered, he regulated our household regime with quiet efficiency, dealing with emergencies such as snakes or bees in his stride. I have a decorative leather-bound tortoise shell, the relic of a Bell's Hinged Tortoise (*Kinixys homeana* Bell) which I picked up one day in the bush. It was the sole capture of a morning's fruitless shooting expedition and I brought it home for O to see. Putting it through its paces before setting it free, O and I admired its agility and turn of speed. Laid on its back it would swiftly flip over and right itself before trundling off towards freedom at a high rate of knots. Charles came out on the stoep and saw it and his eyes lit up. "Mastah, I beg you give me dis small beef. 'E be fine chop too much." Feeling rather guilty, we agreed, O. adding the *quid pro quo* that he return the shell to us once its contents had been consumed. Within the week the polished carapace was back with us, the top and lower parts neatly trimmed with red goatskin, a curious and evocative ornament.

One week-end O. and I were driving the hundred miles or so north to Bolgatanga to see the famous market and to visit a colleague. On a previous visit we had made a short 8mm ciné film of the colourful market. Charles had watched this in our bungalow, exclaiming delightedly at an ancient and somewhat wizened near-naked lady sitting amongst baskets of chickens she was offering for sale. "Dat be my grannie!!!" On our next trip north he came with us intending to visit her. As usual my shotgun was tucked in the back of the car in the event of a bush-fowl or guinea fowl materialising en route. The only wildlife of note that we saw was a pair of elegant crowned cranes (*Balearica pavonina*), some thirty yards from the road edge, engaged in their mating dance and entirely oblivious to our presence, as we watched from the stationary car. The three-foot tall birds pranced and fluttered, lovingly entwining their long necks one with the other. O and I were entranced at the spectacle. Charles however was more practical. When we drove on again several minutes later, he asked plaintively from the rear seat. "Why Mastah no fit shoot one-time? - plenty meat dey - 'e fit catch both dem birds together!"

As the above incidents perhaps illustrate, Africans are rarely sentimental about animals. Sentimentality being an emotion which only the wealthy can afford. It is also an ideal beyond both the reach and the comprehension of much of the world's population. Wild animals are either pests or meat on the hoof - and often both. Domestic animals represent wealth and sustenance. African villagers often kept dogs, not as 'companion' animals but as an alarm system who warned of the approach of strangers and who relied on scavenging for their survival. Some hunting dogs were kept as with the Yoruba 'hunter-men' whom Benjamin Ladipo and I accompanied in later years in Nigeria. But even these privileged dogs were never pets. If one put out one's hand to them, they would cower and cringe. They were scabby and scarred with old wounds from porcupine quills or from savage bites from the orange incisors of the 'cutting grass' giant cane rats. In northern Nigeria, there were occasions when approaching some remote village or compound on foot, I was at times quite prepared to shoot any of the slavering pi-dogs that swarmed about us if they pressed too close, if they were not sufficiently deterred by the stones and clods of earth that we heaved at them to keep them at bay.

O and I left Tamale on an extended six months leave at the end of 1959. I had been required to do a three month stint in Gracechurch Street at the Bank's Head Office before we returned to West Africa. As we drove into the compound on our return, Charles came smilingly forward to greet us. After a few moments he became silent, his face lengthened. He was obviously upset. He took some of our baggage and disappeared inside the bungalow and did not re-appear. O said, "What's up with Charles? Why is he behaving so oddly?" After several minutes and no sign of Charles, O went off to look for him and found him sitting glumly in the kitchen. "It's all right," said O when she came back after a while. "I've sorted it out - Charles didn't recognise me when I got out of the car. We left here six months ago when I had long hair - now it's short again - Charles thought you had ditched me and brought back a new 'Madam' - that's why he took off in a huff!"

In the later years to come in Nigeria, in Kano and Lagos there were more successes and disasters. We accumulated and discarded both stewards and nannies once our two children arrived on the scene. A measure of order finally settled on our last three years on the Coast, with the trio of conscientious Ibos who regulated our more or less efficient domestic economy - Jonathan Njoku, staid and sensible cook and steward; Oliver Eke, the cheerful fourteen or fifteen year-old 'small-boy' saving up to return East to school – (he would read to the children, leading them in their daily exercises - "Knees *bend*! Arms *stretch*!") and cheerful, plump Anna, the 'nanny.' We left them in early 1967 to lead a more settled existence away from Africa. The Biafran War had broken out. I feared for their future and still wonder how they fared. Oliver I know returned East, and at his age would have been at great risk, naught but 'cannon fodder' for the coming slaughter.

CHAPTER 26

Kano and the Bank of the North
(Nigeria Oct 1963 - Apr 1964)

"At nos hinc alii sitientis ibimus Afros"
"But we from here are to go to some arid Africa"
(Virgil 70 - 19 BC)

At the end of August, 1961, O. and I with our 9 month old daughter Isobel, who had been born in Tamale, sailed out of Takoradi on Elder Dempster's regular mail boat SS Aureol, leaving West Africa for a new life (or so we thought then) back in the UK. I had resigned after some eight years in the Gold Coast and Ghana feeling that enough was enough - or at least that I had endured enough, which included an extended bout of poor health on my last tour. To quote Montaigne, *"many of life's permanent decisions are made in a temporary state of mind."*

In the nearly two years that we then spent back in England we started up a boat business from scratch on the Worcester Birmingham canal. After many setbacks we were ready for our second 'make or break' season at the beginning of 1963. This had all been jointly financed with two or three old friends from West Africa, one of whom, Ralph Little from Tamale, was now living in London. In early-January of that year the coldest winter of the century set in. Frost, snow and ice bound almost the entire country in an iron grip for three months. By mid-April when we should have been hiring out our canal cruisers the ice on the Midlands waterways was still strong enough in places to bear the weight of a car. The Inland Waterways maintenance crews were still lighting huge bonfires on the foot-thick ice without risk when clearing brushwood and tangled thickets from the canal banks. By that summer it was patently clear that disaster and possible bankruptcy was now staring us in the face. With two small children to provide for, we were forced not entirely reluctantly, to concede that another spell in West Africa would clear us from the financial problems that beset us. Perhaps foolishly I decided not to swallow my pride and go cap in hand back to my former employers, the Bank of West Africa, although at the time I left the Secretary had generously written to say that if I should later change my mind they would be happy to see me return. I was about to become what was known then as 'a retread.' A worn-out old tyre from the scrap heap roughly patched and put back into service.

I joined the Bank of the North in Nigeria more by accident than by design. In that mid-summer of 1963 it was clear that we would have to sell the boat business as we could no longer continue without injecting more capital which was not a realistic option. I wrote to the British and French Bank in London and arranged an interview, knowing that they had an associate Bank in West Africa. The interview went well. I spoke to the the French General Manager, M. de la Jugie who was visiting London from Lagos and all seemed to augur well for a prosperous return to the Coast in the near future. Then I heard nothing more. It was as if the curtains had come down. The sale of the boat business neared completion and suddenly out of the blue I had a letter from Intra Bank's London office asking me to present myself for interview, as Major Parbold-Plinge, the MD of their own Nigerian associate Bank was on a brief visit from Kano. I had almost forgotten that I had fired off a salvo of job applications to an assortment of potential West African employers. Another shot had struck home! (How easy it was in those far off days to find employment.)

Parbold-Plinge was an agreeable, slightly woofly old bird, ex-military gent - war-time brevet Lieutenant Colonel, Major TD (Territorial Decoration) and not averse to being adressed by his former higher rank. Intra Bank's London manager was in direct contrast, Lebanese or perhaps Armenian, dark and sharp, firing off a machine-gun babble of fractured English and offering coffee and cigarettes. Definitely not your traditional London banker. Parbold-Plinge as I came to realise later was not quite as open and affable as he seemed on our first meeting. For instance, there was a great deal of non-disclosure of pertinent background detail on his part. But equally I was desperate for a job back on the Coast - and as soon as possible. Here was Parbold-Plinge offering me immediate employment in Kano in Northern Nigeria, a comfortable bungalow for O., myself and our two small children, plus £2,000 a year - when could I leave? Had I realised then how desperate he was to get me on his Kano staff, and had I known some of the background and brief history (at that time) of the Bank of the North I might have held out for more money and asked some more searching questions. I accepted on the spot, we all shook hands and I drove home to Redditch.

Within a few weeks we had packed up, sold the car, put the furniture into store with relatives, paid some of our our debts, said goodbye to our respective families and tried to stitch up the loose ends of the boat business for my partner in London, R. (the former polo player from Tamale) to wind up with as little trouble as possible. In the end it was nearly a year before we were clear of the lawyers and the Banks.

On the 24th October 1963, late in the afternoon, our BOAC flight set us down in Kano. To me it felt like coming home. Heat, dust, old familiar tropical smells. At the foot of the airport control tower was the Emir of Kano's official 'Air Traffic Manager,' swathed and turbanned in scarlet and green cotton robes, squatting by his tethered camel, long brass trumpet at the ready. On this he blew a sustained and discordant blast whenever a plane took off or landed - signifying the Emir's token consent to each arrival or departure. I think I could have kissed the ground. After all the financial worries of the past year, the trials of a failing business (while England prospered - "You've never had it so good!" Harold MacMillan had trumpeted), of debt, of risking being without a roof - going back to Africa, although the continent was by now being swept at near gale force by SuperMac's "Winds of Change," was a healing balm. Whatever vicissitudes The Bank of the North might bring - for the moment all was going well.

We were met by Alan Craddock himself ex-BBWA and whom I still see from time to time to this day, forty years on, and by Humbert Flange, another bachelor 'Coaster' - previously with the British and French Bank - as Major Parbold-Plinge had also been as I subsequently learned. Banking in Nigeria was obviously an incestuous business, not as in Ghana a few years earlier where the two British Banks, Barclays and BBWA, by mutual agreement, would not have touched each other's former employees with the proverbial forty-foot barge-pole. Humbert Flange was beginning to go a little 'bush' by this time, although it wasn't immediately noticeable at our first meeting. Later, as I may record, his behaviour became bizarre in the extreme.

Our baggage was rapidly cleared through Customs and my two sporting guns were declared and placed in bond for me to collect later from the Police Armoury. (Imagine the trials and tribulations of travelling by air today with guns and ammunition in one's baggage!). We were driven off to our new home and a beery, boozy, Friday evening bachelor Coasters' welcome to Kano. Our two tired and sleepy children were soon bathed, fed and put to bed in our new bungalow. A baby sitter had been arranged, and the Coast swept us back into its welcoming bosom. Crad took us off to his former BBWA bachelor mess where as ex-colleagues ourselves O. and I were made welcome.

The only thing that I remember in short supply that evening, as always for the British bachelor in West Africa, was palatable food. Considering that the principal occupant of the Mess was John Wright - BBWA's produce 'expert' who roamed northern Nigeria by Land Rover and camel - (accordg to the published official history of BBWA, he was known as 'Camel' Wright, although at the time one never heard this sobriquet) the unsurprising quality of the food was probably an improvement on his usual fare in remote Government Rest Houses. Both Olive and I were exhausted and having persuaded Crad to drive us back to the bungalow, after checking on the children we put ourselves to bed in air-conditioned splendour. Crad took himself off to the Club for a few more Star beers and a game or two of snooker.

We had made it back to the Coast again!

The Bank of the North was a curious hybrid organisation set up by George Bedas, a Lebanese tycoon (who once made the front cover of Time magazine) with the tacit support of the Northern Nigeria Marketing Board and various Lebanese interests. Earlier in the Middle East Bedas had founded Intra Bank S. A., which after a twenty year classic 'Boom and Bust' cycle failed spectacularly after a 'run'in 1966.

The Bank of the North in 1963 was severely under-capitalised which hindered its activities, but as an indigenous Bank it did not need the much larger capitalisation demanded by the government of 'foreign' Banks. Its operations were largely dependant on deposits from the Marketing Board and technically speaking, although viable for the circumstances then prevailing, for much of the time it was operating near the edge of insolvency. The Nigerian Central Bank regulations required a minimum twenty-five percent cash/liquidity ratio and as the new Head Office Accountant I found it difficult at times to 'massage' the figures in our monthly return to the Central Bank to meet these requirements. On one occasion we experienced a true crisis when Humbert Flange, as Branch Manager, refused an overdraft to a local government official - unaware (or simply uncaring of the consequences) that the man had the power to transfer a £25,000 deposit from ourselves to a competing bank. Outraged by Humbert's curt refusal he transferred the money the same day to another Bank. This unexpected withdrawal tipped our always delicate liquidity position into the disaster zone. Technically we could now be closed down. Panic ensued. Parbold-Plinge soundly berated Humbert for his ill-judged action. Humbert was told to apologise immediately to the Nigerian official - this he unsuccessfully attempted to do but it was not in his nature to manage this in a manner which would have mollified the *amour-propre* of our dissatisfied ex-customer. Jim Wood, the 'Wise Owl' of our organisation, which now teetered on the edge of disaster, came up with the only practical solution to save the Bank's official bacon. When the office closed that afternoon and the African clerks had left, the four expats who remained and between us possessed a full set of keys to enter the strongroom did so. Jim Wood took a £500 bundle of notes from the cash reserves, Parbold-Plinge and Humbert signed a debit note charging this sum to 'Advertising Expenses' and the Chief Inspector set off to track down the only man who could save us. In this he was eminently successful and by the following morning the £25,000 deposit had been re-instated in our books and the Nigerian official's ledger account had a new overdraft limit.

The local staff were mainly of Ibo extraction, plus a few Yoruba, which within two or three years was to lead to serious trouble. By 1966 inter-tribal rivalries were leading to widespread massacres and ultimately to the Biafran War. The mainly Hausa speaking Muslim northerners who were sufficiently educated were few in number and went into government service rather than aspiring to become bank clerks. The Bank had only a few Branches, all in the north except for Jos and Lagos. The expatriate staff were a mixed bunch of British, Lebanese, Egyptian and Palestinian bankers.

The Kano Head Office of which I found myself appointed Accountant in late 1963 had only British expats when I came on the scene. There were reasons for this which became clearer the more I learned of the Bank's recent history. There was of course Major Parbold-Plinge, the General Manager whom I had already met in London. Next in the hierarchy was the splendid Jim Wood, the Bank's Chief Inspector, in the war he was a Master Navigator with the RAF's Pathfinder Force who against all the odds had survived two operational tours with Bomber Command. By the time I knew him he was a fully laid-back, fully qualified eccentric. I don't recall ever meeting anyone who was quite so much 'his own man' as was Jim Wood. He had formerly been in the Gulf and the Middle East. His banking knowledge and skills were one of the mainstays of the organisation, and as noted above his skill and coolness under fire were to save us in our hour of need.

Humbert Flange, a bachelor who was acting Manager of Kano branch was beginning to exhibit many of the symptoms of 'going bush.' He was becoming increasingly solitary and anti-social, which combined with mild megalomania (common enough in many Europeans isolated in Africa), exacerbated his already noticeable tendency to pompous irrationality. A few months later this culminated in Humbert driving south one weekend to the town of Zaria, storming into the Club and demanding to be served with a dozen fresh oysters and a pint of champagne on ice. When the steward declined his order on the understandably straightforward grounds of unavailability - Humbert threw a 'wobbly' and had to be forcibly ejected. He then went off on much overdue leave and didn't return. Before he departed he had advertised in the classified columns of a well-known British Sunday paper for a 'companion' to join him on an extended tour of Europe during his leave. Crad, O. and I had all been consulted by Humbert on the form of wording to adopt. All of us had strongly recommended that he clearly specify 'female' companion in his copy but this he declined to do, convinced that his own carefully worded invitation would attract a host of replies from a range of attractive 'Dolly Birds' then supposedly thronging the fleshpots of early Swinging Sixties London. We eagerly awaited the package of replies to be sent on from the newspaper's London office. These were exclusively from male homosexuals, sexually explicit and offering Humbert a range of services and practices, many of them undreamed of in our wildest imaginations. Humbert was shaken to the roots of his being, his already faltering equilibrium was verging on paranoia and by the time we saw him off on leave he was close to nervous prostration.

Then there was 'Crad' - (Alan Craddock) whom I later came to know well. Ex-National Service sailor, ex-BBWA, very definitely a 'one-off.' He was rational and decisive, but as befitted a bachelor Coaster of some standing and experience, argumentative and a mite eccentric. He later became the Kano Manager for the Bank of America and before he retired, a senior Inspector for their Middle and Far Eastern operations.

At this time Crad was a very capable Bills Manager for the Bank of the North. He was already well known in Kano, having once elected, against all advice, to defend himself in the local Magistrate's Court against a series of charges brought against him by the English Chief of Police who intended making an example of Crad with the aim of cracking down on the riotous behaviour of the British bachelor employees of the BBWA for whom Crad then worked. This involved such devious and (for this record)* unspecified matters as *'obstructing trains, general rowdyness and accusations of driving in a negligent manner thereby giving cause for possible breaches of the peace'*

There had been an acrimonious Court hearing with considerable rancour being displayed on both sides. Crad, conducting his own defence had first confounded the Kano local authority police witnesses and then calling the Chief of Police in person into the witness box had bested him in a series of exchanges which resulted in the charges being dropped, thus giving the lie to the saying that anyone who represents himself in Court has a fool for a client. By the time the case was brought to a close, the Court was packed with local onlookers, many of whom knew Crad, if not personally, then by reputation, keenly following the action and at the risk of being ejected, cheering the repartee and the outcome. The native West African is by nature an expert barrack-

---

* Note: These 'crimes' might seem, in cold print, to be both vague and amorphous, but in fact could probably have been substantiated - and had caused the Police Chief considerable annoyance and inconvenience. It is beyond the scope of this narrative to detail them more fully.

room lawyer and has a well developed appreciation of the finer points of the Law. Until the final departure of the expat Police Chief who was replaced by a Nigerian, Crad thereafter had to tread carefully in Kano.

The Bank of the North's premises were situated outside the old city walls not far from the Sabon Gari - the new town or 'Strangers' Quarter' and the main commercial area. The ancient city of Kano inside its thirteen miles of defensive but now crumbling mud walls still remained much as it had for centuries. The Bank occupied a large, rambling and inelegant single-storey building which in one of its earlier incarnations I believe it had once been a nightclub and restaurant.

Our 'Head Office' was surrounded by spreading neem trees in whose shade there lived a mysterious encampment of quasi-Tuareg nomads. I remember there being few women or children, but dogs and goats abounded, plus bubbling and groaning camels hobbled outside their masters' rude matting shelters. The semi-permanent residents of this settlement appeared to spend their time plaiting lengths of coarse sisal rope - a complicated operation carried out from the sitting position using both bare feet as an essential part of the process. I never came to terms with the economics of these semi-nomadic squatters and their hangers-on, for amongst other things it turned out that they were employed by the Bank as watchmen. They were armed with those straight-bladed cross-hilted, double-edged Sudanese swords with tasselled leather scabbards that hung on a cord over one shoulder. In fact they were not Tuareg at all but Busai clansmen from Niger and mere vassals of those stately blue-robed 'Lords of the Desert' to whom they owed allegiance. The Bank paid them a weekly pittance from Petty Cash as a retainer and permitted them to use the compound as their base camp. I think there was also an outside water tap provided. They spoke no language known to me although some of our African clerks must have been able to communicate with them in some version of Hausa.

From time to time they were visited on site by representatives of their Tuareg overlords, veiled and robed in swathes of shiny-indigo dyed cotton, sitting tall on their camels - the purpose of these visits being not to enquire after the welfare of their dependants but almost certainly to extract from them the proceeds of their rope-making activities and whatever was left over from the meagre allowance the Bank paid for their services. The squatters were a genial crew; respectful and punctilious in their salutations to us expatriate employees in our comings and goings. As I shall explain later, the almost total lack of communication and understanding between the various contracting parties in this deal meant that the 'watchmen' had only the slightest idea as to their own particular duties. As with so many Africans untramelled with a western-style education they probably considered that whatever the whiteman did was so bizarre anyway that they might as well go along with it.

Of 'normal' banking business there wasn't a great deal, for the very good reasons that the Bank of the North, being undercapitalised, was limited as to the advances it could make and moreover the other older-established banks had long since skimmed off the cream of local business. However one of the Bank's more profitable activities was what today could possibly be interpreted as 'money laundering.' I hasten to add that it was then all perfectly legal - in Nigeria at least - and it didn't involve drugs, the international trade in anything other than marijuana not having reached Nigeria at that time. What it did involve was being a small but necessary cog in what was then a big international ring dealing in smuggled diamonds. (If my memory serves me I think the opening sequences of the 1960s James Bond film 'Diamonds Are Forever' give an inkling of the general mayhem and illegality then involved at the 'point of production' in Sierra Leone and which still continues unabated to the present day).

Who first thought up the *modus operandi* I don't know, most probably the Lebanese, but the way it then worked is as follows and it requires a certain amount of concentration on the part of the reader to come to grips with the sequence of devious operations involved at that time. The modern turn of the century illicit diamond trade has expanded globally and as well as being the glittering prize for oligarchs such as the (fortunately) late General Mobutu and the Congolese warlords, and is the curse of Angola's and Liberia's civil wars, diamonds have been both the *casus belli* and the source of funding of many African conflicts and rebellions.

In Sierra Leone in the early Sixties an almost unregulated West African diamond boom was gathering momentum. It was a free-for-all firstly by virtue of the fact that the Freetown-based government forces could neither stop nor control the illegal mining of alluvial diamonds which were then being discovered in ever increasing quantities in remote bush areas. CAST (Consolidated African Selection Trust) who held the sole mining concessions were also powerless, in spite of the considerable firepower of their own private army, to prevent hordes of native IDMs (illicit diamond miners) suddenly descending on a site and digging and washing out large quantities of alluvial stones, before being discovered and ejected by force. Secondly, the IDMs and the Syrian, Lebanese and Indian dealers and buyers who followed these 'strikes' ended up with heaps of valuable diamonds that they couldn't legally sell on the world market- that is, not in Sierra Leone anyway.

To sell diamonds in any quantity legally on the international market (which as my readers will already know is - or was - very closely controlled by De Beers and the other big players - like the Russians) requires valid documentation. The most essential document was a certificate of origin giving the stones a provenance. For this purpose it was a matter of great convenience that the country bordering Sierra Leone to the south is Liberia. In 1963 diamonds were not mined in any quamtity in Liberia except by a few wildcat prospectors and then only on a very small scale. A consortium of enterprising Lebanese, Syrian, Greek and sundry other European gentlemen cleverly (or cunningly) based themselves in Monrovia, Liberia's capital, obtained a mining concession from a more than willing Minister for Natural Resources, dug a modest sized hole in the ground on the outskirts of town and declared it a diamond mine. They then bought in at an advantageous price large quantities of diamonds smuggled over the unguarded frontier with Sierra Leone. The diamonds now had a provenance, ie they had supposedly been mined from the hole in the ground outside Monrovia, and Hey presto! They were now legal. Also in 1963 Liberia was virtually an American colony, albeit self-governing (abandoned later by the USA when as a strategic base it ceased to have any further relevance to the stand-off between the Eastern and Western power blocs), Monrovia enjoyed the modest benefits of a western style society, there was an Army which had not yet run riot, a measure of peace and the rule of law (on paper at least) gave the population a degree of security. Fifty years later, Liberia is alas a classic African basket-case country. Its neighbour Sierra Leone also underwent a traumatic period of chaos, but with a limited amount of help from the UK the former colonial power, is beginning a slow process of recovery. Liberia can expect nothing similar from the USA where capitalist economics have the final say.

Who then wanted the diamonds? Well, to name but two - De Beers and the Russians wanted them. Why? Because then, as now, they had to control the market to maintain the price. Parcels of diamonds are released to the world trade only in carefully regulated quantities. Flood the market with the piles of diamonds that exist and the buying public will soon realise, as did Cecil Rhodes when he controlled De Beers at the turn of the century, that not only is the Emperor not wearing any clothes, but that diamonds are a grossly overpriced commodity. The Graeco-Lebanese and Syrian-Liberian buyers therefore sent on their parcels of stones to Beirut where - guess who bought them? Apart from a few independent dealers, De Beers and the Russians! How did they pay for them? In US dollars. Beirut at that time was still one of the world's leading fleshpots - rich, exotically cultured, a paradise for the Arab jet-setters of the Middle East. Beirut was an *entrepôt* where everything was possible - at the right price. Sadly this was all brought to an untimely end when civil war broke out in 1975 and the Lebanon was blown apart. Without an infrastructure, plumbing or communications such fleshpots all too soon crumble into wastelands. To paraphrase the writer P. J. O'Rourke, it is only too easy to blow up the shithouse in an excess of revolutionary zeal, but to rebuild it so that it works as before is entirely another matter.

At this stage the reader needs to change tack. The original illegal miners who you will remember dug up the stones in the first place, had to be paid. They didn't want to be paid in US dollars but with a curious fringe currency known as CFA francs, which circulated in all those former French African colonies that had the sense to remain within the Comité Francaise, thus retaining a measure of fiscal stability. Many of the illegal miners came from the former French colonies of Mali, Niger and Senegal where their poverty-stricken families still lived and where the consumer goods they wanted had to be bought and paid for. This is where the Bank entered into the equation.

Not far to the north of Kano lies the border with the former French colony of Niger, where the CFA franc circulated freely. Because of varying tariffs certain traders from Niger found it profitable to smuggle trade goods purchased in Nigeria north across the border. The principal source of our CFA Francs arose from smuggling groundnuts north to Niger where a better (and more honest) price could be obtained from the French buyers than from the sometimes corrupt licensed sole-agents of the Northern Nigerian Marketing Board. To finance this illegal cross-border trading large sums of CFA francs therefore entered northern Nigeria which then had to be changed into Nigerian pounds (then still loosely tied to the old Sterling Area). This 'money changing' was brokered by a group of mainly Hausa middlemen known as the 'Al-Hajis' - all wealthy traders rich enough to have been on the pilgrimage to Mecca. The 'Al-Hajis' sold large amounts of CFA francs in cash to the Bank which made payment in Nigerian currency - all done over the counter. Each transaction involving up to several hundred pounds it was not long before large piles of high value, dirty, greasy CFA franc notes had accumulated in our strongroom. It goes without saying of course that at every stage of this business a sizeable commission was creamed off by all involved. As far as the Nigerian authorities were concerned these currency transactions were legal but with the French it was a different matter in view of the large sums involved, the trade having become a running sore in the fragile economies of their former territories. We even had a formal visit from a group of French Treasury officials making polite enquiry as to the volume of currency that passed over our Bank counters.

Every few weeks having accumulated a sufficient value in CFA notes, say perhaps thirty thousand pounds worth (then, a great deal of money) – we then packed them into steel-banded wooden boxes with constantly changing coded numbers and differently coloured wax seals - and flew them from Kano via London to a little Swiss bank in Geneva - the Swiss having always been very accomodating in these matters. To avoid any switching of boxes in transit security was made extremely tight by multiple receipts, ciphers and codes, the details of which were cabled to Geneva at the last minute before take-off from Kano. Several months after my departure In spite of all these elaborate precautions a switch was made during transit but the Swiss being a canny lot noticed the discrepancies and refused to accept delivery. I believe the insurers finally paid up in full.

The Swiss bank would give us credit for the shipment, in sterling in London - the CFA francs were then sold on to the Lebanese-Syrian-Graeco-European diamond buying consortium in Liberia in exchange for the US dollars the latter had received in Beirut. The piles of grubby CFA francs were then handed over to the diamond diggers from Sierra Leone in exchange for more dirty cloth bags of raw, uncut diamonds. Full circle!

The above matters had a direct connection with my presence in Kano. When the Bank was first set up a year or two earlier it was alleged that the expatriate managers needed to run the Kano operation had been recruited as a 'job lot' in Europe. Most were Swiss and some were German and it was also rumoured that most of them already knew each other and that having been associated with a dodgy Casino operation it suited some of them to leave the European financial theatre until Time's healing balm had soothed some much troubled waters. Whatever the alleged truth may have been, it had been a difficult period in the Bank's short history.

It is however a matter of record that several months before I arrived on the scene one of the last remaining original expat. staff, the Swiss (or German) manager of the Kano Branch, (at the instigation of the senior management of the Bank) was made *persona non-grata* overnight with the Nigerian authorities. Hereafter for simplicity referred to as 'Willi,' he had decided that since he was making so much profit for the Bank with the CFA currency deals, he might as well divert some of the business into his own pocket. From what I was led to understand Willi made frequent long weekend trips north into Niger – (it was then a simple matter to cross the border, legally or illegally by day or night) – to fly to Liberia, to buy or deal in diamonds direct, then flying back again to Niger where he had left his car, drive down to Kano overnight - and be in his office as usual on Monday morning.

Willi was a man of undoubted enterprise and initiative, but he probably trod on too many toes in the course of his dealings - jeopardising the interests of too many middlemen in the process. The traditional essence and ethics of West African trading are concerned with brokering deals and controlling trade. Everyone must have his cut - smugglers and currency dealers included. Someone complained to the hierarchy of the Bank who then used their influence with the Nigerian authorities. One weekend while Willi was known to be across the border in Niger, his work and residence permits were formally cancelled and all border posts alerted that he was now officially excluded from re-entering the country.

He was turned back from the border. The Kano staff was told that he had been sacked; a new manager was to be appointed. Willi's kit and belongings were packed up to await his disposal instructions. His keys were recovered from the office safe and from his bungalow and everything seemed tidy and secure. Conclusion of episode? Not quite.

Willi was a man of parts. He had stashed away either money - or most probably packets of diamonds in various hidey-holes around the fabric of the Bank premises and these he now needed to recover to start his new career as a diamond dealer. Being a prohibited immigrant posed no problem, as at so many West African frontiers (this was before the days of the trigger-happy *lumpenmilitariat* coming to power), when the official crossing points and the border posts closed their barriers at nightfall, one simply drove off into the bush skirting the frontier post, usually following a well-marked track that rejoins the road a mile or two on. These routes are for smugglers or cattle drovers who having no passports or travel documents see no need for visa stamps or other bureaucratic formalities. Willi arrived at the Bank's offices in Kano some time after midnight. He was of course well known to the Busai watchmen - to a man all fast asleep enjoying a refreshing night's work round the back of the compound.

It seems that because of the communication difficulties with the watchmen/guards, no-one had bothered to tell them that Willi had been sacked and had been replaced as Manager. However, as was subsequently explained via a series of interpreters the following morning, Willi having called up the watchmen had succeeded in making it plain that he (a) needed to get into the Bank, (b) had forgotten his keys, and (c) he would be much obliged if they would harness up their camels, yoke them to the door handles by means of the plentiful supply of handmade rope that was to hand, and (d) pull the doors off their hinges as soon as possible so that he could get into his office where he had urgent business requiring immediate attention.

The Busai watchmen swiftly obeyed these requests. As I noted before, tribal Africans often regarded 'whitemen' as bizarre lunatics and believed it best to go along with any strange behaviour for fear of giving offence - and after all, Willi, so they thought, was their employer. Having gained entry to the Bank and with the aid of a crowbar, wielded in a helpful manner under his direction by the 'security staff' and recovering his property, Willi made handsome 'dashes' to the watchmen - asking them to prop up the unhinged doors in a tidy manner as he left. Before dawn and before the border posts were officially open, he was no doubt safely back into Niger complete with diamonds.

The somewhat bemused bank staff arrived the next morning to find the front doors neatly stacked up against the door casings. Inside there were no signs of a robbery as was feared - but strange trails of random vandalism. The air-conditioning units in both the manager's office and the boardroom had been prised loose from their wall mountings. Ventilator grilles had been ripped off and ceiling fans were dangling loose from their fittings. "Yes" said the Busai watchmen (through a hastily recruited interpreter). "Manager - he take plenty small ting, small-small packet from inside de wall an' de roof. He very happy for we when he look-um, he dash us plenty before he say Bye-Bye."

When I arrived in Kano some months later, recruited to replace the first wave of expatriate staff that by now had all left, the rough and ready repairs to the walls, the fan fittings and the air vents were still plainly visible.

It was with a not unwelcome *frisson* of pleasure, that I realised I was back in the real world of the Coast once more.

CHAPTER 27

"In Nothing else so Happy"

"I count myself in nothing else so happy
As in a soul remembering my good friends."
(Wm. Shakespeare Richard II)
or
".....as good people's wery scarce, what
I says is, make the most on 'em." "
(Sketches by Boz - Charles Dickens)

    I have written very little about the many Africans I knew over the years. Reading these pages it may sometimes seem that expatriate life was an island of white culture amid a sea of black faces. If that is the impression received then it is false. During the years I spent in Africa, daily contact with a wide spectrum of African society was part and parcel of existence and any expat European who deliberately tried to detach his or her life from such association was doomed to a sterile isolation.

    I have come to realise that to some degree I fell into a social trap that was in a way peculiarly British and no doubt was factored in to the collapse and final dissolution of the Empire. The British Empire builders of the 19th and early 20th centuries had created a colonial system of benign despotism (or was it well-meaning paternalism?) that eventually brought into being a significant and powerful native bourgeoisie. This was an entirely different philosophy to that pursued by the French, who had colonised a much larger area of West and Central Africa over a longer period of time than had the British. The French aimed to produce and educate a minority African élite who would regard themselves culturally as French men and women, albeit black, able to become the administrators, military leaders and governors[*], acting even as deputies in the assemblies in Metropolitan France itself. The French also actively encouraged their own nationals to settle in their 'black' colonies, establishing businesses and owning land and property. Even after the successive waves of African independence movements in the 1950s and 1960s the post-colonial rulers were often a black Francophile élite with an interest in retaining strong economic, defence and cultural links with France.

---

[*] General Dodds who 'conquered' Dahomey in the 1870s was of mixed race and in 1940 the governor of Chad, the first overseas French territory to declare for De Gaulle, was black.

Still None The Wiser

Those territories which decided they wanted greater freedom were cut adrift from the generous support of Metropolitan France and were abandoned to sink or swim by their own efforts. Many of them then quietly stewed in their own juices, a classic example being the former French colony of Upper Volta (now Burkina Faso), bordering northern Ghana, which within a matter of ten years or so from 1960 had transformed itself into a terminally poor country wracked by revolution and military coups. The other route was adopted by the Ivory Coast, which retained strong links with France, and sustained at the time of independence a population of some 30,000 white French settlers - traders, administrators, farmers, shopkeepers, even bakers and bar-keepers - most with a personal stake in the country. Only now, after more than forty years since Independance have national upheavals reversed that situation reducing the country to 'basket case' status (in common with many other sub-Saharan countries) with a mass exodus of the expatriate business community, leaving only the Lebanese (as usual) to pick up whatever crumbs of profit are salvageable from the economic and political chaos. Almost certainly *les évolués* motivated by French cultural values will also have fled their native land as its once prosperous economy turns to dust and ashes.

By comparison, the territories which comprised the Gold Coast (which became Ghana in 1957) had been amalgamated as a full British colony for little more than fifty years and where few whites had been allowed to settle on a permanent basis[*]. Land owning by non-natives was either actively discouraged or forbidden. Many Lebanese and Syrian traders of course took local citizenship - while retaining undercover dual-nationality passports in reserve and it it was not unusual for the same Levantine or Indian family to include British, US, French and various West African nationals among their numbers. Contrary to their policy in East Africa in the early part of the 20th Century, in West Africa the British seem to have understood (counter to much received European thinking at the time) that Africa was not a no-man's land awaiting settlement. It had been difficult for the European to understand the concept that tribal 'land' is common property that confers no long term rights to the individual. As long as he occupies it is his, but he, the occupier, has no right to dispose of it. In legal terms *'There is no property in land.'* The principle of non-alienation of land is basic

---

[*] My friend Richard Steimann in Sekondi was deported from Ghana in 1958, soon after Independence in 1957, unable to renew his work or residence permit. Likewise 'The Uncrowned King of Tarkwa' John (C. J.) Green, manager of Tarkwa branch of BBWA since 1933. He was long retired and lived locally as a 'Chief' with several 'wives' and many children. In 1957 he was forcibly deported back to England where he swiftly expired. Is it perhaps an ironic co-incidence that fifty years later so many citizens of Britain's former colonies now have inalienable rights of residency in the United Kingdom and the EU?

to many African societies and it continues to lead to problems where government (and their foreign concessionaires) usurp land or mineral rights - as in the Niger Delta today. On the Gold Coast the European trade forts and castles since the 16th C. had invariably stood on land leased from the local chiefs and were always subject to protracted disputes over boundaries and rents. In its successor state, Ghana, there was a mostly transient European expatriate community of administrators, traders, businessmen and missionaries, doctors and teachers which rarely exceeded a total of 4,000 or so. In the late 1950s Britain (perhaps with a hint of reluctance) put into action its long term policy of 'freeing' its extensive colonial Empire (though Mary Kingsley's earlier description of British colonial policy as *"a coma interrupted by fits"* was always apt). Native movements for independence hastened the process but were not crucial. An orderly handover was the aim, leaving behind (it was hoped) a working infrastructure and a trained and competent civil service – both to be manned by a large body of educated African workers who had been schooled as well as a benevolent colonial government could afford and manage. Alas, the level of education widespread as it was, proved too little and too late. The educated elite tended to produce a class of intellectuals whose principal interests veered towards the law and politics rather than to the practicalities of running a newly independent state.

I wrote earlier that I fell into a peculiarly English 'social' trap in my relationships with the Africans with whom I associated outside the work context. If I digress then perhaps the reader will come to understand the dichotomy into which the average expatriate found himself propelled willy-nilly in West Africa.

Edward Blyden (1832 - 1912) the West Indian born abolitionist and pioneer Pan Africanist wrote as follows:"*(There are) four classes of European that a negro meets, first the professional philanthropic, going into ecstasies over "This Man and Brother" putting themselves to all sorts of inconveniences to prove to the unfortunate fellow that he is a fellow member of the human race. Second, those who adopt every expedient and on every occasion exhibit their vehement anatagonism. Third, regard with contemptuous indifference, exhibiting neither favour nor dislike whatever his merits. Fourth, those who treat him as they would a white man of the same degree of culture and behaviour, basing their demeanour upon the intellectual or moral qualities they see.*" Most of us would have liked to see ourselves in the fourth category, but as in earlier colonial days who is to blame the Old Coaster in his off-duty hours for preferring the company of his own kind at the Club once the novelty of living in a culture vastly outnumbered by blacks with its own rules and customs had worn off?

Still None The Wiser

In 1787 Thomas Clarkson, the English Quaker and fervent abolitionist (then aged twenty seven and presumably both resilient as well as philanthropic) wrote (as he would be unable to do today) of his visit to Sierra Leone to see matters for himself at first hand, *"The fatigue and unpleasantness of such a visit is not to be described. So many people jabbering together, others speaking to you through an interpreter, and the whole drinking to excess."* Marcus Garvey, the contemporary of another leading Pan Africanist W. E. Du Bois and a mentor of Kwame N'Krumah said, *"The prejudice of the white race against the black race is not so much because of colour as of condition."* To which I would add that it might not be a bad thing if meaningful comment on relations between the races were not bedevilled by the repressive rules of political correctness which has become the enemy of rational thought and action.

That last statement in itself is more than enough to have me denounced as a racist by any spokesperson of the flourishing race relations industry at the end of the 20th Century. Only in their terms do I plead guilty, I am white, I am English, I have lived in Africa - QED. (By the same criteria the feminist sisterhood would also accuse me of being sexist - to which charge I plead *not* guilty but being a middle class male, white heterosexual, I therefore stand condemned).

Throughout my African years once one understood a few basic rules and customs I found (and I hope offered) mostly courtesy, a natural friendliness, little hostility of any kind (with *some* notable exceptions) and a degree of tolerance and hospitality towards strangers in their midst - which if the situation were reversed would not be reciprocated in most of Europe. As Richard Burton observed of the 18th century explorer Mungo Park, who died in a fracas near Bussa on the Niger, what was *really* surprising was that Park with his white companions had survived so long and had travelled so far, opening fire on passing tribesmen as he did, making no concessions to the various nations he passed through, and dressed all the while in conspicuous European costume. Burton remarked that had a similar group of armed and openly aggressive Africans in native costume attempted to force a passage up the Thames or the Grand Union Canal in a dugout canoe, they would similarly have been massacred by the otherwise kindly peasants and burgesses of 18th century England. 19th century travellers such as Livingstone, de Brazza or Mary Kingsley who often journeyed alone in the bush met with general courtesy from the natives. Those like H. M. Stanley, who frequently encountered hostility, were conversely those who provoked and expected it. At the end of the colonial era in the 50's and 60's I suspect that relations between the races were more cordial than forty years later when the numbers of unaccountable UN and international Aid Agency employees in Africa greatly exceed the total of the former expatriate colonial services (and where the rule of law and order no longer runs).

The colonial Englishman, though invariably middle-class habitually aspired, even if in trade, to 'upward mobility' and on arrival in his new sphere, would promote himself to the upper middle class as overlord of the subject races. In other respects he followed the example of the British upper classes in choosing to associate only either with their perceived social equals or the working classes in the personae of nannies, grooms, gamekeepers and servants - regarding with distaste the middle-classes engaged in trade or the professions. Thus the average class-conscious colonial *arriviste* (and of the English fifty years ago - it was a rare bird among us then who did not share the nation's still-continuing obsession with class.) nurturing his new found pretensions also preferred to associate with the native aristocracy (in the person of the rulers) or the peasants - the latter as servants or hunters. This had been particularly true in 19th Century India and the same social pattern was repeated in the late 19th and early 20th centuries in Britain's African colonies. Either deliberately or by default the colonialist (not *the colonists* of Australia or Canada who either massacred or otherwise sidelined the indigenous populations) tended to regard with distrust and disdain the new native middle classes, the merchants, the clerks, the lawyers and the teachers - the very strata of society that colonialism's more benign policies had deliberately created. This distrust and disdain eventually became mutual as these were the people who would provide the mainspring of the independence movements throughout the colonial empire - surely a not insignificant factor that led to the ultimate eviction of the white man from the English speaking African colonies.

There were characters I knew who still stand out from the passing parade of memory - people with whom I was at ease and with whom informality and friendship were the rule, whatever the original basis of our relationship might have been.

In Sekondi, in my bachelor days, I can no longer remember how I first met them, were the two Gold Coast lawyers, John Abbensetts and Howard Christian[*]. Both were of West Indian or Creole ancestry, John, tall and fine featured, in his late twenties was a partner in his father's local law practice. Howard, an older man in his forties, ex-Winchester and Balliol - whose mother had been a pioneering midwife in the colony - was an urbane and charming man with a noticeably pock-marked face - who lived in faded style below Fort Orange in an old three storey stucco house that boasted

---

[*] See my earlier reference to his relationship to Moira Stewart, the British TV presenter.

a billiard room. At that time both of them were I think seriously underemployed, certainly understretched intellectually and wondering perhaps what the future held for them as Independence and 'Freedom' approached. Both of them were openly (or at least to me) scathing and mocking in their opinions of the new breed of fire-eating and self-seeking politicians who would soon hold the reins of government and patronage. John I would meet sometimes in Mrs. Kings' tiny bar (more of a shop) in the quiet road below the fort to laugh and crack jokes over a cold beer, Howard Christian would sometimes drop in to while away an hour or two. In his time Howard had acted for the defence in several high profile political and criminal cases in the colony and was therefore regarded with a certain amount of suspicion by Old Coasters such as Colin MacLeod who disapproved of my socialising with him. Like many barristers he had a fund of amusing anecdotes concerning the Law. One would also meet John Abbensetts at the local dances, then much frequented by the young expat bachelors 'on the prowl.' He always seemed to be on the committee of some church or social club or indigenous charity.

Neither of course were members of the Sekondi Club, whose rules no doubt had originally excluded 'blacks.' By 1954 many of the European Clubs in the Gold Coast were under pressure to admit African members, the Accra Club in particular which was seen by local politicians as a last bastion of colonialism. When the rules were amended (as they were bound to be) a few senior African civil servants and judges duly applied and were accepted, but after after they had made their token appearances the Club's active membership remained almost exclusively European. The French, Syrian and Lebanese Clubs had always been social gathering places for their own nationals but came under no pressure to open their doors. Such exclusivity was not seen as politically acceptable for the predominantly British Clubs established by the former colonial masters. In Sekondi there was a multi-racial Club established at about that time, named the 'Arden Club' (after the Governor, later Ghana's first Governor General. Sir Charles Noble Arden-Clarke) but although admirable in principle it attracted little active membership in practice, nobody, black or white, wanted to patronise a Club that anyone could join.*

---

* The influence of 'the Club' in British (or rather English) colonial society is deserving of a major research study, it has been as much neglected in the social history of recent times as has the (mostly ignored) important role of the Greeks in the early settlement and modern development of much of Africa.

The last time I saw John and Howard together was in 1958 in Accra. O. and I, newly married, were out one evening at the Ambassador Hotel when they walked in with a senior African judge in tow and John with the very pretty West Indian girl he had recently married. They were in Accra for the opening of the Assizes and held forth at some length on the discomfort of 'processing' through the streets to the Law Courts in the midday heat in black jacket and waistcoat, striped trousers, stiff collar, bands, gown and horsehair wig while the judge had come close to fainting in his knee breeches, heavy robes and shoulder length wig. In retrospect it was a sad occasion for it was the last time I spoke to John. A few months later (he must have recanted - or at least kept quiet about his view of politicians) he was appointed Attorney General. Within little more than a year he was dead, struck down by hepatitis at the start of what would have been a notable career.

At the other end of the social ladder, was the Hausa trader Mallam Salifu, a travelling dealer in African trinkets and curiosities, who I also encountered for the first time in Sekondi. He dressed in spotless blue and white cotton robes and with embroidered hat on his shaven head, always accompanied by one, sometimes two, labourers carrying his wares, would turn up on my verandah, leave his yellow Moroccan slippers at the threshold. Sitting cross-legged on the floor he would prepare himself for an hour or two of talk, of bargaining - if there was anything I wanted to buy - or simply discussing at length whatever was going on in our respective worlds. He was probably fifty years of age, stately, tall and smooth skinned. His command of spoken English was good and I have no doubt that he spoke many other West African languages including a smattering of French. His twinkling eyes matched his sense of humour. As a 'mallam' he would have professed a knowledge of the Koran in its original Arabic but he could neither read nor write English. He claimed to come from Kano but I think like many traders at that time his territory extended across much of West Africa, national borders meant little to him.

I passed eight years in Ghana and wherever I was Mallam Salifu would eventually turn up, sometimes after intervals of many months, invariably lodging in the local 'Zongo' or strangers' quarter of town (throughout West Africa the equivalent of a *caravanserai*). He would make some transaction at the Bank involving receiving or sending money, usually to Kano, and if he had any curiosities (about which, if genuine rather than 'tourist art', he was well informed) which he thought would catch my eye he would eventually arrive at my bungalow. After several months in Sekondi I had developed an interest in the traditional Ashanti *cire-perdue* gold-weights (made of brass and bronze) and started a small collection of these fascinating miniatures which eventually totalled nearly four hundred items by the time we left Tamale in 1961 when original pieces had become increasingly rare. At that time the Ashanti had been under direct British rule for little more than fifty years, and as the older generations died off their descendants with either little interest or knowledge of tradition were disposing of much of their cultural baggage, sometimes selling the brass and bronze castings merely for their scrap value.*

Mallam Salifu was always my principal source of these intricate miniature sculptures. On one memorable occasion he appeared in my office in Tamale in 1960 with one hundred and fifty gold-weights, most in identical sets of six, representations of tiny stylised animals, birds, fruits, and human figures engaged in a great variety of activities – sometimes illustrating obscure proverbs and sayings. At that time it was still possible to buy (after a suitable period of bargaining) a common 'proverb' weight, often seventy or more than a hundred years old, for as little as five shillings (twenty five pence) - a fraction of their true value once their rarity and cultural significance was recognised in later years. My own collection, before its unfortunate forced sale, had been loaned to the Bristol Museum as the centrepiece of a special exhibition. Its loss to me remains a matter of regret. I accept that in this particular case, the collection being part of Ghana's cultural heritage although unrecognised and uncontrolled at that time - Proudhon's maxim '*All property is theft*' may well have had some relevance. Nevertheless I would have enjoyed the opportunity to remain the collection's temporary custodian for my own lifetime.

In Takoradi in 1956 my fellow expat and friend Jack Hollinshead was engaged in the business of buying in and shipping out scrap metal, mainly non-ferrous, for re-smelting in Belgium, (for very obvious reasons telegraph wire, railway track and rolling stock were prohibited exports.) Over a period of a few years he had accumulated two forty-gallon steel drums filled with brass and copper manillas, tribal bracelets and anklets, innumerable Ashanti gold-weights, masks and figurines - sufficient to stock the ethnology shelves of half a dozen museums - which his African agents had bought in for their simple value as scrap metal. Jack finally shipped these out as part of a much larger consignment, the two drums carefully marked for setting aside for his personal

---

* Alas during a period of temporary insolvency a year or two later in the UK the majority of these had to be sold, leaving only a small core collection. Much to my chagrin an American coffee table 'art book' purporting to be a definitive work on the subject was published a few years later, illustrating several unique pieces that had formerly been in my own collection.

attention on arrival in Antwerp. A few months later he was in Belgium and asked his agent to produce his property. "What drums might those be?" The agent said, "The whole shipment went straight off to the smelter as usual. *Why* are you shouting Monsieur?? Is there something wrong? Please to pacify yourself!!"

A few months after I first arrived in Lagos in 1964, my friend Crad who by then had come down from Kano to take over the Bank of the North in Lagos told me that he had met someone who would interest me. One Sunday Crad had driven out of Lagos for several miles on the Ikorodu road towards Abeokuta. Stopping the car near a village on the banks of the Ogun River he had gone for a walk upstream along a narrow bush path. There he chanced upon Benjamin Ladipo, checking and emptying fish traps. Walking back to the village together, Crad learned that Benjamin was checking the traps for a 'German'* who had a business exporting live tropical fish for European collectors. When later I met Benjamin myself I learned that he was a keen 'hunter-man' and that he would be glad to let me accompany him in his forays into the Ikorodu bush along with the pack of wooden-belled hunting dogs he and his fellow Yoruba employed in harrying the 'small beef' and bushmeat that formed their quarry. It was the beginning of a rewarding friendship that would last until O. and I finally left Lagos in 1967.

Ben Ladipo would have been in his mid-forties by 1964. I learned that as a young man he had enlisted as a soldier and had gone off to war with the Nigeria Regiment of the WAFF (West African Frontier Force), first of all to Egypt guarding the Suez Canal and later to Burma with the 81st West African Division where he had fought the Japs with General Slim's Fourteenth Army during the Arakan campaign. After the war he had been a golf caddy at the Ikoyi Club in Lagos, but by the time I knew him he was headman of his home village beside the Ogun River. He was also a part-time auxiliary policeman - or at least he occasionally wore bits of uniform and headgear which identified him as such, and he wielded a degree of authority in his locality that came with age and personality.

---

* I believe this 'German' was in fact an unusual Swiss, a self-styled 'adventurer' named Heinrich Görtz who based himself in Southern Nigeria for several years until the mid-1960s and in 1975 published (in German) a lurid account of his exploits entitled 'Elefanten, Löwen und Grüne Mambas' ('Elephants, Lions and Green Mambas'). An English translation, less sensationally called 'Beyond the River Bend' was published by Cassell in 1979 - in which I recognised some of the places he wrote about - but seriously questioned the scale of his adventures.

Ben had, as I discovered, an interest in politics. Partisan and sometimes violent civil wars had been a frequent feature of Yoruba life throughout the 19th Century - and as soon as British colonial rule came to an end the old patterns of violence and prejudice in the area now known as Western Nigeria came swiftly back to the boil after the brief sixty year span of *Pax Britannica* - and by 1964 were spilling over again. I will not attempt a resumé of mid-20th century Yoruba politics, but to describe the situation as gang warfare carried out by the politicians' thuggish henchmen operating under the thinnest veneer of democracy would not be far wide of the mark. Immediately prior to the first military coup that overthrew Nigeria's civilian government in January 1966, Chief Samuel Akintola, premier of the Western Region, was shot dead in Ibadan by rebel soldiers; there had already been bloody and violent political riots with many deaths in the preceding months. Ben Ladipo was a supporter of an opposition faction and heard early rumours of Akintola's demise. He told me that on hearing the news he had travelled post-haste by 'mammy' lorry to Ibadan and made straight for the hospital mortuary, where he 'dashed' the attendant a shilling and joined the queue to view the corpse, to make sure that Akintola was in fact genuinely dead and not playing his usual deceitful tricks. Considering that Akintola had been shot at least thirteen times Ben soon came away convinced that the rumours had been true and that Akintola was not shamming.

Ben became my mentor in the high forest and the dense bush along the Ogun River and around the farms in the Ikorodu region (I subsequently discovered that much of the area we ranged through were forest reserves where all hunting was forbidden - but Ben when he admitted this said that the forest guards got 'plenty dash' (the sum of five shillings being mentioned) from him to cover their 'fee.') Without Ben I would probably not have ventured into the high forest, totally unlike the savannah and orchard bush of the north where I had always felt at ease and free to wander at will - and to find my way home with the aid of a compass if necessary. At first I found the forest dangerously confusing away from the narrow bush tracks. One could easily become lost, particularly because the dogs as well as Ben and the other hunters roamed at random wherever the chase might lead. The quarry was almost anything that walked, climbed, flew, slithered, swam or scuttled. As with the Cantonese – anything that could be killed, cooked and eaten was fair game.

We would take to the bush together on Sundays at least once a month, meeting shortly after first light in the cool of the morning, with another eight or ten Yoruba hunters armed with their local blacksmith-made muzzle-loading guns, long barrelled flint and caplock muskets, heavily charged with shot rather than ball as the

Still None The Wiser

latter would have made the whole proceedings even more dangerous than they already were. Ben had a breechloader that was his pride and joy - an old double 12 bore Damascus barrelled hammer gun by the English maker, Hollis. The 'hounds' were a nondescript pack of small prick-eared pi-dogs, motheaten and piebald with scarred hides and bitten-through muzzles, the result of their encounters with the razor sharp incisors of the giant cane rats, the spines of their cousins the porcupines, or the tusks of the bush pig or perhaps they had been sent flying by the iron hard, ridged tail of a large monitor lizard. The dogs hunted mute, their pace marked only by the rhythmic 'clonks' of their wooden bells. I remember the eagerness with which they clustered around their master at the start of the day's chase, begging impatiently for the bells that he took from his bag to hang around their necks.

As often as not I would take a friend along, lending him if necessary my spare gun. Paul Gautier (now also in Lagos) sometimes came with me as did Crad or Gareth Plinge (and his Irish namesake one Finnbar O'Plinge). It was useful to have a companion with whom I could communicate easily, in case we became lost or if the worst happened perhaps injured. Otherwise Ben and I passed the day in 'pidgin.' Ben's English possessed a marvellous variety but at times it could be impenetrable. I recall a visit to his village to arrange for a future hunt. He said he had recently met with some success. He had shot and killed, so he said, an 'Ironer.' After several minutes' close interrogation I had established little except this was a quadruped with large teeth. All was made clear, when in a final effort to explain, he said. "De 'Ironer' 'e catch spots for him belly. 'E smell plenty bad for 'e larse an' you no fit savvy if 'e be man or woman - but de meat 'e sweet too much." "Ah-hah!" I said, all revealed. "You done kill a *Hyaena*!!" "Yaas," said Ben, "What I done tole you already - an 'Ironer.'"

On another occasion Ben and I together, without dogs or other hunters, had gone towards Ijebu Ode to hunt bush fowl in the farms on the edge of the forest and as I was following Ben down a narrow path he suddenly leaped backwards as a long black snake, head and neck erect, whipped at speed across the path almost in front of our feet. "Oh Lordy!" he said, mopping his brow with his hat, "Dat de biggest cobra* I ever done see, 'e fit spit for my eye - an' den 'e fit bite *you* - an' we both done lib for die one time!" Several minutes later as we proceeded quietly, calm restored, he waved his hand

---

* *(Note:-These aggressive ring-necked spitting cobras were doubly dangerous, both spitting and biting. From a distance of several feet they can project a blinding spray of venom accurately into their victim's eyes. I noticed that some of Ben's fellow hunters wore a shiny piece of tin pinned to their smocks - this was a diversion intended to give any angry cobra they might encounter an alternative target to the reflection from their own eyes

behind him to stop me in his footsteps. He whispered "You hear dat smell? Monkey dey for dat big stick!" Raising his gun, he crept forward, fired and down plummeted a monkey out of the topmost branches of a tall tree, crashing to the ground with a thump. "Dat be plenty fine chop too much!" Said Ben as he tied its tail to its forearms as a convenient carrying handle.

I remember how alert the hunters were, using all their senses in a way that town bred Europeans (and Africans too for that matter) have lost. As for smell, though I still smoked cigarettes in those days even I could smell monkey - once Ben had told me what it was. But the behaviour of birds was another giveaway. Once when all the hunters insisted that a python was close by - we never found it, but I am sure they were right. The hunters communicated with each other in thick bush by imitating the soft 'hoo hoo' call of the grey hornbill (which given half a chance they would also shoot and eat). To them, the bush and its creatures was like an open book which they already knew by heart. Most successful hunters develop an affinity with their prey, fish, fowl or fur. Indeed it is necessary if they are to take their quarry consistently; and in truly primitive societies such as those of the bushmen of southern Africa it is firmly believed that the spirits of the hunter and the hunted are interconnected.

To ask questions of my group of Yoruba was not an easy matter with Ben acting as interpreter. I remember once asking Ben the name of a spectacular forest tree which was in full flower, meaning I suppose its vernacular name, with hindsight a pointless exercise. However Ben and the hunters then went into a huddle, engaging in a long and heated discussion, until at last Ben said triumphantly, "Ahah! - We done savvy proper how you call um. We call um *Tree*!" Another time on the edge of an abandoned clearing we had found a cashew tree (*anacardium occidentale*) in fruit, the pale yellow plum-sized fruit each with its comma-shaped nut at the end. The astringent, refreshingly juicy and sweet fruits were at their rarely found peak of perfection. The hunters stuffed their bags with those they could not eat. Making a play of reluctance as he gave me one, to roars of laughter Ben said "Dat no be fit for white-man - dis be proper black-man chop!!"

Except for the occasional bush fowl I rarely took anything from the communal bag. In fact on these forest hunts for fear of shooting a dog or worse, a fellow hunter, I seldom fired a shot at anything except the occasional monkey for the benefit of the others. I caught fleeting glimpses of antelope, mainly the grey forest duiker, and the large 'cutting grass' cane rats (sometimes euphemistically called 'rabbit) which whizzed past closely pursued by the dogs with their clonking bells. I even saw a snake shot out of the crown of a palm tree by Paul Gautier and stuffed still wriggling into a hunter's bag.

Monitor lizards were sometimes cornered by the dogs and despatched by cutlass or expired in a cloud of white smoke and slugs from a muzzle-loading gun. All was grist to their mill. I never saw a bush pig in the Ikorodu forest, but Ben said they were often taken in the wet season when they would be found on higher, dryer ground in dense bush. He said it was vital for the hunters to follow the dogs closely then and to kill the pig before it killed the dogs.

At midday we would rest for a while, on the edge of a clearing, sometimes perhaps in the shade of a palm-thatched shelter with our nostrils assailed by the peculiar rank sour smell of cassava soaking in a nearby muddy puddle. In the noonday heat the dogs would lie twitching, their lolling tongues and eyes pestered by swarms of flies. Sometimes a farmer working his patch of cassava or yams with hoe and cutlass would bring us a gourd of refreshing palm wine. The only time I would drink it was on these occasions tapped straight from the crown of the tree that same morning when it was still only mildly alcoholic, frothing and cloudy like fresh lemonade. Then perhaps I would buy a calabash full of palm wine and take it home for O. in my own water bottle. It needed drinking the same day for left for any longer it swiftly fermented, becoming sour and undrinkable to my palate. Many Old Coasters of former years aquired a taste for it by adding a tot of gin to the fresh sap.

Some of Ben's exploits he regaled me with were of a dubious nature by today's standards. He told me of one occasion when hunting antelope in the forest reserve at night, with a dim carbide headlamp, (a brighter lamp curiously enough is less effective) he had disturbed a family of sleeping chimpanzees and having fired and as he thought killed one, he was then closely pursued in fear of his life, by an angry old male hot on his heels. He came to the river bank and started to wade across in the moonlight with the fearsome chimp breathing down his neck. "E fit kill me one time, 'e vex proper bad, lef small I go die-oh!!" "What did you do?" I asked? "Ah," said Ben, "When I no fit run no more, I stop and he deh-dey, he stop too an' I give him de udder barrel in de chest, an den I run until reach de village safe. I never go back, maybe he no be dead an' 'e still vex."

Once Finnbar O'Plinge and I persuaded Ben to take us on a hunting trip up the river by canoe. We arrived at Ben's village two hours before dawn and in a dugout with Ben and three other Yoruba we pushed off in the light of a setting full moon. The paddles rose and fell silently leaving a dripping trail in the placid dark water. Sir

Richard Burton described in '*Abeokuta and the Cameroon Mountain*' (pub. London 1863), how he set out on an identical journey in 1861 en route to Abeokuta in the company of Commander Bedingfield RN from Lagos and a Mr. Eales as a sightseer, the latter being remarkable only for his *idée fixe* that unicorns abounded in northern Yoruba. Burton noted that at times "*a dense and dripping fog concealed the surface of the river*" and that among the irritations of the journey were "*fishing ropes stretched from bank to bank with wicker cone-shaped fish traps suspended.*" By 1965 nothing had changed. Burton referred to the "*long, loud cries*" of the 'pataku,' the bush dog. As we in our turn passed the dark, wooded banks of the reserve in the dim light of pre-dawn we heard the 'bush dog' yapping away in the forest. Ben said, "....dat de 'pataku' - you no fit see-um with light" indicating that their eyes were small and deep set. Burton wrote that "*the pataku is dangerous only to pigs and children.*" Ben would only say that it was definitely not an '*Ironer.*' In several reference books I have failed to find any variety of hyaenas or any other small carnivore to match. Perhaps the *pataku* is some local species still unidentified and unknown elsewhere. But both Burton in 1863 and Ben Ladipo in 1965 knew of it - and I have heard it.

I still retain a vivid memory of another occasion accompanied by Crad. One Sunday morning an hour or so after first light and before the heat of the day, while our hunting party were crossing the single track Bailey bridge that spanned the river by Ben's village. A passenger lorry, a 'mammy' wagon, came hurtling up behind us barely slowing its headlong pace, rattling over the planks that formed the narrow roadbed and forcing everyone on foot to leap for safety into the girders that supported the bridge. All that is except for Ben's young son, a lad of nine or ten who was carrying his father's gun and hunting bag. The lorry struck him a glancing blow and with a piercing wail he fell between the girders into the river below with an almighty splash. The lorry, its passengers shouting the alarm, juddered to a halt once across the bridge and everyone including the driver spilled out onto the roadway to watch the drama. The boy struggled and splashed to safety on the shore below and to our amazement he was still clutching fast to the gun and the hunting bag remained strung across his shoulder.

Once Ben had checked that the boy and his equally precious gun had come to no great harm, he turned on the lorry driver. What followed can only be described as 'big palaver!' The driver claimed it was not his fault and some of his passengers backed him up. Generally it is true to say a European should be slow to interfere between Africans in what at first seems to be a potential riot but which may only be a spirited argument. They should be allowed to let off steam and talk themselves out - or that at least is how as an Old Coaster myself I would advise someone in a similar situation.

Crad and I stood back on the fringe of the crowd as more and more people flocked over the bridge from the village and joined their voices to the general uproar. As the din grew louder and the temper of the altercation became more outraged both Crad and I observed that in the heat of the moment, not only were our group of hunters armed with loaded guns, but cutlasses, invariably carried as a naked blade, were now being brandished. The moment when violence would openly erupt seemed imminent. At the back of our minds we both knew that drivers involved in road accidents and held responsible for injury or death could be savagely beaten and sometimes killed by the onlookers, as often as not before any survivors were attended to.

Crad shouted to me above the uproar, "If this goes on any longer we can kiss our day's hunt goodbye - and *we* are going to end up as witnesses to murder!" Seizing a brief hiatus in the pandemonium, he pushed his way through the bedlam of gesticulating, shouting Yoruba and climbed up onto the bonnet of the lorry. From his vantage point he caught the attention of the mob. Waving his arms he bellowed "QUIET!!! I beg you, LISTEN TO ME!!!!" The crowd momentarily stilled and in the sudden silence gazed at him expectantly.

Crad kept his arms above his head, and spoke. "De piccan he OK now, nobody get hurt at all. I beg you all go 'gree with me one thing for now! ALL LORRY DRIVERS ARE BUSHMEN!!! NO BE SO???" The crowd roared their agreement, several by now falling about with laughter. The driver looked rueful, but laughed as well. Crad continued, twice striking his hands together in front of him in that peculiar gesture understood by all. "PALAVER DONE FINISH!!!" The villagers filed back over the bridge, the passengers climbed back on their wagon and waving to us through the dust drove on to Abeokuta, and we went hunting.

O. remembers Ben well. We once went together to his village as I wanted to see him about something or other, perhaps the flintlock gun that Jimoh Babatunde, the blacksmith at Ikorodu was then making for me. Ben greeted us and asked us into his hut to discuss the matter in hand. I gave him some shotgun cartridges I had brought as 'dash' and from beneath his bed he pulled out a box from which he took a bottle. He poured neat gin into three tumblers, filling them to the brim and giving us one each he took the third which he drained with gusto, smacking his lips. I sipped mine gingerly. Burton once referred to *"the delights of the social glass of gin for breakfast at 8 am."* If it was anything like that warm, heavily scented Portuguese gin smuggled from Fernando Po that we were offered - then forget it! It was like drinking a warm slug of aftershave. O. took a sip and gagging and spluttering asked Ben for a little water to dilute it. In the interval while Ben went to fetch a jug of clouded water from the river she managed to pour away most of the contents of her glass into the ground and was smacking her own lips appreciatively when he returned. I was not so lucky and drank my bitter cup to the dregs under Ben's watchful eye, praying that the gin would kill whatever livestock the water might contain. O. asked him to show us around the village. Moored to poles along the river bank were the country boats and big dugouts which in years gone by would have brought down puncheons of palm oil from up-river, the boats being loaded by first sinking them in shallow water, floating in the kegs over the gunwales and then furiously baling out to re-float them. Their modern cargo was clean river sand for building purposes to be taken downriver and across the lagoon to Lagos.

In one large swish-walled-tin roofed building, empty now but which in a more prosperous past had been a trader's warehouse, a bundle of rags lay in one corner on a heap of rubble where the wall had partially collapsed. A half-full bottle of some liquid that was plugged with coco fibre lay on its side next to a carved wooden image; this was about eighteen inches high, roughly whitened with clay or flour which to me looked like a figure of a schoolboy wearing a peaked cap. It was clearly a makeshift altar with a votive offering. Ben became highly agitated and started shouting at the small group of people who came to see what was causing the disturbance. Ben said to O. and me, "Dis some dam' fool ju-ju, somebody make fetish to Mammy Water* dat why de wall fall down!" He angrily kicked the pile of rags and the bottle aside. "When I find de man who done dis-ting- I mek him plenty sorry!"

By the second half of 1966 with the increasing risks imposed by the violence of the military coups and the now widespread brigandage outside Lagos, my occasional weekend hunting trips to the open country north of Ibadan and Iseyin in company with Paul Gautier and two Greek friends, Spiros Mavromatis and Tasso Leventis, were abandoned. On our last trip our car was surrounded by an angry mob south of Abeokuta at about 5 am, the scene lit by a nearby blazing vehicle (what they wanted we never knew) and Gautier wound down his window and showed them his shotgun barrel before they let us pass, brought it home to us that any future excursions were now too risky. Even closer to Lagos there were many times when it was inadvisable to leave the environs of the city. In early 1967 when O. and I had made up our minds to leave West Africa, Ben came to Ikoyi to say goodbye for the last time. As a parting

---

* Mammy Water, a (usually) malign female water spirit, worshipped as a sub-cult - probably originating with the occasional appearances of the manatee or dugong, or perhaps the formerly plentiful and potentially dangerous hippopotamus in the rivers and creeks of some parts of the Niger Delta, which some ritual masks in fact resemble.

Still None The Wiser

gift I gave him all my remaining shotgun cartridges (praying that his ancient gun would hold together when he used them). A remarkable and likeable character, for me Ben remains a happy and lasting memory from those difficult last years in Africa.

In 1985 at home in the Lake District one evening I switched on a television programme on the traditional drumming and dancing of the Dagomba people of northern Ghana - having been subjected, not always unwillingly, to many hours of the real thing in years gone by. The camera suddenly showed 'the Paramount Chief of the Dagomba' emerging through the low doorway of a hut in his palace compound, swaying and dancing (in a very measured and dignified manner it must be said) to the rhythm of the drums. To my surprise it was my old friend Yakubu Tali - or more properly to give him his full title, His Excellency Alhaji Yakubu Tali, the Tolon-Na.

I first met him in Tamale in 1959. One morning I was talking to a clerk behind the counter when a large American car drew up outside and as the passenger emerged from the back seat a crowd swiftly assembled around him and commenced that curious greeting peculiar to the northerners - clapping their hands softly, shuffling down on their haunches, bowing ever lower and saying the word, repeated several times, that I can only describe as "Na!" A tall and stately man, clad in flowing pale blue robes was obviously making for the Bank as the gathering crowd parted before him like the Red Sea before Moses, "*Sanu da zuwa. Nagodia!*" they repeated in polite welcome.

The clerks and the two messengers, Peter and Winfriend started to show signs of panic. Wonderful N.Storph,* then my Chief Clerk, (later the manager of Yendi Branch), said in a tone of considerable alarm "My God! It's the Tolon-Na!" Their mood was infectious. If he was coming to see me then I too needed time both to compose myself and to clear space among the piles of papers and files that cluttered my desk, (I have always subscribed to the theory that a clean and tidy desk is the symptom of a sick mind). Peter the messenger shoved his head inside my door, without knocking, the whites of his eyes staring, "Manager" he said, "De Tolon-Na say he done come!"

At that time Yakubu Tali was the most powerful politician as well as the most important tribal chief in the north of Ghana. What made him the more remarkable was that he was no lackey of Kwame N'Krumah's Convention Peoples' Party which had spearheaded the Gold Coast's drive to independence. He would have been in his late forties when I first knew him. He had been the first ever northerner to gain a formal education at Achimota College, later Ghana's premier University and ranking on the

---

* I can no longer remember what the initial 'N' stood for.

West Coast with Ibadan in Nigeria and the once equally well-known Fourah Bay College at Freetown. Having first qualified as a teacher, he later became an MP, for a while serving as Speaker. I think he had been a member of the old colonial Gold Coast Legislative Council and he had early been made a Paramount Chief of the majority Dagomba tribe in his home town of Tolon to the northwest of Tamale. The Moral Re-armament Group claimed him as one of their leading converts and supporters in West Africa.

In the post war years of Britain's Labour government as he once told me, he had led a delegation of northern chiefs to London to protest the Northern Territories' loyalty and to petition the Crown not to hand them over to amalgamation with the Gold Coast Colony and Ashanti whenever independence was eventually granted. The NTs had a very good case being originally constituted piecemeal as a Protectorate by a series of treaties signed by individual tribal chiefs and countersigned by Queen Victoria herself. The northerners had well-founded fears of economic and political exploitation by the more numerous and better educated coastal tribes. They suspected the Colonial Office would abandon them to their fate as 'hewers of wood and drawers of water.' By both religion and culture the northern tribes were more closely allied to the arid sub-Saharan countries to the north of Ghana's borders than to the forest dwelling Ashanti or the Ewe and Akan peoples of the Atlantic coastal plains. Ernest Bevin, at a meeting with the delegation, blunt and plain speaking as always, had told them in short order.

"Fat chance! When the time comes yer'll all be part of whatever country *we* decide the Gold Coast is to become. Like it or lump it!"

According to Yakubu Tali that was the substance of the message. They accordingly lumped it and left.

My own dealings with Yakubu Tali were much less blunt. A long and circuitous discussion, full of courtesies and dissembling occupied a full half hour once he had entered my office. I found him a man of great intelligence, charm and manners and like so many Ghanaians possessing a considerable sense of humour. Eventually he came to the point of his visit. It was, he said, a matter of some circumspection. Secrecy and absolute confidence being the crux of what he was about to say.

After more than forty years, with Yakubu Tali long gone to the grave, his reputation and memory secure, I now feel free to reveal the substance of his request.

"Manager," he said, "I have come to ask you for a loan of £5,000."

This immediately put me in a quandary; Yakubu Tali had only a near-dormant current account with a balance of some seven shillings and sixpence (old money – now 35 pence). My own discretionary lending limit at that time was no more than £1,000,

(£5,000 then was probably £75,000 today). The matter was clearly out of my hands, I would have to consult 'Duggie' Medcalf my fractious, fire-eating District Manager in Accra. "What is the loan for?" I asked. "I need to know."

Yakubu Tali hesitated, lowering his eyes, "Manager," he said, "It is necessary to start up a pig farm. You will understand that as a strict Muslim I cannot in any way be associated with this project. The money will be given over to my 'brother' who is a Christian and who will deal with everything on my behalf. It will be very profitable." (This term 'brother' indicates a wide range of tenuous relationships and in business terms sets off all sorts of alarm bells!)

'I phoned Duggie Medcalf, indicating the delicate circumstances and the need for secrecy. To my surprise he immediately approved the advance and a simple letter arrived a few days later authorising the transaction without any mention of its purpose. By the time I left Tamale two years later in 1961 the loan had been repaid in full.

Whenever Yakubu Tali was in Tamale thereafter he often came to see me, simply to engage in conversation and to exchange information. I took pleasure in his company and still feel flattered that he took the time to visit me.

In Lagos some three years later I saw that he had recently arrived as Ghana's High Commissioner to Nigeria. I called in to see him one afternoon at the High Commission at the top of a nondescript office block; he greeted me enthusiastically, wearing his usual flowing robes. He confessed his pleasure, as I did also, at meeting an old friend far from his home ground. I think now that he felt isolated, both personally and geographically. As a politician he had been sidelined by the Ghana government, who being unable to sack him because of his northern power base, sent him instead to Lagos where at that time the Nigerian northerners, mainly Muslim, dominated what passed for a democratically elected government. For the remainder of my time in Lagos he remained as Ghana's High Commissioner, surviving both the military coup that removed Kwame N'Krumah from power in Ghana and then the succession of Army revolts that toppled Nigeria down the slippery slope into anarchy and the Biafran War.

I saw Yakubu Tali on many occasions thereafter. If I finished work early, having phoned to confirm his presence, I would sometimes call in at the Residency in Apapa for an hour or so, for tea or beer. Always he seemed alone, except for a discreet houseboy - almost certainly a fellow Dagomba and the large house seemed otherwise empty and deserted.

Still None The Wiser

In late February 1966 while working temporarily in Apapa and on my way back to Lagos I called in to see him late one afternoon. The day before, news had broken of a military coup in Accra, deposing the President, Kwame N'Krumah, but as with all such events hard information was in short supply while censorship ruled and rumour proliferated. Yakubu Tali was delighted with the news. He provided me with graphic descriptions of the fighting in Accra, with patriotic Ghanaian soldiers storming the Presidential Palace, the hand-to-hand fighting with N'Krumah's hand-picked and heavily armed praetorian guardsmen who fought like rats, trapped in the secret tunnels which honeycombed their fortress, until tanks and armoured cars blasted them from their concrete lairs. He mimed the action from behind a settee, shooting an imaginary machine gun and throwing hand grenades at the doomed defenders. N'Krumah was believed to have been spirited away to Russia. It was all tremendously exciting and I felt privileged to have this first hand information which had reached Yakubu Tali by telephone from Accra.

Alas, to coin a simple phrase, it was all total bollocks. A virtually bloodless coup had taken place while President N'Krumah was in Peking attempting to re-plant himself on the world stage by brokering a cease-fire in the Vietnam War. He never returned to Ghana, seeking refuge in the left wing state of Guinea and dying a few years later in exile. The Ghanaian public welcomed the army into power. N'Krumah had become a despot and his socialist inspired Five Year Plan introduced in 1963 had quickly reduced the already damaged economy to ruin and chaos. One party rule (voted in by 'referendum' with a 'ninety nine' percent majority in favour) swiftly led to government by decree and detention without trial for opponents of the regime. In late 1965 the final straw arrived in the shape of N'Krumah's plan to invade Rhodesia to depose Ian Smith. The great pan-African ideologist and self-styled 'Redeemer' had, his generals decided, finally achieved total detachment from reality.

When O. and I left Lagos in early 1967 I lost contact with Yakubu Tali, but seeing him on television in March 1985 I wrote to him, care of Tamale Post Office and a few weeks later he replied. Modesty forbids that I should repeat in full the text of his letter. To proclaim that my *'features'* remained well-remembered in Tamale (after nearly twenty-five years absence!) and that many of its now prosperous citizens ascribed their present enviable condition to my personal concern for their welfare and efforts on their behalf in past years, I regard as honeyed hyperbole - but none the less flattering.

In his letter Yakubu Tali outlined his career since we last met. He left Lagos shortly after we did, in 1967 - no doubt because so many of the northern Hausa and Yoruba muslims in the Nigerian government were murdered or removed in the various military coups of the previous year. He then spent several years as Ghana's Ambassador to Yugoslavia, Romania and Bulgaria, living in Belgrade. He wrote in his letter "*I am still a capitalist though!*" Later, following another military coup in Ghana which removed K. A. Busia's civilian regime, Yakubu Tali was sent to Freetown as High Commissioner to Sierra Leone and Ambassador to Guinea. At the end of 1975 he said "*I returned home to live among my people as their chief and have taken up farming quite seriously.*" He ended his letter with a warm invitation to visit him when "*it would be my pleasure and pride to show you around ..... And if your daughter could come, to see where she was born.*" As I re-read the letter today I can still hear his resonant, dark voice that typified his benevolent presence, the warm intelligence, his good manners and his natural generosity that personified him..

The years pass and in 1997 my son, at the Ghana High Commission in London to obtain a visa for a short working visit which included Tamale, asked if Yakubu Tali was still 'on seat' as paramount chief of the Dagomba. The Ghanaian official sighed, "The Tolon-Na? I remember him well..... that tall black man, alas, he is dead."

Of the many others I remember, there was Issah Kanjarga, the elderly Superintendent of Police in Tamale, long past retirement age, but still in harness. I was a fellow guest the night we were both 'dined in' at the Army mess. Grey haired and ramrod straight he wore a starched white mess jacket displaying the glittering medals of two World Wars. One of the English subalterns asked him about the East African campaign of 1915 - 1918 when the Allies had vainly pursued the wily German general Paul Von Lettow-Vorbeck and his handful of white colonial officers and tough native 'Schutztruppen' (of that same breed as Stanley's Zanzibari askaris of forty years before) across half the African continent. Issah Kanjarga's eyes twinkled as he recalled his time as a young soldier serving in the WAFF and how the Gold Coast men had frightened their Kikuyu carriers half to death. Leaving Nairobi by train for the front the soldiers found a rabble of carriers already occupying all the seats. Issah Kanjarga said that the East Africans naively suspected that the WAFFs were cannibals who ate human flesh at every opportunity. The Gold Coasters looked knowingly at each other, and then directed their gaze at the Kikuyu while smacking their lips, rubbing their stomachs and miming anticipatory noises of the coming feast. The carriers quailed before them and fled and the soldiers then travelled in comfort while the porters trembled in fear on the carriage roofs and in the cattle wagons.

On his off duty days Issah Kanjarga sometimes wandered around the town dressed in a ragged cotton smock and sometimes slightly the worse for a proffered drink or two in the way of hospitality, visiting offices and stores, the Banks and trading companies to chat and pass the time of day with his cronies. My friend T. (whose predecessor Robin Greenwood, had known Issah well), newly arrived as District Manager of the United Africa Company was taken aback one afternoon when Issah appeared at his office door unannounced, well refreshed and waving a bottle. T. called a strangely reluctant messenger and told him to remove the unknown scruffy intruder, by force if necessary. The messenger demurred, mumbling that he was "*No fit.*" T. only narrowly avoided manhandling the old man when a clerk rushed up and said "Sah! I beg you not to vex so, dis be de Chief of Police - he come to greet you!"

Another old soldier still serving in the Gold Coast regiment of the WAFF in the early fifties was a veteran sergeant major who by special dispensation wore the ribbon - and on high days and holidays the insignia of the Iron Cross which he had won while serving with the German colonial troops in Togo in 1914. Issah Kanjarga and men like this had lived out the entire colonial period, being born in the north before the British arrived brandishing their blank treaty forms, (already signed in triplicate by Queen Victoria), and surviving for sixty years or more until the white man finally relinquished control and departed.

I realise with hindsight that excepting the trader Mallam Salifu, whose own unchanging lifestyle transcended centuries of changing borders and cultures, all the other Africans whom I have attempted to portray in this chapter were men of a particular time, unique creations of the colonial period. John Abbensetts and Howard Christian were Creole incomers practising the whiteman's law. The Yoruba hunter Ben Ladipo, Burma veteran then golf caddy and village elder. Yakubu Tali, the first Dagomba to receive a formal western education, Member of Parliament, ambassador, statesman and finally Paramount Chief in active retirement. Issah Kanjarga who had enlisted as a soldier in the WAFF to serve in East Africa, and forty years later was still in government service. They were all men I am proud to have known, and in bringing them back to brief life in these pages I hope the impressions of the chaos and cruelty of modern Africa often given by television and sensational journalism will somehow be tempered. It was not always thus, and need not be always so in the future.

CHAPTER 28

Lagos 1964 - 1967

"Ye shall hear of wars and rumours of wars: see that ye be not troubled: for all these things must come to pass but the end is not yet."
(Matthew 24:6)

In April 1964 after six months in Kano we moved to Lagos - another job, another employer. It was, to repeat Montaigne's maxim but *"another permanent decision made in a temporary frame of mind."* Perhaps more correctly it was *"out of the frying pan and into the fire."* The Bank of the North, entertaining though it was had not been a good career move and its future prospects seemed obscure - an aspect which had been highlighted when I discovered that some of the expatriate staff withdrew their monthly salary in cash as soon as it was credited to their account, Major Parbold-Plinge kept his in his private safe, others presumably paying it into another bank (ostensibly on the grounds that they did not wish their colleagues to know how they disposed of it). I wondered at times if it indicated a lack of confidence in the Bank's somewhat shaky foundations.

In those far distant days I realise now that I must have still thought in 'career' terms so I was flattered when I was approached by the French manager of the United Bank for Africa in Kano who confirmed that in spite of the long delays since my interview in London the previous year they still wanted to employ me. Parbold-Plinge was understandably annoyed when I resigned and I later learned that he had contemplated cancelling my residence permit so that O. and I and the children would be forced to leave Nigeria before my new employers could regularise my presence with the Immigration authorities. As in many West African countries the dilatory processes of bureaucracy could be spurred into action by judicious venality - or even political pressure and O. and I in the event were spared the necessity for a temporary stay in the neighbouring Ivory Coast.

In early 1964 Lagos was still relatively civilised both in political terms and in its infrastructure. The water and electricity flowed - if somewhat intermittently at times; the police directed road traffic in a manner still calculated to expedite the movement of vehicles rather than as a simple method of augmenting their personal cash flow; the Courts, in theory at least, exercised the rule of law and an elected government held sway (I hesitate to use the word *'democratically'* elected). The army and the 'young

Turks' - their officers - remained in barracks and the Federal regions remained attached by open lines of communication to the administrative centre. Nigeria still seemed to have a bright future after four years of independence. In the short space of another eighteen months all this was to prove a false calm before the coming storm. By the beginning of 1966 the first of a series of military coups accelerated the long slide into the swamplands of near anarchy and civil war with the seccessionist East, while corruption and oligarchy ruled under the sway of a culpably inefficient military kleptocracy which by its own unaided efforts would soon reduce the oil-rich country to virtual bankruptcy and hopelessness.

We moved into a comfortable third floor flat in the residential area of Ikoyi, a pleasant island suburb to the east of the city, mainly inhabited by expatriates and well-to-do Africans. We met up with many old friends from earlier years in Ghana. As a fluent French speaker O. soon found a job with the Ivory Coast Embassy as personal secretary to the Ambassador, which being a diplomatic post fell outside the strict labour laws governing the employment of expat wives. Her hours were far from onerous and the embassy furnished us liberally with duty-free liquor and cigarettes. Our remaining debts from the UK had been cleared and once more O. and I had our heads above water. We bought a boat and at weekends idled around the extensive creeks, lagoons and beaches beyond the main harbour. We had a new team of efficient house servants. The domestic side of our life had reached a calm and sunny plateau -for the time being.

The major fly in the otherwise soothing ointment of our latest migration south from Kano was the organisation I had now joined. Not for the first time I realised that I was totally unsuited to the corporate, bureaucratic life style to which I had once again committed myself. The near anarchic days of the old Bank of British West Africa I had joined in the Gold Coast ten years earlier were ancient history and the antics of my recent employers in Kano were but an entertaining memory. In Lagos the expat bureaucrats, the number-crunching bean-counters, the grey men in grey suits, were already taking over from the 'Old Coasters.' Gradgrind was in control. Spontaneity, imagination and any idea of joy were definitely out. Concrete air-conditioned offices, reams of deadly statistics and a suffocating hierarchy meant ever longer working hours. Ineffable tedium ruled. The ethos of the multi-national Bank I had now joined, under the influence of the French majority shareholding, encouraged confusion and crisis. I discovered the drawbacks of working with a polyglot mixture of French, Italian, Irish, Scots, Dutch, English and American, Australian and New Zealand expatriate colleagues, several seconded from their parent Banks (who were also part of the consortium) for one or two years to gain (or offer) experience on their fast-track career ladders as the case might be. Individually many were likeable characters and good company. En masse their effect on our working environment was both confusing and indigestible and eventually I think it made me physically ill. Looking down from our multi-storey office block on Broad Street in the commercial centre of Lagos, I now felt an almost total isolation from everything that had attracted me to Africa. This is not to say that there were not brief moments of passing interest. There were times when groups of strikers or protesters threatened public order and a phalanx of Riot Police would clear the street below our office windows - the whiff of tear gas being barely detectable in our sterile air conditioned offices and the cries of innocent passers-by bludgeoned into the gutter by the staves of the Riot Squad reduced to a distant murmur through the plate glass. Another spectacle to be seen from the office window was the annual appearance of the 'masqueraders,' dangerous personifications of a Yoruba 'orisha,' the cult of Egugun, masked and dressed in ritual costume lurching through the streets on short stilts - armed with clubs and whips, who were by custom taunted by the wary spectators who followed them, the 'masquerader' darting at the crowd and on occasion catching and mercilessly beating the less agile or fleet of foot among the audience. Women were noticeably absent from these performances and I believe that they were forbidden to witness either the display or even to speak the name of Egugun. They were certainly forbidden to witness the rites of 'Oro,' another powerful and more violent 'orisha' which was banned in Lagos. Europeans with any sense kept well clear on these occasions, being regarded as prime targets for these ritual assaults. *(Note: 'Oro' like 'Egugun' is a 'policing' orisha and according to Burton writing in 1860 its victims were crucified on rude crosses, or clubbed and impaled, on a small island at the back of Lagos town off King Dosumu's palace. All male dogs were forbidden and if found were strangled to ward off evil influences, split, trimmed like sheep and hung up at the door of some great man where rows of of the putrid carcases of their brothers were to be seen. At the vernal equinox wrote Burton *'a young female was impaled alive to breed plenty in the land.'*)

Another memorable event that once briefly relieved the weekday tedium was when I was summoned as a juror to the Lagos High Court. I attended the opening of the Assizes where the cases were arraigned - there were twenty eight cases of murder, one of rape and one case of slave dealing. I would have preferred to hear the last. I certainly had no wish to be implicated in sending anyone to the gallows, for the death penalty was mandatory for murder and the prosecution evidence invariably strong - of that variety involving severed heads and dripping cutlasses, the accused being apprehended at the scene of the crime and confessions extracted on the spot. What I got was the rape case. This was complicated by the fact that charges should probably never have been brought in the first instance, but once the Police became involved matters had inexorably taken their course. It concerned a white teenaged girl on holiday from the UK, the Nigerian houseboy, the girl's irate father and other relevant and confusing circumstances which I shall not go into. I was the only white in a jury of otherwise 'good and true' Lagosians. The Nigerian Judge's summing-up was both wise and just, and unanimously we found the accused houseboy 'not guilty.' I have never had any doubt it was the right decision in the circumstances. But I would still have preferred to hear the case of slave dealing.

There were also the occasions when if one held a key to the strongroom one was obliged to stay late in the office after the African staff had left, to pack up large amounts of cash in smart, new suitcases to be carried off by 'executives' representing major clients who already had, or hoped for profitable government contracts. In today's terms these sums would have been between £250,000 to £500,000. No questions were ever asked and no answers were required, one simply assumed the 'usual' destination was some Minister or other official requiring 'dash.' (This was long before anyone had heard of the terms 'compliance officer' or 'slush fund'). The then going rate was anywhere between ten and fifteen percent or more, of the expected contract price. The extra sums involved were always factored into the tender price.

The old days of keeping 'government hours' of 7.30 am to 2 or at the latest 3 in the afternoon were definitely over. We rarely finished before 6.30 pm - a mere nothing in today's turn-of-the-century terms and the 24 hours a day 7 days a week commitment asked of many employees, but then thank God, the advent of the all-powerful computer was still lurking hull down on the horizon and there were as yet no satellite or mobile phones or pagers to disturb us away from the office. Nevertheless in spite of one free Saturday morning a month, the underlying pressure was relentless.

We were to spend three years in Lagos and with hindsight this was the nadir of my banking career. I loathed my job with ever increasing intensity. Lagos was beginning its long descent into becoming one of the world's most unpleasant and dysfunctional cities. My crutches were my wife and two children, our friends and all the time I could still snatch away either in our boat or in the bush at weekends - for within a few months of arrival I had entered once again the network of like-minded old friends from our earlier days in Ghana and Northern Nigeria, whose principal pleasures like mine, lay in fishing and hunting away from the teeming streets of Lagos.

Paul Gautier and his wife Juliette, old friends from Tamale, lived nearby on Ikoyi Island. Jacques Spencer-Chapman, still the feckless companion of my bachelor days in the Gold Coast, but now married, was with a French oil company in Lagos; Crad - from Kano - was now living in Apapa close by on the mainland. Other 'Old Coaster' friends and aquaintances from happier times past now re-surfaced in Lagos. These were the dying years of a post-colonial false sense of security, those early years of Nigerian independence when the stirrings of imminent strife and civil war muttered and grumbled, mostly ignored and half-heard like the echo of some distant thunderstorm beyond the horizon. For those who had ears to hear and eyes to see, the signs were but thinly veiled. Even superstition played its part - in 1964 and 1965 the waters of the lagoons and distant creeks which surround Lagos were fouled with the bloated carcases of tens of thousands of silver, eel-like 'lancelets' - primitive, blind, primaeval fish whose festering and stinking remains littered the shifting sand bars and mangrove islands swept by the tidal currents. Local tradition held that their death in such huge numbers presaged imminent disaster. How right they were.

1966 was not a good year for Nigeria. The first military coup masterminded by mid-ranking army officers took place in January. In Lagos the Federal Prime Minister, Alhaji Sir Abubakar Tafewa Balewa, a northerner and a respected Commonwealth statesman, was murdered (his severed head allegedly despatched to his widow in a laundry basket). The influential, heavyweight and flamboyant Minister of Finance, Chief Festus Okotie-Eboe, a Calabari (whose traditional dress inluded a straw 'boater') from the Rivers State, was also assassinated in the early hours of the same morning. His official residence adjoined that of the Prime Minister backing on to Five Cowries Creek. Okotie-Eboe was a ruthless and unpleasant forerunner of the many politicians and soldiers who subsequently plundered and robbed Nigeria blind of its oil revenues at the expense of the general population, (my colleague Gareth Plinge who claimed to have had dealings with him always prefaced any mention of his name with the honorific "Shagnasty"). He was undoubtedly tortured to reveal details of his overseas numbered bank accounts before being murdered. It was rumoured that he had either been buried head down in an unmarked hole in the ground, or hacked into pieces to forestall any traditional funeral rites. Other senior ministers were either killed or arrested. In the north, the most powerful of Nigeria's political and religious leaders, Ahmadu Bello, the Sardauna of Sokoto, was murdered by rebel army officers. A second stage military coup swiftly followed and in time-honoured fashion the first wave of plotters were arrested and executed. Strict martial law was imposed under the figurehead of a respected moderate and professional soldier, Major General Aguyi-Ironsi, an Ibo. The stage was now set and Nigeria was on course for disaster.

Curfews, roadblocks and 'stop-and-search' checks became part of our everyday existence. Military governors (including my old Epsom College schoolfellow Colonel Chukwuemeka Ojukwu) took over in the Provinces and the Regions. A series of soothing letters emanated from the British High Commissioner, Francis Cumming-Bruce, advised us to keep calm and *"not to offend local susceptibilities."* We promptly made certain that our personal details were on record at the High Commission and other nationalities did the same at their own Embassies. O. was now working for the ILO, a United Nations agency, having left the Ivory Coast Ambassador's employ as the result of an *Ivoirien* directive on 'foreign' employees in 'sensitive' posts. (She remained on good terms with her former 'Patron' and our welcome perks of diplomatic liquor and cigarettes continued.) As a UN employee she was now on their books, and from UN sources we received highly alarmist reports on the political situation. Her UN pass was useful and usually ensured safe passage through the road blocks.

During the next six months the situation steadily deteriorated. Travel by road away from the towns became risky (the *lumpen-militariat* and associated *banditti* were unpredictable and potentially dangerous) and shortages of basic foodstuffs became common. O. recalls that during one strike when Lagos ground to a standstill, I surreptitiously collected flour and other supplies from the back door of a Syrian store while pickets blockaded the main entrance. Infinitely more serious than such minor inconveniences was the unrest in the regions. Rioting and bloodshed in the northern cities of Kano, Kaduna and Zaria led to many thousands of deaths and a mass exodus of Ibos back to their homeland in the East. At Makurdi, the rail and road crossing of the Benue River, Ibos in their hundreds were massacred on the river bank. The Ibos in the East duly retaliated, killing every northerner they could lay their hands on.

At the end of July 1966 units of the army at Abeokuta in the west, mutinied and fought each other. The unrest spread to Ibadan and at the Ikeja barracks outside Lagos where there was heavy fighting between rival army factions involving civilian casualties, including an English expat killed in the crossfire and the country's main airport was closed for several days. I cannot remember now for how many days the uncertainty continued. Curfews were in force throughout Lagos and businesses and offices were shut. We remained at our flat in Ikoyi along with the other residents, all of them fellow employees and their families. We sat companionably drinking beer, uneasily enjoying the enforced holiday, keeping the children occupied and listening to the radio. The TV screen was blank and played the same endlessly banal tapes of martial and classical music broadcast by all the Lagos radio transmitters. At irregular intervals a recorded announcement said that *"An official statement will be made shortly."* Most of us realised that the timing of this depended on which faction came out on top. The BBC World Service told us little that we did not already know. So we waited.

Rumour was rife, hard information non-existent. John West, a colleague, went downstairs to our single communal telephone in the lobby and rang the Lagos Radio Station (reportedly surrounded by soldiers) to demand more definite news. After several minutes his call was answered. "Please ring off *immediately*, I beg you, this place is *too* dangerous now!" whispered a frightened voice.

About mid-morning on August 1st 1966, the radio crackled to life, the Nigerian national anthem was played and on our black and white TV screen an unknown (to us) army officer appeared. "This is Lieutenant Colonel Yakubu Gowon, Chief of Staff Army speaking to you. My fellow countrymen ...." So we now knew who had come out on top - at least for the time being. General Ironsi, Colonel Gowon's predecessor, had disappeared *"in unexplained circumstances"* (if later rumour was to be believed a selection of *his* body parts had been sent as a gift to the late Prime Minister's widow in the north to avenge her husband).

For much of the time our daily life now continued more or less normally while the situation deteriorated. Nigeria was beginning to split along tribal lines with the Ibos in the East against the rest of the country in the north and the west. Like many other expats in Lagos who had a boat, I kept ours in a state of readiness on its trailer in the garage with two full tanks of fuel. We were ten minutes away from a launch site on Five Cowries Creek. 'French' territory at Porto Novo in Dahomey (now Benin) was little more than sixty miles and a few hours away up the sheltered waters of Badagry Creek across the open water of Lagos harbour. At times we heard totally unfounded rumours that an Anglo/US fleet was lying hull down beyond the horizon ready to evacuate expatriates. Area wardens and local leaders had been appointed by the UK High Commission and the various embassies and the UN for their expat communities. Both the UN and The UK High Commission advised us to accumulate enough tinned food for a week and to keep suitcases ready packed together with supplies of drinking water and our passports on our persons. If it came to the crunch, servants and pets were to be abandoned.

It was fortunate that none of these emergency measures were ever put to the test in view of the total chaos that would have ensued. O., sensibly displaying a healthy scepticism of officialdom in such circumstances thought she would check out the *bona fides* of our own area warden. Walking down the road in Ikoyi to the address we had been given, O. knocked on the door of what was in fact the official residence of the Indonesian Ambassador. His Excellency while sympathetic expressed total ignorance of his alleged responsibilities and confirmed that in the event of an emergency arising he would be otherwise pre-occupied.

There was an undercurrent of unease, particularly amongst those with families. Those of us with long experience of Africa knew how volatile the situation could become without warning. O. and I had been in Tamale in 1961 when the first European refugees came out of the Congo. We had known people who had been killed there, others taking refuge in Ghana recounted their terrifying experiences. In 1964 the Congo blew up again and whites held as hostages were massacred in Stanleyville by the 'Simbas.' Refugees, many of them badly injured and with horrifying tales to tell were evacuated by air through Kano. Much of what I heard in person from people who were there I have tried, unsuccesfully, to forget.

Biafra under Colonel Ojukwu threatened secession and I briefly considered sending him a telegram of encouragement quoting our old school motto *"Deo non Fortuna Stop Floreat Epsomia."* Wisely I refrained; the risk of being taken for a spy sending secret messages was too real. The rumoured foreign involvment in the coming war and the arrival of white mercenaries in the East was fast becoming fact. Today, Kate Adie would arrive on the scene at this stage.

In the bar of the Ikoyi Hotel I bumped into Colonel Duggie Cairns, late of the WAFF and the Ghana Army, whom I had last met in Tamale and who was now an official 'observer' for the British government. (He, together with General Henry Alexander and the young Jonathan Aitken were soon to achieve a brief notoriety in the so-called 'Daily Telegraph Secrets Case' involving alleged breaches of the Official Secrets Act and the UK's undercover involvement in the Biafran war.) The occasional bomb exploded in Lagos, more or less at random. The roof of a house in Ikoyi near the golf course was blown off in an explosion (putting at least one golfer of my aquaintance off his stroke during a Sunday morning round), the result of a premature detonation which splattered the would-be bomber's body in a brownish mush all over the now exposed inner walls of the bedroom which I passed each day on my way to and from the office on Lagos Island. Random shootings and murders, mostly politically motivated, were occurring in the residential areas around Lagos. We dined one evening with a Swiss UN colleague of O.'s in a house formerly occupied by a senior army officer.

Above the dining table the ceiling was still stitched with a ragged pattern of bullet holes, some with ominous stains, which marked the recent demise of the previous occupant, shot dead as he lay in bed in the room above.

O and her colleagues were trapped in the ILO offices one day as automatic gunfire crackled from the nearby army barracks and random bullets smacked into the building. Whoever was shooting at whom and why was never explained. (Who was the wise journalist who said "The bullet with my name on it doesn't worry me nearly as much as the one addressed 'To whom it may concern'?)

We were due for leave within a few months. The whiteman's day in West Africa was fast coming to a close and I could see no further useful role for myself nor could I see any long term future. With a young family to consider the time was also fast approaching when our children would have to go to school away from the Coast, where only the French had the facilities and their Alliance Française schools and teachers to educate their offspring within their own national curriculum.

In January 1967 we packed up our household for the last time in Africa. We paid off Jonathan and Anna; Oliver, the 'small boy' had already left for the East. Apart from providing references and three months' pay, there was nothing else we could do. As Ibos in what could now be a hostile country we feared for their uncertain future.

I first went to West Africa as a young man in 1954, leaving for the last time some thirteen years later, older, sadder and perhaps still none the wiser even if I had learned much in the years between. In the many decades that have since ensued, I have never again set foot on those blessed and blighted lands that lie below the Sahara. A part of me forever remains in exile - from a place that perhaps has only ever existed in my own imagination.

And there is hardly a day since, when unbidden, the Africa of my youth does not come to life again in my mind. Strangely, the happy times come to me again in my waking hours – but at night the dreams that trouble me are of a difficult and darker world from which I cannot shake myself free.

From the times of my childhood until the present day I have come to see my past life as a series of cardboard boxes, one inside the other, in a manner not unlike some Russian doll - each part fitting neatly to the next in sequence - some easily accessible, a few important, some dusty and half forgotten. But not the African box that lies outside and apart from the others. The contents of that box, into which I am driven to peek, if not every day, then at random and unexpected moments, are an entirely separate and complete chapter of my life. The box contains its share of darkness, its cobwebbed nooks and crannies, its matters of guilt and regret that still trouble my dreams. There are things that happened a long time ago that still pursue me like some dogged and ancient enemy who creeps up from behind to tap me on the shoulder; as if to say "I'm still here!" However hard I try I cannot purge them from my memory. I have in the end become like that troubled and legendary fugitive who joined the French Foreign Legion "….to forget a girl called Sandra."

But that strange box from my past also contains much that still has the power to delight me when I open it and start to put it all back together once more.

A PARTIAL BIBLIOGRAPHY

FOR 'STILL NONE THE WISER'

Ade Ajayi & Smith, R. S., *Yoruba Warfare in the 19th Century*, Cambridge U. P. 1964

Alexander, H. T. Major General, *African Tightrope*, Pall Mall Press 1965.

Allen, Charles, *Tales from the Dark Continent*, MacDonald Futura, 1979

Allison, Philip, *Life in the Whiteman's Grave*, Viking 1988

Bannerman, David, *Larger Birds of West Africa*, Penguin 1958

Booth, A. H., *Small Mammals of West Africa*, Longmans, 1960

Burton, Sir Richard Francis, *Abeokuta and the Cameroon Mountain*, London 1863

Burton, Sir Richard Francis, *Wanderings in West Africa*, London, 1863

Burton R. F.and Cameron V. L. *To the Gold Coast for Gold*, London 1883

Cansdale, George, *Reptiles of West Africa*, Penguin 1955

Clifford, Lady (ed.)' *Our Days on the Gold Coast*, John Murray 1919

Conneau, Capt. Theophilus, *A Slaver's Log Book*, Hale 1976

Crowder, Michael, *The Story of Nigeria*, Faber 1962

Crowder, M, Ed., *West African Resistance*, Hutchinson 1971

Dorst & Dandelot, *Larger Mammals of Africa, a Field Guide*, Collins 1970

Fry, Richard. *Bankers in West Africa*, Hutchinson 1976

Gwynn, Stephen, *Life of Mary Kingsley*, Macmillan 1932

Horn, Alfred Aloysius, *The Waters of Africa*, Cape 1929

Horn, Alfred Aloysius, *The Ivory Coast in the Earlies*, Cape 1927

Howard, Cecil, *Mary Kingsley*, Hutchinson, 1938

Huxley, Elspeth, *Four Guineas*, Chatto & Windus 1954

Kingsley, Mary. *West African Studies*, Macmillan 1899

Kingsley, Mary, *Travels in West Africa*, Macmillan 1897

'Langa Langa,' *Up Against It in Nigeria*, Geo. Allen & Unwin 1922

Leeson, F., *Snakes of the Gold Coast*, Crown Agents, London, 1950

Myatt, Maj. F., *The Golden Stool, Ashanti 1900*, Kimber 1966

Oakley, Richard, *Treks and Palavers*, Seeley, Service & Co. Ltd. 1938

Rattray, R. S, *Tribes of the Ashanti Hinterland*, Gold Coast Government pub.,

Thomas, Hugh, **The Atlantic Slave Trade**, Simon & Schuster, New York 1997

Thorp, Ellen, *Ladder of Bones*, Cape 1956

Ward, W.E.F., *A History of the Gold Coast*, Geo. Allen & Unwin, 1948

Willcock, Gen. Sir James, *The Romance of Soldiering and Sport*, Cassell 1925

Williams, Chief Elwyn, *Oyinbo Banki, A White Chief's Nigerian Odyssey*, Elna 1996

If you have enjoyed reading **'Still None the Wiser'** and have not yet read the first volume of this two part mid-century memoir 1932 – 1967, **'None the Wiser'** 1932 – 1952 covers the pre-war years and the author's later experiences as an RAF National Serviceman in Malaya; first published in 2005 by **Hayloft Publishing Ltd., Kirkby Stephen, Cumbria, CA17 4DJ. (www.hayloft.org.uk)** ISBN I 904524 25 7, price £14 from good bookshops or direct from the publisher plus £2 p. & p. .252 pages including many photographs and illustrated by Caroline Elkington.

Of the two part memoir, Eric Robson, broadcaster and TV presenter wrote:-

"Paul Adamson is a self confessed hoarder and in **'None the Wiser'** *his magpie tendencies have served us well. His rummage through the dusty attics of family history set against an historical background of Britain at war and mislaying an Empire gives us a fascinating glimpse of a lost world............"*

'Searchlight' Magazine, Journal of the RAF Seletar Association, also wrote of **'None the Wiser'** *"The section dealing with his service in the Far East .... Is really first class .....His version of Seletar is exactly as most will recall from later years."*

Joyce Wilson, 'Literary Lookaround' Keswick Reminder, said:- *"For those who were privileged to serve His/Her Majesty during those years this book will evoke both painful and hilarious memories. The line drawings by Caroline Elkington ...... delightfully complement the spirit of the text."*

Printed in the United Kingdom
by Lightning Source UK Ltd.
122705UK00001B/157/A